Teaching Ten to Fourteen Year Olds

Teaching Ten to Fourteen Year Olds

SECOND EDITION

Chris Stevenson
University of Vermont

 LONGMAN

An imprint of Addison Wesley Longman, Inc.

New York • Reading, Massachusetts • Menlo Park, California • Harlow, England
Don Mills, Ontario • Sydney • Mexico City • Madrid • Amsterdam

Acquisitions Editor: Virginia L. Blanford
Associate Editor: Arianne J. Weber
Project Coordination and Text Design: Ruttle, Shaw & Wetherill, Inc.
Cover Designer: Chris Hiebert
Cover Photo: c1997 PhotoDisc
Electronic Production Manager: Christine Pearson
Manufacturing Manager: Willie Lane
Electronic Page Makeup: Ruttle, Shaw & Wetherill, Inc.
Printer and Binder: The Maple-Vail Book Manufacturing Group
Cover Printer: Phoenix Color Corp.

Library of Congress Cataloging-in-Publication Data

Stevenson, Chris.
    Teaching ten to fourteen year olds / Chris Stevenson. — 2nd ed.
        p.   cm.
    Includes bibliographical references and index.
    ISBN 0-8013-1582-4
    1. Teaching. 2. Middle school teaching. I. Title.
    LB1025.3.S74   1998
    371.1'02—dc21   97-9971
                                                                     CIP

ISBN 0-8013-1582-4

12345678910—MA—00999897

Peter Stevenson   Bill Balentine   Robby Robinson   Whit Stevenson   Emily Balz   Lonnie Pirkle   Jeremy Cohen   Todd Gordon   Ben Kahn   David Wolk Lisa Brothers David Wollins Mark Gilston Lisa Banasch Laura Larson Lorna Aikman Celia Blumenthal Sabra Hull Eileen Lockhart K.C. Gordon Kim Sweet Mark Fischer Mary Lee Bell Christina Lord Louis Derry Mark Woodin Jonathan Leinbach Lucy Smith Sean Moriarty Charlie Brake Danny McKay Martha

Bramlett

Morgan

McAlpin

Allen Black

Shawn

This book is lovingly dedicated to all those young people who taught me about themselves and, in so doing, also taught me a great deal about how to teach them and others. Some of their names are listed here, but there are many, many more.

Herrity Heather Pierce Fay Howell Jeanetten King Debby Jamison Julie Ridley Helen Rudolph John Wiley Mary Jane Smith Lucy Aikman Win Pound Martha Pentecost Sam DuBose Michael Slade Peter Bevington Sarah Croft Erica Johnson Luck Gambrell Blake McBurney Ben Simms Billy Horton Lauran Wilson Marshall Eubanks Jan Thurman Eloise Black Sam Austin Julia Moore Rip Black Rhodes Perdue Ann Armsby George Yancey Rufus Dorsey Rob Hancock Joe Whipple Joe McDonough Claire Schackelford Marie Christiansen Bob Schneider Randy Siegel Cathrine Crowe Brenda Peskin Connie Neely David Towles Margaret Howell Meredith Culver Annette Rice Jane Tuttle Owens Chapman Tom Gray Carl Hartrampf Elizabeth Appleby Laura Heery Carol Miller Valerie Fiel Cathy Floyd Mary Sidney Anderson Kathy Davidson Monica Slate Bo Newton Harriet Hall Sarah King Michael Cacciamani Christy Cole Billy Sweet Phil Frank Sharon Silverman David Harrington Kevin Redmond Eric Johnston Steve Banasch Terry Martin Buddy Wright Marty Marks Tracy Foster Elizabeth St. John "Paddington" Hub Moore Susie Sweet Brooke Ackerly Shenandoah Arnold Rob Allen Peter Ackerly

Contents

Foreword

As a college professor, I seldom used textbooks. They were too encyclopedic, too pedantic, too sterile, simply too "textbookish." The existing stereotype of boring textbooks was, it seemed, well founded. But every now and then the exception that proves the rule comes along. And *Teaching Ten to Fourteen Year Olds* is that exception. Here is a book that breaks new ground, that departs significantly from the traditional textbook pattern. Chris Stevenson's book is the most exciting, nonstandard education text that I've seen in more than forty years in education.

Many recent education texts have tried to be nontraditional. They have employed add-ons or gimmicks like cartoons or boxed anecdotes to entice the reader, rather than really altering the style by which the facts and advice are presented. Here, however, is a book with an engaging style that is solidly grounded in human growth and development and never departs from that proper foundation no matter what the topic. It is thoroughly and consistently kid-centered. The book, written in first person, is scholarly and well documented. Excellent references and supporting activities accompany each chapter.

The consistency of its philosophy gives the book a particular strength. No attempts are made to appeal to all sides or persuasions. Its philosophical orientation, which is pure middle school, pervades every chapter.

"The proper study of mankind is man," claimed Alexander Pope in an oft-cited bit of wisdom. And so the best way to study early adolescence is by becoming acquainted with young adolescents. Here, *Teaching Ten to Fourteen Year Olds* rises to admirable heights in following Pope's advice, for this volume contains a rich abundance of vignettes about actual young adolescents—Erica, Gordon, Kevin, Eric, and Travis, to mention a few. These are not hypothetical cases contrived to illustrate a particular point; rather, the points are usually made simply by presenting these genuine samples of life among young adolescents. There are also instances in which teachers like Mr. Barrett and Martha Melton are brought to life.

These valid examples are from a man who has lived and taught among young adolescents for years. Chris Stevenson knows young adolescents and has a remarkable knack for expressing their experiences. That he was, and is, a highly successful teacher soon becomes evident. His sensitivity to individuals, inherent goodness, and masterful, low-key approaches to instruction, though never directly claimed, come through. Rare will be a reader who does not say to himself or herself, "How I wish my child might have had Chris Stevenson as a teacher."

As a textbook this treatise is not a self-contained course, ample as it is. It bids—in fact, obligates—you to go outside its pages to learn about ten to fourteen year olds in your setting and school, to examine its propositions, to gather data on which to draw your own generalizations. One cannot read it without asking and answering many questions about one's own beliefs, attitudes, and standards. Honest, probing classroom discussions will emanate from a group's common reading of this material. Such discussions will not be artificial or perfunctory; they will get at the difficult issues that are inevitably involved as middle level education seeks to implement a developmentally responsive and intellectually challenging program.

The appearance of this book is especially timely, for the burgeoning middle school movement is catching up teacher preparation programs in its wake. Long-reluctant colleges are now offering courses specifically designed for middle level teachers, and they need materials that truly reflect the middle school concept. *Teaching Ten to Fourteen Year Olds* more than fills the bill. Through this single volume, students can gain a grasp of the middle school concept, its foundation in the developmental nature of the age group, the school's special mission, its need for a distinctive curriculum and age-appropriate methodologies. While it is not a catalog of methods or activities, readily usable techniques are inherent in many chapters. The treatments of experiential learning, evaluation, and discipline, to cite just three examples, are superb.

I enthusiastically endorse *Teaching Ten to Fourteen Year Olds* and commend it to a wide array of readers without any reservations. Future generations of middle school teachers who cut their professional teeth on this book will be able to step into education's most critically important classrooms far better prepared than their predecessors. For those now teaching at the middle level who were denied the benefit of specially focused preservice programs, this book will be a delightful tool for use in staff development programs. Indeed, even parents will find this volume to be particularly helpful in understanding their young adolescent children and the type of school program Chris Stevenson and his thousands of active colleagues in the middle school movement are seeking to provide them.

Some who read the Foreword to the first edition of this book might have thought the unbridled enthusiasm for it was more a testament to my rhetoric than it was to the book's quality. In the five years since its release, however, the accolades received from hundreds of student users and professors have proven the strong endorsement made in 1992—which has been repeated above—was justified by the quality of the book.

In this revised edition nothing that made this text so atypical, functional, and engaging has been lost. But some additions have incorporated recent educational developments and approaches. References have been updated. *Teaching Ten to Fourteen Year Olds* remains the quintessential text for use in preparing teachers for the middle schools of tomorrow. It is still unmatched.

John H. Lounsbury
Dean Emeritus, School of Education, Georgia College, and
Publications Editor, National Middle School Association

Prologue

This book has been built gradually over the thirty-five years that I have worked alongside young adolescents, mostly in schools but also in a variety of other settings. The work is inevitably grounded in reflections and revelations about my own early adolescence as well as parenting four children. I also learned from the wisdom and candor of my parents, Margaret and Frank Stevenson, as well as that of parent friends—notably Mary Scott and John Arnold. My teaching career, always challenging, has been particularly blessed with opportunities that produced momentary insights refined and confirmed by later development.

Research, theory, and innovative practice are blended here with what I readily acknowledge are my own idiosyncratic perceptions about living and growing through the crucially important years from ages ten to fourteen. In this manuscript more than any other, I have presented what I believe to be the most important lessons of my personal and professional career.

This chronicle of a personal quest toward particular ideals I have for the school life of each emerging man-child and woman-child describes my most enlightening struggles and portrays the inspiring work of some exceptional teachers with whom I've been privileged to work.

The patience, optimism, and generosity of so many young adolescents I've known inspired this book, and thus it is dedicated to them.

A POINT OF VIEW

In reviewing the evolution of the study of adolescence, Carol Guardo (1975) suggests that we attempt an integration of what she refers to as "adolescence-in-theory" and "adolescence-in-fact," the latter referring to adolescence as described by research. She further proposes that we proceed in terms of the "adolescent-in-reality—living in his (or her) day-to-day environment, similar to all adolescents in some respects, yet totally different in others." Guardo captures the spirit of the approaches I've taken as a teacher, and that spirit will, I believe, be self-evident throughout this book. I am totally committed to the belief that the highest calling we have as teachers is to employ our wisdom, abilities, instincts and energies toward cultivating the essence that lies within every child. In so doing, we also attend responsibly to our own growth.

USING THIS BOOK

This book is over 50 percent longer than I had originally intended. Anecdotes and materials collected over the years were more extensive than I had anticipated—a common problem, I am told, for many authors and for those whose feelings about their work run very deep. Both descriptors apply to me. My initial intent was to produce a book that could be a reference for a single course that prepared teachers for work with students in middle level schools. The result is material sufficient for a two- or three-course sequence as well as a resource and reference for practicing teachers.

The text is divided into three parts. Part One establishes an educational context and guides the reader through some developmental considerations of young adolescents; Part Two surveys numerous curriculum possibilities and recommends pedagogy that is responsive to these young people's development; and Part Three is directed especially toward the more personal opportunities and responsibilities of teaching in a middle level school.

HOW THE BOOK IS ORGANIZED

Chapter One sets the stage for Part One as well as for the rest of the book. It describes the most noteworthy underpinnings of middle level education and establishes a context for your personal and professional development as a teacher of young adolescents. The current movement is grounded in its twentieth-century antecedents, and the most esteemed and celebrated past and current policy decrees are excerpted. The chapter closes with principles and rhetorical questions that, in my judgment, are crucial for both aspiring and teachers in service to contemplate.

Chapters Two and Three guide the reader in utilizing shadowing and inquiry techniques as methods for observing and learning from and about young adolescent students. Chapter Four organizes selected data concerning young adolescent development according to what I refer to as interactive domains. I hope that the process of carrying out and sharing shadowing and inquiry techniques will substantially enhance the reader's insights about young adolescent development—the understanding of which is so vital to the decisions we make as teachers.

Part Two builds on the insights acquired from the processes and content presented in Part One. The four chapters in this section focus on conceptualizing, organizing, presenting, and assessing the effectiveness of schooling that will complement the developmental conditions of young adolescents. I believe that teachers and curriculum designers should reconsider the question "What should the middle level curriculum be?" as "*How* should the middle level curriculum be?" Stevenson, (1991). The answer to this question lies in understanding how children go about the business of learning and how we teachers guide, support, and monitor their learning. With the content of Part One as a prerequisite, Part Two could also serve as the focus for a materials and methods course.

Chapter Five begins Part Two by examining pedagogy, and Chapter Six follows with an examination of the principles and guidelines for choosing curriculum. Developmentally appropriate designs for organizing young adolescents into teams, strategies for grouping students within teams and classes, and classroom and team management approaches constitute Chapter Seven. The final chapter in this section reveals ways to assess and evaluate what is taking place in the educational program—a responsibility that is rightfully shared with young adolescents.

Part Three examines the teacher's personal context—selected roles and functions of middle level teachers that define our work in ways that contrast with the exclusively subject-matter priorities of a traditional junior high school. Chapter Nine emphasizes the commitment necessary to see that interdisciplinary team organization works satisfactorily not just for students but also for teachers. Chapter Ten examines teacher advisories, underscoring the benefits to both generations. The final chapter shows how we can cultivate our most influential allies—our students' parents. In each chapter I have attempted to concentrate on the personal as well as professional benefits of being a middle level teacher. Part Three could be the text for a course or seminar during and following an internship or a semester of student teaching.

ONE FINAL SUGGESTION

A suggested itinerary for reading this book is to first read the Introductions to the three sections. The imagery is deliberate, and these introductions are included to establish a frame of reference for everything that follows. Then, before delving into the individual chapters, read the Epilogue. This final piece emphasizes the importance and limitless potential of the work we undertake when we choose to live, work, and learn with young adolescents. An initial reading of those overview sections will establish a context for the study of the individual chapters.

Teaching, perhaps more than any other profession, is a personal odyssey. Each of us brings to it and carries through it a unique complex of assumptions, expectations, and personal aspirations. This book recounts my odyssey, and it has been written with the hope that it will help you, the reader, find greater meaning and personal fulfillment in your own odyssey.

ACKNOWLEDGMENTS

Hundreds of adults and young adolescents have contributed to this project. I will not attempt to name everyone, lest I unwittingly leave someone out. I must mention, however, a few individuals who have been particularly influential. My parents, Margaret and Frank Stevenson, were the first to encourage me to write about my work. Their confidence sustained me in the face of considerable self-doubt. Mike and Allen, my brothers, are teachers who complimented my letters and other short pieces, and they also encouraged me to write for publication.

In 1989 Longman's education editor rebutted my criticism of textbooks about middle level teaching by challenging me about what I thought such books should include. My long-winded, impassioned (and probably tiring) response was essentially an outline of what has turned out to be the contents of this book, and an invitation to write it was immediate. Thus, an hour's conversation launched a working relationship between author and publisher that from my perspective became a "dream come true."

Two Johns—Arnold and Lounsbury—are the quintessential colleagues with whom I wish every teacher's life could be blessed. Both are possessed of a depth of personal spiritual commitment to the work of educating young adolescent children and their teachers as well. Both are gifted thinkers and writers who have been liberal with astute criticism and suggestions as well as exceedingly generous with their encouragement and praise. They have continuously inspired and reassured me countless times in my effort to make the book just right. My personal and professional life are inestimably richer for them.

Numerous leaders in middle level education, especially university professors, have been exceedingly generous in using the first edition with their classes and subsequently sharing ideas and providing suggestions. Some of them are Ken Bergstrom, Ed Brazee, Ken Brighton, Jody Capelluti, Judy Carr, Tom Dickinson, John Duval, Tom Erb, Jim Garvin, Tom Gatewood, Janet McDaniel, Ken McEwin, and Julia Thomason. I have especially enjoyed and benefited from teleconferences with their students. I would also like to acknowledge the countless readers who have written or telephoned or e-mailed or introduced themselves at professional meetings to speak with me about the book. Your affirmation has been far more gratifying than I can adequately express, and I hope that you will recognize in this edition the ideas and suggestions you shared with me. I hope I have represented you and those improvements well.

I would also like to thank my original editor, Naomi Silverman, as well as those manuscript reviewers who gave me valuable input as I prepared for the second edition: Susan A. Adler, University of Missouri, Kansas City; Harold L. Chapman, Jr., Fort Valley State University; Charlene M. Czerniak, University of Toledo; James Dick, University of Nebraska, Omaha; Cheryl K. Kish, Northern Illinois University; Wanda Price, Longwood College; Charles Robinson, Bridgewater State College; Adele Sanders, University of Northern Colorado; and Marvin Silverman, San Francisco State University.

My unofficial editor and official lifemate, Katherine Jacobs Stevenson, has, through her suggestions, editorial feedback, and ever-present good humor, continued to prove our partnership to be the best contractual arrangement I ever made. I simply could not have accomplished this project without her scholarly and spiritual companionship. I think she knows how very, very much I appreciate her.

Finally, my colleagues in the Department of Education at the University of Vermont have always been conspicuously prompt and cheerful as they rushed to help me sort out the multifarious complexities of microcomputers and photocopiers. Donna Flanigan, Darlene Nelligan, Susan Symula, and especially Donna Rowe provided me with abundant patience and friendship as well as technical know-how, and I am indebted to each of them.

Chris Stevenson

NOTES

Guardo, C. J. (1975). *The adolescent as individual: Issues and insights.* New York: Harper & Row.
Stevenson, C. (1991, November). "You've gotta see the game to see the game." *Middle School Journal, 23*(2).

PART ONE
About the Kids

INTRODUCTION TO PART ONE

This book chronicles my pursuit of some particular ideals I hold for the schooling of young adolescent students, and it discloses a few of my most enlightening struggles. My career has been particularly blessed with opportunities that produced momentary insights refined and confirmed by later development, always with interesting challenges. Throughout the saga I have marveled at kids' chutzpah, the resilience of their human spirit in the face of my failures to understand. But perhaps most dear of all qualities has been their quickness to forgive—a lesson students can often teach their teachers.

After I had been teaching for several years, I undertook to learn another complex of understanding and skills that had been lying dormant with me: *sailing*. As I worked to become a perceptive and competent sailor I also began to recognize interesting parallels between teaching and sailing, especially when they are done well, but also when they are attempted haphazardly. As you carry out your own teaching voyages, I hope you will accept a few words of welcome from a fellow seafarer.

Dear Shipmate,

Don't be put off by the mariner's greeting!

Teaching is often described as a journey, an odyssey of personal experiences and insights that one hears about in teachers' day-to-day give and take with one another. Sailing likewise is a trip, also characterized by tales swapped by old salts. Both travels are highly personal, sometimes life-threatening, and they both perpetually challenge the voyager to apply wits, energy, and self-discipline in order to achieve an itinerary. Teaching well and sailing well are a lot alike.

Let's begin by recognizing that both good sailing and good teaching make use of an enormous natural energy. For sailors the energy comes from the wind and sea, and the challenge is to adapt those energies in order to achieve locomotion toward one's chosen destinies. The fastest, most favored courses follow the wind or go across it, using its force to push the vessel forward toward selected goals. Sometimes the destination lies directly beyond the wind's direction, so one must sail diagonally back and forth across the wind, using its force to draw oneself steadily but more slowly forward. Attempts to sail directly against it, however, will render the vessel stalled, dead in the water. Navigation that complements the predictable times of flooding and ebbing tides likewise enhances the voyage. Extremes of storms and doldrums always come from time to time, but they are anticipated by prudent sailors who take precautions, understanding that surrounding conditions are by their nature always changing—even though sometimes the changes are imperceptible.

The energy tapped by successful teachers is that which abounds in young adolescent students and flows naturally from them. I refer to their vigorous mental activity, not just their well-known physical energies. Each youngster's mind is working all the time on ideas, questions, intuitions, and theories of interpretation that for often imperceptible reasons drive his or her thoughts. This ever-present mental activity is the energy that provokes inquiry, challenges, speculation, learning, and scholarship. It is the essential energy we teachers must learn to complement and steer. When we are responsive to that energy, we create ways for it to propel students and ourselves onto new passages. Without their energy, we all drift, often mindlessly. Conflicted, aimless, meaningless schooling becomes the shoals of education that must be avoided at all costs.

Maintaining the principle of balance is essential in both sailing and teaching. Wise sailors preserve balance by adjusting the boat's rigging, sails, and direction to achieve maximum benefits from the combined forces of wind and sea. Prudent teachers likewise try to achieve a balance of expectations for learning and types of teaching and learning activities. They understand that middle level education at its best is an accomplishment shared by students and teachers. The goal to achieve balance between the adults' agendas and the students' priorities must guide every educational decision, just as the wary sailor constantly strives to achieve maximum speed without capsizing.

Teachers and sailors must be vigilant learners, expanding and refining their own wits, testing possibilities, learning from every encounter, and continuously growing in wisdom through experience. Because the surrounding conditions are fluid, varying sometimes from hour to hour, it is necessary for them to be good observers, continuously monitoring changes and taking corresponding deliberate actions to accommodate the circumstances. An essential navigational skill is the ability to correctly assess directionality and velocity of the energy. Just as light breezes necessitate lots of sail, and stronger winds require that sails be shortened, teachers adjust their demands and strategies according to shifting conditions of student energy. And in a gale, prudent sailors and prudent teachers both batten the hatches and ride it out, keeping things simple and remembering that all storms pass.

Finally, good sailors and good teachers both show personal courage. In the face of adversity that may sometimes seem life-threatening, they show faith and determination. In spite of fear of failure or impending disaster, they muster the mettle and self-discipline to remain poised and rational. Roland Barth (1990), teacher and sailor, writes about his own profound learning experiences on occasions when he summoned his courage and took chances, "when the boat was heeling and water was washing over the gunwhales. Learning seldom comes from passively sitting still in the water with the sails flapping."

In this book I have tried to explain the possibilities and the storm signs in terms that will serve the novice sailor as well as the old salt. I alert you now, however—you won't learn either sailing or teaching by merely reading. No, you must move into the wind, allowing its embrace to guide you into a host of challenges and new realizations. You must do it to learn it. I hope this book will help prepare you and make sense of the voyages ahead, enabling you to realize new possibilities for teaching as a wiser, more skilled navigator and pilot, encouraged about your own potential and readiness. As we begin, I wish you fresh breezes and fair tides!

Chris Stevenson
Burlington, Vermont

Now sits the wind fair, and we will be aboard.

Shakespeare, *Henry V*

REFERENCE

Barth, R. (1990). A personal vision of a good school. *Phi Delta Kappan, 71*(7), 513.

Chapter 1

A Rationale for Responsive Schooling

○ *What is a responsive middle school?*

○ *How does it differ from a junior high school?*

○ *What should be the purposes of schooling for young adolescents?*

ASSIGNMENT

Before reading further, sketch on a large sheet of paper a ten-, eleven-, twelve-, thirteen-, or fourteen-year-old student. Draw either a girl or a boy, whichever suits you. Don't worry about the artistic merit of your sketch—keep the emphasis on portraying what you think. When you've completed your sketch, label all the parts that come to mind. When you're satisfied with your drawing, set it aside. We'll come back to it later.

TEACHING IN THE MIDDLE GRADES—THE NATURE OF THE WORK

There are passionate advocates for teaching all age or grade levels and proponents for many different approaches to teaching. Kindergarten teachers love the innocence and wonder of five-year-olds. First grade teachers want to launch their children successfully into a lifetime of reading and loving literature. High school teachers cherish the opportunity to organize their disciplines to teach them to late adolescent students, who offer an expanding consciousness and ability to think like adults. For a long time, those of us working at the middle level, however, have had to overcome a somewhat dubious identity in both public and collegial perceptions. Our choice to teach at the middle level raises a fundamental question we must examine and answer clearly if we are to understand ourselves in relation to this important work.

Why Does Anyone Deliberately Choose to Work Daily with Young Adolescents?

Stereotypes emerge from exaggerated characteristics that obscure the facts of individuality. A particularly harmful stereotype has long been associated with young adolescent children. In general it portrays these youngsters as rebellious, frantic, confused, irresponsible, inattentive, and driven by obsessions about boy–girl issues. G. Stanley Hall's early two-volume study of adolescence proffered the "storm and stress" theory that emphasized an emotional instability in this age group (1904). Over the years, distortions of that influential work have been popularized into much more superficial, inaccurate characterizations contributing to the stereotype.

Because these young people are changing so rapidly from the physically smaller stature and more typically docile, obedient temperament of earlier childhood, ten- to fourteen-year-olds pose a difficult challenge to any single definition of who they are and what matters to them. Perhaps that is why so many descriptors are used in reference to these youngsters: in-betweeners, transescents, pubescents, junior high kids, middlers, teenagers, emerging adolescents, early adolescents. We must think of these variably developing children in terms of a period of several years during which the transition from childhood to full adolescence is accomplished.

Prevailing stereotypes of young adolescents have done enormous harm to both the public's and educators' perceptions of students during this particular time of their developmental lives. Of course, not all of them are obsessed with sex, rebellious to adults, or uninterested in intellectual matters. Among the few accurate generalizations that can be made is that these children change immensely in lots of ways during these years and that variability among them is common. Sweeping generalized definitions of who they are, how they are, and what they care about should be treated with caution if not outright rejection.

These several years of a child's accelerated development in the transition toward adulthood are often confusing to parents and teachers. Relative consistencies and predictability from earlier times are no longer comfortably dependable. Activities that were happily shared in the past are less appealing to children. Their withdrawal from efforts to please their adults and their sometimes outright challenges to adult authority are upsetting. That these and other changes are confusing to adults is not surprising, so understanding what is happening and what to expect is essential to working compatibly with children in this age group.

Some Generalizations You Can Trust

For three decades I have worked with young adolescents, observing and contemplating their day-to-day lives. I have recognized five motives that have applied consistently to every single student I have come to know well. These truisms may also apply to students of other ages, but my interest has been primarily occupied by ten- to fourteen-year-olds. When all five of these needs conditions are satisfied, children perform well by all measures of academic learning and citizenship. While it may be far-fetched to expect each teacher working alone to ensure these conditions for every student, I have seen that in schools or on teams where teachers embrace these propositions and work to achieve their fulfillment, remarkable accomplishments proliferate.

Every Child Wants to Believe in Himself or Herself as a Successful Person

> A little boy was asked how he learned to skate. He replied, "Oh, by getting up every time I fell down."
>
> *(Dale, 1984, p. 80)*

I've never known a youngster who didn't care very deeply about being a success. Our life instinct is to become accomplished in whatever ways matter and feel correct to us, and young adolescents are growing rapidly in self-awareness and aspirations. Each of us is gifted, and we need to find expression for those gifts and accomplishments that validate our existence. Watch the toddler's attempts to walk. Tumbles and bumps dissuade him only temporarily before he's back for another attempt. Once early locomotion is accomplished, the explorations expand to new opportunities now within reach that weren't previously viable. This incremental process of exploring, testing, and accumulating experience—assimilating, in Piagetian terms—is simply the way we are as humans. It is from natural curiosity and exploration of our world that we learn or—again in Piagetian terms—accommodate. The successes we have from our earliest experiences as toddlers feed this human process of seeking and valuing success.

By the time youngsters reach the middle grades, they have already had lots of experience pursuing success. Most of them have succeeded often enough for their natural striving to still be functional and for them to be optimistic about continuing success. Others, however, have had a much harder time of it.

The circumstances of many children's lives are astonishingly difficult given the assortment of social problems affecting them today. For example, only about a third of them live with both parents. What is truly remarkable about young adolescents, however, is that no matter how badly things have gone for them in past years, they are eager to be optimistic, receptive to a genuine invitation to make a fresh start, willing to try again. What a precious opportunity for those who teach them!

Those of us who elect to work with these youngsters must never lose sight of their desire to be successful and their resourcefulness in spite of past experiences. We must also be especially mindful that the array of legitimate opportunities for success that we provide must be much more expansive than those that schools traditionally allow through honor rolls and interscholastic sports. Our challenge is twofold: to look to the children in order to understand what matters to them and to find ways to provide for their collective and individual interests so that they have successes at school. This challenge necessitates our looking well beyond traditional schooling. Our success is essential to their becoming the healthiest, most fulfilled people they have the potential to be.

Every Youngster Wants to Be Liked and Respected

> People develop feelings that they are liked, wanted, acceptable, and able from having been liked, wanted, accepted . . . successful. One learns that he is these things, not from being told but only through the experience of being treated as though he were so. Here is the key to what must be done to produce more adequate people.
>
> *Arthur W. Combs (Dale, 1984, p. 37)*

Much has been written and said about the power of peer influences on kids' values and behaviors. Peer pressure has become a familiar term. During these transition years from childhood to adolescence, there is a gradual shift from parents as the primary influence to a growing predominance of selected peers and peer groups (Elkind, 1984). Further, the "Steinberg accelerating hypothesis" suggests that parent–child distance accelerates pubertal maturation (1988). The essence of the issue, however, is often overlooked. Youngsters want to be liked and respected not just by age-mates but by both generations—peers and adults, including parents. As their teachers, we must devise ways to be responsive to this natural craving for recognition and respect.

Erik Erikson has written about the desire for approval from adults as a central motivation in the "industry need" (1968). Children want to be recognized as producers, people who can make worthwhile contributions to society. They need to be seen as positive contributors, and they take great satisfaction in receiving the approval of selected adults. Often there is disparity between what the child perceives as worthy of adult recognition and what the adult in question regards as meritorious. Teachers and other adults who work closely with these children need to be watchful for such tension so as to avoid costly misunderstandings and setbacks to confidence.

A tragic circumstance of schools and other social settings is the instance in which children are roundly rejected by other people, regardless of their generations. Even simple indifference from another person whose responsiveness is valued may be construed as rejection by one whose need for approval is particularly urgent. We all know about social isolation from our own experiences growing up. When children ache for belonging but are ignored or outwardly rejected, the pain runs deep and may profoundly affect the youngster's relationship to society. Teachers cannot override all conditions of peer rejection, of course, but there is much we can do to increase the probability that every student will find another student or group where membership is possible. How we group children for instruction and activities, how well we establish and preserve communications about interpersonal matters, and how well we recognize the worth and contributions of every student have enormous potential in helping children achieve the friendships and respect they need.

Every Youngster Wants to Do and Learn Things That Are Worthwhile

The media have recently and appropriately reported the action of some eleven-year-old boys and their teacher of shaving their heads in support of a classmate. Scott Sibelius had begun to lose his hair in clumps as a result of chemotherapy treatments he was receiving for lymphoma, so he had his head shaved rather than endure an irregular and embarrassing process of shedding. In a demonstration of compassion and support for Scott, his classmates and his teacher, Jim Alter, likewise shaved their heads. No one could deny that these young adolescents acted admirably, but just imagine the affirmation Scott experienced and the gratification his buddies felt for what they did. They all recognized the importance of this outward sign of loyalty and the value in doing it.

Craig Kielberger, a twelve-year-old Toronto student, became concerned about the exploitation of children as industrial workers in countries that were trading partners of Canada (and also the United States). With remarkable determination, he and several friends created an organization to lobby against the exploitation of child labor wherever it was occurring. In just a few years "Free the Children" has become a recognized, effective movement, taking Craig and others on speaking tours around the world and before committees of the Canadian Parliament and the United States Congress.

It often seems that too much of early adolescence is spent waiting. Kids typically have few real options for actions such as these examples that they recognize as immediately important. With the possible exception of a few youngsters who have a paper route or regular baby-sitting or lawn care work, they are also financially dependent. Their time for first employment, driving a car, and making consequential decisions may be only a few years away, but their need for authentic, worthwhile engagement is at the moment.

John Arnold uses the term *empowerment* in referring to young adolescents' need for experiences that are to them self-evidently worthwhile (Arnold, 1993). He argues for school curricula that "will enable young adolescents increasingly to assume control over their own learning, exercising initiative and responsibility . . . helping (them) make sense of themselves and their world . . . rich in meaning, dealing with issues worth knowing . . . exploring values . . . [contributing] to the well being of others" (p. 7). While much more will be said on this subject in Part Two, the urgency of their need for such authentic experience merits early and frequent mention. Whether students are conducting a study of their neighborhood or community or providing a volunteer service to primary children or senior citizens, they need to be engaged in activities they recognize as having both learning value for them and a positive impact on others. The inevitable outcome of such authentic experience is that students will perceive themselves as needed and worthwhile. Remember Scott Sibelius, Craig Kielberger, and their classmates.

Every Youngster Wants Physical Exercise and Freedom to Move

Over the years I've spent working with young adolescents, I've listened to hundreds of conversations in which kids talk about themselves, what they enjoy doing, and what they believe they do well. I have also formally and informally interviewed lots of them, asking them to simply "tell me about yourself." Two themes relative to physical freedom and expression predominate throughout this discourse. One theme is that lots of physical activity, ranging from relatively mild to moderate to highly vigorous, is essential and central to their daily lives. An overwhelming majority of children respond to the question "What things do you do well?" with references to physical activities and individual pursuits such as running, swimming, bicycling, skating, four square, and gymnastics as well as team sports, especially soccer, baseball, football, basketball, volleyball, dodge ball, and so on. As responsive educators we must meet these exercise needs through physical education classes and intramural events, but we must also look for additional ways to help children find outlets.

These youngsters have also been eager to talk about what works well for them at school as well as what causes them problems. A second theme relative to their commentary about physicality in their lives concerns the movement they enjoy during the school day. A common difficulty they cite is confinement. One report of adolescents who do well in school revealed that among the factors to which they attributed their successes was the freedom they were allowed to move about the classroom and work with classmates (Beane & Lipka, 1986). Teachers who provide an assortment of groupings and activities are being responsive to kids' natural needs.

It has become clear that young adolescents are most comfortable when they have reasonable freedom to move about the classroom and school as their needs dictate rather than according to the limitations of a bell schedule enforcing thirty-five- or forty-minute periods. It appears to me that they associate such relatively free movement about the school with an attitude of advocacy for them and their needs, while the more restricting character of desk confinement and a traditional bell schedule are adversarial.

Youngsters Want Life to Be Just

> Integrity without knowledge is weak and useless. Knowledge without integrity is dangerous and dreadful.
>
> *Samuel Johnson (Dale, 1984, p. 94)*

What would we do in schools if our primary purpose was to educate children to be moral?

John F. Arnold (1989)

At first glance, one might assume that in school and family situations where children are being successful and enjoying satisfactory relationships with peers and adults, life is good. Indeed, such youngsters have the outward trappings of the good life. But there is another dimension to "good" that must not be overlooked: the life that is morally and ethically good. Young adolescents are aware that conceptualizations of interpersonal ethics and moral order exist. Regardless of their home or community contexts, only under the rarest of circumstances does one of them live in a moral vacuum.

Regardless of children's social and economic backgrounds, they live in a world of constant debate around questions of right and wrong. The omnipresence of the media—especially television—and the consistency of prosocial values taught from the child's first experiences in schools ensure that the basic conceptual dichotomies of right and wrong, justice and injustice, truth and falsehood, good and evil, courage and cowardice, loyalty and betrayal are established in their consciousness. Whether or not they always act as we would like, it is the exception when a child does not understand the choices.

What is particularly wonderful and at the same time almost overpowering is that during these middle years one dimension of the changes children experience has to do with how they assess the world they inhabit. This is an era in which youngsters face a great deal of internal struggle between what they may believe and what they wind up doing. Here's the time when the standards and behaviors we model become so very critical to their private challenges. One student commenting about his teachers' participation in public protests said, "These teachers don't just talk that talk, they walk that walk." What are the special implications for us as teachers as we contemplate moral and ethical issues?

In interviews, youngsters most frequently defined the good life as one that is "fun." Read carefully here: Their use of "fun" does not mean playing and joking around, although those activities may be a peripheral part of a setting they would describe as "good." No, by "good life" they refer to characteristics such as fair, safe, interesting, and exciting to conditions that show them they are special and worthwhile and that they are accomplishing good work and doing important learning. Where students are voicing their ethical dilemmas, working peacefully and purposefully together, and manifesting good humor and contentment with each other, the good life in their terms prevails.

The Norm: Constant but Irregular Changes

What is normal and predictable about children during the several transitional years of early adolescence is that individual and group change will be constant but irregular. By *irregular* I refer to differences in timing and intensity of changes from child to child. Consider the most visible of adolescent changes: the body. Many children's bodies will change dramatically, while others will appear to change very little. It is not uncommon for two children of the same age to vary in height by a foot and in weight by as much as sixty or seventy pounds. A normal time for the beginning of physical changes is any time within a period of approximately three years beginning about ages ten and eleven.

An earlier developmental time when children are becoming facile with language and able to communicate easily with a variety of other people is sometimes referred to as the age of reason. The young adolescent years might be considered the second age of reason, because there are notable changes in the way youngsters think. Some of them will show surprising evidence of new intellectual sophistication, while the thinking of others of the same chronological age remains essentially childlike. Materials they become interested in reading, things they choose to do with leisure, and the points of view from which they assess events in their daily lives and in the world further reflect the variety that is common to this transition period. Teachers who recognize these natural growth processes find satisfaction in working with changing youngsters, discovering compatibility and mutual benefits in learning from them while guiding their healthy development.

The central difficulty in describing young adolescents is that although some generalizations may be made about selected dimensions of change they undergo, there is no typical youngster. Although we may find ourselves easily slipping into generalizations such as "eighth graders are obsessed with sex," there remains in truth a tremendous variety of developmental circumstances pertaining to children of the same chronological age. It becomes necessary, therefore, to conceptualize early adolescence as the developmental span overlapping the approximate ages of ten to fourteen. During this time there are multiple interactions between genetically determined physiological changes and elements in one's living and learning contexts that affect the progress and adjustments of individual youngsters. In order to reasonably comprehend this multifaceted, dynamic developmental state, we must visualize development through a multifold, interactive framework.

One particularly helpful conceptualization of this dynamic developmental era is offered by John P. Hill of Virginia Commonwealth University (1980). In his synthesis of developmental research, six classic psychosocial issues are referred to as Secondary Changes (see Table 1.1). We might think of these issues as human development tasks that are especially sensitive during early adolescence, although their resolution is not limited to this period. In considering these psychosocial issues, it is important to remember the variables of

TABLE 1.1   Psychosocial Issues in Adolescent Development

Issue	Adolescent Change
Attachment	Transforming childhood social bonds to parents to bonds acceptable between parents and their adult children.
Autonomy	Extending self-initiated activity and confidence in it to wider behavioral realms.
Sexuality	Transforming social roles and gender identity to incorporate sexual activity with others.
Intimacy	Transforming acquaintanceships into friendships; deepening and broadening capacities for self-disclosure, affective perspective-taking, altruism.
Achievement	Focusing industry and ambition into channels that are future-oriented and realistic.
Identity	Transforming images of self to accommodate primary and secondary change; coordinating images to attain a self-theory that incorporates uniqueness and continuity through time.

(SOURCE: J.P. Hill, Understanding Early Adolescence: A Framework. Carrboro, NC: Center for Early Adolescence, University of North Carolina at Chapel Hill, 1980. Reprinted by permission)

(a) each youngster's context, (b) the timing of the onset of change, and (c) the relative intensity of changes among individuals.

Hill's framework, shown in Figure 1.1, illustrates the complex interactions of biology (Primary Changes) with context (Settings) and adolescent developmental tasks (Secondary Changes). While no model can adequately accommodate the manifold idiosyncratic issues and interactions youngsters engage in during these years, this configuration stands as a durable organizational model for understanding both established research and more contemporary inquiries. Readers are encouraged to study the full explanation of Hill's framework for a fuller conceptualization and understanding of the dynamic forces of early adolescence.

Cultural Recognition of Early Adolescence

Many so-called primitive cultures have long recognized the changes occurring in the transition from childhood to adulthood. Margaret Mead's (1950) classic anthropological studies of the 1920s documenting community life in Pacific island cultures noted formal community recognition of this several-year passage from early childhood dependency on others into the fuller participation of adulthood. Ruth Benedict's (1934) comparative studies of the Pueblos of New Mexico, the Dobu of New Guinea, and the Kwakiutl of the American Northwest Coast further showed that although rites of passage and ceremonies vary considerably among peoples, each culture recognizes the maturational significance of

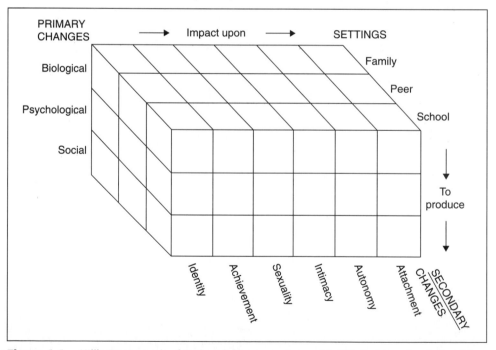

Figure 1.1   Hill's Framework of Early Adolescence   Source: J. P. Hill, Understanding Early Adolescence: A Framework. Carrboro, NC: Center for Early Adolescence, University of North Carolina at Chapel Hill, 1980. Reprinted by permission.

the transition. The "walkabout" custom of Australian aboriginals is an adventure in which the young adolescent boy leaves the family circle and strikes out alone to demonstrate his readiness for manhood and ability to be self-sufficient. Such events constitute cultural markers that indicate progress along the path to full adult status in the culture. Markers vary from culture to culture, and they may consist of demonstrations by boys that they have achieved warrior status or can stoically tolerate physical pain.

In some cases the rites are primarily associated with physiological changes. Menarche, the signal event for girls, may bring about temporary banishment from one cultural group, while in others it may be regarded as a manifestation of supernatural blessings. In yet other cultures the physical events of puberty are subsumed in a more comprehensive recognition of growing up. The community acknowledges that youngsters are growing and changing steadily as they progress toward full adult status. As Benedict reminds us, "the puberty they recognize is social, and the ceremonies are a recognition in some fashion or other of the child's new status of adulthood" (1934, p. 25). This notion of social puberty is significant as we think about the ways in which contemporary American society recognizes early adolescence.

The highly pluralistic and changing nature of our contemporary culture obscures the few remaining markers for our youth. Yet, our young adolescents may still be recognized and celebrated as a consequence of their membership in their families and a few subcultural groups. For example, children who are Roman Catholics or members of many Protestant religions usually study the catechism or other components of faith before they pass through rites of confirmation to new status in their churches. Jewish boys and girls likewise experience similar specialized religious schooling that culminates in the ceremonies of bar mitzvah and bas mitzvah. These ceremonies, usually occurring at the age of thirteen, signify acceptance of these youths into adult status in their religion. Certainly our cultural definition of early adolescence is much more obscure than it was in earlier generations and today remains in other cultures. American children see differences between membership in Cub Scouts or Brownies in the elementary grades and Boy Scouts or Girl Scouts in the middle grades as a matter of one organization existing for children, the other for adolescents. Parents often make determinations of such matters as allowance, chores, bedtime, and dating age on the basis of their own sense of family tradition and interpretations of cultural standards. Defining this period of life in terms of developmentally appropriate expectations, responsibilities, and opportunities is a task that educators must perform in order to reestablish a sense of place in American society for young adolescents. As David Elkind laments, "Vanishing markers give ample evidence that there is no special place for teenagers in today's society" (1984, p. 113).

In spite of the traditional elementary–secondary division in education in the United States, we have come to recognize the need for schooling that is conceptualized, designed, and administered to be mindful of individual and cultural conditions of the ten- to fourteen-year-old's time of life.

Responsive Schooling for Young Adolescents

Just as the students are variable, so must their schooling provide complementary diversity—choices of curricular content, multiple approaches to teaching, diverse grouping formats. Expecting every student to learn the same material at the same time as a result of the same exposure is contradictory to their developmental diversity. Expectations that young adolescents will thrive in a teacher-focused, textbook-centered classroom hour after hour, day after day is at the very least naive. Teachers who expect and seek that type of uniformity should stay away from the middle grades, where at any moment authentic learning reflects learners engrossed in studying a multitude of topics employing a wide variety of learning activities, much of which they sustain themselves.

Since the mid-1960s a gradual but steady reform has been taking place in the design and practice of education for students at the middle level of American schools (Lounsbury, 1984). While the contemporary middle school movement is seen by many as a recent development, it is in fact the most comprehensive professional response ever made to the long-standing realization and belief of many educators that schooling at this level should be responsive to young adolescents' changing developmental nature. It is also important to note a somewhat subtle distinction in semantics associated with middle-level education and middle schools. One-third of all the students in public schools may be referred to as being in the "middle level" or "middle grades" (5–8). However, they attend schools that are organized according to a variety of configurations: K–6, 7–12, K–8, K–12, 7–9, and so on. The reference is to the group of students in the middle of the twelve-year spectrum of public education.

Middle school refers to a school that is organized to include some combination of the grades between 5 and 9. In one of their several studies describing middle school practices, William Alexander and Kenneth McEwin report that the dominant organizational trend is to include grades 6 through 8. They explain that a "major development in American school organization and programs during the twentieth century is from two-level elementary and secondary school organization to a three-level organization: elementary, middle and high school" (Alexander & McEwin, 1989, p. 3). In comparing data collected in similar ways from 1968 and 1988, they conclude that the traditional grade 7–9 junior high school organization has declined dramatically in favor of 6–8, 7–8, and 5–8 configurations. They go on to emphasize that "most important is the evolution of the school once created which in impressive numbers succeed in becoming real middle schools" (p. 5). Their data confirm the continuing trend toward more widespread schooling that is increasingly responsive to youngsters' needs at this time of life rather than practices that remain mindlessly bound to traditional ways of doing things that may be contrary to healthy child development.

The junior high school movement of the late 1920s and early 1930s was previously the most focused attempt to create distinctive schooling for the middle grades. That movement reflected educators' recognition of students' developmental transition and the need for schooling that responded to those conditions. This trend was short-lived, however, succumbing to a lack of clear identity and understanding by both the public and the profession (Briggs, 1920). The many similarities between traditional junior high schools and their senior high counterparts that persist in many schools today derive from educators' failure to understand and make commitments to schooling that is responsive to the developmental needs of young adolescents.

A central reason for the durability and promise of the current middle school movement is that its specialized mission and exemplary practices have been clarified and well publicized. The flow of publications concerning the education of young adolescents has grown and expanded steadily since the decade of the 1920s. (For an annotated bibliography see Lawton, 1989 and Totten, et al., 1996.) Publication of *The Middle School We Need* in 1975 succinctly offered clarity and direction to the movement (Gatewood & Dilg,

1975). This widely disseminated publication has been an often-cited antecedent of public positions taken by learned societies that are especially influential in giving direction to educational reform. A brief review of two of those benchmark publications is appropriate.

As it became increasingly evident that the middle-level education movement presented a serious opportunity to create more responsive schooling for young adolescents, the need for a professional association to communicate pertinent educational advances and insights became more urgent. Thus, the National Middle School Association (NMSA) was founded in 1973, an outgrowth of the Midwest Middle School Association begun three years earlier. This new national organization, committed to furthering specialized schooling at the middle level, quickly became established with a central office, publications, and conference services. Membership growth and expansion of services have been steady, and since the 1980s NMSA has been the dominant voice for middle-level education. A recent revision of the original 1982 publication of *This We Believe* articulates the guiding beliefs and characteristics of schools that excel in service to youngsters at the middle level (NMSA, 1995). That document is outlined below, but readers are urged to obtain and study its full text.

Effective middle (level) schools share these major characteristics:

A shared vision
Educators who are committed to young adolescents
A positive school climate
Adult advocates for every student
Family and community partnerships
High expectations for all

This benchmark document goes on to spell out essential elements of "effective middle schools":

A challenging and exploratory curriculum
Varied instructional practices
Assessment and evaluation that promotes learning
Organizational flexibility
Health and wellness policies and programs
Comprehensive guidance and support services

In recognizing the need for differences in schooling for younger and older adolescents, the National Association of Secondary School Principals (NASSP) formed a Council on Middle Level Education composed of established leaders in the middle-level movement. Their 1985 publication of *An Agenda for Excellence at the Middle Level* stated positions compatible with NMSA's document and added explicit programmatic recommendations for schools. Explications from those philosophical statements are briefly sketched below. Again, readers are encouraged to study the full text of this excellent document (NASSP, 1985).

1. *Core values* must guide both the individual behavior and institutional policies and practices and must address personal responsibility, the primacy of learning and intellectual activity, and respect for diversity found in the school and the society that nurtures it.

2. *Culture and climate:* School improvement depends on change—not on the addition of certain program elements that seem to appear in effective schools, but change that supports excellence and achievement rather than intellectual conformity and mediocrity.

3. *Study development:* Schooling should focus on the practice and mastery of personal attributes and behaviors related to a realistic adjustment to adult life.

4. *Curriculum* must balance skill development with content coverage intellectual skills, and an understanding of humankind that will permit the student to gather information, organize it in a meaningful fashion, evaluate its veracity and utility, form reasonable conclusions about it, and plan for individual and collective action.

5. *Learning and instruction* should be characterized by teachers who are caring, enthusiastic, optimistic, and well versed in pedagogy and their subject areas, and who have high expectations and are accessible, patient, and quick to reward good student performance.

6. *School organization* should encourage the smooth operation of the academic program, clear communication, and maximum teacher and student control over the quality of the learning environment and should contribute to a sense of belonging and militate against anonymity and alienation from the primary mission of the school.

7. *Technology:* Students should learn to use technology competently and thoughtfully in their study of specific subjects and in their approach to complex problems.

8. *Teachers* who model intellectual growth and excitement of learning understand the subjects they teach and the development of young adolescents. They require special preparation in human development, counseling, differentiating instruction, classroom management, and home–school cooperation.

9. *Transition:* A main responsibility is the smooth transition from elementary to high school through coordinated plans to integrate curriculum across all grade levels.

10. *Principals* should provide strong administrative leadership and have a clear sense of mission and confidence in the capacity of administrators to handle problems that interfere with the learning program of the school.

11. *Connections:* The school must work harder today to maintain good relations with its constituent community.

12. *Client-centeredness:* Teachers should understand the relationship of development to learning so that students are not asked to violate their development in order to participate fully in the educational program.

Since public education is organized, administered, and funded primarily at the state and community levels, the enactment of the aforementioned policy recommendations has been patchy. In spite of such irregularity, however, the movement toward specially written policies and technical assistance for the middle grades is growing rapidly in approximately half of the states (Children's Defense Fund, 1988). Several major state reports have given explicit direction to the creation of responsive education for young adolescents. Further information about state-approved policy definitions and programs for the middle level can be found in *Middle Level Education: An Annotated Bibliography* (Totten et al, 1996).

The urgency of continuing reform in schooling practices at the middle level is documented in studies of dropouts and the reasons they give for their decision to leave school prematurely (Wheelock & Dorman, 1988). This study reports that the school-leaving syndrome is rooted in loss of self-confidence and disillusionments exacerbated by alienating practices and conditions in the middle grades. Among the factors cited most frequently are retention in grade, tracking and ability grouping, discrimination based on standardized tests, boredom with standardized curriculum and instruction, punitive practices, suspension and expulsion practices, school climate and rules, and fragmented school organization. The report suggests numerous remedies and alternatives—all of which are discussed in subsequent chapters of this book.

Perhaps no document concerning the education of young adolescents has achieved such widespread public and professional attention as the prestigious Carnegie Corporation's (1989) publication of *Turning Points: Preparing American Youth for the 21st Century* by its Council on Adolescent Development. This report was prepared differently from all of the preceding ones in that the task force members were not middle-level education specialists. For the first time a council composed of political leaders, policy specialists, researchers, and other lay leaders promoted an educational agenda that is responsive to the needs of young adolescent students. This excellent report confirms the momentous developmental changes of young adolescents, warns of the many risks encountered by multitudes of contemporary youth, and makes recommendations for transforming middle grades schools. Six years later (1995), an overview of the progress being made by schools, gains made by students, and continuing initiatives being required was given by the same council in *Great Transitions: Preparing Adolescents for a New Century*. Readers are again urged to study these full reports in detail.

The executive summary of *Turning Points* appears below.

The Task Force calls for middle grade schools that:

Create small communities for learning where stable, close, mutually respectful relationships with adults and peers are considered fundamental for intellectual development and personal growth. The key elements of these communities are schools-within-schools or houses, students and teachers grouped together as teams, and small group advisories that ensure that every student is well known by at least one adult.

Teach a core academic program that results in students who are literate, including in the sciences, and who know how to think critically, lead a healthy life, behave ethically, and assume the responsibilities of citizenship in a pluralistic society. Youth service to promote values for citizenship is an essential part of the core academic program.

Ensure success for all students through elimination of tracking by achievement level and promotion of cooperative learning, flexibility in arranging instructional time, and adequate resources (time, space, equipment, and materials) for teachers.

Empower teachers and administrators to make decisions about the experiences of middle grade students through creative control by teachers over the instructional program linked to greater responsibilities for students' performance, governance committees that assist the principal in designing and coordinating schoolwide programs, and autonomy and leadership within subschools or houses to create environments tailored to enhance the intellectual and emotional development of all youth.

Staff middle grade schools with teachers who are expert at teaching young adolescents and who have been specially prepared for assignment to the middle grades.

Improve academic performance through fostering the health and fitness of young adolescents, by providing a health coordinator in every middle grade school, access to health care and counseling services, and a health-promoting school environment.

Reengage families in the education of young adolescents by giving families meaningful roles in school governance, communicating with families about the school program and student's progress, and offering families opportunities to support the learning process at home and at the school.

Connect schools with communities, which together share responsibility for each middle grade student's success, through identifying service opportunities in the community, establishing partnerships and collaborations to ensure students' access to health and social services, and using community resources to enrich the instructional program and opportunities for constructive after-school activities. (Carnegie Corporation, 1989)

The majority of states have published within the last decade some form of state policy guidelines for the middle level. A few of them include curriculum mandates and other regulations that pertain specifically to the middle level. Some initiatives to develop and publish these policy positions arose from the encouragement and support of the Carnegie Corporation. Others arose from the momentum of local educators working in partnership with lawmakers and state department of education officials. This emergence of state policies signals the growth and significance the middle level has achieved in recent years.

Almost every state also now has a professional middle level organization that is represented in the fifty-two affiliated members of the National Middle School Association. Affiliated organizations exist in several provinces of Canada, and there is an active European League of Middle Schools. The National Collegiate Middle School Association exists to support college students who are preparing to be middle level teachers, and it sponsors special events and publications for its membership.

Further information about all these affiliated associations can be obtained by writing to NMSA, 2600 Corporate Exchange Drive, Suite 370, Columbus, Ohio 43231–1672 or by telephoning the toll-free number: (800) 528–NMSA (see also Totten et al., 1996, pp. 355–366).

From these reports of national policy developments and initiatives by professional associations, one might assume that there has been a new unanimity of purpose among educators plus a felicitous transformation of schooling practices. The fact is, however, that actual change in schools seems to occur very gradually in spite of such compelling developments.

For a long time those of us involved in middle level innovations have had to rely mostly on personal empiricism, descriptive accounts of exemplary practice, and policy initiatives such as the aforementioned ones to affirm our vision. We have long believed deep down that if we organized ourselves and our students into small learning communities such as teams, *of course* students would perform better as learners and as citizens. We have likewise believed that if every student had an active adult advocate such as a teacher advisor, *of course* they would feel safer and would reciprocate the social values we embody. And many of us have never doubted that when curriculum is authentically integrated, *of course* students will achieve the greater depths of knowledge and meaning that indicate high standards of academic achievement. Studies generating hard data are beginning to appear, and these research reports are encouraging if not downright exciting.

Of particular importance is the massive ongoing longitudinal study of approximately 100 middle level schools that have incorporated Carnegie's previously mentioned "Turning

Points" (Felner, et al., 1997). In order to assess the impact of those reforms, the schools were separated into high, partial and low levels of "implementation" for data gathering and analysis.

First published reports indicate that the more extensively schools implemented reforms such as teaming, advisories and curriculum integration—the higher the students' achievement and the lower the levels of behavior problems (p. 544). In spite of such compelling evidence, however, too many educators have remained reluctant to change. Some merely pay lip service to reform or only make isolated, short-lived, and piecemeal attempts to change their schools. This research also showed that such modest, disconnected changes were unlikely to produce much improvement in students' performance, cautioning that ". . . successful reform must be comprehensive and integrative, with careful attention to sequencing and establishment of some . . . building blocks on which other elements can be mounted . . . there are clear patterns of interdependence" (p. 547).

It is in the day-to-day implementation of visionary propositions such as "Turning Points" that actual changes come to pass. The essential, indispensable ingredient in such change is the teacher and his or her commitment to a shared vision. Because we teachers have spent so many impressionable years in schools, we are often the people who historically have had the greatest difficulty stepping outside our personal situations to look at schooling more holistically and propositionally. We too often dismiss visionary initiatives as simply high-sounding rhetoric, rationalizing that it is easy for one to imagine from the outside how things might be without having to actually do it. But as the Carnegie Task Force also points out,

> "The success of the transformed middle grade school will stand or fall on the willingness
> of teachers and other staff to invest their efforts in [their] young adolescent students.
> Teachers must understand and want to teach young adolescents and find the middle
> grade school a rewarding place to work." (1989, p. 59)

It is in recognition of the possibilities and a personal disposition toward reform for improvement that large numbers of middle-level teachers have addressed the challenges of their circumstances, evolved a common vision, and acted to bring lasting reform to middle-level education. The essential ingredients in this conversion are disposition and collaboration in forming and implementing a common vision.

The Essential Component: Vision

Our belief systems are all-important to the way we assess things, the decisions we make, and the things we do with students. Every middle-level teacher, like every parent, should as a matter of course reflect on "how can I nurture these kids' healthy development and learning?" It's natural to dream of how schools might be and to imagine students working together in cheerful collaborations, taking responsibility for themselves and their learning. The image of students loving to learn and teachers working happily alongside is intoxicating! Such dreams, thoughtfully studied and refined, can become visions—realistic plans to achieve coherence between the ideals we wish to achieve and how we actually function each day. The research literature shows us that in the great schools, vision is always present, giving purpose to teachers' decisions and practices (Lipsitz, 1984).

When schooling is organized around a common vision and translated into statements of mission that spell out steps and processes for implementation, teachers and kids know what the school stands for and where they are headed. A unified purpose grows from such common understanding. I encourage every middle-level teacher to dream on a grand scale, to imagine every possibility, and then to plan realistically for his or her given circumstances. Progress grows incrementally as we take modest but well-conceived steps, studying the results as we go and learning from day-to-day experience.

Sweeping advances may ultimately result from such applied vision—whether the advances are technological, political, or social. The best schoolwide examples of middle-level education have grown from past educators imagining what might derive from programs based on students' particular needs rather than benign generic traditions. The visioning process began when someone looked at students in existing circumstances and imagined possibilities not yet realized. Eventually the envisioner explored those alternatives by trying out innovations with students, learning about the efficacy of the idea from their responses, and shaping and reshaping the activity as suggested by firsthand observations until the innovation became a "new tradition."

Consider this example. At some point during the middle grades, students usually enter a departmentalized program after spending several years in self-contained elementary classrooms. Sometimes the change occurs as early as the third or fourth grade, but more often it comes between the fifth and seventh grades. Regardless of where the change occurs, children move from belonging to a small group into the relative impersonality of multiple classes. Kids usually welcome the change at first, believing that this change marks their movement into schooling associated with more grown-up students. But once the novelty has passed, kids experience varying degrees of confusion. Sometimes their confusion is disabling.

It is not at all difficult for an experienced teacher to recognize the signs of apprehension and confusion as these children are removed from a setting in which they spend the bulk of their day with one adult to one that includes multiple teachers and a school day of continually changing classes geared to bells. This high-school–like configuration disregards children's basic needs to feel a sense of belonging with a more familial group and to know that they have a valued place in a smaller assembly of people. Observant, thoughtful educators have envisioned other less confounding possibilities for organizing students and teachers.

One of the more successful of these innovations is teacher advisories—ideally sized groups of ten to twelve students who meet daily with one teacher who is an advocate for those advisees. (See Chapter 10.) Another creation is the organizational practice of interdisciplinary teams by which several teachers provide the core instruction for a group of 60 to 125 students. (See Chapter 9.) These innovations have now become central organizational features of exemplary middle level education, although originally they were created to work toward a vision about how schools might be better organized to serve young adolescents' needs.

Since the beginning of the middle-level reform movement of the 1960s, several organizational and curricular features have been tried out in numerous middle schools. The observed benefits of those innovations have become widespread, and there are now accepted practices and standards for exemplary schools. The previously cited position statements by NMSA and NASSP went on to include implications for schools. Alexander and

McEwin combined those documents and list "earmarks considered as critical in achieving educational quality in middle schools" (1989, p. 1):

1. An interdisciplinary organization, with a flexibly scheduled day
2. An adequate guidance program, including a teacher advisory plan
3. A full-scale exploratory program
4. Comprehensive curriculum provision for the broad goals of personal development, continued learning skills, and basic knowledge
5. Varied and effective instructional methodology for the age group
6. Continued orientation and articulation for students, parents, and teachers

While others will undoubtedly add their own preferences to this listing of characteristics for exemplary middle level schools, these items are essential. Each allows for the design of programs that will accommodate the developmental conditions of the students they serve. Those already teaching in the middle grades and those anticipating that experience might use this list of program implications to assess the schools they know best.

Impediments to Vision

We are living in the time of the parenthesis, the time between eras. We are clinging to the known past in fear of the unknown future. The time of the parenthesis is a time for change and questioning.

John Naisbitt (1982, p. 279)

Presumably Naisbitt did not have the middle-level reform movement in mind when he wrote these words, but he could not have better articulated teachers' central dilemma—the tension between the "known past" and the "unknown future." Even though the middle level movement is here to stay, most schools do not yet fully manifest the aforementioned "earmarks." Reading and using books such as this one, visiting innovative programs and exemplary schools, and attending workshops and conferences are appropriate forms of questioning during this time of parenthesis, but in themselves they do not constitute the change that requires collaborative vision, action, and mutual support. Change in how middle-level schools function requires collective vision and volition.

In 1970 Charles Silberman charged American education with "mindlessness," especially in junior high schools. He argued that schooling then was largely an uncritical perpetuation of traditions, however ineffectual. That indictment continues to be valid in too many classrooms and schools. Timidity and loyalty to traditions have proved to be rigid limitations on the capacity of many educators for overcoming or transcending whatever may be accepted conventional practice. "Because that's the way we've always done it here" is too common a justification for keeping things the way they are and rationalizing decisions about single issues isolated from larger conceptions of purpose.

An unfortunately persistent example of continuing mindlessness is the practice of tracking students for instruction by so-called ability measures even though comprehensive analysis of research data does not support the practice (Slavin, 1987). Four out of five schools persist in this practice with students at the middle level, although virtually all outstanding middle schools place students in heterogeneously grouped teams (George,

1988). No matter how compelling the case may be for replacing tracking with groupings better suited to the full range of kids' needs, habitual beliefs carry enormous influence when grouping decisions are made. This issue is examined comprehensively, and developmentally appropriate alternative grouping strategies are described in Chapter 7.

Another impediment to vision is teachers' preoccupation with their own performance. While it is natural for the one in charge to be concerned with how he or she is performing in the classroom, what is most important for middle level learners is what they are doing. It is easy to slip into a teaching mode in which all students in a class are expected to be doing or learning the same things at the same time according to a single mode of instruction. Certainly there are lessons and particular content most appropriately presented via simultaneous direct instruction to whole groups, but exaggerated reliance on teacher-centered instruction is inappropriate for highly diverse middle level learners.

Closely akin to the myth that "everyone must be doing the same thing at the same time" at the middle level is the apparent assumption that the most necessary learning derives from prepackaged instructional materials: textbooks, workbooks, kits, and a vast assortment of instructional systems. By this statement I don't question the propriety of selectively employing packaged materials for learning particular concepts or procedures that are well organized and presented in a particular volume. The notion I challenge here is the practice day after tiresome day of directing and regulating youngsters through textbook and workbook materials, ingenuously assuming that such so-called disciplined repetition produces meaningful learning. As every thoughtful, experienced teacher knows, certain words will dampen enthusiasm for learning: "Now, open your textbooks to page. . . ."

While there is no question that having every student working out of textbooks or on worksheets is more efficient and easier to control, we have to look well beyond what I suggest are primarily management strategies if we are to envision the learning of which authentic scholarship is made. We have to acknowledge that simply keeping kids busy and out of trouble isn't the best way to develop their potential as scholars or lovers of learning. Purposeful reading, writing, computing, and the many other manifestations of intellectual activity prevail where youngsters are motivated by genuine interest and purpose, not just mindless obedience. Thus, we have to envision how students can be involved in firsthand learning in ways that differ from our benign tradition of textbook-centeredness. We must look beyond sincere but simplistic apprehensions that "if they don't cover the book, there'll be gaps in their knowledge." Alternatives to these textbook-centered assumptions compose the heart of Part Two of this book.

A final barrier to creating a vision and subsequent innovation that I will mention briefly is the fear that departures from prescriptive curricula will result in lowered standardized test scores. The prevailing logic is "If I don't teach the text, they won't do well on the tests." Horsefeathers! There are no data showing that digressions from lockstep curricula result in lower test scores. Goodlad's (1984) research suggests that published curricula often have very little bearing upon what teachers actually do. I'm not suggesting nihilistically that the curriculum be ignored or discarded. I do mean that selective departures from prescribed curricula and textbooks are not hazardous to student learning, assuming the alternatives are at least equally if not more engaging. Perhaps the most important longitudinal study ever carried out in American education, *The Eight-Year Study,* showed that students who attended innovative secondary schools that did not follow externally prescribed curricula did as well as or better than cohorts who attended traditional secondary schools (Aikin, 1942).

Visions of schooling that transcend many of our traditional practices at the middle level are not uncommon. Many teachers over the years have known in their hearts that better ways of educating emerging adolescents could be found. Many of those teachers acted on their visions and created innovations for the moment, some of which endured. Others dreamed of possibilities for innovation but, for the preceding assortment of reasons as well as others, chose not to act. The momentum of the middle level movement provides unprecedented support for moving beyond traditional practices in order to enhance the efficacy of schooling for emerging adolescents. They must have teachers who are likewise questioning, changing, and eager to grow with them. Where teachers lack vision, their actions become "reflexive, inconsistent, shortsighted . . . [trying] to quickly put out the fire [so that they] can get on with putting out the next one" (Barth, 1990, p. 151).

The Essential Catalyst: The Teacher

Every thinking person will surely agree that teachers are closely connected to the quality of any school. When teachers are committed philosophically and by personal actions in support of common purposes, they achieve remarkable results. Even in the face of serious limitations of resources, teachers bonded by shared purposes effect an aura of purposefulness through their work and optimism through their presence. Their confidence and vitality sweep up students and often the rest of the community into a realm of learning and living that goes well beyond the usual.

When groups of such teachers function synergistically as a team or faculty—each one doing his or her share as well as contributing to everyone else's effort—schooling and education can become synonymous. Occasionally we see this quality of teamwork in a theater group or a basketball team or a music group where the performance reflects selflessness and commitment to common goals. Accomplishments seem to be greater than the sum of the individual parts, yielding outcomes that transcend more ordinary expectations.

The challenges of teaching at the middle level are such that teachers and teachers-to-be should forthrightly examine themselves and their motives. I recommend that everyone considering this career candidly contemplate and respond to several self-assessing questions:

What do I have to offer?
What am I willing to do?
What am I unwilling to do?
What are my motives?

No particular answers to these questions are presupposed as criteria for acceptance as a middle level teacher. It is very important to everyone's welfare, however, that one's responses be consonant with the values and policies discussed in this chapter. Efforts to achieve even better matches between schooling practices and the developmental circumstances of young adolescents must characterize the continuation and expansion of the middle level movement. Consider these several dimensions of teaching at this level:

The Teacher as Curriculum

During the years that I have been a university teacher I have interviewed students who are planning to be teachers about their recollections from the middle grades in their school lives. The interviews begin simply with the invitation "What can you tell me about your memories of being in the middle grades?" Responses are predictably wide ranging, but virtually all respondents name one or more teachers at least once in the interview. If the students aren't adequately explicit in describing the teachers they've mentioned, I say, "Tell me about teacher X." I've rarely encountered anyone who was indifferent to all of his or her teachers. Typically the students comment emphatically, sometimes passionately, often offering illustrative anecdotes. These perceptions of their teachers figure strongly, although they are not necessarily central, in how the students recall these years of schooling.

Some of their recollections of teachers are merely names and roles, for example, "Mr. Washburn taught social studies and Miss Hood was the counselor." But those teachers who are described in detail or who are figures in the stories they share tend to fit one of two general categories that occur fairly equally.

One category is made up of teachers recalled with fondness, sometimes even devotion. It is not uncommon to hear "Mrs. X saved my life!" The stories offered to explain such a dramatic assertion usually contain an example of adult intervention and kindness at a time when an advocate was needed. Many of us experience real or imagined crises during these years, and a benevolent adult who makes a point of conveying humane sustenance makes all the difference in how we get through our episodes. Less sensational comments relate beliefs that a teacher really cared about the student, that she was understanding and forgiving in a crisis. In general these teachers are very much admired, and when asked whether that teacher was in any way an influence on the student's interest in becoming a middle grades teacher, the response is often affirmative.

The other category is the polar opposite: antipathy for the remembered teacher. Usually the student recalls a disliked teacher as someone who either didn't care about kids or even openly expressed dislike for them. Often there are references to these people being unfair. Occasionally the dislike is even stronger, even expressed as impassioned hatred. Incidents of embarrassment or even humiliation in front of classmates are often related as examples of this degree of enmity. I am often struck by how vulnerable these students saw themselves as young adolescents and how much weight they attached to how kindly and lovingly their teachers treated them.

Given the importance students attach to how they perceive their relationships with their teachers, it is especially important that those of us planning to work with them or already working with them assess ourselves as a curriculum of sorts. It may be that during these years our students learn or accommodate more pertinent, enduring knowledge of who we are than they retain from the intended curriculum. Let's consider some of the dimensions of this idea of the teacher as curriculum that will become central to your students' perceptions about you and about their relationships with you.

Your Dispositional Nature. In their study of adolescent self-concepts and self-esteem, Beane and Lipka (1986) asked students who were successful at school to identify factors that they attributed to their success. One of the primary factors identified in this important study was "nice teachers." Although "nice" may be difficult to define from a research perspective, we all know in a general way what that means. Furthermore we're likely to have some personal preferences about the attributes of "nice."

My interviews of university teacher education students likewise generate numerous references to "nice." Their examples of "nice" include references to "friendly, easy to be with, easygoing, helpful, accessible, cheerful, positive, congenial." They make numerous references to their favorite teachers' sense of humor, often citing both "fun" and "funny" about the same individual. These choice teachers are also assessed as "reasonable, fair, and willing to work things out." While these examples are dispositional attributes that could apply at any age or level of schooling, they seem to be especially important as adolescents and young adults recall their middle grades teachers.

My interviews with young adolescents also reveal that they are quite aware that even the most appealing people may yet have bad days. After all, these youngsters are experiencing a time of life when mood swings show firsthand what it is to have a day when lots of things seem to go wrong. They recognize that there are times when for unknown reasons one just doesn't feel good, isn't "on their game," so to speak. These transient moods are forgivable, however, as long as they don't lead to abuses that hurt others. It becomes important, therefore, that teachers have knowledge of their own dispositions. Simply being a nice person should not be unnatural. A generous capacity for tolerance is basic, because students will fall short of your hopes and expectations. Inconsistency is common when children are in the state of flux that is early adolescence.

Your Human Nature. How do you describe yourself intellectually? Aesthetically? In terms of personal courage? What teachers know and can do becomes increasingly important to kids during their middle grade years. It's harder for teachers to achieve credibility without substance and evidence of themselves as knowledgeable people who can do things worth doing. This credibility includes, but is not limited to, how much one knows about the particular subject matter being taught. Hobbies, athletics, outdoor sports, experiences in life other than being a teacher—all these elements of who you are convey you as a resource and ensure your creditable identity as a learning, doing person.

If, for example, you love literature and share your favorite fiction or poetry by occasionally reading aloud to your students, whether or not they care for the particular sample you offered, they'll internalize your nature as a lover of literature. And remember—the emphasis is on sharing your passion for literature, not simply using it to impress your students with your erudition. Freely and comfortably sharing your loves—of music or cooking or fishing or the Red Sox or whatever—helps your students know you better and identify possibilities on which they may be able to begin building a relationship with you. Every time I encounter a twelve-year-old girl who lives in my neighborhood, she asks, "Have you been sailing lately?" It doesn't matter that it is winter or summer; the point is that her knowledge of my love of sailing has become a conversation starter and thus a basis for the friendly relationship enjoyed by two people forty-five years apart in chronological age. Don't underestimate the value youngsters place on knowing much more about you than merely your name and the role you play at school.

Your Nature as a Learner. Evidence of the developmental change process in early adolescence can be seen in the growing incidence of youngsters who have expertise their teachers may not have. I recall several incidents years ago as some of my eleven- and twelve-year-old students worked earnestly to teach me how to ski. Their general goodwill and earnest efforts assured me of their warmth and caring at moments when I was otherwise preoccupied with apprehension, if not outright fear. Their examples and patience with my errors as I progressed unevenly over several seasons from snowplows to stem christies to schussing were particularly satisfying.

A wonderful but potentially disconcerting by-product of the technology boom that has brought microcomputers into classrooms is that middle grades students are often ahead of their teachers in learning how to use them. Many young adolescents converse regularly on the Internet (Burkhardt, 1996). It is not uncommon for those who have advanced in both keyboard and programming skills to become resources to teachers. Students' expertise and the teacher's need for immediate help create a healthy climate of give and take as long as the teacher is comfortable with revealing what some people might construe as a personal deficit.

Another dimension of your nature as a learner is your attitude and what you actually do in order to learn about new things. So much is worthwhile to learn that choosing and following through may be difficult. Nevertheless, being an ongoing learner not only is necessary to lifelong learning but models a central quality for everyone—especially young adolescents becoming aware of so many options. A vibrant middle level school is a place where both students and teachers are engaged in continuous learning. A friend who taught the seventh and eighth grades took up piano at the age of forty-five, never having been able to read music or play an instrument of any kind. She openly shared with her students the challenges and satisfactions of being a struggling learner, and at the end of the year she performed a private recital for her students. Another teacher and coach responded when he saw that some girls in his advisory were learning knitting from their mothers. He solicited an introductory lesson from his wife in order to share the craft with his students and seek their help when he had difficulty. The importance of modeling with one's students what it means to be a lifelong learner cannot be overstated.

Being With-It. The term *withitness* was coined by Jacob Kounin (1970) to characterize a quality possessed by teachers he studied who appeared to "have eyes in the backs of their heads" in that they seemed to know what was going on at all times in a classroom. My adaptation of Kounin's term here as "being with-it" extends the idea of knowing what is going on from the classroom to the adolescent culture. In brief, a teacher who is with-it is able to converse with students about elements of their culture they choose to share, such as clothing fads, favorite musical groups, and television shows. I am not suggesting in any way that the teacher must try to be like them, for that is awkward and inappropriate. I do suggest that if teachers are to build constructive relationships with adolescents, they must have some knowledge of their students' culture (see especially Chapters 2 and 3).

The most direct way to learn a close-knit culture is to live with it and study it first-hand—observing, listening, inquiring, recording, interacting with the constituents. Anthropologists document the way of life of the people they study in order to describe and explain it in nonjudgmental ways to others. While it isn't necessary for middle grades teachers to go to the same lengths as those necessary for a scientist studying an alien culture, an anthropologist's attitude is not only appropriate but necessary if a teacher is to understand her constituency. An eighth grade English teacher transferred to a new school noted that the girls in her classes talked a lot about a rock group unfamiliar to her. She conscientiously listened to kids' conversations, noting their agreements and differences—especially when boys participated. She recognized general differences between girls' and boys' enthusiasm for the group and their music. Subsequently she asked to borrow a record in order to hear the music. By selectively expressing what she liked and disliked about the music, she participated peripherally in her students' culture without losing her separate identity as an adult and teacher.

There is an important distinction here between "being with" students and "being as" students. "Being with" them simply means being consistently attentive to who they are: their interests and concerns, habits and customs. The teacher's ongoing purpose is to understand their culture. "Being as" students refers to the always awkward situation in which a teacher seeking acceptance or popularity tries to join the student culture. In their zeal to be a friend to kids, beginning teachers sometimes lose their way and slip into the certain confusions that derive from trying to be part of the child's culture for which they have adult responsibilities. The challenge is to be with them without being like them; that distinction preserves generational distinctions while at the same time building important bridges of communication and trust.

A POSTSCRIPT

The opening part of this book begins with a letter to those who will read and use it. That letter addressed you as "shipmate" and referred to some parallels between teaching well and sailing well. There's a final similarity I want to draw in closing this introductory chapter.

Experienced sailors know that when equilibrium has been achieved between the energy forces of nature and the adjustments (trim) of the vessel, the helmsman feels a subtle but exciting sensation referred to as "the groove." When sailing is said to be "in the groove," a physical complementarity exists that can be accomplished only through the sailor's study, analysis, and deliberate actions. Balanced forces not only propel the sailor toward a charted destination but provide a priceless bonus: the life-enhancing exhilaration of harmony and belonging. That combination of personal affirmation and renewal explains why sailors return to the sea.

Teachers who have learned how to educate by complementing their students' natural life energies also know the groove. They know the special signs and sensations when, in their vernacular, "everything works." The balance between youngsters' energies and the teacher's educational plan brings about a state of being that elevates schooling far above the ordinary. While this kind of "working" is only partly explainable in the quantified terms of physics that explain sailing, the life-enhancing consequences for teachers are nonetheless real. It is the appeal of this groove that draws us and its actuality that holds us. It is this very relationship between teachers and young adolescents that is the rationale for this book—lives lived "working in the groove."

Unlike sailing, however, teaching well cannot be reduced to quasi-scientific explanations that focus on the teacher and the mechanical processes embodied in such alien rhetoric as "delivering instruction." We must shift our investment of faith and energy from the curriculum more toward the children themselves—individually and collectively. They are the goal, not the means to the exploitive goals of high test scores or championships. While wise teachers remain very attentive to lessons from the science of teaching, they recognize that fundamentally their work remains an art. The life energies of young adolescent children are idiosyncratic, incidental, irregular, unpredictable. Nell Noddings argues that we must "be clear and unapologetic about our goal . . . to produce competent, caring, loving, and lovable people" (1992, p. 174). Every community, school, and group of students brings its own distinctive conditions that affect our pursuit of this ultimate overarching goal. Therein lies the wonderful challenge of teaching at the middle level.

Supporting Activities

1. At the beginning of this chapter you were invited to sketch and label a young adolescent student. Study your sketch. What assumptions about this age group are suggested by your work? Exchange drawings. What assumptions are suggested by your classmates' drawings? Save your drawings for review and possible alterations upon completing Chapter 4.

2. Review the propositions stated under "Some Generalizations You Can Trust." List recollections of your experience as a middle grades student as they relate to these propositions. Share examples. Add further propositions that you believe might be included.

3. Briefly interview three or four classmates who are not reading this text about their recollections from being in the middle grades. Find out what they recall about what was successful in their schools. What are their recollections about friendships? About schoolwork? About teachers? About activities?

4. Compare the philosophical belief positions about middle level education taken by NMSA, NASSP, and *Turning Points*. What value positions are shared by these documents? List your ideas about how these beliefs were or were not part of your experience as a young adolescent. Share them with classmates.

5. Get informed. Find out what your state's and district's policies are with regard to the middle level. What certification/licensure is required? What committees responsible for the middle level exist locally? What programs are recommended or required for middle level students? Compare and assess your local policies with those cited in this chapter. Does your state have a middle level association? What does it stand for? What services does it offer? Determine how you and your classmates or colleagues can contribute and benefit from becoming involved.

6. Assess yourself in light of the four questions asked under "The Essential Catalyst: The Teacher." Write a 750-word essay that spells out and explains your perceptions of your potential as a middle grades teacher.

REFERENCES

Aikin, W. M. (1942). *The story of the eight-year study.* New York: Harper.
Alexander, W. M., & McEwin, C. K. (1989, September). Schools in the middle: Progress 1968–88. In *Schools in the middle.* Reston, VA: National Association of Secondary School Principals.
Arnold, J. F. (1989, July). *On the moral education of adolescents.* Lecture at the University of Vermont.
Arnold, J. F. (1993, Fall). A curriculum to empower young adolescents. *Midpoints,* 4(1). Columbus, OH: National Middle School Association.
Barth, R. S. (1990). *Improving schools from within.* San Francisco: Jossey-Bass.
Beane, J. A., & Lipka, R. P. (1986). *Self-concept, self-esteem, and the curriculum.* New York: Teachers College Press.
Benedict, R. (1934). *Patterns of culture.* Boston: Houghton Mifflin.

Briggs, T. H. (1920). *The junior high school.* New York: Houghton Mifflin. (Also cited by G. Melton in Lounsbury, 1984, 6.)

Burkhardt, R. (1996, Spring). Clueless kids/dangerous minds. *Becoming, 7*(2).

Carnegie Corporation. (1989). *Turning points: Preparing American youth for the 21st century.* Washington, DC: Carnegie Council on Adolescent Development.

Carnegie Corporation. (1995). *Great transitions: Preparing adolescents for a new century.* Washington, DC: Concluding Report of the Carnegie Council on Adolescent Development.

Cawelti, G. (1989). Middle schools a better match for early adolescent needs, ASCD survey finds. Washington, DC: Association for Supervision and Curriculum Development.

Children's Defense Fund. (1988). *Survey of state policies and programs for the middle grades.* Washington, DC: Author.

Dale, E. (1984). *The educator's quotebook.* Bloomington, IN: Phi Delta Kappa.

Elkind, D. (1984). *All grown up & no place to go: Teenagers in crisis.* Reading, MA: Addison-Wesley.

Erikson, E. (1968). *Identity, youth, and crisis.* New York: Norton.

Epstein, J. L. & MacIver, D. J. (1990). *Education in the middle grades: Overview of national policies and trends.* Columbus, OH: National Middle School Association.

Felner, R. D. (1994). *Lessons learned through self-study and cross-site findings: structuring and using data to facilitate school change.* Burlington, VT: Council of Chief State School Officers.

Felner, R. D. Jackson, A. W. Kasak, D. Mulhall, P. Brand, S. & Flowers, N. (March 1997). The impact of school reform for the middle years. *Phi Delta Kappan,* Vol. 78 (7), pp. 528–550.

Gatewood, T., & Dilg, A. (1975). *The middle school we need.* Alexandria, VA: Association for Supervision and Curriculum Development.

George, P. S. (1988, September). Tracking and ability grouping: Which way for the middle school? *Middle School Journal, 20*(1), 21–28.

George, P. S., & Oldaker, L. (1985). *Evidence for the middle school.* Columbus, OH: National Middle School Association.

George, P. S., & Shewey, K. (1994). *New evidence for the middle school.* Columbus, OH: National Middle School Association.

Goodlad, J. I. (1984). *A place called school: Prospects for the future.* New York: McGraw-Hill.

Hall, G. S. (1904). *Adolescence.* New York: Appleton-Century-Crofts.

Hill, J. P. (1980). *Understanding early adolescence: A framework.* Carrboro, NC: Center for Early Adolescence.

Irvin, J. A. (Ed.) (1992). *Transforming middle level education: Perspectives and possibilities.* Needham Heights, MA: Allyn and Bacon.

Kounin, J. S. (1970). *Discipline and group management in the classroom.* New York: Holt, Rinehart & Winston.

Lawton, E. J. (1989). *A journey through time: A chronology of middle level education resources.* Columbus, OH: National Middle School Association.

Lipsitz, J. (1984). *Successful school for young adolescents.* New Brunswick, NJ: Transaction.

Lounsbury, J. H. (Ed.). (1984). *Perspectives: Middle school education, 1964–1984.* Columbus, OH: National Middle School Association.

MacIver, D. J., & Epstein, J. L. (1993). Middle grades research: Not yet mature, but no longer a child. *Elementary School Journal, 93*(5), 510–533.

Mead, M. (1950). *Coming of age in Samoa.* New York: New American Library.

Naisbitt, J. (1982). *Megatrends.* New York: Warner Books.

National Association of Secondary School Principals. (1985). *An agenda for excellence at the middle level.* (Council on Middle Level Education). Reston, VA: Author.

National Middle School Association. (1995). *This we believe.* Columbus, OH: Author.

Noddings, N. (1992). *The Challenge to Care in Schools.* New York: Teachers College Press.

Silberman, C. (1970). *Crisis in the classroom.* New York: Random House.

Slavin, R. E. (1987). Ability grouping and student achievement in elementary schools: A best evidence synthesis. *Review of Educational Research, 57,* 293–336.

Steinberg, L. D. (1988). Reciprocal relation between parent–child distance and pubertal maturation. *Developmental Psychology, 24,* 1–7.

Totten, S., Sills-Briegel, T., Barta, K., Digby, A., & Nielsen, W. (1996). *Middle level education: An annotated bibliography.* Westport, CT: Greenwood.

Wheelock, A., & Dorman, G. (1988). *Before it's too late: Dropout prevention in the middle grades.* (A report by the Massachusetts Advocacy Center, 76 Summer Street, Boston, MA 02110 and the Center for Early Adolescence, Suite 223, Carr Mill Mall, Carrboro, NC 27510).

Chapter 2

Awareness through Shadow Studies

○ *How do young adolescents learn?*

○ *How do they deal with problems?*

○ *How do they react to their mistakes?*

○ *How do they get along with one another?*

○ *What is it really like to be in seventh grade?*

○ *What do sixth graders talk about? Seventh? Eighth graders?*

Professional literature and national reports beseech middle level educators to provide schooling that complements the developmental nature and needs of young adolescent students (National Middle School Association, 1982; National Association of Secondary School Principals, 1985; Carnegie Corporation, 1989). This is a compelling invitation because we know that when schooling does not match well with the nature of its constituents, it will likely produce indifference if not conflict and ultimately, academic and social failure for many. Often that is just what many youngsters experience in the middle grades—a perpetual disharmony between the school's expectations and agenda, on one hand, and their own priorities and interests on the other. The long–term price of such a standoff is exorbitant to everyone at the moment as well as in the future.

Given the enormous variety of developmental levels and idiosyncratic interests among young adolescents, what kind of schooling makes the most sense for them and to them? Educators and parents make decisions about how to raise children: "Trust us—we know what's best for you." Since we have all lived through our own early years of adolescence, it's natural for us to trust our assumptions that our special insights about what these youngsters need are valid. But once we have created what we believe are programs that are responsive to their nature and needs, how do we know to what extent they are achieving the goals that precipitated the design?

There are certainly lots of answers to these questions—theoretically, as many as there are students and teachers. Each person's reality is idiosyncratic; the events of a school day are perceived and internalized according to each individual's frame of reference. A student who is involved and doing well in a study of the Civil War may speak quite positively about himself. On the other hand, a youngster who is disoriented and uninvolved may describe the very same class as "boring and tiresome." Therefore an explanation of the way things are is subject to the discriminations of the person offering the description, especially when the respondent is a young adolescent.

How, then, can educators assess and understand the efficacy of the match between students and their schooling? The answer to this fundamental but often overlooked question is surprisingly complex. The question also must be raised with the humility that accompanies an open mind. We're familiar with all sorts of professional and political claims and generalizations about "what kids need" and "how they're doing in school." But given the enormous variability among them, responsible educators have to look more carefully and precisely at the daily school experiences of individual students in order to gain an informed grasp of their actuality. Shadow study is a technique designed to produce documentation for just that kind of summation.

DEFINING "SHADOW STUDY"

A useful framework for observing and documenting any individual's school life is to carry out a systematic observation and recording of the events in the subject's day. By steady compilation of an anecdotal account at short intervals, usually every five to ten minutes, a student's behavioral responses to events and activities can be itemized. A follow-up interview gives the observer a chance to gather further information and to explore questions that may occur during the course of the observation. Once these two tasks have been accomplished, the observer synthesizes the information gathered and produces a summation of this single day in a student's school life.

The goal of the shadow study, sometimes referred to as a quasi-ethnographic procedure, is to enhance our understanding of a single youngster's or teacher's life at school. It is essential to understand that the information or data it generates pertains only to the single case of the individual being observed on the day of the observation (Lounsbury & Johnston, 1988). Conclusions are not interpreted as global in the sense that formal research is considered generalizable, but a collection of several studies randomly selected will contribute significantly to our understanding of the actuality of the school lives of students and teachers.

The National Association of Secondary School Principals, the National Middle School Association, and the Association for Supervision and Curriculum Development have led the way in publishing summaries of five national shadow studies of middle grades students, each of which has been guided and written by John Lounsbury. (See Lounsbury et al. [1980] for titles of specific studies.) Each of these publications also includes samples of representative studies. The reader is urged to review these excellent publications to understand the broader context of students' school lives across the country.

WHO CAN BE A SHADOWER?

Anyone who is willing to stick to the documentation protocol for a full school day can carry out a shadow study. No particular expertise is necessary. What is essential is attentiveness. Ongoing thoughtful analysis of the documentation generates organic questions that can be asked at the end of the observation period. The subject's responses help clarify the actuality as well as his or her perceptions of the school day.

University students who are interested in young adolescents and their schooling constitute an especially effective pool of potential shadowers. Although they are students themselves, they have usually been removed from young adolescents and the middle grades for several years. Often they have insights that escape people even more distantly removed from that level of schooling. The only hitch I've occasionally encountered is that the procedure requires a full day away from university classes and other commitments. Shadowers must have a full day to devote to the study.

Parents are also a potential source of shadowers. Every school has in its parent population some individuals who are willing and can do an excellent job of shadowing. By using parent helpers in this way, the school also demonstrates its openness and interest in closing any gaps that may exist between homes and the school. It is prudent, of course, to assign parent shadowers to classes other than those their own youngsters are in. It may be wise to invite only parents of primary grade children to shadow in the middle grades, since their presence would be least likely to distract older students and their teachers.

I once used the shadow study technique as a teaching device with some of my seventh and eighth graders. Our "Who are We? Who am I?" unit focused upon the changes my students were experiencing, and one of my goals was to have students focus carefully and systematically on a randomly selected classmate in order to better understand the other kid. They literally drew names from a hat and then created fictitious names for their subjects in a vain attempt to preserve anonymity. (Although no one admitted it, I suspect they had all told each other whose names they had drawn before the end of that day.) During the week designated for the shadow studies, each student shadowed his subject on any single day he preferred. Observations were recorded at ten-minute intervals. Once the documentation was complete, I helped them identify questions they'd like to ask their subjects. Our final treatment of the documentary and interview data was to address two questions: What have you learned about how your subject plays? What have you learned about how your subject works?

This modification of shadowing worked very well in this particular unit. Students did an excellent job of documenting, and their interviews appeared to be especially challenging and pleasing. I was also satisfied that for a few of my students this was the first time they had looked objectively and uncritically at one of their classmates. I hoped that looking so carefully at their chosen students would help them gain more enlightened perspectives on all of their classmates. And, perhaps, it would help some of them become more tolerant and patient with themselves.

ORGANIZING A SHADOW STUDY

The initial step is, of course, to make arrangements with the principal and teachers to conduct a shadow study in a particular school. This is best done by first explaining the technique and the rationale, and by offering examples such as those excellent published ones already mentioned or the excerpts included in this chapter. People in schools are often sensitive about outside evaluation, so it is imperative to explain that the process you'll use is one of documentation and not evaluation. Once permission has been given, the following steps should be taken.

1. *Choose a focus.* What do you wish to learn? Clarify your priorities for yourself in advance. If your purpose is to document a representative student's school day, ask your

host to randomly select a subject for you. You might wish to observe a student who does particularly well or one who doesn't do well or one who embodies some other differentiating characteristics, such as a special education student who is being mainstreamed in a regular class. Whatever focus you wish to take, be candid in making your purpose known to your host. Sometimes the host will see your study as an opportunity to gain some insights about a single student, so your project may present an opportunity to give something back to the school. The imperative issue here is that you and the school representative openly discuss and plan according to your and their priorities.

2. *Making arrangements.* The shadow study reports cited earlier include "Directions for Observers" that are quite explicit and standardized because observers were participating in nationwide research in which uniformity was necessary—a condition that does not necessarily pertain to the studies suggested here.

   Ordinarily, the student being shadowed is not told in advance that he or she is the subject of the study. The purpose is to document a typical or representative day. If the student knows in advance that he or she is being observed, that knowledge will affect the authenticity of the observations. If your purpose is to shadow a teacher, however, his or her permission should be obtained prior to the study. Furthermore, you should initiate a preliminary conversation with the teacher, preferably in person but at least by telephone. Explain your purpose, what you'll actually be doing, and how you'll use the data you obtain. Confidentiality must be assured, even to the point of your using a pseudonym for the teacher. I have always required students to give a copy of their study and their analysis to the teacher when the study is complete. After all of this explanation, however, if the teacher wants no part of the process, we are obliged to honor that choice. If the teacher agrees, however, the final step is to obtain a copy of the subject's schedule for the day of the observation, so that shadowing can begin as the subject begins the school day.

3. *Exit interview—tentative format.* As already mentioned, before you carry out the documentation portion of this study it is important to list things you'd like to know more about, then phrase questions that you think will help you access the desired information. Some answers may emerge from your observations; others will result from questions you'll ask the subject near the close of the day. For example, if you'd like to know your subject's favorite times of day, you might be able to infer the answer from what you observe of her behaviors. There are also subjects who are uniformly enthusiastic as well as those who seem to be chronically indifferent to everything that is going on. In all cases, however, subjects may provide far richer responses as an outcome of direct, verbalized queries.

   You should also anticipate that during the course of your observation you'll have some additional questions. That is an inevitable and natural derivative of this kind of observation. I recommend that you write those questions on the observation sheets and then underline them in order to locate them quickly at the end of the day. You can then judge whether or not to ask them.

   Unless you serendipitously engage in conversation during the day in which you indicate your interest in asking the subject some questions at the end of the day, you need to request the interview before the subject is getting ready to leave. The request should be simple and direct: "My name is _____, and I've been observing the school today. I've seen you in several classes. May I ask you a few questions?"

Listed below are some standard questions the novice shadower might consider in preparing a tentative format for the exit interview.

On a scale of 1 to 10, with 1 being "poor" and 10 being "great," how do you rate this school?

What changes can you think of that would make the school better?

What are some important things you are learning here?

What advice would you give to a new student coming into this school?

Preface the next two questions by explaining that you'd like the subject to think first about things that work well for him and then about what works well for kids in general.

What works (best/worst) for you personally here?

What changes would make the school better for all kids?

A good closing query is this:

Is there anything else you can say to help me understand the school?

4. *Arranging an introduction to students.* Unless you are shadowing in a school that is constantly being visited, you should ask to be introduced, at least to the first meeting or class you attend. Students will take note of your presence and some of them may ask you why you're there. Be forthright in explaining that you are an observer, but don't go so far as to say, "I'm here to observe Suzie Sweet." You need to be a complement to the school—as unobtrusive as possible.

CARRYING OUT THE STUDY
Observation and Documentation

The school day begins when the subject arrives at school, so if at all possible the observations should begin with his or her arrival. Students usually mill about in conversation in halls and classrooms before the official day begins. It is important to observe that time to gain a full picture. Teachers usually arrive well before the first-period classes, so observation of a teacher ought to begin with his or her arrival, too. Once you are present in a group of students being directed by a teacher, you should be introduced by name as "a visitor who is observing us today."

Sheets of paper organized into columns for recording times and observations should be prepared in advance. Columns should be spaced as well as possible to provide room for notating time; behaviors or activities; environment or context description; and impressions, comments, and questions. Six to ten pages will be needed to cover the whole day; you may wish to make additional copies in order to be able to edit your entries after the study is completed. Be sure to prepare all sheets in advance.

The "Study Observation Form" used for the national sixth grade shadow study (Lounsbury & Johnston, 1988) was organized as follows:

	Specific Behavior		Impression/
Time	at 5–7 Minute Intervals	Environment	Comments

This division works well because it provides an expanding perspective of the observed incidents. Once the time has been recorded, the specific behavior is noted and then followed by a somewhat broader description of the context before the observer adds more inferential commentary. The format I have used with university students is somewhat more abbreviated and can be seen in the examples included in this chapter.

It is difficult to be completely unobtrusive. Sometimes a student will ask, "Are you watching me?" A suggested response is "Yes, I'm observing kids to understand what they do and how they learn. May I also ask you a few questions at the end of the day?" The statement is nonevasive and honest. Furthermore, following that admission with an invitation to help encourages the student to contribute further to the visitor's understanding of the school. Of course, the student may also refuse the request for an interview. Friendly exchanges of conversation throughout the day will in all likelihood soften that initial rejection and enable the shadower to obtain the interview after all.

Finally, don't skip any activities during the school day except for those that are self-evidently private. Students reveal much of what they think and believe outside their classes and at times when they are less closely directed by teachers. Therefore, you ought to continue documenting during recess periods, lunch, and activity periods—the total school day.

Exit Interview

Now is the time to reconcile the tentative interview format you prepared in advance of the observation with the situational questions that have emerged over the course of the day. Because you must now restructure the exit interview and you don't want it to require more than a few minutes of the subject's time, the final exit interview format has to be quickly edited. I urge students to underline their questions as they occur over the course of the day. That additional step makes it easier and faster at the end of the day to locate those organically derived questions, reexamine the original tentative interview format, and then determine their relative priority before the exit interview.

By the close of a school day most students and many teachers are usually eager to get on their way. Therefore, the exit interview needs to be as brief as possible while covering the issues you need to address. I encourage you to tape-record this five- to ten-minute encounter. The recording makes it easier to attend to the subject during the interview and to follow up statements with requests for clarification, elaboration, or examples. The recording also makes it possible to accurately review the interview as many times as you wish. The tape not only provides a certain record of the dialogue but also frees you to concentrate on your questions and the subject's responses.

Assimilating, Digesting, and Summarizing

There's no single recipe for pulling together the results of a shadow study; it is a subjective process of looking for themes and noting things that appear to be characteristic. However, some suggestions will help you keep your insights fresh and clear.

As soon as possible following the close of the exit interview, review all of your material. Edit your notes for clarity and consistency. If it isn't feasible to do so before you leave the school, be sure to do so that evening. If you have recorded the exit interview, listen to it at least once right away. Immediacy is primary.

You will have some dominant impressions, perhaps some conclusions. List your major impressions about the subject and the context while they are fresh in your mind. Explain them thoroughly in this initial step of analysis. Your observations will also generate somewhat more tentative conjectures. Describe those also in language that will be adequate to clarify your recall when you review these materials later.

I suggest to observers that once these initial reviews and edits are accomplished, they set them aside for a few days. Allowing the events and impressions to settle aids their digestion. Then it is important to write an analysis—usually just two or three pages—that presents your perspective on the school life of your subject. Where you make claims, be prepared to support them with observation and/or interview data. You can expect to have some unanswerable questions. Include those questions as if you were going to continue this study with further observations and interviews with the same subject. Finally, be sure to remember to share a copy of your analysis with the cooperating teacher and offer to respond to any subsequent questions he or she may wish to raise.

SHADOWING STUDENTS: A SAMPLE STUDY

In order to become truly effective middle level teachers, we must understand the students in our constituency and complement their developmental conditions. Even though we have already lived through these years of change ourselves and may believe that we understand this time of life, we must go further. Our personal experience is valuable, but alone it is inadequate. We have to achieve a broad general understanding of the physical, intellectual, and psychosocial context of early adolescence as it is available through pertinent theory and research about human development. That essential knowledge must then be augmented by our own firsthand studies of youngsters in accessible settings.

The most direct route to gaining observed knowledge is to shadow students through a school day. This technique is informative both to university students preparing to be teachers and to experienced teachers, because it forces us to focus upon one subject's experience of the schooling process and perspective on it. It requires that we exercise humility in acknowledging that in spite of our age and experience, there are still valuable insights we can yet gain by observing and listening to children.

Bonnie is a third-semester teacher education student who hails from a rural community of fewer than 4,000 residents. Her own schooling occurred in her town's K–12 school. Although she'd felt certain since childhood about becoming a teacher, she was uncertain about which age or grade level to choose. She admitted to "feeling intimidated by eighth grade boys," so it was fitting that she chose to shadow an eighth grade boy.

The fifth to eighth grade middle school where Bonnie carried out her study enrolls approximately 350 students in a working-class neighborhood of a small eastern city. Most of the students live in relatively modest homes, and while they are not wealthy, neither are they undernourished or neglected. The school has been a traditional junior high school since it was founded as a consequence of district reorganization some fifteen years earlier. A few months prior to this study, the school had instituted a teacher advisory program as the first step in a gradual movement toward middle school organization. Jake, the subject of Bonnie's study, was suggested by the principal after Bonnie asked him for an opportunity to shadow an eighth grade boy. The following pages are a slightly edited version of Bonnie's study. Note that she underlined questions (italicized here) that occurred to her while she was shadowing.

Bonnie's Observation of Jake

Time	Activity	Comment/Question
8:05	Kids milling around lockers visiting, waiting for advisory	J chatting, laughing with 3 boys—all shorter than J. He seems to be the central person in the group
8:15	Advisory: 9 kids, Mr. M. (t'cher) roll call, announcements, Mr. M. introduces me as visitor; talk: soccer game after school, report cards coming	Relaxed, informal, J seems well-liked, wears Redskins jersey, jeans, Reeboks, laces untied. J "fits in." *What does he think of the advisory?*
8:22	J volunteered to take attendance to office; returns promptly	
8:30	Advisory ends, kids leave cheerfully: "G'day, Mate" (*Crocodile Dundee* movie?)	J leaves with Sam (?) talking about math homework. Two others follow and listen. *Is J a leader?*
8:40	Study hall, J does math HW, most kids just "hanging out," minor disruptions squelched by teacher who is grading papers	*Why start the day with study hall?* This period is mostly wasted time
8:48	J still doing math	23 in class, only 3 really working
8:55	J watching 2 girls to his left looking at him, whispering, giggling	Math finished—J "eyeballing," smiling at girls, being "cool"—his legs wiggling, flicking his pencil. *Why is he nervous?*
9:05	Teacher selling lunch tickets	J combing his hair
9:15	Math class, J chooses front row seat, greets teacher	Only 1–2 minutes between classes, kids hurrying but many speak to J.
9:25	Reviewing HW, J raises hand often, has correct answers	J is good at math. *Is there a hard subject for him?*
9:35	Swapped HW papers, going over answers	J is confident, smiles a lot, comments to kids sitting around him
9:45	Classwork on 2 pages in book, teacher working at his desk	J seems bored, making hand signals to boy two rows away, legs wiggling
9:55	Science—2 kids per table, J talking to boy he was with before advisory	Another rush between classes! Help!
10:05	T on stool in front calling on kids for answers to chapter review—test on Mon.	J seems to know answers but bored, playing slap game with partner when T isn't watching. Combs his hair
10:15	T still doing same thing	J jumps up twice and shouts out answer. T warns him, threatens to take points off his test grade
10:25	Silent study assigned	J and partner playing tic-tac-toe, pretending to be studying

10:35	Social Studies—J in group of 4 making mural of costumes worn in Elizabethan England	J and Sara competing for leadership of group. He backs down. *Why?*
10:45	Mural work continues	J works with Jason and the 2 girls are together—subgroups. J is relaxed but is working—seems content
10:55	T reads from Romeo and Juliet—she stops frequently to make sure they understand	J is very attentive as are most kids. T reads and explains well. J is stretched out in desk, hands behind his head
11:05	T reviewing due dates for group projects	J asks if they can have more class time for project work—answered "yes" he smiles, bows, says "thank you, mum"—T and kids laugh, J smiles
11:18	Just settled in French class	Another rushed change. *Why don't they have more time so it won't be so frantic?*
11:25	3 kids reading a skit in French in front of room	J sitting in middle of class, hasn't spoken, watches dramatization
11:35	Groups of 3 practicing same skit	J with 2 girls who seem to speak well, J reads with hesitation, seems awkward, blushes when one girl helps
11:45	Still reading skits	J is annoyed with girl who helps with pronunciation—"Just let me do it!" *What kind of work groups does he prefer to work in?* J seems subdued
11:58	J in lunch line with Sam	Kids rushed to cafeteria—very noisy and crowded, tables seat 6–8, some kids have bag lunches. After J gets his tray he saunters entire length of cafeteria like he's a celebrity. Several kids watch him with smiles
12:10	J and Sam at table with 5 girls dressed a lot alike in sweaters and skirts—they look/ act like "preppies"	J and Sam have their collars turned up and are acting macho to girls' delight. Lots of hand and body gestures, acting cool. J seems very self-assured, even cocky
12:23	Language Arts class—J is sitting with girl from lunch and telling her a story I can't make out	Class hasn't started—kids are still arriving from lunch (I wolfed my apple)
12:30	T points out rhyming scheme of poems in textbook	J and Annie swap glances, smiles
12:40	Students volunteer to identify rhyme schemes	Annie volunteers successfully. J gives her big smile and thumbs up signal
12:50	Seat work with partners to label poems on ditto sheet	J and A work together—noted their shoulders touching/pressing for last 4–5 minutes. *How do you like working with girls?*
1:00	LA about to end, teacher assigns reading	J and A turned facing each other and he's telling her something—A looks solemn, starts staring at the floor
1:10	Fine Arts class just beginning, T to show slides of Eskimo artifacts	J sits in back of room at a single desk near back door; rest of kids at tables. *Why did he sit alone?*

1:20	Slides of carvings	J stretched out in desk watching, fingers in his mouth, legs twitching
1:30	T in front of room asking ?s	J very fidgety now, avoids looking at T, playing with pencil like baton, aiming it like a pistol
1:33	T asks J about examples of realism in Eskimo art	J stammers, vague about "lines, shapes," blushes, twists in his seat, flicks his pencil vigorously, stares angrily at a student at table next to him after T asks another student to answer. *What is going on here?*
1:38	Slide discussion continuing	J very restless now, twitching, watching clock
1:45	J dressing for Phys Ed	The moment the bell rang J was out door like a sprinter and I lost him. Something is wrong; I want to know. *Tell me about Fine Arts*
1:55	Boys are running up and down the gym in pairs tossing a ball back and forth—lots of yelling and friendly taunting	J looks surprisingly boyish in gym clothes— tall but not yet muscular. He isn't very adept at the activity, and his face shows a partial grimace. He seems annoyed, and he's not clowning with the others
2:05	4 rows of boys—2 rows dribble to one end of the gym and then hand off to another boy who dribbles back. Still lots of cheering	J has a hard time with this activity. He is slower than average, and he has lost control of the ball each of the 2 times he's tried it. His body language has changed from swagger this morning to a slouch now! *What sports do you enjoy most?*
2:15	Boys have returned to locker room to change	J's afternoon was completely different from this morning. He was on top of the world then and looks like he's lost his best friend now. *What happened?*
2:32	Afternoon advisory and silent reading period. Mr. M. tells J that he "heard good things about J's math." J smiles but doesn't speak	J is reading *Late Night with David Letterman: the Book*—a funny book but he doesn't smile and slouches on the floor leaning against the wall. *How do you like the Letterman book?*

Bonnie's Exit Interview with Jake

In a quick preparation for the exit interview, Bonnie did a good job of extemporaneously editing her preconceived questions in order to add some of those that emerged from her observation. However, she reported that she had assumed prior to carrying out the study that she would gain a fuller understanding of her subject than she actually did. Her preconceived questions are marked with an asterisk.

B:* What things do you like best about this school?
J: I dunno. [shrugs] The kids, I guess. Some of the teachers are pretty nice, too. It's a pretty good school.
B: Tell me about the advisory.

J: It's when you get together with your advisor in the morning and before you go home to see how you're doing. It's good. Last week our advisory went to [see a movie]. Mr. M stays on top of us. We're all doing pretty good.

B:* What is your best subject?

J: Math. [pause] I make As and Bs mostly in everything.

B:* What is your hardest subject?

J: Hardest? Hmm. I dunno. None of them are really hard. Sometimes I don't get what the teacher is saying—like in Fine Arts. I don't know what she wants.

B: Tell me about Fine Arts.

J: What do you mean?

B: How do you like it?

J: I dunno. It's OK, I guess. [pause] I'd rather do math. Is this gonna take much longer? I've gotta go.

B: Just a couple more questions. How do you like working with girls?

J: [blushes slightly, smiles, looks away] It depends. If you can pick the girls it's OK, I guess. Some of 'em are a real pain, though.

B: How are you liking the Letterman book?

J: Huh? [looks surprised] It's pretty funny. Not as good as the show, though.

B: Do you get to see it very often?

J: Yeah, a couple of times. It comes on pretty late.

B:* Is there anything else you'd like to tell me about the school?

J: Nah, That's about it. It's a good school. Are you coming back?

B: I hope so. Would that be OK with you?

J: Sure. Look me up anytime.

Summary Excerpts

Jake could give lessons to a peacock. From his preoccupation with his hair to his concern with wearing the right clothes to his practiced strut across the cafeteria, he gives the impression of a male bird in full plumage preparing for a mating ritual.

Most of the teaching was routine and fairly boring, but the students seem to be fairly tolerant of it. Jake does all right by just giving back what the teachers want, but I think he has some real ability that isn't being used, especially in math. I hope he doesn't become so bored with school that he doesn't take learning seriously.

I think I learned a lot about Jake, but he's also still a mystery to me. I'd love to spend more time observing and talking with him. I have a lot of questions. Why did his mood change so much from the morning to the afternoon? What happened between him and the Fine Arts teacher? What does he like to do with his spare time? I also feel like he has potential to become a leader in this school. Mr. M may be the key.

An inherent liability in using the shadow study technique is the facile assumption we find ourselves making that after observing and interviewing another person, we should be able to explain that person. While it is natural to speculate about causes and possibilities, the temptation to interpret and theorize motives must be kept in its proper perspective. Shadowing is not a psychoanalytic method; it is simply a documentation technique. Nor are we qualified to make psychological interpretations. We can log the events of the subject's day and capture the gist of one day of school life. This study served Bonnie well in that it reminded her of the complexity of human personality and the difficulties and limitations inherent in trying to understand behaviors.

This shadow study is particularly interesting because Bonnie became intrigued by the change of temperament she perceived in Jake's apparent attitude and responsiveness to school from the first half of the day to the second half. She expressed genuine concern that the school didn't have much to offer Jake except the chance to be with other kids his age. After Bonnie had presented her study in class at the university, she challenged her classmates for ideas about how the school might be organized so that students like Jake wouldn't become bored or alienated. Her challenge accomplished the original aim of the assignment—to study young adolescents in order to identify ways to present schooling that will more fully complement their developmental nature and needs. And finally, Bonnie's earlier apprehensions about eighth grade boys changed to intrigue.

SHADOWING TEACHERS: A SAMPLE STUDY

While the primary use of a shadow study is to advance understanding of the school lives of students, the technique is also useful for observing the life of a teacher at school. An effective way for an aspiring teacher to gather insights about what teachers do is to shadow a teacher through a school day. Consider this excerpt from one student's observations of an hour and a half of an eighth grade social studies teacher's day. The host school is called a middle school because it includes grades five through eight. With the exception of two teams of students and teachers, however, the school actually functions as a junior high school with departmental organization, an eight-period bell schedule, and so on. Note again the italicized questions Melanie, the observer, noted to ask Ken, the subject, at the end of the day in an exit interview.

Melanie's Observation of Ken B.

Time	Activity	Comment/Question
9:10	Answering questions about project assignment	Kids seem unsure of what Mr. B wants
9:15	Talking about Renaissance as rebirth and humanism	Kids listening
9:20	Talking about Renaissance artists	Ditto
9:25		Ditto
9:30		Ditto
9:35	Writing names on board: Botticelli, Da Vinci, Giotto, Durer, El Greco, Raphael	Most kids are copying; kid next to me is drawing airplanes
9:42	Assigns pages to be read and tells them to read for the rest of the class period	Kids are restless; *is this a typical class?* They're fairly attentive but they don't seem very interested
9:45	Talking to a girl; girl is called to desk as bell rings	Most kids are reading; *what was the conference about?*

Time	Activity	Comment/Question
9:50	Standing in hall supervising	Kids talking, going to next classes
9:55	Mimeographing U.S. maps to use later in 7th grade class. This is a prep period for him. We're in teachers' work room	I help and we talk about last class. He describes class as below avg., that he worries about them. Girl he spoke with is failing the course
10:00	Stapling maps	I help. Mr. B asks me about [college]
10:05	We have coffee, he tells me about control and preparing lessons that keep kids busy	K is a nice person, and he is very well organized. I think I might like to intern with him
10:10	K talks about the principal who retires this year and that he's sorry to see him go	
10:15	K calls his dentist to make an appointment for his son	
10:20	K grades spelling tests	I want to ask K why he likes to teach middle school instead of high school
10:25	Ditto	
10:30	Ditto	
10:35	We're in a 7th grade geography class. K tells kids to take their seats; he's annoyed	The kids mostly ignored him until bell rang. Then they all sat down. They're very independent, unafraid!
10:40	K uses a wall map to show where he was born (Colorado) and is showing states where kids in the class were born	Why don't they already know the states? The kids seem to be going through the motions

The excerpt is typical of this particular shadow study. The student did a good job of documenting the teacher's behaviors at regular intervals. Taken as a whole, the shadow study shows a rather routine workday of a nice person whose manner of instruction is probably familiar. The observer's Comment/Question column notes reveal that the student warmed up to the teacher as a person, is impressed with his organizational manner, and is already even imagining the possibility of working with him as a student intern. On the other hand, the student also questions the ordinariness of this teacher's style and his students' general diffidence about their studies.

This particular excerpt created a good deal of discussion back in the university class. Photocopies of the shadow study were distributed to the observer's classmates and read prior to a class discussion. That discourse focused on two issues: the teacher's domination of "air time" and his adherence to "the curriculum," the propriety of which the university students challenged. An important outcome of this dialogue was our resolve to include the following question in subsequent shadow interviews: What do you do when the curriculum and the students don't match?

Let's consider one more excerpt from a shadow study conducted by another student on the same day in the same school. In this case the observed teacher is a member of a three-teacher team that works with approximately eighty sixth and seventh graders. The team is housed in two large rooms and two small rooms located at the end of a wing of the school. Their space is decorated in the team colors of green and white, and signs proclaim it "Crusader Country" because the team name is Crusaders.

The time block excerpted from this shadowing exercise is what the Crusaders call "Prime Time." Prime Time begins when the morning class meeting ends, usually about 8:45 or 9:00, and it lasts until all Crusader students have math at the same time, 10:30.

Andrew's Observation of Peggy

Time	Activity	Comment/Question
8:45	Class meeting being run by 2 girls. "P" (teacher) hasn't said anything yet	This is amazing! The teachers are sitting in the group and raising their hands to speak, same as the kids do
8:50	Meeting has just ended. P asked 8 kids to bring their writing folders and meet with her first thing during PT. She is showing them how to structure their paragraphs, topic sentence, etc.	
8:55	P shows them how a paragraph ought to look like an upside-down triangle	
9:00	P and students are writing	
9:05	Kids take turns reading what they have written	P is an incredible teacher. She is showing them how to do exactly what they don't understand. They obviously like her a lot, too
9:10	P is showing two boys on a computer how to "debug" something in a program	
9:15	Listening to a girl's poem	
9:20	Shows a parent visitor how to interpret the language kids invented for a project where they created a fictional culture	
9:25	Still talking with the parent; they had to stop when a boy asked P to explain difference between "its" and "it's"	P is always on the go. The longest she has stopped is 15 minutes, and even then she was interrupted a lot
9:32	Conferencing with B, who has been goofing off. He argues, but P has the upper hand	P is firm, yet gentle. Amazing!
9:45	3 girls report that they have talked to 2 florists who will let them be apprentices in December	There's so much going on! I have trouble remembering to watch the clock
9:50	P joins 4 boys and listens to them discuss *Treasure Island.* She asks them to write and illustrate an advertisement so that other kids will want to read it	I wish I'd counted the number of different interactions she's had today. It's like being in charge of the control tower at a busy airport!
9:55	P talks with the parent visitor	
10:09	P checks with the boys on the computer. They seem to be OK	P asked Sam (student) to answer the parent's questions about the culture project. (Oops! I was listening to Sam and forgot to record on time.)

10:15	P has gone to the rest room	It's amazing! She's out of the room and everything just keeps humming along
10:20	P moves through the room, mostly observing like I am but offering suggestions or help	Kids just keep working normally as she passes by or stops to observe
10:27	P asks people to wind up their work for math class but to first listen to decisions the Halloween Committee has made	I'm amazed! 100% of the kids have worked almost the entire time and they've had easy access to P almost the entire time. How does she keep up with what each one is doing?

LEARNING FROM SHADOW STUDIES

The first use of shadowing is to document the events of another person's day in order to better understand the experience from that individual's point of view. To paraphrase an old saying, "Don't judge another person until you've walked a mile in his Reeboks." Although the curiosities and priorities may be different between university teacher education students and teachers who have been in the field for several years, shadowing is a technique equally valid for both groups.

When the class project for teacher education students was to become thoroughly acquainted with a practicing teacher, the observers went considerably further than the initial shadow study (Stevenson, 1987). Working in pairs or small groups, they spent several days with their subject in a variety of settings—sometimes even visiting in the teacher's home. Following these visitations they compared observations and further refined their focus. The final projects were videotaped "portraits" of their subjects that were presented to the class. Their periodic reports to class and the final projects showed a vividly realistic grasp of a teacher's life—documenting that individual's satisfactions, challenges, and concerns.

Shadow studies have also been carried out by experienced teachers observing middle grades students in schools other than their own as a project in graduate courses. The reflections of these observers are remarkably similar to those of preservice and undergraduate students. They also report the recurring incidence of becoming bored, weary from so much sitting and inactivity, finding themselves vulnerable to distractions, and clock-watching. Regardless of the observer's prior role in schools, doing at least one shadow study of a student is essential to recognizing what schooling is like from the other side of the desk. Using the technique forces the observer to experience school from the perspective of the student and, in so doing, to raise pertinent issues and questions for further study. One's professional development can then be assessed in terms of responses to those issues.

John Lounsbury, a highly regarded proponent and user of shadow studies as a technique for understanding students and schools, summarized what had been learned from the five national studies that he has helped direct (1989; personal correspondence, 1990). In reporting the major insights and generalizations gained from sixth, seventh, eighth, and ninth grade studies, he described "good things schools do" as follows:

1. Schools are important and valuable to the youth of America apart from their primary value as academic institutions.

2. Schools are well organized and efficiently operated.

3. Students are well behaved and cooperative.

4. Teachers, with limited exceptions, are conscientious, supportive, and well intentioned.

5. Students perceive their teachers and their schools in a positive light.

These themes are at least encouraging in that they convey a somewhat benign positiveness about middle level schooling. Certainly there are many people who do not admit even this level of accomplishment in public education. Lounsbury's analysis of twenty-five years of shadow studies goes on to spell out substantial "areas of concern."

1. The school day, as typically operated, is physically demanding.

2. Students, although well behaved are, as learners, too passive.

3. Meaningful intellectual interaction between students and teachers is lacking.

4. The textbook dominates the instructional program.

5. The instructional program is fragmented, disjointed, and excessively compartmentalized.

Lounsbury added that the studies also showed that a good bit of time was wasted; that teachers were more concerned if not preoccupied with "covering material" rather than accomplishing the substance of learning, and that scarcity of time limited interactions between kids and grown-ups beyond "the lesson."

These themes identify excellent issues for both the novice shadower and the experienced observer of schooling to consider when they carry out their own studies. Although it must be remembered that the primary purpose is documentation, assessment derives from careful observation and study. Themes previously cited identify prevailing conditions in middle–level schools, so they also constitute criteria that can guide conceptualization of pertinent questions for exit interviews.

Bill Hull (1970) listed another excellent collection of questions and issues for observers to think about while observing. Some of those questions relevant to shadowing young adolescents are

Do students talk with each other about their work?

Do they initiate activities which are new to the classroom?

Do they persist . . . on things which capture their interest?

Do they exhibit any initiative; have they developed any skill in finding out what they want/need to know?

Can they deal with differences of opinion or differences in results on a reasonably objective basis without being swayed by considerations of social status?

Do they continue to explore things which are not assigned—outside of school as well as within?

Do they challenge ideas and interpretations with the purpose of reaching deeper understandings?

Are they charitable and open in dealing with ideas with which they do not agree?

Can they listen to each other?

Are they willing to attempt to express ideas about which they have only a vague and intuitive awareness?

Are they able to make connections between things that seem superficially unrelated?

Are they flexible in problem solving?

Can they suspend judgment?

Do they know how to get help when they need it and refuse help when appropriate?

Can they accept guidance without having to have things prescribed?

Are they stubborn about holding on to views which are not popular?

Can they deal with distractions, avoiding being at the mercy of the environment?

Do they recognize conflicting evidence or conflicting points of view?

In order to design schooling that is complementary to the pressures and changing conditions of young adolescents' lives, we must begin with knowledge of who they are, how they function, and what their interests and capabilities may be. It is appropriate for middle level educators to adopt an anthropologist's attitude in trying to understand our students' culture from their perspectives. While we may hold special biases and priorities based on our own growing-up years, our viewpoints may not always correspond with those of youngsters in our contemporary classrooms.

It is likewise prudent for teachers to remember that even though many of our students may appear on the surface to be very much alike, they in fact remain unique, and they are growing, developing, and learning idiosyncratically. It is necessary, therefore, that middle level educators create circumstances by which we can learn directly from the students whose education is our responsibility. The shadow study is one excellent technique for advancing our understanding. Inquiries presented in the next chapter constitute another avenue for our efforts to grow in understanding of our particular student constituencies.

Supporting Activities

1. Review the steps in organizing and carrying out a shadow study. Develop one tentative interview format for a student and another for a teacher. Try them out with classmates.

2. Shadow a middle level student in a neighboring school, following the guidelines presented here. Present a summary of your work to your classmates. What are your most important learnings about your subject? About the school? What are some implications for teachers who work with your subject?

3. Shadow a middle level teacher. Present a summary to your classmates. What are your most valuable insights and questions about your subject? About being a middle level teacher in the host school? About being a middle level teacher anywhere?

REFERENCES

Carnegie Corporation. (1989). *Turning points: Preparing American youth for the 21st century*. Washington, DC: Carnegie Council on Adolescent Development.

Hull, W. (1970). Things to think about while observing. In *ESS Reader*. Newton, MA: Education Development Center, 153–154.

Lounsbury, J. H. (1989, October 28). *Life in middle level classrooms: Findings and techniques from 25 years of shadow studies*. Paper presented at the 16th annual conference of the National Middle School Association, Toronto, Canada.

Lounsbury, J. H. (1990). Personal correspondence.

Lounsbury, J. H., & Clark, D. C. (1990). *Inside grade eight: From apathy to excitement*. Reston, VA: National Association of Secondary School Principals.

Lounsbury, J. H., & Johnston, J. H. (1985). *How fares the ninth grade? A day in the life of a 9th grader*. Reston, VA: National Association of Secondary School Principals.

Lounsbury, J. H. & Johnston, J. H. (1988). *Life in the three sixth grades.* Reston, VA: National Association of Secondary School Principals.

Lounsbury, J. H., & Marani, J. V. (1964). *The junior high school we saw: One day in the eighth grade.* Alexandria, VA: Association for Supervision & Curriculum Development.

Lounsbury, J. H., Marani, J. V., & Compton, M. F. (1980). *The middle school in profile: A day in the seventh grade.* Columbus, OH: National Middle School Association.

National Association of Secondary School Principals. (1985). *An agenda for excellence at the middle level.* (Council on Middle Level Education). Reston, VA: Author.

National Middle School Association. (1982). *This we believe.* Columbus, OH: Author.

Stevenson, C. (1987, November). How does a student decide to become a teacher? *Teaching Education 1*(2).

Chapter 3

Understanding through Inquiries

○ *What are my students' values?*

○ *What are their interests? Concerns? Ideas?*

○ *How are they alike? Different? Are there gender differences?*

○ *What do they think about themselves? Each other?*

○ *What would they like for me to understand about them?*

○ *What do they like about school? Dislike?*

○ *What are their thoughts about how to make our school better?*

Inquiry Excerpt 1

There appeared to be four fairly well defined informal groups among the fifty-three students in the two seventh grades: eight to ten *jocks,* five to eleven *preppies,* four to six *do-gooders,* and exactly four *punks* (a.k.a. *weirdos*). The main reasons the kids gave for explaining "how you know which group a person belongs to" are by (1) how they treat each other and other kids, (2) their clothes and hairstyle, and (3) how they talk. Of the twenty-one students we interviewed, five acknowledged that they belonged to one of these groups. Their explanations for why they were in a particular group were (1) they're my friends, (2) we get along with each other, and (3) I can be me. One especially interesting thing was that all eleven students referred to at least once as *preppy* were girls.

Inquiry Excerpt 2

The most surprising thing we learned from the time-use study was how much time the eighth graders spent talking on the telephone. Everyone used the telephone at least once during the week, and the average use was eleven times a week. The average length was just under twenty-eight minutes for each student per school day, but several students talked up to an hour and forty minutes on a single day. Only five of the twenty-five students in the class reported that they spent five minutes or less talking on the phone. Six girls reported that they talked to friends an average of an hour a day after getting home from school. Students who used the phone the most called each other on the weekend, but the conversations were a lot shorter.

Inquiry Excerpt 3

There's a lot of difference in the amount of money these sixth graders have and spend, and in how they get it. Almost half the kids get a regular weekly allowance; the least amount reported is $2 and the most is $15. All the students who don't get a regular allowance reported that they do receive spending money from parents "when I need it." Seven kids who don't get allowances said that their parents give them money for doing chores such as washing dishes, babysitting (siblings), cleaning the house and yard, etc. Four kids who receive allowances, and eleven who do not, also earn money outside their homes by babysitting, delivering newspapers, and doing chores such as mowing grass for neighbors or family friends.

One boy reported that combining his allowance with money he earns from a paper route and picking up odd jobs gives him between $35 and $40 a week. He also wrote on his sheet that his older brother in high school has two jobs—one at night in a fast-food restaurant and one on the weekend at a convenience store. He added that his brother has to earn the money to pay for his car insurance.

These excerpts are taken from inquiries carried out in public middle level schools by university teacher education students who attempted to become better acquainted with and more directly knowledgeable about a group of students. The inquirers had some general theoretical knowledge about early adolescence as a developmental period, and each of them had personally experienced those developmental years relatively recently. However, they needed to augment that foundation with insights obtained from deliberate, firsthand investigations involving the particular groups of students with whom they worked most closely. Part of this getting-to-know-them process consisted of designing and using a formal inquiry to explore in detail some aspect of early adolescence that held particular interest for them.

Excerpt 1 is taken from an inquiry carried out by Gail and Helen, two university students who were particularly interested in young adolescent group dynamics, clique membership and identity, and kids' use of stereotypes. Their interest was spawned by a formal research study they had read about how youngsters perceive informal groups in middle schools (Castlebury & Arnold, 1988). After having spent two days during a two-week period earlier in the semester doing shadow studies in a local school and thereby becoming somewhat familiar to and with seventh graders there, they returned for an afternoon to interview students randomly. From several brief discussions they learned that "who you're connected to and with" was indeed a high priority, but—at least as far as the interviews revealed—there were some intriguing qualifications. They were particularly intrigued that while the youngsters they interviewed told them that other kids felt strongly about being part of a particular group, the interviewees saw themselves as being more independent. Almost all of the interviewees denied that they themselves belonged to a stereotype group.

Helen intuitively speculated from her interviews that perhaps some of the kids thought an admission of group membership might be perceived as a weakness. Gail was less certain of this assumption. Who knows? The point is not to make absolute pronouncements but to become sensitive participant-observers in a typical twelve-year-old cultural context in order to gain a clearer sense of its dynamics. Such informal investigations can do much to help grownups working with them to understand better how students perceive and treat one another.

The second excerpt is taken from an inquiry carried out by Pat, a middle school math teacher–graduate student, who wanted to know more about how his students spent their hours out of school. He designed tally sheets for nonschool hours that began on a Wednesday afternoon and continued until bedtime on the following Tuesday night (Fig-

Date: _____		Student: _____	
Time	Activity	Time	Activity
6:00 AM		3:00	
7:00		4:00	
8:00		5:00	
9:00		6:00	
10:00		7:00	
11:00		8:00	
12:00 NOON		9:00	
1:00 PM		10:00	
2:00		11:00	

Figure 3.1

ure 3.1). Each student agreed to keep a careful record of what he or she did and for how long each activity was done on each of the seven days of the study. Pat reminded them each morning and again in the afternoon classes that their homework assignment was to maintain up-to-date records of how they were spending their time according to the tally sheets. Students then turned in their sheets to Pat each day in math class until all seven days had been logged and collected. He also urged them not to compare their data until the week had ended.

Upon completion of the study week, Pat taught them how to organize and total their data according to categories before entering it on a computer spreadsheet he had programmed to correspond to the study. Not only did he and his students gain lots of insights about where their time went, but the project produced numerical data he then used to teach a unit about graphing.

The third investigation of money in a self-contained sixth grade class was made by Jeff, a university junior who was working his way through college as a bicycle and motorcycle mechanic. Given his personal concerns about paying his own bills, he became interested in knowing more about how kids think about their finances, their money values, and their spending habits. Because his work schedule limited the time available to him to spend in a school, he visited one class for a couple of morning hours, during which he did some tutoring and talked with kids informally about money. He then designed an anonymous survey that asked kids to answer questions he created as a result of his visit. Once the teacher had made some wording suggestions and approved the anonymous format, she made copies for every student and asked them "to help Jeff with his homework" by answering the questions.

While Jeff gained several tentative insights from the kids' responses, it was the teacher who turned out to be most surprised by the results. Just as Pat had employed his time-use data for a graphing unit, she also used the allowance information for arithmetic lessons. Since she had never done such an inquiry herself, the insights this inquiry produced about her students' awareness and use of money prompted her to carry out subsequent inquiries of her own interest.

Inquiry such as these examples illustrate is simply a process of exploring a curiosity by asking students to "tell you how it is." The action is characterized by the humility that accompanies honest questions and by an earnest intention to understand how others perceive things. The query may be as routine as asking a class how difficult a homework assignment was, or it may be a systematic study of how kids use time on a scale as extensive as Pat's project. In all cases, the investigation is an attempt to understand more fully some aspects of other people's lives. Inquiry is a process that "involves a way of thinking and functioning as a teacher-learner that grows and improves through experience" (Stevenson, 1986, p. 43).

WHAT IS INQUIRY?

> The secret to a powerful inquiry lies in not knowing the answer. I don't mean just the student, I mean no one, including the teacher, knows the answer.
>
> *Jim Burns, middle school teacher (Shinas et al., 1994, p. 19)*

As already indicated, inquiry at its simplest is simply *asking*—asking others to tell you how they see things. A teacher's Monday morning query "How was your weekend?" is an inquiry. A librarian's survey of favorite books is an inquiry. Any request for a show of hands that asks the respondents to express personal preferences is an inquiry. What is especially helpful about middle level educators' use of inquiry is that, like shadow studies, it provides a window with which to view and better understand our students' circumstances.

Consider these sentence completions used by some Illinois middle grades teachers: (Mee, 1995, p. 5)

A good teacher is . . .
A good student is . . .
I worry about . . .
Advice I'd like to give the principal . . .
I would like to advise teachers . . .
I would like to tell my family . . .
Rules are . . ."

Sometimes more formalized inquiry is called action research to emphasize that the one is formally investigating a research interest. In some cases teachers collaborate with professors or professional researchers to collaboratively explore a question or hypothesis. The emphasis intended for inquiry, however, is on teachers working alone or in collaboration with colleagues to enhance their understanding of *their students' perceptions, ideas, and beliefs*. The information that comes from students is valuable, and educators whose disposition is toward knowing "the world according to kids" generally enjoy good rapport with them. An assortment of communication strategies appropriate for young adolescent students is described later.

Casual inquiries generally produce both information and discussion. "Which rock singers do you like?" "What are the best computer games?" "What are you going to do this weekend?" While these momentary inquisitions may satisfy a fleeting curiosity or provoke the discussion the asker desires, the most enlightening inquiries require forethought and planning that go well beyond these examples of more serendipitous exchanges. In this chapter we will examine an assortment of issues in youngsters' lives that through well-placed inquiries may be better understood by those of us who work with young adolescents. We will also examine techniques for collecting information from students, and later in this book we'll look at how inquiry also serves as a developmentally appropriate learning tool for young adolescents to use themselves.

Of particular interest are areas of concurrence or disagreement according to gender. Many times I have uncovered points of view that students hold according to their gender. Academic preferences are very important to understand, and differences in musical tastes are often interesting to explore. A question that I often use is "List three significant events in the history of the United States." Usually one gender group predominantly cites wars and assassinations, while the other's responses tend to be much more diverse. Getting it right or wrong is superfluous to the question; everyone is right in that everyone's opinion is equally valued. However, it becomes very interesting to speculate with students about their different ideas, and particularly rich discussion usually occurs when differences appear to be gender-related.

Perceptive, attentive teachers learn a lot about their students on a day-to-day basis through their academics, observed work ethic, and interpersonal exchanges. Many youngsters want adults to be interested in the things that are on their minds, and they often reveal bits about themselves through anecdotes about their activities outside of school. Such incidents constitute an invitation to learn more. At the other extreme, however, are youngsters who have become distrustful, even suspicious of teachers. They may offer no clues whatsoever to their true natures. Given the pluralism of backgrounds, talents, attitudes, predispositions, and a host of other idiosyncratic characteristics at play in the middle level setting, even the most perceptive of teachers can still use inquiry as a vehicle to better understand what is going on within this predictably diverse constituency. And not surprising, teachers' credibility with their students is enhanced by inquiry; young adolescents like to be asked what they think and believe.

Inquiry requires only curiosity and access to candid respondents. It should not be confused with formal educational research. Traditional educational research necessitates a carefully constructed research paradigm for examining hypotheses or research questions derived from articulated theory. A primary purpose of formal research is to produce generalizable findings—results that are applicable and likely to occur in comparable settings. While pertinent research such as that reviewed in the subsequent chapter provides invaluable guidance to classroom teachers, inquiry is simply a strategy one can use to gain insights and promote communication with a single group of people—usually students. The same rationale and techniques may be used to learn what colleagues or parents think as well.

It should be emphasized again, however, that this chapter is about inquiry to understand one's immediate students better. Although the inquirer may have hunches or assumptions or even a personal theory about a matter being explored, no formal hypotheses or theoretical justifications for inquiry are necessary. The only requirement is curiosity—an interest in understanding one's immediate constituents. Likewise, no sampling techniques are required, no presumptions of objectivity are alleged, and in no sense should the results of inquiry be regarded as generalizable to any other people or situation. It is also a mistake to approach inquiry with an expectation of *proving* anything. The strongest claim any inquirer can make is "that is what I asked, and this is what they told me."

One further qualification of inquiry is appropriate here: inquirers and respondents improve with experience. My university students and I have found a great deal of diversity in the ways young adolescents react to their initial experience with inquiry. It usually turns out well, though, because we've learned that once they get into it, kids enjoy and appreciate being asked for their opinions. Sometimes, however, they are wary and suspicious of the inquirer's motives. Obviously, this kind of reaction raises doubts in our minds about the candor of their responses. In reflecting on the limitations of a first inquiry with adolescents who were troubled and suspicious, one professional inquirer-writer wrote:

> They worked hard on the questionnaires and in the end it was readily apparent that in comparison with the depth, breadth and "truthfulness" of what it had been possible to achieve through sustained participant observation, the questionnaire method was impressively shallow: the results were too meaningless and too incomplete (and often illegible) to include in the study. (Ross, 1979, p. 174)

Like any other skill, inquiry requires practice that is acquired over time and through firsthand experience. The more inquiries we create, administer, and interpret, the better we become at those processes and the more confident we feel about doing them. Likewise, the youngsters providing the information also get better at it with experience. Once they've had a good experience, they become more trusting and therefore more willing to cooperate. Sometimes they will even want to carry out their own investigations.

Consequently, first-time inquirers should not be surprised either by their own feelings of awkwardness or by wariness from kids for whom it is also a first inquiry. Undergraduate students are well advised to anticipate this likelihood and look for ways to make improvements in subsequent inquiries. Teachers have a valuable opportunity to use inquiry to construct modes of communication that, over time, help establish and maintain trust between generations.

WHY USE INQUIRY?

> If I ever needed convincing about how important the relationship is between teacher and student, the experience of these inquiries over the last two years has taught me a lesson which I thought I knew but really didn't. The value of personal reflection is only beginning to be tapped. (Harrington, 1993)

Regardless of how generally knowledgeable a teacher may be about adolescent development and social dynamics and human behavior, inquiry enables him or her to understand a single constituency—a particular class or advisory or the teachers on a team or the parents of a school. A lyric from *Music Man* reminds salesmen that "you gotta know the territory." Inquiry helps teachers do just that, and "the territory" they must learn in order to have authentic communication is their constituents' social and cultural context as they perceive it.

Even a teacher who has many years of experience continuously encounters new students and groups of students who have unique priorities and perceptions. Although they are similar in many ways to their predecessors, they are also distinct. Just as every human personality is unique, every combination of personalities has its own dynamics. And just as individuals are growing and constantly changing, group priorities and mores change. Building and maintaining mutually satisfying communication must be an urgent priority for middle level teachers.

Communication

True communication is at least a two-way exchange requiring both listening and telling. Schools are customarily organized so that most of the telling is done by adults, and most of the listening is expected to be done by students. But where the best communication occurs, there is balance and everyone functions in both modes. Teachers who recognize this truth and who value good communication with their students work conscientiously at establishing themselves as thoughtful, responsive listeners. Inquiry is their invitation to students to be the tellers. Thus they demonstrate their interest in understanding how the kids see things. When a teacher goes to the trouble to develop an inquiry and then in turn earnestly and responsibly shares what he or she has learned, credibility and sincerity as a communicator are being demonstrated in certain terms. Every effort teachers make to demonstrate their trustworthiness to children contributes to the strength of the communication bridge between generations.

Adult Understanding

Teachers often express such views as "What a terrific group last year's sixth grade was" or "This is an immature class." Inquiry enables us to go beyond these kinds of generalizations, because it provides us with more complete understanding about our students individually and collectively. We have to work continuously to keep up with our students and to understand them as fully as we are capable of knowing them if we are to provide education that is truly grounded in their developmental nature and needs. As one middle level educator put it:

> in one word, the total realm of middle school can be brought into perspective; that word is *understanding*. Understand that real life needs are hidden inside those large or small bodies. Understand that a variety of experiences must be given so that an experience can be enjoyed. Understand that never before have they experienced this crossroad. Understand. Understand. Understand. (Knight, 1988, pp. 99–100)

The only way we can understand is to earnestly and honestly open our minds to the lessons others can teach us, especially the ones children can give us about themselves. The essence of inquiry, then, is an attitude—an attitude that values children's impressions and points of view about their own circumstances. The spirit of inquiry is humility—the modest realization that we don't always know just how things are with them. Inquiry techniques constitute some useful things we can do in what must be an ongoing effort to educate ourselves about them, all the while demonstrating our humanity.

Students Knowing about Each Other

One of the most beneficial by-products of classroom inquiries is the extent to which they generate information that the kids themselves want to know about each other. In a very real sense, kids themselves are a curriculum. In fact, no group is more interested in learning about the dynamics of early adolescence than young adolescent youngsters themselves. What do their peers think, do, and expect? They are living in a social and cultural context that they have not previously experienced and for which there are no clear directions.

Any inquiry that solicits information from students must also be reported back to them. In the previous Excerpt 2, Pat found that his students were intensely interested in each other's daily lifestyles. While he had intended all along to use the kids' data for a graphing unit, he did not quite expect their enthusiasm for making comparisons with each other. Pat also observed that enough data for an entire semester's mathematics curriculum had been collected through the inquiry.

Reflection and Speculation

An endearing attribute of young adolescents is their growing tendency to reflect about their past experiences. Often in casual conversation they demonstrate this inclination by recalling childhood events, sometimes sentimentally and other times with amusement at how they've changed. This is also an era when they are increasingly inclined to think theoretically—especially about themselves, their social dynamics, and their generations. I have often been impressed by the intricate theories youngsters conjure up to explain everyday incidents that entail values such as prejudice or hypocrisy. Inquiries inevitably produce findings that invite kids' participation in explanation and interpretation. The results often become the subject of much considered reflection and speculation. These processes are valuable exercise as well for developing students' perceptions and other intellectual capacities.

Modeling

The inclination to ask comes early in the human process of language acquisition. Even if there were no other justification, inquiry is worthwhile on the basis that it models what an educated person does when understanding is needed that can't be found in books or deduced from experimentation. Teachers who easily acknowledge that they don't know something are demonstrating candor. And even though they may not know something, when they do know how to find out and act upon that knowledge of process they *exemplify* the maturity and responsibility students need to be able to draw on as their own sophistication as learners evolves.

WHAT DO YOU WANT TO KNOW?

I stumbled onto my first inquiry by attempting to resolve what was to me a somewhat tiresome argument among several of my students. Their dispute was about who was the most powerful character among several they had been watching on television (Stevenson, 1986). I suggested that we find out what other people thought by doing a survey. They leaped to the opportunity, and once the questionnaires had been collected, they loved comparing responses. Subsequently, they came up with additional questions. Their enthusiasm led me to further inquiries in order to better understand, in their vernacular, "where they were coming from." In the course of that year, inquiries became as common to my teaching style as any other technique. I learned a great deal about my students that otherwise would not have been available to me.

This is a good place to review the excerpts from the three inquiries that introduced this chapter. Each of those projects grew out of a complex of questions and assumptions the inquirers wanted to explore with students. The most appropriate inquiries spring from such curiosities. Using different techniques for accessing information, each inquiry produced information that helped answer the original questions. The first challenge, then, is to focus on a topic of personal interest that lends itself to inquiry. What aspects of the young adolescent community interest you? Intrigue you? Bewilder you?

After I had carried out inquiries with my ten- to fourteen-year-old students for several years, I compiled a list of topics that had been helpful to explore—those that helped me learn more about my students and their priorities or were important to my students. Over the years that list has grown steadily. Topics explored by undergraduate and graduate students have been added to total more than 400 that might be useful to teachers wishing to use inquiry to learn their territory. The following list of some issues in kids' lives has been drawn to stimulate possibilities for your consideration. It is not an exhaustive list, of course, but it shows the scope of possibilities.

ABOUT SCHOOL
Features of school that I most like/dislike
My views about school rules, discipline policy, homework, cafeteria
Things that happen at school that cause me to feel: safe, well liked, happy, secure, successful, proud, stressed, worried, afraid, nervous, embarrassed, pressured, discouraged, defeated, like quitting school
What adults think of me (classmates, teachers, coaches, principal)
Favorite people at school (kids and adults)
The best/worst parts of my school day
The day of the week at school that I most like/dislike
What it was like to be a new student in this school
Changes I would make to improve our school
Things about our school that I would never change
Times of day when I'm most ready to work or it's hardest to concentrate
Advice I'd give to a new student about how to make good grades, get along with other kids, get along with teachers, have a good time here
Things I'd like to do more of or more often at school
Needs I have that don't get met at school
Things I'd like to learn about that haven't been taught
What I contribute to my advisory/class/team/school
Things I most look forward to next year/in high school/as an adult
People at school I admire
The most powerful/influential/likable people at school
The best/worst/most exciting/most embarrassing thing that ever happened to me at school

Favorite school activities/clubs/sports/events
Most/least important things I learn at school
Safest/unsafest places to be at school

ABOUT TEACHERS
Things about the teacher I most admire/like/dislike
Things teachers have done that made me feel good/happy/successful
Things teachers do that help/hinder me as a person
Things teachers do that help/hinder my learning
Things I like/dislike about a teacher's personality
Things the best teachers do to help kids learn and get along with others
What teachers expect of me
My favorite thing a teacher once did for me
When a teacher was unfair/unkind/mean
What makes a good teacher
What I'd do if I were a teacher

ABOUT LEARNING
What I most enjoy learning
Things that are easy/hard for me to learn
Things I know I can learn if I work hard enough
Things I don't think I can learn no matter how hard I work
Things I don't want/like to learn
Times of day/week/year when I learn best
Important things I've learned about outside of school
Changes at school that would help me learn better
The best time of day/week for me to learn/study
Ways I like to show what I have learned or can do
Important things I've learned today/this week/term/year
Things I do/learn better than other people realize
Things I'd like to learn a lot more about
Things people do that are helpful/harmful to study habits

ABOUT PARENTS/FAMILY
What my parents expect me to do at school, home, neighborhood, community
Ways my parents help me
Favorite times with my parents
Good advice my parents have given me
Things that are hard/impossible to talk about with my parents
Things about me I wish my parents valued more
What my parents think about my schoolwork
Consequences when I do something wrong/bad
Favorite things to do with my parents/siblings/family
Family routines/traditions/rituals/celebrations
Rules/chores at home; after-school routine/activities
Favorite relatives
Favorite stories my parents/relatives tell

ABOUT OTHER KIDS
Important things about best friend(s)
Things friends have done for me and/or things I do for my friends
Things other kids do that they should not do
Things kids have tried to persuade me to do that I didn't want to do
Other kids I know I can go to for help if I need it
Things some kids do that make me feel sad, hurt, disappointed, betrayed
Things about kids whom I don't like to sit next to/be around
Things I'd like to do with my best friend(s) or other kids I don't know well
Things other kids do that make them successful/unsuccessful

ABOUT MYSELF AND OTHERS
Ways in which I am a responsible person
Ways in which I am confident about myself
What I've learned to do to cope with difficult situations
Things I do/have done to help other people
Ways in which our society needs to improve
Things about me that make me a good friend
Things about me that are special that other people may/do not know
Things I have read/like to read for pleasure
How I'm like other people and different from other people
Beliefs about religion, racial discrimination, ethnic groups
Things I most like to do with my free time
Rights that kids my age ought to have
My greatest fears/worries
Things I have that I value the most

FAVORITES
Food
Music
Clothes
Games
Sports
Television/movies
Travel

COMMUNITY ACTIVITIES
Scouting
Organized sports
Church groups
Music
Dance
Other lessons

MISCELLANEOUS
Allowance/money
Chores
Jobs
Pets

Hobbies
Possessions

JUDGMENT AND CHOICES—ISSUES IN KIDS' LIVES
Experimenting with or using tobacco/alcohol/drugs
Peer pressures relating to using harmful substances
Going to parties, dating, going steady, sex
Damaging another person's property by accident or deliberately (vandalism)
Stealing from classmates, parents, teachers, stores
Cheating on homework, in class, on tests
Telling the truth: exaggerations, fibs, white lies, lies
People who abuse kids
Adults/other kids I turn to for support/advice

EXERCISING DISCRETION

As should be obvious from this list, it is extremely important for inquirers to exercise a great deal of discretion in selecting topics. Inquiries that solicit information that is particularly personal—especially some of the topics related to family—should not be attempted until or unless the teacher has established trusting communication with parents. Advisors who meet with their advisees daily have a particularly promising opportunity to build such trust over time. It is inappropriate, therefore, for an outsider or even a regular teacher who is a first-time or occasional inquirer to probe topics that are likely to be sensitive.

Peter, a teacher with more than a dozen years of experience, who has been highly respected by parents and students, wanted to help his seventh graders and their parents overcome some communication awkwardness about growing up. His inquiry was done first with his students' parents at the annual open house early in the fall term. He asked them to anonymously complete a survey about their memories from years ago when they were in the seventh grade. A few weeks later, he shared the summarized data with his students in a health class, where they'd completed the same survey. Peter opted not to reveal the source of his data. The students confirmed that the data reflected an accurate understanding of what it was like to be a twelve-year-old. Only at the close of the lesson did he reveal that the data he had given them were their parents' recollections of being twelve. The kids were predictably amazed. Their subsequent assignment was to show their parents what they had learned from the two surveys.

As a general rule, I urge that kids' participation in inquiries be both *elective* and *anonymous*. No one should be compelled to provide personal information unless he or she freely elects to do so. Likewise, students who wish to participate anonymously must be assured of their privacy. Of course, some of the strategies used for collecting information described in the next section mitigate against anonymity, so they would be inappropriate if it is important to maintain privacy. I recommend that first-time inquirers plan to collect their initial data anonymously, allowing for the possibility of a less anonymous follow-up if additional information is desired. Excerpt 1 is an example; Helen and Gail had established enough credibility with two classes of seventh graders to enable them to collect students' ideas in a manner that was neither embarrassing nor obtrusive. As a general rule, however, university students carrying out an inquiry should design it to ensure that it is both elective and anonymous.

There are numerous topics in the preceding listing that a first-time inquirer could safely and fruitfully explore, and further examples are included later in this chapter. First, however, let's examine some ways to go about collecting information from kids at school. You may even have occasion to use these techniques with parents, as Peter did, or with colleagues—depending upon whom you wish to understand better.

WAYS TO COLLECT KIDS' THOUGHTS

The strategies used to find out what kids think have a great deal to do with the quality of the responses you'll get. Ask a flippant question, and you'll probably get a flip response. On the other hand, when an inquiry has been well thought out, carefully prepared, and unpretentiously introduced, you'll usually find the sincerity of your effort reciprocated. It is also important to be candid with the respondents about the interests and seriousness that motivate you to create and carry out the inquiry. You can equate how they respond to the inquiry with their readiness to trust you.

Once the topic and focus of a project have been selected, look for ways to present it that appear most likely to both provide the information you seek and make the experience interesting and enjoyable for the youngsters. As an experienced inquirer, I am accustomed to students afterwards showing their interest in why I asked particular questions and what I hoped to learn. Invariably, kids like to tell other people what they think, and since the topics inquiries explore are usually about matters that concern them, they also care about the results. As you go about designing your project, then, do your best to shape the procedure along lines you believe students will enjoy.

There are lots of ways to collect other people's ideas, perceptions, and opinions. A private one-to-one interview is excellent but time-consuming. Surveys and inventories have become commonplace, but their impersonal nature might be taken less seriously than you'd like. The more experience you gain with an assortment of information gathering techniques, the more savvy and inventive you are likely to become.

Once again, a central matter to consider in shaping an inquiry concerns the privacy of the respondents. Regardless of how the inquiry is to be carried out, provision must be made for anonymity. Likewise, all inquiries must be optional; students should never be coerced if they do not wish to participate. While the vast majority of inquiries are not so personal that respondents would be concerned about their responses being kept anonymous, careful explanations and the option not to participate or to participate anonymously must always be made clear. Depending on the topic you wish to investigate, it may also prove useful to look at responses according to differences between the sexes or among ages or grades if you're considering expanding beyond a single class. Remember, the overarching purpose of inquiry is to advance understanding, communication, and learning—the bedrock of trust.

Below are brief summaries of inquiry techniques and guidelines that many of my undergraduate and graduate students and I have used successfully to advance our understanding of young adolescents. These and other methods are described more fully elsewhere (Stevenson, 1986).

Questionnaire/Survey

By far the most common collecting strategy, one that is especially popular with first-time inquirers, is a questionnaire or survey made up of items that usually look a lot like the standardized ones we've all experienced. Individual items on these homemade versions tend to be pretty much alike, although sometimes the inquirer varies the ways questions are asked to add variety. One important caveat must be remembered, however. Don't take for granted that it is easy to write short structured items when your original overarching purpose is to provoke students to share their thoughts as freely and directly as possible. How questions are asked affects how they are answered.

Writing items for inquiry is just like any other form of precise writing in that drafts and revisions are necessary to create the most accurate phrasing possible. I usually avoid asking questions that can be answered either yes or no, unless that particular item helps classify or sort the survey forms for subsequent analysis. If, for example, your inquiry is about kids' use of the telephone, you might first ask whether or not they have a telephone in their room or whether or not anyone is at home when they get home from school. Establishing such information early helps when sorting and comparisons are made later.

Begin by writing draft items according to whatever format you prefer. Then ask a classmate or colleague to answer or respond to them, adding whatever suggestions he or she thinks will improve the wording. On the basis of this feedback, edit as you think best. Repeat this kind of field testing until you think your items are as nearly perfect as you can get them. Then try them on a few youngsters of the ages of those with whom you'll use the survey. Ask them to not only answer the items but also tell you what they understand you to be asking or directing them to do. Having completed these developmental steps in producing a survey, you'll have a better chance of getting precisely the information you seek.

There are several effective formats for soliciting youngsters' responses that will be briefly summarized and exemplified in the following pages.

SHORT-ANSWER AND MULTIPLE-CHOICE ITEMS

Group A Fill in the blanks:

The best hours of the day for me to learn something difficult are _____.

If I could visit anywhere in the world, I'd go to _____.

Group B Circle your answers:

The approximate amount of time I usually spend on homework is:

15 min.   30 min.   45 min.   1 hour   75 min.   90 min.

The ways I usually feel about doing homework are:

I'm willing   I'm bored   I'm eager   I hate it   I don't care

By the middle grades, all students and teachers are familiar with items written like the ones in these two groups. Workbook exercises and tests composed by teachers often require one- or two-word responses designed much like those in Group A. Standardized tests rely more heavily upon multiple-choice items. Both types of questions are easy and efficient to score, but the specificity may limit kids' range and depth of thought.

STATEMENT COMPLETIONS

Complete the following sentences according to what you believe:

1 I am a responsible person because . . .
2. I like school best when . . .

Young adolescents routinely respond to completion items like these with a single distinct idea expressed in just a few words. Sadly, too many of them have grown to dislike writing so much that their responses may be minimal. Yet, as they become more accustomed to this format in free writing exercises as well as inquiry, the texture of their responses will become richer and more complete.

LIKERT SCALE RATINGS

Circle your answer:

1. Students who misbehave usually get the punishment they deserve.

    Strongly Agree   Agree   Undecided   Disagree   Strongly Disagree

2. My best friend always tells me the truth.

    Strongly Agree   Agree   Unsure   Disagree   Strongly Disagree

Comment:

The primary advantage of this format for presenting items is that it invites respondents to go beyond simple agreement or disagreement to indicate the extent of the value they associate with the issue. Item 2 invites further comment—an effective device as long as the survey is one page or less. Kids are inclined to pass over opportunities to comment on a long survey, unless they have particularly strong views about the item. This format also allows for indecision or uncertainty.

RATING ITEMS

Rearrange the following lists so that the most important to you is "1," next most important is "2," and so on so that least important is last.

1. (a) Science textbook 1 _____
   (b) Social studies textbook 2 _____
   (c) Literature book 3 _____
   (d) Math textbook 4 _____
   (e) My notebook 5 _____

2. (a) Having a best friend 1 _____
   (b) Making the honor roll 2 _____
   (c) Staying out of trouble 3 _____
   (d) Having a boy/girl friend 4 _____
   (e) Pleasing my parents 5 _____
   (f) Other: 6 _____
       (explain)

These items invite the student to be reflective in terms of criteria and comparisons that are not always easy to resolve. Likewise, they tend to generate lots of questions and discussion about how others rated the items. It is a good idea, therefore, to capitalize on their curiosity with follow-up discussion as soon as the inquiry has been completed.

LISTING QUESTIONS

List all the words or phrases you use to describe your best friend:

My five favorite activities to do on weekends are:

An advantage of listing questions is that they require original thought and deliberation rather than limit the respondent to rearranging preconceived items. Everything students offer comes from their individual consciousness, for how the item appears doesn't offer any guiding or qualifying suggestions or clues.

COMBINATIONS

First, list all the things teachers do that help you learn. (Pause while the students write.)

Next, put a "1" next to the most important thing you have listed, a "2" next to the next most important, a "3" next to the third most important, and so on.

Sometimes it is helpful to combine techniques if you can do so without causing too much confusion. Combinations that work well together are "Listing" and "Rating," like the example above. Although there are lots of additional ways to ask questions and package individual items, these examples should be adequate for getting started with drafting potential items for a survey or questionnaire.

Some Final Suggestions

If you decide to use a survey/questionnaire to collect students' ideas and beliefs, consider these guidelines. Following them will help you reduce the likelihood of confusion and redundancy.

1. Remember to draft each question/item several different ways, then choose the one that you think does the job best. Try out your items with a few friends or, even better, with a few students of comparable ages in another class or school. *Never* administer a questionnaire without first testing it with others and considering their suggestions for improvement.

2. Write concise, well-articulated directions. If the format for responding to a new set of items is different, make sure the new directions are clear.

3. Keep the number of items brief; five to ten items is a good range.

Reflection and Speculation

One of the most appealing indications of change in ways youngsters think during the early adolescent years is their growing inclination to share thoughts that are increasingly reflective and speculative. The astute observer will notice the frequency of expressions such as "I remember the time when . . ." and "When I was little we used to. . . ." Youngsters are also becoming more inclined to imagine alternative ways of doing things or resolving contrary issues as expressed by "What if . . .?" These evidences of intellectual transition invite some distinctive forms of inquiry. Youngsters' reactions to problems—real and fictitious—may help the inquirer learn more about not only the students but also their ideas. Interests and curiosities they share may also suggest areas for curriculum development.

Inquiry that springs from students' interests and questions is self-evidently authentic. For example, a study that was loaded with geography and mathematics grew out of an inquiry with seventh graders about "work I'd like to do if I could begin right now." Several boys and one girl reported that they might like to be truck drivers. Others reported "travel agent, airline stewardess, mechanic, engineer" and so on. Their teacher subsequently shaped a transportation unit around their career interests that related to individual interests. Ross Burkhardt uses inquiry very successfully in designing successful interdisciplinary curriculum units (1994). He recognizes the urgent importance of his students learning how to carry out an inquiry process. More will be said about inquiry in curriculum in Chapter 6.

A sampling of some techniques that are likely to encourage reflection and speculation is offered here.

DILEMMA

Ann is a very shy seventh grader who has only one close friend: Mary. Although Mary is quite popular and outgoing and has several other friends, she's always remained loyal to Ann. They have been next-door neighbors since first grade, and their families have also become friends. Last August the two families went to the beach for a week's vacation together, and they are planning a ski weekend together next month.

As the two girls walked to school together this morning, Mary unbuttoned one of her sleeves to show Ann how she had written answers for the science test on her arm. Although Ann knew that on a few occasions Mary had told fibs and shoplifted candy or gum, she'd never known her to deliberately cheat on schoolwork. During the test she saw Mary using the crib notes on her arm. What should Ann do?

This dilemma can be approached by asking students to look at and respond to this issue from several points of view. Foremost, of course, is the quandary Ann faces. If she does anything to expose Mary's behavior, she risks losing the only real friend she has. On the other hand, Ann knows that her school's honor code posted in the classrooms and on book covers requires that students turn in cheaters to the teacher or principal. What should she do? How will Mary react? Will she regard Ann as a traitor, betraying their long friendship? Finally, look at the issue from both sets of parents' points of view. How will Mary's parents respond to her cheating? And how will they react toward Ann for turning her in? And what happens to the friendship between their families?

This dilemma was real; it occurred just as described here. Our everyday lives often include such dilemmas. What hard decisions have your students confronted? Once you have worked through Ann's dilemma, invite students to write out dilemmas they have faced or to create fictitious ones around issues of concern. Published examples may also be helpful (see Casteel, 1978).

REFLECTION

How do you remember learning to swim? To ride a bicycle? To take a bus alone?

By the time youngsters have entered their early adolescent years, they are increasingly able to contemplate prior events in their lives in ways that give rise to interpretation and theorizing. They also recall events anecdotally, often somewhat differently from how the same event may be recalled by someone else who was also present. This growing readiness to conceptualize, reflect, and analyze major events, turning points, and breakthroughs makes inquiry that seeks reflective responses particularly interesting and often revealing as to how an individual thinks.

> Tell me about yourself.
>
> Can you tell me what it's like to be your age?
>
> What are your thoughts about your life as a child/twelve-year-old?

WHAT IFS?

> What if you could change any one thing about yourself?
>
> What if the president of the United States asked you to be his advisor about schools?
>
> What if a movie was being made about your life? Tell about it.
>
> What if you found $1,000 cash in a paper bag with this note: "Whoever finds this money may keep it. I am throwing it away."
>
> What if you were to encounter a flying saucer the size of our classroom? A warm, friendly voice invites you aboard, promises not to harm you, but does not promise to bring you back. What do you do (a) if you're alone? (b) if you're with a parent? (c) if you're with any friend you choose?

John Lennon's haunting lyrics expressed in "Imagine" capture the human tendency to fantasize about how things might be "if." Imagining is especially natural to young adolescents as they begin to think in new ways about their lives and issues in the world they're becoming more aware of. Inviting them to suppose actions and consequences is an especially effective stimulus to imaginative, large-scale thought. I created the examples above to provoke imagination, speculation, and reflection. Usually they provoke an immediate, superficial response, but as discussion continues there is often a qualitative change in tone and substance. Very contemplative individual thought and spirited group discussions are aroused.

Interviews

When you want to know what other people think or believe about something, the most direct way to find out is to ask—directly, in clear language, and with the nonjudgmental earnestness that conveys respect to the person being asked. Teachers, parents, and other adults are wise to listen to their youngsters in this way. After years of interviewing middle grades students, I have found that when they are satisfied that I really want to know what they think, and that I am not evaluating them or rating what they have to say according to any external expectations or comparisons with what anyone else has said, they reciprocate my attitude. In chance encounters with parents, I've gotten comments about how much their son or daughter enjoyed our interview. I've learned that with rare exception, kids delight in this opportunity to express themselves. Our children are the experts in knowing what they personally think and believe, and if we're to understand them we must acknowledge their expertise by listening openly and earnestly.

The one-to-one interview is generally the best way to solicit direct responses to inquiry. Face-to-face conversation is direct, potential confusions or uncertainty about the question can be cleared up on the spot, and the interviewer has an opportunity to build rapport with the student, even if the interaction lasts only a few minutes. Despite these advantages, however, it is often difficult to conduct more than a few interviews because they are so time-consuming for both interviewer and subject. Given this constraint, it is particularly important that the inquirer prepare thoroughly and ask only a minimal number of questions that have been carefully worded in advance.

The previously mentioned inquiry by Gail and Helen is a good example of effective use of one-to-one interviewing. The tentative interview format they had prepared was first approved by the cooperating teachers. On the morning of the inquiry, the teachers announced that Gail and Helen would be visiting again in the afternoon and that they were interested in talking briefly with some eighth graders about social groups. Between the two of them they managed to interview seventeen of the fifty-three students in the eighth grade. None of the chats lasted more than five minutes, so the flow of afternoon periods, one of which was a study hall, was not seriously interrupted for students or teachers. Helen and Gail added that many more students were willing to participate than time permitted.

Group interviews are customarily thought of as discussions, but they are also common ways teachers try to find out what and how students think. When a teacher asks, "How did you like *Where the Red Fern Grows*?" a group interview is initiated about an experience those students have in common—they all read this particular book. If the interview is authentic, the teacher genuinely wants to learn the students' thoughts; further instructional efforts might be set aside until later.

Two generally unavoidable conditions handicap group interviews. First, securing enough time for every student to express his or her view is difficult to achieve in heavily planned schedules. Second, interpersonal dynamics may intimidate some students from saying anything, while others try to dominate air time to advance their own agendas. Given these constraints, the smaller the group, the more likely it is that each student will participate.

Depending on the subject of the inquiry, using a group of student interviewers to conduct one-to-one sessions may prove to be the best way to collect information. If the topic isn't particularly sensitive or threatening, students who are equipped with a common set of questions and have been rehearsed in conducting interviews can gather the needed information themselves.

Some guidelines follow for using interviews successfully.

1. The very best entry into an interview I have found is either "Tell me about . . ." or "Tell me your thoughts about . . ." This petition invites the respondent to offer whatever he or she wishes, assuring that the student remains in control of the discussion. From there the interviewer may use probes for elaboration or clarification as needed. Sometimes a student will respond with "What do you want to know?" An appropriate response is "Whatever you can tell me." It is important that the respondent feels that he or she is in full control of the discussion.

2. Write your questions in draft form prior to the interview. Field-test them on colleagues or with students if possible, and edit them to ensure that they are understandable and succinct.

3. Once the interview has begun, avoid paraphrasing questions unless the respondent simply does not understand what you are asking.

4. The interviewer should *never* interject a personal opinion about a respondent's comments, even if the interviewer agrees wholeheartedly. It is very important not to influence what the student thinks. Afterwards it might be all right to swap points of view, but the interviewer must remember that during the interview the purpose is to understand the respondent's viewpoint.

5. Tape-recorded interviews can be particularly helpful, because they enable the inquirer to concentrate upon the respondent's monologue without the distraction of taking notes. If the interviewer wishes to make a recording, however, respondents should be asked ahead of time how they feel about it. Sometimes students who are willing to be interviewed are uncomfortable about being recorded. Again, the emphasis here should be upon assuring the respondent that he or she is in control of the situation.

Documentation

The purpose of documentation is to teach students how to keep an ongoing record of selected representations of their lives and learning. For example, a file folder or portfolio (see Chapter 8) containing every math practice sheet, homework paper, test, self-assessment anecdote, and other pertinent material for a student is a documentation of his or her math experience. Study of the contents of that folder will reveal insights about the youngster's performance and progress in that class. It does not tell everything a teacher might wish to know, but it constitutes primary source material for study.

The best ways I have found to comprehend the personality and character of a student's life over a year or more have been to use combinations of documentation strategies. Day-to-day interactions certainly offer lots of clues to the major themes in kids' lives, but continuity emerges only from longer-term documentation. Undergraduate university students may not find this process immediately feasible, since they usually have limited and irregular access to students. During internships and practice teaching, however, the possibilities for studying individual students increase. Once one interacts daily with them, documentation engenders insights into how individual students function best and also how they view their schooling.

Topical Discussion

There is no shortage of current issues that young adolescents care about and are eager to discuss. For example, a recent newspaper editorial argued for support of mandatory school uniforms in public schools. My casual mention of that proposal in a middle grades classroom I was visiting aroused spirited reaction from students. The editorial argued for uniforms as a way to reduce school violence—a point of view most of the students supported. On the other hand, they also saw clothing and fashion as a personal choice issue, and none of them could easily let go of that felt freedom. Consider also the advertising aimed at adolescents—especially those for tobacco, fast food, and clothing. One student observed that "Joe Camel is as well known [to us] as Mickey Mouse." Discussions about books they have read, especially those that purport to speak on behalf of their generation, invite discussion about the veracity of the depiction. Movies and television, especially situation comedies that dramatize kids their ages, are ripe for their discussion. When youngsters willingly engage each other and adults about such topics, they open windows for us into their thinking, their beliefs and values, and their needs. Prudent teachers take full advantage of such opportunities to learn about their constituents.

Documentation related to assessing and evaluating learning will be discussed further in Chapter 8. Several methods of documenting assorted aspects of young adolescents' school experiences deserve at least a brief explanation here.

Video/Audio Recording

Contemporary technology offers inexpensive, easy-to-use ways to create a record of every student. The most fascinating and informative inquiry I have ever carried out consisted of a series of five- to ten-minute videotaped interviews with students in a middle school. The four-year sequence of interviews commenced when they were in fifth grade and continued annually through their eighth grade year. The format was consistent each year, and it began with the entreaty recommended earlier in this section: "Tell me about yourself." Students talked about things they liked to do, their accomplishments, and what they enjoyed doing with friends. Occasionally, when they seemed tongue-tied or couldn't think of what to say, I used gentle probes such as "What things do you do best?" "What things do you like to do with friends?" "What things do you do that you'd like to do better?" "When you have some free time, what do you like to do?" Because I happen to be particularly interested in any thoughts they might have about their future lives, I also ask, "What are your thoughts about what you might do when you're a grownup?"

It was a simple matter to set up the video recorder and microphone in a small room where the session could be private. I kept individual videocassettes for each student so that each year's interview simply followed the one from the previous year without requiring any editing or splicing. So that what they chose to say in one year's interview would not be affected by their having seen their previous interviews, I didn't let them see their tapes until the end of their eighth grade year, six months after the final session. At that time I gave each student a copy of his or her four interviews. Not only did these interviews help me and my colleagues understand these youngsters better, but they became a cherished souvenir of their middle school years and a graduation gift for them and their parents.

This same type of documentation process can be carried out with an audiocassette tape recorder. While audiotapes cannot capture the visual evidence of often dramatic changes in physical development, body language, and hair and clothing styles, they are easier to set up and administer. It is also possible for the recording to be made without the teacher's presence. One teacher friend required her students to tape-record "the story of my life" at two-week intervals as a warm-up activity for writing autobiographies. The teacher then listened to the tapes during her forty-five-minute commute each way to school. She also tape-recorded private feedback to them at regular intervals, taking advantage of otherwise lost time on her daily commute. Students loved the opportunity to tell their personal sagas to someone they recognized as caring so much about them.

Journal Writing

A journal is simply a book of blank pages into which the journalist writes experiences, thoughts, observations—whatever one wishes to express and record. Sometimes people will keep such a record of thoughts and experiences over an extended period of time, even years. Journals kept by young adolescents often include drawings as well as words, and sometimes young authors also opt to include photographs, clippings, or copies of pieces they find appealing in other publications. At their best, journals are personal accounts of "how things are" that with passing time become records of "how I was."

Journals are comparable to diaries in that they are personal records that are available for others to read only under conditions agreeable to the author. Academic journals emphasize writing about one's perceptions of academic material—what Fulwiler refers to as "I–it" (1987). Teachers expect to review these journals as a way of understanding what the student understands. Personal journals are less restricted accounts of experience. Often, however, students will permit trusted teachers to read them as a way to help the teacher understand the student's life and reflective thoughts about what he or she is experiencing. It is essential to preserving trust and fostering teacher credibility, however, that everyone fully understands from the beginning the ground rules about who is authorized to read journals and under what circumstances.

Journal writing can be an effective device to help reflective students learn to assess and write more holistically and analytically about their school lives, looking for patterns in their decisions and choices. When they are written candidly and are shared in trust with a teacher, they also convey the authors' perceptions of their circumstances. Journals may also be used for recording ideas and understandings about curriculum, a use that is further described later. For excellent detailed suggestions about journaling techniques and uses, see *The Journal Book* (Fulwiler, 1987) and *Coming to Know* (Atwell, 1990).

Logs

At the opening of this chapter is an excerpt from Pat's inquiry that involved eighth graders keeping records of how they spent their out-of-school waking hours. That inquiry is an excellent example of building one type of log. Students kept personal activity and time data according to the framework Pat created (see Figure 3.1). They subsequently converted those entries into statistical data that included setting up frequency distributions, determining ranges, and making limitless calculations of averages and percentages. Through this study of their uses of time they were also able to identify personal time use patterns and group trends. Pat learned a great deal about his students individually and collectively, and he captured their interest in using mathematics for analyzing personal habits and lifestyle.

We know in a general way that our students spend a good bit of time watching television. From time to time we see newspaper accounts of research that warns that contemporary youth is spending more time in front of the television set at home than receiving instruction in school. While such results catch our attention, they don't tell us anything about the particular students in our advisory or class or team. Another legitimate topic especially appropriate for inquiry, therefore, is our students' television viewing habits. Using logs to record the programs they view each day for a week will produce much more pertinent information about how much time they spend watching television and what programs they watch alone, with a friend, and with a parent. Like Pat's time use study, these logs will also generate data that can be used for both math and social studies lessons.

Another application of logs as ways of knowing our students better is the use of reading logs. How much time do they spend reading as a matter of personal choice? What do they read? With whom do they exchange their reactions? Are they swapping materials? These important questions are best addressed for a large number of students by having them keep individual reading logs first, then following up with a survey that asks specific questions such as those stated above. These records identify the specific literature youngsters are reading as well as their appraisal of it, reflecting their taste and often their expectations and standards.

Logs may also be used for assigned entries about the literature being taught in class. In this application the teacher asks students to write in response to a particular prompt in order to access reactions to a particular issue or event. Prompts usually solicit youngsters' feelings and thoughts about a character or event. The appendices of Nancie Atwell's (1987, 1990) books contain many excellent prompts. Learning logs are used not for evaluation and grading but for assessment—a way for the student and teacher to understand what and how the student has learned. Academic learning logs are described further in Chapter 8.

In a special application of logs, one teacher offered blank books to his eighth grade students at the beginning of the school year with the following provisos: (1) students would make a minimum of two entries per week, (2) only second or final drafts could be entered, (3) all entries had to be written in ink in one's best handwriting, and (4) the logs would be stored in the teacher's cabinet. When a student was ready to enter something, he or she would ask the teacher for the log. What the students did not find out until the last day of the school year was that the teacher had designed a year-ending surprise. Using a dry-mount press, he had attached a black-and-white photograph of each student inside the front cover of his or her log. Then he had the student's name and the school year embossed on the outside cover. The logs constituted an immediately accessible archive of some of each participating student's work that kept the teacher informed about each student's personal standards. They also became treasured keepsakes for the students.

Teacher's Log

The frequency of interpersonal exchanges, some of which may be somewhat intense, is so great that even our very best efforts to remember the details and understand them on reflection are frustrated. Though a single interaction may present some new or previously unnoticed insights about a student, hanging on to those thoughts is jeopardized by the continuing flow of other interactions and events of a typical day. Occasionally a teacher-writer develops a participant-observer's discipline by maintaining shorthand notes of these interactions (Paley, 1981). Paley's documentary writings provide exceptionally valuable insights about the thought of primary school children and portray the atmosphere and vitality of their environment. Those of us at the middle level, however, do well to salvage at best a few notable insights from a day at school unless we develop a way to systematically document our experience.

While some of us may be able to simultaneously document and teach, most of us are well challenged by either task, much less attempting both at the same time. For me, an efficient and satisfactory way to keep a running record of pertinent interactions and incidents has been to maintain a three-ring notebook of observations, hunches, and questions I want to be sure to remember. In the binder are pages tabbed for each student, where I jot notes about important thoughts and incidents as they occur. Sometimes I have anecdotally recorded an event that involved several students, later cross-referencing the entry to other students' pages. By keeping such a log I can construct a fuller representation of what I am learning about my students.

For the first few months that I used this system, students were not permitted to read my notes. I reasoned that this was my private record. I soon discovered, however, that the book was becoming a barrier to our communication. They were suspicious about the book, and my insistence upon its privacy, no matter how rational, was breeding distrust. Consequently I rescinded the original privacy policy and invited them to look at anything I wrote on their individual pages. Other students' pages had to be kept private between them and me. For a while there was a great deal of interest in checking out my notations, and sometimes kids challenged my account of an event. On those occasions the big gain was, of course, that I learned even more. Keeping such a notebook requires self-discipline, but it is well worth the effort when it enables us to gain in our efforts to understand students' individual needs and readiness.

Letter Writing

Among the several forms of communication that occur routinely in schools, letters between teachers and students have a unique character. First, letters are direct expressions between two individuals in a context where most of the communication is oral and group-directed. Only one-to-one interviews bring the two communicators into more direct dialogue than letter writing. And because letters are a more intimate communique between people, they tend to be more conscientiously thought out than other less personal writings that occur in school. Often a focus of such writing is a class or activity both parties experience, and the letter shares a point of view about that common experience.

Another valuable but sometimes overlooked feature of letters is that aside from the literal messages they may bear, their mere existence is evidence of the author's respect. One doesn't take the time and energy to write a letter unless she cares about communicating with the recipient. Children recognize this fact, and they understand that letters represent more than simply a vehicle for sending someone a message that could be delivered more quickly in person or by telephone.

Young adolescent students can also recognize that because they outnumber teachers by such a large margin it is impractical for a teacher to correspond regularly with every student. Therefore, the best routine becomes one in which students write to the teacher at one- to two-week intervals, and teachers respond by either writing on the student's letter or by attaching a return note to the letter. I went one step further and asked students to maintain both their original letters and my replies in their portfolios where we could both have access to them as we made periodic reviews of their progress and personal history.

During the last several years I taught middle grades students, I was part of a team made up of sixth, seventh, and eighth graders. During the summer my teammate and I wrote notes or brief letters to our fifty or so students who would be returning in the fall. Most of the kids responded in kind or by telephone, and in these ways we maintained an ongoing dialogue, slowed but not broken by the summer vacation. Occasionally we followed the letter exchanges with a rendezvous such as a baseball game or a drop-by visit. Writing and these occasions of visiting helped me know these young adolescents better than would have been the case without the exchanges. These contacts also conveyed the importance we placed on their ideas and aspirations. I believe these letters did more than any other single thing I did as a teacher to build communication with a few individuals.

One particularly memorable exchange took place with Sabra Hull, a seventh grader spending her summer in Maine. I had written about what was an uncomfortably hot, humid August in Boston, and I must have conveyed a good bit of envy for her refreshing summer in the cool Maine woods. Her return "letter" was simply an aromatic sprig of balsam. My appreciation and understanding of Sabra grew more as a consequence of the sensitivity she revealed in that action than any other single exchange we had during our three years together on that team.

Suggestion Box

Many years ago, while teaching about adolescent sexuality, I learned about using a suggestion box to help students anonymously raise questions or issues that they might be embarrassed to verbalize in class or directly to an adult. The box itself was simply a cardboard shoe box with a slot cut in the lid. At the end of class each day I'd ask everyone to write questions or suggestions they'd like to have me address in a subsequent class on a piece of paper, then fold and put it in the box as they left the room. I asked them to put a folded note in the box even if there was nothing in particular on their minds. That strategy ensured that no one was singled out; anonymity was assured. On a few rare occasions I found playful chits, but most of their questions and suggestions were self-evidently sincere, reflecting genuine concern or confusion, and they guided my effort to be responsive to the issues on their minds.

Noting the effectiveness of the suggestion box in that particularly sensitive setting, I opted to continue using it as an effective communication vehicle. Once or twice a week on average, especially at the close of a team meeting when our discussions might have been somewhat emotional or shown sharp differences of opinion, I'd employ the suggestion box both to offer an outlet for students who needed it and to collect the views of kids who hadn't spoken. Again, participation was mandatory. Although this is an excellent assessment device for teachers working every day in a middle level school, it also serves well for inquiry being done by undergraduates who may have access to students only occasionally.

Portfolios

The inquiring teacher can also gain fuller understanding of individual students through having them maintain a comprehensive file of their work, including periodic self-evaluations. This process is detailed in Chapter 8.

THE CASE FOR INQUIRY

How does a middle grades teacher respond to the dinner party query "What do you do?" What, indeed, does one do? The foremost occupational hazard of our profession is our tendency to become so preoccupied with covering material, getting through textbooks, calculating grades, and performing other duties familiar to teachers that we may not be getting to the larger goal of helping students develop competencies and character. The most important single characteristic of the middle school movement is the commitment to schooling practices based on the nature and needs of young adolescents. Both teachers and the public are becoming increasingly mindful of reestablishing the primary focus upon our constituency—our students. This mentality is reflected by our responses to the above question: "I teach young adolescents" or "I teach young adolescents about math and science," rather than "I teach math."

Inquiry allows us to gain a critical grasp of how our students comprehend their school experience. Although they are no longer completely dependent young children, neither are they fully self-sufficient adults. We must understand how the school appears to them, setting aside our own assumptions for a moment in order to understand their points of view. How do they think about the purposes of their schooling? The ways it is organized? The expectations teachers have for them? As I have already shown, there is a myriad of pertinent questions we can well afford to ask youngsters about the efficacy of how schools function.

Inquiry is also the most direct route for us to learn about our youngsters as individuals. Inquiry revealed to me "Silent Ben's" passion for anything having to do with archeology, and I was able to be a much better, more responsive teacher for him as a result. I also discovered that Marian's favorite readings were plays—especially those of Shakespeare. That insight led me into a vigorous exploration of how it was that she had such esoteric intellectual interests and tastes while at the same time she was perceived by all of her teachers as just another "average student." And it was also through inquiry that I learned that Sean, a troubled thirteen-year-old who presented a continuing discipline problem, was obsessed with aeronautics, constructed radio-controlled airplanes, hung around a small private airport, and knew far more than his teachers about aviation and airplanes. To gain such valuable insights about our students' interests, aptitudes, talents, curiosities, and points of view, we must deliberately listen to and trust their responses to our genuine inquiries. Understanding their personal interests and learning traits is far too important to be left to chance encounters and indices from standardized tests.

If We Are to Understand, Then We Must Ask!

Even if a teacher doesn't care (heaven forbid!) how students perceive the school or what personal interests occupy their minds, surely all teachers have an undeniable obligation to be informed about how their students learn. That obligation is one of the principal attributes that distinguishes teaching as a profession. We need to know as much as a teacher can know about what instructional practices work for students and what hinders their learning. The kids themselves are the experts on these issues. If we teachers are to establish enlightened, functioning matches between what we do as schooling and how our students learn best and grow most healthily, we must create circumstances by which kids can tell us their experience and identify their personal tendencies.

A colleague and I used an assortment of inquiry methods to assess some fifth and eighth graders' learning and perceptions about units they had been taught (Rogers & Stevenson, 1988). We found lots of differences between what kids appeared to know, based on their performance on tests administered at the end of the units and what they evidenced in interview situations and on test items presented weeks after the unit. Working with other teachers, we also devised many strategies for finding out what students believe. Inquiry is, after all, a form of assessment—a way of finding out how things are, independent of any evaluative criteria.

It is appropriate in closing to remind the reader again that the focus of this chapter has been on using simple inquiry strategies to enhance one's knowledge of his or her particular students as individuals as well as to better understand the specific culture of the student group. Well-done inquiry based on genuine curiosity develops professional insight. Remember, though, that establishing generalizable truths or proof is not the purpose of inquiry.

To Professors

Teachers of young adolescents are not the only ones who benefit from inquiry. I have learned a lot from my university students about how well programs and courses are actually working, and their candid input has also been helpful to me as an advisor on numerous occasions. There is also something to be said for the effects of catharsis. Simply telling someone else in a credible, trusting context about a traumatic time can help lighten burdens. Journals, logs, the suggestion box, and invitations to free-write have been especially successful ways of both gaining insights about my students and helping them come to better terms with personal issues. To illustrate this point, one of my students allowed me to include here the following excerpt from her reflective course journal:

> Many experiences have helped shape who I am today, but one experience has had the greatest impact on my mind and soul. I changed schools when I was in the eighth grade. I went from being a popular happy child to being a disliked and unpopular student. My new peers were cruel and mean to me. They picked on me until I would cry. The girls started an "I Hate Susan Club," and it was the "in thing" to make me aware of how much everyone disliked me. One incident really devastated me. A group of four girls became very friendly with me and invited me to a party. I was very excited and happy to have finally found some friends, and I spent hours getting ready for the party. When I arrived I was greeted by unusually warm smiles and friendly gestures. I mingled and was really enjoying myself until the real motive of the party became apparent. These people who had become my new friends had actually lured me there with the intention of ridiculing and belittling me.

Susan's journal continued with this sad account of her struggle, and although she was now twenty-one, the effects of that incident were lasting. She later wrote about how that experience became a deliberate part of her resolve about herself as a teacher:

> That experience taught me how important it is for people to learn to be loving and accepting of each other, even toward people they don't particularly like. My classroom will be a safe place for all students. No one will ever be allowed to put another person down. I don't want any student to go through the hate and self-doubt I went through. I will always remember this experience, and I will use it to educate my students to be kind, considerate human beings who treat others as they want to be treated.

Supporting Activities

1. Review the inquiry topics suggested in this chapter. Which of these topics do you feel most certain about in terms of your present understanding of young adolescent students? Which of them do you know little or nothing about?

2. Conduct an informal interview with at least one young adolescent about two or three topics from the two listings you created in responding to Activity 1. You might conduct your interview at a local shopping mall, fast-food restaurant, or arcade where you're likely to find some kids hanging out.

3. Design, field-test, modify, and carry out an informal inquiry about one or two of the topics listed in this chapter. Summarize your data and present your insights to your classmates.

4. Write a brief overview of your inquiry, observing the following framework:

   > *Rationale* (why you investigated the topic; who are the participants)

   > *Procedure* (how you arranged cooperation; how you obtained the information)

   > *Results* (what you learned from the inquiry)

   > *Implications* (how a teacher could use the information)

   > *Reflections* (what you'll do differently next time)

REFERENCES

Atwell, N. (1987). *In the middle: Writing, reading and learning with adolescents.* Upper Montclair, NJ: Boynton/Cook.

Atwell, N. (1990). *Coming to know: Writing to learn in the intermediate grades.* Portsmouth, NH: Heinemann.

Burkhardt, Ross M. (1994). *The inquiry process: student-centered learning.* Logan, Iowa: Perfection Learning.

Casteel, J. D. (1978). *Learning to think and choose: Decision-making episodes for the middle grades.* Glenview, IL: Scott-Foresman (Goodyear Series).

Castlebury, S., & Arnold, J. (1988). Early adolescent perceptions of informal groups in a middle school. *Journal of Early Adolescence, 8* (1), 97–107.

Fulwiler, T. (1987). *The journal book.* Portsmouth, NH: Heinemann/Boynton Cook.

Harrington, D. (1993). Personal correspondence.

Knight, A. (1988, November). The magic word for middle level educators. *NASSP Bulletin, 72* (511), 99–100

Mee, C. (1995, December). Middle school student voices. *AIMS Newsletter* (19)2.

Paley, V. G. (1981). *Wally's stories.* Cambridge, MA: Harvard University Press.

Rogers, V., & Stevenson, C. (1988, February). How do we know what kids are learning in school? *Educational Leadership, 45* (5), 68–75.

Ross, P. (1979). *Trouble in school: A portrait of young adolescents.* New York: Avon.

Shinas, K., Jeffryes, L., & Burris, J. (Spring 1994). *New Mexico Middle School Journal,* (4), 19–22.

Stevenson, C. (1986). *Teachers as inquirers: Strategies for learning with and about early adolescents.* Columbus, OH: National Middle School Association.

Chapter 4

A Teacher's View of Development

○ *What's happening to these kids?*

○ *Why are their interests changing?*

○ *Why are they so restless? So loud?*

○ *Why are they so hard on each other?*

○ *What are their parents doing to them?*

○ *Why don't they pay more attention to me?*

○ *Why aren't they more like they used to be?*

Several notable memories from my first years of teaching young adolescents thirty-five years ago remain remarkably clear. Although some recollections are still somewhat painful, the perspective of age has made me somewhat more tolerant of earlier good intentions gone awry. One particularly memorable experience was the very first formal teaching I ever did—eighth grade English. Over the summer I had carefully prepared a unit about American short stories to teach to three eighth grade sections in the opening weeks of September. Assuming it might be difficult to get them interested in classic literature, I took care to see that the stories we studied included a lot of humor, such as Mark Twain's "The Celebrated Jumping Frog of Calaveras County" and James Thurber's "The Secret Life of Walter Mitty." I also selected some gripping adventure stories such as James B. Connolly's "Dory-Mates" and Richard Connell's classic, "The Most Dangerous Game." I was determined to hook them on good literature by starting out with pieces I was sure they'd enjoy and that would represent the short story genre well.

As an undergraduate psychology major preparing to teach, my study of educational psychology and learning theory had been preoccupied with behavioral approaches to teaching. The emphasis in these courses was almost exclusively on what my instructors referred to as "organizing and delivering instruction." I recall that my study of adolescent development was essentially detached from pedagogy. Instructional planning was organized around general goals and specific objectives. Since I loved the planning process and designing lessons, I began the year with confidence that my students would be pleased with the class activities and comfortable with the materials I had prepared. I recall being so eager for the school year to begin that I could hardly sleep. On the first day of classes I was waiting for the custodian to unlock the door at six o'clock in the morning!

As I recall, most of those classes went fairly smoothly with regard to my covering the stories and content I had planned. I divided our time between giving my lectures, taking turns reading aloud, defining vocabulary and language idioms that weren't familiar, and discussing somewhat erudite dimensions such as style and theme. If the kids became restless or inattentive—as was particularly true of a section that met right after lunch—I shifted to assigned deskwork to make sure they stayed busy. I don't recall whether or not anyone raised any original, introspective questions about substantive issues in the readings, but it is also fair to say that as a rookie teacher preoccupied with my performance, I might have had difficulty recognizing such a curiosity.

The unit was planned to last three weeks, culminating in a Friday exam. Although I'd given several short quizzes I called vocabulary checks, the bulk of the unit grade would be based upon students' performance on the culminating exam. With the same egalitarian sense that had led me to build in a variety of types of classroom instruction, I produced a four-page exam constructed around what I believed was balance and a wide array of items: short answer, vocabulary and definitions, matching, fill-in-the-blank, multiple-choice, sentence completion, and short essay.

Because there were 103 students in the three sections, I ruled out longer essays, knowing that they would take too many hours to grade. I also deliberately included somewhat obscure items here and there because I had absorbed from years as a student that such items were the necessary sorting device for distinguishing the most thorough, well-prepared students from their classmates. I had gullibly accepted that it was my duty to separate sheep from goats. I was very proud of my exam, and just as on the opening day of school, I couldn't wait to see how my students would do. On the appointed Friday, while the second section took the exam, I began scoring papers from their classmates in the earlier class.

I still feel queasy about that day. The kids' performance was disastrous. As the day wore on and I scored more and more exams, the disaster's magnitude grew. Not a single one of my students had scored as high as 70—the minimum passing grade. Their failure was my failure, total and absolute. Hours of work every day for weeks appeared to be a waste. I left school that Friday afternoon feeling completely defeated and thinking, "I could round up kids off the street, and they'd probably do just about as well." Over the weekend, disillusionment began to evolve into anger. From the beginning I'd been confident that I'd designed an excellent unit, and I believed all along that I was teaching it well. Now I was angry, because the kids hadn't done their share. I thought, "These ingrates don't deserve me!" I began to seriously contemplate other careers.

Wisdom combines an understanding of the past with responsive and responsible actions thereafter. Given my investment in the short story unit, it was very difficult for me to be wise, to understand what had happened, and to make responsive modifications for the future. It was much easier to rationalize that these kids hadn't done their share by listening in class and studying for the exam. Diatribes against kids by a few veteran teachers in the teachers' lounge, which I had previously ignored, began to sound more plausible. With an arrogance that still causes me to wince, I recall justifiying myself by agreeing that most of the kids simply were not very bright, were lazy, and came from poor backgrounds.

I regret to add that it took several more years for me to gain enough insights about the schooling process itself plus wisdom about my own expectations and standards to begin to become the responsive teacher that my students deserved. It was difficult to see the way and to venture beyond how things were and seemingly always had been. Even today, I see teachers struggling against the same conditions that thwarted and almost disillusioned me three decades ago.

Joseph Chilton Pearce (1971) warns us about *ideation*—complacency with our own personal ideas about how things are and are supposed to be. In the foregoing illustration, I was an unwitting victim of ideation. I was not alone then, nor am I yet entirely free of that reflex. Yet, I take no comfort from knowing that others were and are similarly going about their day-to-day work accepting only superficial evidence that truly authentic education is taking place. There is, I believe, a traditional institutional ideation—*schooling*—that is grievously insufficient for the needs of young adolescents. I continue to explore, to try to better understand how we can know what our youngsters are actually learning in school (Rogers & Stevenson, 1988).

To put it simply, our traditional schooling ideation is that school is where children come to learn an appreciation for our American heritage and traditions, the basic academic skills, and a liberal education in the arts, sciences, and humanities. According to this ideation, children are expected to conform obediently to sanctioned points of view. The presumption is that individual digressions from this monolithic procedure must be postponed until higher education. Each generation becomes empowered through knowledge and contributes in turn to the enhancement and improvement of what I'll generalize as "our way of life." These goals are much like those in any other nation, although the content varies according to setting, of course. There is also nothing wrong with these goals except, perhaps, that they are too briefly stated here.

The most severe problems with this ideation arise not so much with the conception of purpose as, in the kids' vernacular, "where the rubber meets the road." I refer to how we go about trying to achieve these goals. My short story unit is just one of countless examples of similar teaching that have over the years become our norm—processes that are preoccupied with what the teacher does, with content and skills, and with test performance and grades as the valid measures of learning. These understandable concerns often divert our attention from what is actually going on in students' minds and lives and how our expectations and standards correspond with their readiness, priorities, and concerns.

TEACHING THINGS AND TEACHING PEOPLE

Two concerns have historically dominated teachers' thoughts: What is the most important curriculum to cover? What is the best way to "get it across"—that is, to teach it? Just as I went about designing my short story unit, so teachers generally seem to reflexively think first about *what to teach* in a particular unit. Implicit in this action is an apparent assumption of equivalence between what is taught and what is learned. Every textbook, curriculum guide, and content-specific professional organization make compelling cases for what ought to be taught. Specialists in subject matter areas produce carefully wrought curriculum plans that organize their fields of knowledge into scope and sequence charts. Sometimes a specific curriculum is mandated, and a condition of the teacher's assignment may be the promise to "cover that curriculum." A greater, more varied selection of prepackaged curricula is available today than has ever before existed. Countless instructional programs, kits, and packaged learning schemes are being touted with promises of higher test scores, magical effects on students, and promises to make teaching easy and learning fun.

There is also an equally abundant variety of often persuasive arguments for *how to teach* selected content and skills. A portion of any responsible teacher education program includes a study of learning theories and child development. In the best of circumstances an attempt is made to link this theoretical orientation, usually presented in university classes, to examples of exemplary practice in local schools. Courses often titled "Methods and Materials" are concerned with instructional planning and organization, delivery systems, and other references intended to guide a teacher's choices of how to teach chosen content and skills materials.

The glut of commercial textbooks, workbooks, instructional kits, and programs or whole-school instructional systems can be overwhelming—especially to the novice teacher who may never have faced such an abundance of points of view and possibilities. My undergraduate teacher education students are routinely amazed by the expanse of options in a single subject matter area. They often challenge me to spell out exactly what is to be taught and how it should be presented. They are often made uncomfortable—at least initially—by their growing realization that there are no absolute, universal truths in responding to these earnest, legitimate questions. Their concerns highlight the crux of this professional dilemma about teaching subjects and teaching people.

It is vital that middle grades teachers serve a highly diverse constituency in ways that are responsive to the students' contextual and developmental circumstances. In my experience, we tend to choose content and mode of presentation, using a general but vague sense of the readiness or performance level of a particular class. Judgment is a function of past experience. John Goodlad's monumental study of American education revealed that "teachers saw themselves to be in control of what they taught and how" (Goodlad, 1984). I want to introduce here the same equation I present to my students as they tackle these knotty but essential questions.

$$\frac{\text{what to teach and how to teach it}}{\text{developmental assessment}} = \text{Responsive Education}$$

In other words, it is our purpose to provide education that is responsive to the developmental needs of young adolescents. Our decisions about what to teach and how to go about presenting it must be calculated on the basis of what we know about the multifaceted development of our students. We need to be informed by a sound general knowledge of their changes during these transitional years, against which we can understand our specific students as they reveal themselves to us through day-to-day interactions and through techniques such as shadowing and inquiries. Nothing is gained and much is risked when youngsters are confronted with learning tasks they simply aren't ready to accomplish.

What Is Meant by Developmental Needs?

Humans grow according to an individual inner schedule—an essentially biological timetable. We vary a lot with regard to the timing, duration, and intensity of developmental events, and there is further variability within and between the sexes. Barring exceptional circumstances of genetics or personal living or both, however, we progress in our own time through a common series of changes.

Growth spurts can be observed in most girls between the ages of nine and ten and, on average, approximately two years later in boys. Timing within each gender will vary widely, however. Pediatricians usually assess girls' physical maturity in terms of stages of breast development; boys' stage of physical maturity is indicated by stages of genital development. Increases in sexual interest and arousal are believed to derive from higher levels of testosterone, although one should not conclude that this change also increases sexual activity. Adolescent development is also very much affected by social conditions, of course. For a long time our culture has treated boys and girls differently in early adolescence. We seem to become more anxious about what I suggest we think of as a "woman-child," and we increasingly try to protect them from ourselves. An interesting corollary is that we are more inclined to celebrate the emergence of the "manchild." These differences don't seem to be as great as they were when I began my teaching career, but vestiges of those biases remain. Regardless of the influences of a particular setting, however, the changes of puberty in a changing national culture, as represented by the omnipresent media, assures the urgency of distinct human needs associated with the adolescent experience. Responsive schooling must be built on this understanding.

The greatest single variable in development, however, is individuality—the unique congenital and cultural nature of each young person. Needs rise from individual experiences, and needs dispose individual students toward often idiosyncratic interests and particular social affiliations. These inclinations rise from that individual's existential circumstances, and in referring to them as "needs," it is important to emphasize that no weakness or deficiency is implied.

These few years are also a time when youngsters are moving back and forth on a continuum between virtual dependence on others—adults in general, but especially parents—and the relative independence they will have in their own adulthood. Some of their personal needs at this time become especially intense. Ideas, realizations, and emotions not previously experienced often preoccupy them. Since they are experiencing many of these needs for the first time, their unsophistication in handling changes may prove unsettling. They are not unlike young birds balancing on the edge of the nest, contemplating a venture forth to try survival on their own, but wary of the risks inherent in taking off too soon.

Four Caveats

Because variability among individual youngsters is so great, the extensive changes occurring in early adolescence can only be generalized. However, in contemplating this developmental stage, it is essential to keep in mind four caveats relating to children's growth in these years.

1. *Early adolescence is a time when all youngsters change in many ways.* Adults, especially parents, are probably most conscious of the often extreme changes in their children's physical development during these transition years. Growth spurts that change physical proportions, from shoe size to the size of appetite, are well known. Keeping kids clothed in ways that suit their tastes at a time when their bodies seem to grow almost overnight poses a major challenge for parents and the household budget. Less obvious,

perhaps, but equally profound are the changes in how youngsters think. What amuses them, and their ideas about what family members ought to do and be, may even become contentious. Furthermore, the basis on which they choose their friends often changes, and dynamics of relationships within their individual families take on new dimensions. It is accurate to say that these changes in human beings—taken as a whole—are greater and more profound than the changes occurring during any other equivalent time in the schooling years, including the years in higher education.

2. *Changes occur at idiosyncratic times on a common schedule.* How predictable and much simpler it would be to plan responsive schooling if all children changed in the same ways at the same time and at the same pace. Except that girls as a group appear to experience physical changes a year or more ahead of boys as a group, predictability and simultaneous changing are illusory. Young adolescents don't begin changes at the same time, nor do they progress at the same rate through the same developmental periods. What can be said is that individual variability is the norm. We can observe differences among children in a group of toddlers, but those differences are much more subtle and are multiplied many times over ten years later when they develop so idiosyncratically during early adolescence. Furthermore, changes do not appear to happen in any particular order, nor is growth in one developmental domain equaled by concomitant growth in another domain. A boy whose legs and feet begin to grow in this period may remain less sophisticated in terms of thinking and judging than a smaller age-mate whose body development is only slight.

3. *Home, neighborhood, prevailing gender roles, and racial and ethnic identity influence development.* While every individual has unique inborn potential, the expression of that potential is influenced by the life circumstances in which the child grows up. The outlook of young adolescents living in rural poverty differs from that of their age counterparts from the suburbs. Youngsters who grow up with a strong ethnic identity are more likely to understand their origins and their culture's expectations. Children whose parents listen to them, support their interests, and routinely engage them in dialogue tend to be more likely to perform responsibly in school than those whose parents either ignore them or administer their authority dictatorially. Not only is there great diversity in personal development schedules, but the pluralistic complex of early adolescence is further exacerbated by social, economic, and ethnic influences.

4. *The influences and effects of early adolescence are long lasting.* Physical changes influence personal adjustment in early adolescence. Longitudinal data indicate that how early- and late-developing boys perceive themselves persists well into adulthood (Jones & Mussen, 1957). A major study of dropout prevention indicates that alienation occurring in the middle grades forms the basis on which, a few years later, many students exercise their legal prerogative to drop out of school at sixteen (Wheelock & Dorman, 1988). As we'll see in the subsequent discussion of the "introspective domain" of change, how a youngster perceives himself or herself has a great deal to do with the choices he or she makes in these years as well as later in adulthood. It is therefore critical that middle grades teachers find ways to help youngsters be successful and feel positive about themselves and their potential.

Bearing these four guidelines in mind, let's now look at more specific elements of change.

THE DOMAINS OF ADOLESCENT DEVELOPMENT

The following generalized treatment of early adolescent development is specifically intended for middle level educators. It is not meant to be a formal and comprehensive study of the discipline, although such a study is strongly recommended. This treatment provides an overview of essential information for those intending to work with these youngsters in schools. Development will be discussed in terms of broadly grouped domains that constitute windows through which schooling can be considered.

In delineating these domains, I refer to a broad conceptualization of change that is grounded in selected theory and research and in my years of firsthand experience as a teacher. I am not a developmental specialist, so my choice of organization does not reflect any recognized criteria in the field of human development that is familiar to me. Rather, this is a framework that has emerged from my years of interactions with students and from studying research reports and other practitioner-focused literature written to explain these developmental circumstances. This construction of domains of change is not intended as a substitute for the formal study of human development. All that follows has antecedents in earlier childhood and corollaries in full adolescence and adulthood that are worthy of more concentrated study. After all, human development is ongoing "from cradle to grave," and it would be a mistake to presume that developmental needs pertain to only a few years of life. Life *is* development—active, incremental, and continuous.

These domains may be thought of as "centers of similarities" for youngsters between the approximate ages of ten and fourteen (Lipsitz, 1980). These centers are delimited only by reference to their titles and the principal knowledge that comprises them. Domains also refer to highly interactive and overlapping changes, and the reader should not be distracted by an expectation that developmental conditions must be categorized and explained or justified in a particular way. For example, a young girl's more adultlike appearance may or may not be related to changes in how she contemplates her identity as a daughter. Knowing all the factors involved in that self-perception is impossible even for her, not to mention those who are her teachers. Besides, what really matters most is that she is reflecting upon herself—not a presumptuous assertion that "she is breast-budding, therefore she is . . . ," no matter how well intended.

Another proviso about this homespun approach to comprehending young adolescent development is that I make no claims about causal links between developmental needs and heredity or a specific familial or cultural context. While the temptation is great for teachers and others to assert that particular causalities exist, the complexity and the unknown are far too great to justify the proposition of any type of developmental laws. Again, the point here is for us as teachers to view the spectrum of human development that most directly relates to the young adolescent of middle years—approximately ages ten to fourteen. We can speculate about specific individuals only as we come to better know their circumstances through shadowing, inquiry, and day-to-day interactions with them.

Finally, this conceptualization is organized into five domains (see Figure 4.1), one of which is both central and preeminent. Since the mind is the quintessence of the person, and the seat of perceptions that controls every thought and choice, what I have elected to refer to as the Introspective Domain is the preeminent domain and the focal point of this discussion. This domain is affected by and interprets changes in the other domains. It also guides the individual's responses to those same changes. The Somatic Domain refers pri-

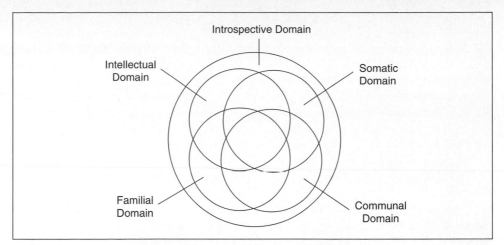

Figure 4.1 Domains of Development.

marily to physiological development and the general human aspirations to feel good and to be physically well. The Intellectual Domain is thinking, learning, knowing, and judging—which continues to be superficially regarded simply as IQ. The Familial Domain refers to the family-specific contexts within which a child resides. The Communal Domain concerns the human desire for fraternization. Note that the domains as graphically represented in Figure 4.1 are overlapping, signifying their interactivity.

The Introspective Domain

Now that I've been a kid for thirteen years, I realize how important everything is.

Jeff

I look into the mirror.
I see a face.
Whose face?
My face.
Who am I?
Molly is only my name.

In just a few lines, eleven-year-old Molly has articulated the quintessential enigma of human life: Who am I? The innate egocentric issues of her earlier childhood have culminated in the ultimate existential question Molly acknowledges in a poem written in the fall of her seventh grade year. Of all the changes taking place during these transition years, none is more central to a child's growth than the continuously shifting product of introspection: how she perceives herself. Self-assessment in the light of previously unrecognized personal or family conditions or societal expectations and possibilities is a complex undertaking at any age. Ten- to fourteen-year-olds are not very experienced at such introspection, especially when it becomes pressing in the midst of so much change. Consequently, they need the respect that is exemplified through patience and understanding from those of us closest to them.

Early adolescence is not, of course, the only time when humans ponder their identity. When my own children were much younger than Molly, they asked their mother and me, "Where did I come from?" and "Why are you my daddy?" Perhaps the elderly person approaching this life's end has the most profound ruminations of all about who he or she is. What is distinctive about this identity introspection at this time in Molly's life is that the way she thinks about herself is changing from how she contemplated herself in the past. She has become aware of issues and possibilities previously unnoticed. She is growing up with a new consciousness of what being a unique person really means. She is coming to grips with the abstract concept of a self. As Mary Pipher puts it, this is the time "when many battles for the self are won and lost." (Pipher, 1994, p. 264)

Because every child is changing in a peer population where everyone else is also changing, previous answers to the question "Who am I?" may no longer fit as automatically and comfortably as may have been the case in the past. It becomes increasingly difficult to be satisfied with simply "I'm Peter. I'm nine. I play soccer. I have a dog." Now comes the ability for Peter to think about himself as a particular entity and to think about the way he thinks. These realizations generate self-examination if not some uncertainty about personal identity. This somewhat fragile state is a time during which the child needs to be able to show himself as well as others that he is competent and is worthy of stature and respect.

While trying to realize personal identity at this time of life is a highly individual and private process, it doesn't take place in isolation. Children naturally think about their age-mates, making comparisons such as "I am a faster runner than . . . or . . . prettier than . . . or . . . not as smart as. . . ." Sometimes they offer these kinds of self-enhancing or self-effacing assertions to others—especially parents and teachers. Since the characteristics and conditions of their total peer group are in a state of flux, how any child sees himself may be in a perpetual state of transition.

Teasing is a particularly interesting behavior of some young adolescents. Taunting that plays upon what appear as weaknesses in another youngster may temporarily exalt the self-importance of the teaser while causing a great deal of anguish for the victim. Kids whose self-concept is dubious are especially vulnerable to teasing. Another type of teasing appears simply to be part of the subcultural repartee. Street kids I've engaged in conversation who tease each other are actually conveying acceptance of each other into their subcultural group. These two distinctive manifestations of teasing are both common among young adolescents. Before intervening, thoughtful teachers must be carefully attentive in order to understand exactly what is being communicated.

Some psychologists suggest that both the self-concept (how one sees oneself) and self-esteem (degree of self-satisfaction) undergo virtually complete reexamination and reconstruction during the early adolescent years (Beane & Lipka, 1987). Introspection and the gradually emerging self-definition are highly complex personal processes affected by everything the child experiences and contemplates.

Erik Erikson's Stage Theory

The wisdom of Erik Erikson (1968) is particularly helpful to an understanding of the development of personal identity, especially in the late childhood–young adolescent years. His stage theory shows a progression from childhood concerns with self primarily in relation to family/parental expectations toward an increasing awareness of oneself in relationships with age peers and sometimes other adults. Of particular interest to those of us concerned with young adolescents are the "Industry versus Inferiority" and "Identity versus Role Confusion" conceptualizations. A brief overview of these concepts is relevant to our understanding and to our efforts to undertake responsive educational planning for middle grades children.

Ten- and eleven-year-olds are inclined to describe themselves in terms of what they can do. Being a worker and a producer and being known by others for those traits become increasingly essential to healthy identity development—especially at school. Failure to be accomplished in ways that are personally and socially esteemed damages the individual's picture of himself. When a child is consistently unsuccessful and is seen as a failure in other people's eyes as well as his own, identity damage can be overwhelming. Self-esteem then has to be sought from activities outside those that are sanctioned by parents and the school.

Youngsters need to believe that they are becoming more skillful and competent. They prize concrete evidence of accomplishments, whether it is a 100 percent correct spelling test, a bookshelf constructed in a woodworking class, or a ribbon for winning a footrace. Successful participation in a concert or sports activity or a play or a presentation to other students or parents provides tangible evidence not only that my work is meritorious but furthermore that "I am a worthwhile person." One's need for recognition and approval from classmates is especially strong and frequently outweighs the need for approval from parents or teachers. Self-confidence may be shattered by peer disapproval or rejection. Sometimes peer standards and adult standards are in conflict if not directly contradictory. Being a good student becomes something worth working for when the child can see evidence of his or her progress. When one is surrounded by circumstances that are wrong or inadequate, one will also become increasingly inclined to see oneself accordingly.

Erikson refers to these desires for accomplishment and recognition as manifestations of the industry need. Given kids' necessity to successfully resolve this developmental stage, teachers' expectations, opportunities, and standards in the instructional program must be broad and varied enough to bring successes within the grasp of all children in the class. Since variability among kids is so prevalent and profound at this time, there must be options and choices that will accommodate even the widest ranges of individual differences and idiosyncracies—including mainstreamed students. Failure to achieve healthy identity development will produce alienation, withdrawal, and sometimes the antagonism that is all too familiar.

Failures or dissatisfactions with attempts to achieve success also breed inferiority feelings. When a school's recognition system is limited to competitive awards such as the honor roll and individual athletic awards, only a few children will receive the recognition that all of them need. Competition is, after all, exclusive in that there is usually only one final winner. Children who do not receive competition-based awards or equivalent recognition from classmates and adults are unnecessarily subjected to the enormous risk of believing that "I can't do," and (therefore) "I am not as worthwhile as the others"—a grievously damaging self-perception.

This criticism of excessive competitive awards often raises an emotional but false controversy, namely, that providing recognition for all students is tantamount to lowering standards. The key ingredient in this discussion is first that the child knows he is improving in ways endorsed by teachers and other adults because he has evidence of improvement.

Then, the payoffs that come from others who help celebrate accomplishment are the ribbon on the gift. How unfortunate but commonplace it is to encounter children only ten and eleven years old who talk about their inadequacy and mediocrity, who demean their own schoolwork, and who accept that they aren't good students. To compound this tragic belief, lack of school successes and recognition lead them to accept themselves as "dummies."

The urgency of children to accomplish their industry needs successfully in early adolescence can hardly be overstated. If they are to achieve healthy, orderly development into later adolescence and adulthood, they must be successful in socially sanctioned endeavors undertaken as young adolescents. Children have a formidable task in learning about themselves and how their world functions at a time when they and their friends are also experiencing so much change. They hunger for opportunities to show what they can do and also for recognition of their accomplishments. Furthermore, these are not transient, one-time needs. During these critical years, children must have continual successes and recurring recognition. They are passing through a period of profound introspection and continuing vulnerability to failure and self-doubt. Our task as teachers includes devising ways by which they can satisfy these hungers, enabling them to grow in the belief that they are capable and praiseworthy. Who knows how often children who regularly encounter failure and who receive little or no approval from peers and adults develop a deep-seated belief that they are incapable of learning and performing successfully?

According to Erikson, introspection and possible anxiety about personal identity definition begin to intensify in early adolescence. That intensity may persist only for a few years or, regrettably, for as long as a lifetime. For the identity formation process to be complete, the individual must successfully rework previous resolution of the needs for trust, autonomy, and initiative. Through this process emerges a revised sense of self that enables one to function comfortably and effectively in multiple roles.

David Elkind on Constructing Personal Identity

Psychologist David Elkind's (1984) long study of adolescents has provided valuable insights about societal and family-based stresses on the identity development process. These understandings are particularly pertinent to teachers. He explains that youngsters develop personal identity either by integration or by substitution. The former process is the slower but healthier and ultimately stronger, more durable of the two. It is a process whereby we

> must encounter a great number of different experiences within which we can discover how feelings, thoughts and beliefs are different from other people. At the same time, we also need to learn how much we are like other people. As a result . . . of differentiating ourselves from others, in terms of how we are alike and yet different . . . , we gradually arrive at a stable and unique perception of our self. (Elkind, 1984, pp. 15–16)

Adult and peer pressures on contemporary youth to act like and be like other individuals or group members are considerable, however. Young people are bombarded by the media as well as by their immediate circumstances with multiple examples of how one should be. Adaptations that serve the exigencies of the moment are substitutions that represent a temporary adjustment but do not contribute meaningfully to the development of an inherent, true sense of personal identity. Such a sense of self simply copied from others is what Elkind describes as patchwork identity, constructed like the quiltmaker's creation of a patchwork quilt. This distinction between identity development based on integration versus that based on substitution is extremely important for us to understand. Educational planning must reflect our appreciation of the relationships of authentic interactions with varied people to the development of healthy identity.

Young adolescents today lack role definition that corresponds to their needs for personal empowerment and responsibility. Elkind laments the dissolution of markers, "external signs of where we stand" (1984, pp. 96–99). These signs confirm for the child and everyone else the progress achieved to date in the extended process of growing to full adult maturity. In the past, the types of activity, clothing, and relationships with authority that Elkind describes made it much more possible to identify just how much independence and responsibility a youngster had earned. Over the course of this century, however, societal changes related to employment, mobility, and family structures appear to have blurred the distinctions in the passage between childhood and adulthood. In our contemporary culture, neither youngsters nor adults seem to be clear and in agreement about their understanding of just what is appropriate to expect of young adolescents.

An intensified preoccupation with how one appears physically to oneself and therefore to others also influences self-perceptions. Elkind describes the power of this phenomenon in his discussion of the "myth of the imaginary audience," the "feeling that everyone else is looking at me" (1984, pp. 33–36). Hair, complexion, and body development are features of special significance to physically changing children. Those of us who spend a lot of time with these children recognize and respect the intensity of this process of self-examination and sometimes subsequent self-criticism. We are often called upon to reassure a child who thinks her nose is too big or one who fears his complexion will never clear up. The ambivalence children may feel between welcoming more adultlike bodies, on one hand, and being apprehensive about what happens next, on the other, challenges their self-confidence. Therefore, looking good becomes an urgent priority.

"Tell Me About Yourself"

One of the most intriguing characteristics of children in these years is how they have responded to my invitations to "tell me about yourself." For several years I have been videotaping brief interviews with ten- to fourteen-year-olds, documenting their comments in response to this invitation. They appear to appreciate this opportunity to think out loud about some of the issues and questions passing through their consciousness. Sometimes they appear to be figuring out what they believe—at least for the moment—by listening to themselves talk about themselves. They offer simple theories and rationalizations about what is meaningful in their lives at the moment, as well as their ideas about their future lives. The idea to carry out this inquiry came from the long-standing work of James Beane and Richard Lipka, who used interviews with young adolescents as a way to understand them in terms of self-concept and self-esteem (1980, 1986, 1987).

When children at ten and eleven and often at twelve respond to my entreaty to tell me about themselves, they usually define themselves in terms of two categories: "things I can do" and "things I have." Consider this example of Christina's remarks over the years. She opted in fifth grade and again a year later in sixth grade to tell about herself by comments such as "I have an older sister and two parents. I take karate. I love animals. I have a pet tarantula. I play the harp." She made lots of additional comments, but they were all of the same type—either things that belonged to her or things she did. In seventh grade she continued to mention things she did or owned, but there was a new element: "I'm just me. Just Christina. And all I want is to just be me." Another year later she ruminated about feeling tension between her growing desire to be an actress and strong feelings that "I need to do something useful . . . like join the Peace Corps . . . or get money to take care of abandoned animals." In brief, she presented herself as a young person with a growing need to be responsible to worthwhile causes.

Beane and Lipka found a similar pattern (1987, p. 11). They characterized youngsters' initial self-definitions as a dichotomy: "I am what I have" and "I am what I do." Soon thereafter they noted a shift toward "I am who I am." Adults working with young adolescents must not fail to recognize this subtle and ever-important introspective transition; it signals the unfolding of womanhood from womanchild, manhood from manchild.

A natural tension exists between what a youngster perceives others as believing and his or her own personal, private hunches. Alternative explanations, multiple solutions to a problem, assertions that are contrary to fact—all these deliberations become increasingly accessible to young adolescents pondering their existence and taking personal belief positions about matters that have ethical content. From all of this thought, personal principles may emerge, even if they are articulated only to settle a momentary issue.

Even under the best of circumstances, ethical behavior takes time to mature. It is especially important, therefore, to help children examine their beliefs, inclinations, and questions as position taking that occurs in a context that both honors individual expression and appreciates that such ideas evolve over an extended course of time and experience. Perceptive and responsive adults help youngsters in the natural processes of introspection that helps them clarify what they believe and confirm their right to their own views, even if they don't coincide with prevailing adult opinion.

How productively youngsters deal with the simultaneous occurrences of personal introspection and external expectations should be of great concern to every parent and everyone who works professionally with young adolescents, especially those of us who work daily with them in schools. Most children who feel respected by nurturing adults during these potentially stressful times appear to grow through this transition successfully. Many others who are neglected by adults also develop healthily in spite of deficiencies in their circumstances. Tragically, however, there are far too many whose potential is lost, owing to adult indifference at the least and outright abuse at the worst, as they ponder the questions of personal introspection and struggle to achieve healthy, integrated identities.

The Basics of Personal Efficacy

"What are the essential requirements for healthy adolescent development? In my view, it is essential that we help young adolescents to acquire constructive knowledge and skills, inquiring habits of mind, dependable human relationships, a reliable basis for earning respect, a sense of belonging in a valued group, and a way of being useful in their communities. These are the fundamental underpinnings of healthy development during adolescence for all young people, in our society and throughout the world. (Hamburg, 1993, p. 467)

Again, I make no claim to being a developmental psychologist. Yet, my reflections on interviews with hundreds of young adolescents over many years have brought to the surface some recurring themes in their commentaries that complement Hamburg's point of view and are worthy of inclusion here. If we agree that every youngster needs to feel an authentic state of personal efficacy as a human being, then we can expect to recognize their self-perception or self-concept in five forms.

1. *"I'm good at . . ."* I've never met a young adolescent who doesn't care a lot about being personally competent. I believe that every interview of any length that I have conducted with a young adolescent has included a revelation about what the interviewee sees himself or herself as being good at. Whether it is being a good speller or a fast runner or a good friend, personal competence is always a theme. Often implicit in that commentary is a consciousness that the areas of competence help define oneself. Students also frequently offer support for the self-perception by commenting about a particular success or recognition that offers supporting evidence. I am convinced that a responsive education, such as that to which we are committed in middle level education, will always see to it that every student is affirmed for his or her competencies.

2. *"I take care of . . ."* Demonstrating personal responsibility is important evidence that an individual is making the transition from the dependency of childhood toward the self-sufficiency of adulthood. My experience with young adolescents has taught me that youngsters who have responsibilities like to talk about them, and their discourse is often illustrated with anecdotes and comparisons. I have often been impressed with a sense of what I would call "healthiness" as they describe others' roles or responsibilities relative to their own. A balance is struck in locus of control between choices and decisions made because of one's personal initiative and the expectations of others. It is as if to say, "I am accountable for myself and what I do."

3. *"I belong and get along . . ."* Being affiliated with something good seems to be a part of every youngster's self-description. Whether it is a sports team or an informal group or one's family, kids talk about themselves in terms of their affiliation with at least one other person, usually a peer, or a defined group of some kind. It is common for kids to mention a best friend or several significant friends. Only rarely have kids indicated to me that the friend was a sweetheart. Sometimes the group connection is relatively extreme, as is the case with allegiance to a rock group or a particular way of dressing. In the case of what I would judge as "healthy affiliation," however, kids talk about being part of a mutually important friendship or belonging to groups that are sanctioned in the school or community, where there is usually a reference to an adult leader or mentor.

4. *"I know what's going on . . ."* Being "cool" or "with it" is the extreme manifestation of kids' apparent need to believe that they are savvy and to be somewhat playful in explaining things. I find especially intriguing their personal reflections about events that they judge to be important to them as well as explanations or theories about how things are with their peers. There seems to be a new urgency about being on top of things. There may also be some correspondence between being savvy and being resilient in the face of interpersonal and institutional pressures to do and be in particular ways. It is especially notable when kids talk about themselves in the context of their time of life, "adolescence," expressing insights about adults and other kids now being generalized as "society."

5. *"I'm a good person."* Over my desk is a time-worn sign that reads, "Every Kid MUST be a Hero!" I'm convinced that virtually all kids want to do good things for the benefit of others, for in that doing they gain personal affirmation. Hence, sensitive adults

look for ways to help kids help each other, younger children, senior citizens, and people in their community. While it is important that youngsters receive recognition and affirmation for what they do, even more important is that adults join them in conversation about matters of equity and justice and citizenship.

One teacher-writer laments that "we don't even talk with them about democracy anymore" (Keizer, 1988, p. 11). If our young people are to move toward adulthood in confidence with optimism about themselves and our society, we must acknowledge and act upon their need to believe in their own basic goodness and promise. Two published young adolescent writers, Latoya Hunter (1992) and Zlata Filipovic (1994), reveal vividly through diaries kept in their respective communities, the Bronx and Sarajevo, the extent of their introspection. Their thoughtful, reflective and perceptive ruminations about their challenging life circumstances document this quality more eloquently than I can. Both are painfully aware of the risks they face day to day, both reflect an expanding awareness of and impatience with absurdities in the adult world, and both manifest personal choices and commitments that shape character.

A more experienced but similarly insightful writer about adolescents, who reflects empathy and understanding but who is an adult, summarizes themes found in the children's writings:

> All adolescents, regardless of economic background, race and ethnicity, gender and geographical region or country, have basic needs that must be satisfied; to experience secure relationships with a few human beings, to be a valued member of groups that provide mutual aid and caring relationships, to become a competent individual who can cope with the exigencies of everyday life, and to believe in a promising future in work, family, and citizenship. (Takanishi, 1993, p. 459)

Knowledge and satisfaction with one's self-definition grow from an integration of everything the youngster has learned about himself or herself from the assortment of roles he or she has filled: son or daughter, grandson or granddaughter, sibling, friend, student, athlete, and so on. Resolution of the question "Who am I?" evolves gradually from the individual's idiosyncratic internalization and consolidation of past and current interactions with others. Role confusion may persist well into adulthood if one fails to resolve identity definition during middle and late adolescence. Quite obviously, the urgency of a child's need to perceive himself or herself in a positive light has direct implications for how his or her educational experiences should be conceived and organized. Too many students pass through these years never seeing themselves as positive, responsible, contributing people. A realistic but also affirmative, optimistic view of oneself as a learner and as a person must be the foremost goal of schooling—especially in the middle grades.

The Somatic Domain

> There were a lot of guys a lot bigger than me, but I wasn't a shrimp. The main thing was they had a lot more hair than me "where it really counted." I *hated* the showers after gym class because we were all naked in front of each other and everyone else knew. I used to cut up a lot and show off and have a smart mouth so the guys wouldn't think I was a geek. Afterwards I'd feel sick to my stomach. Even though I'm caught up [in physical development] now, I still feel uncomfortable about that time.
>
> *George, age nineteen*

This excerpt from the writings of a college sophomore reflecting on his life as an eighth grader illustrates how intensely he felt about physical differences between himself and his age-mates. How George saw his body relative to those of his friends, his dissatisfaction with that perception, and how he saw himself more generally remain benchmarks in his ongoing introspection. How helpful it could have been if George had understood the stages of boys' growth in early adolescence. As is evidenced in his words, not only his perception of his physical and genital development but also his efforts to establish or preserve status with peers were at stake.

Puberty is probably the most familiar term used to describe the extensive physiological changes of this period. Various definitions of the term agree in their emphasis on puberty as the age at which boys and girls are capable of reproduction—approximately age twelve for girls, fourteen for boys. The customary use of the term, however, is to indicate that a young person has experienced the initial growth spurt that signals the well-known era of physical transition from childhood to adulthood. This spurt occurs as much as eighteen to twenty-four months earlier for girls than for boys, and there is often great variability in the timing of puberty for both sexes. Because growth is typically irregular, teachers need to remain mindful that puberty constitutes a broad, inclusive developmental stage spread over several years rather than a single fact of development.

Physical growth is triggered by hormones produced primarily by endocrine glands. Small amounts of these hormones are released into the bloodstream and travel to target areas of the body, where they influence the production of other hormones and subsequent physical growth and development in that area. Growth rates in height accelerate from an average of 5–6 cm (about 2 inches) a year during earlier childhood to 6–11 cm (2–4 inches) for girls and 7–13 cm (2.5–5 inches) for boys (Rieser & Underwood, 1989). Adults are accustomed to the self-consciousness of young adolescent girls, who are growing rapidly and are often noticeably taller than boys. The redistribution of body fat into more womanlike proportions and breast budding further intensify self-awareness. In boys, feet that are suddenly much larger, elongated limbs, and voice changes are parallel changes that signal this growth spurt and the accompanying self-consciousness.

The concept of body image—how one sees oneself, or one's self-picture—is also important to bear in mind while thinking about physical development. Girls are especially vulnerable to "lookism," the ways in which the media in our culture define how females are supposed to look. Sometimes those definitions are subtle and implicit, but more often there is a clear-cut stereotype for adolescent girls: tall, slender to a point of near-anorexia, sensual, and full-breasted. Hair, teeth, and complexion "must" be flawless, and one is challenged to find in the depiction of fashion any differences between adolescents and young adults. The magnitude of this lookism phenomenon constitutes a substantial challenge to the self-perception of most young adolescent girls.

Girls may also be more prone than boys to feel apprehension relating to their physical development, because they experience menarche—what might be regarded as more nearly a single event marking the passage into womanhood. There is no equivalent event in male development. George felt deficient relative to his cohorts, and he was able to see at a later age how that self-image affected his behavior. How good it would be if everyone at nineteen were able to recognize and accept himself as George did. Introspection is common to us all, however, and since physical changes are so variable and uncertain, adults must be especially sensitive to kids' body image concerns during early adolescence.

Girls' Physical Changes

Early adolescence sees multiple physical changes in girls. Changing hormonal structures affect height, weight, shape, and numerous other physical attributes that have a powerful influence on how girls perceive themselves.

> The preoccupation with bodies at this age cannot be overstated. The body is a compelling mystery, a constant focus of attention. At thirteen, I thought more about my acne than about God or world peace. At thirteen, many girls spend more time in front of a mirror than they do on their studies. Small flaws become obsessions. Bad hair can ruin a day. A broken fingernail can feel tragic. (Pipher, 1994, p. 55)

Physical size and sexual maturity are just about the same for most ten-year-old girls. There are exceptions, of course, but at this age most girls have not yet begun the growth spurt that signals a host of physical changes that will occur during the next few years. That sequence usually begins with a growth spurt in height accompanied by a gradual redistribution of body fat and breast budding. Individual variability in the timing of the growth spurt and rates of development is common, but the sequence is the same for all. Girls in general show these physical signs of approaching adolescence eighteen months to two years ahead of boys.

Girls today are generally aware that menarche—their first menstrual period—and breast development are approaching, so they become increasingly curious about this looming passage. As they turn eleven and twelve and more of them show growth spurts, breast budding, and pubic hair, the differences among them become more noticeable. By the end of the twelfth year, girls who are developing according to the average will have achieved more than 95 percent of their mature height (Ames, Ilg, & Baker, 1988). Teachers and others working with girls in groups will note this physical variability, especially in height, weight, and breast development. They may also notice fluctuations in their energy levels, an increase in restlessness, and greater need for recuperative time after a lot of physical exertion. Evidence of approaching womanhood is also evident in grooming habits, dressing choices, poise, body language, and social behaviors toward both sexes.

The association of female attractiveness with breast development in contemporary culture places special pressures on girls whose development begins late or occurs more slowly than that of their peers. The timing and degree of breast development frequently become a basis of peer status, and girls whose breast development is not yet evident may experience a good deal of associated anxiety. Uneven breast development is common, one breast developing faster than the other. The slight nipple hypertrophy occurring early in this growth period gradually evolves toward fuller breast development, sometimes accompanied by slight but conspicuous and potentially disturbing physical pain. Accelerated growth toward sexual maturation makes the seventh and eighth grade years a time for special sensitivity by teachers and others working with girls. They typically feel a great deal of concern about their appearance; "looks" tends to be their greatest single concern (Benson, Williams, & Johnson, 1988).

Menarche is imminent during the seventh grade year, and in girls developing at an average pace it occurs between their twelfth and thirteenth birthdays. The first several menstrual periods are usually irregular, and they vary in intensity and flow. In young adolescent girls who follow a strict training regimen such as that necessary for participating in ballet or highly competitive sports, menarche may be slightly delayed. In spite of the high incidence of first menstruation between ages twelve and thirteen, however, individual variability is still so great that its earlier or later occurrence should not be a cause for alarm as long as general physical health is good.

By the eighth grade the rate of physical change is beginning to slow for most girls, especially those whose growth spurt occurred earliest. It is important to recognize here that this decline is in the *rate* of development, however, not development itself. Single developmental features such as height, weight, and breast maturity will almost certainly continue; it is the rate of their development that is slowing. During this gradual slowing-down of developmental rate, the menstrual cycle becomes more regular, and girls become calmer and more at ease with themselves. Their appearance and many of their social manners increasingly approximate those of adulthood.

It is important to reemphasize that the timing and pace of these physical changes vary a great deal from girl to girl. Regardless of when the initial growth spurt occurs and how rapidly a young girl changes, these events are very significant to her. Body changes, or the lack of them when friends are changing, become a matter of self-examination that is sometimes intense and arouses feelings of inadequacy or deficiency. The natural introspection previously discussed is affected by questions and thoughts about her physical self. Both male and female teachers must be sensitive to these issues and responsive to the anxiety girls may be feeling about specific bodily changes as well as their overall appearance.

Boys' Physical Changes

Although boys also experience a major physical transition during the early adolescent years, their development has a timing and sequence different from that of girls. The fact that the commencement of puberty occurs up to two years later for boys means that by the upper end of early adolescence, about age fourteen, most girls are coming out of a growth period while most boys are at or near the peak of theirs. Confusion and curiosity about same-sex differences in rate of development is exacerbated by kids' consciousness of differences between the sexes. Contrasts within and between the sexes is a rationale within itself for purposeful study of early adolescence and for the creation of an educational context where boys and girls can work together relatively free of the tensions associated with the sexuality issues of later adolescence.

Growth spurt differences among girls that begin to be visible during the tenth and eleventh years are not as evident in most boys of those ages. Even though boys may put on additional weight earlier, more visible physical changes are evident in them by age twelve. The most observable changes are growth of bone size, evident in overall height, length of arms and legs, and gradually widening shoulders. After an initial period of awkwardness, by the eighth grade boys slowly become noticeably more measured and poised in their movements. This recognizable but difficult-to-describe change in carriage augurs coming manhood with much the same certainty with which the changes in girls promise approaching womanhood.

By ages thirteen and fourteen, boys developing at an average pace are distinctly different from their more slowly developing counterparts in terms of increased height and more masculine-shaped shoulders, back, hips, and limbs. Musculature has become more pronounced, a voice change has occurred or will soon occur, and facial and axillary hair is often evident. Changes in sex characteristics for boys are not so outwardly visible as those for girls, although this change does bring about more adultlike genitalia and the growth of pubic hair for boys. Genital changes begin on the average during the twelfth year, but that development persists over several more years before full maturity is reached later in adolescence. Although we are quick to point out facial resemblances with infants, family resemblances in the emerging adolescent are even more recognizable.

Sexuality

During these transitional years, both sexes are becoming much more curious and perceptive about human sexuality than they have previously been. Although they have been very much aware of each other as members of the opposite sex, young adolescents' interests in sexuality become more specific. In just a few years their interests become more focused on each other. However, there are also important differences in the contexts of interest between girls and boys—differences that are especially important for professionals to understand. By *context* I am referring to the predominant ways each sex thinks about human sexuality.

As fifth graders, most boys and girls know in general how babies come into existence. Although their knowledge about the details of sexual intercourse may be vague, they understand that it is a natural part of adult relationships. Part of their curiosity comes from a desire to clarify unconfirmed ideas about sexual behaviors, and part arises because they are beginning to contemplate and anticipate their own future experience. As they move further into their own development in sixth and seventh grades, most girls know they will soon experience a coming of age through menarche. Most boys are likewise aware that girls have periods, although they haven't yet acquired knowledge of the full significance of that event. Sexuality holds a good bit of intrigue for boys, and they have lots of curiosity. Jokes, anecdotal stories, and an array of licentious publications become a source of miseducation about human sexuality. Many boys will have had erections and experience with masturbation by the time they are in sixth grade.

Generally, boys and girls have developed differing orientations toward sexuality by the eighth grade. Many girls tend to view sex in romanticized ways, as portrayed in the pulp novels many of them read and talk about. Love is often highly fantasied, and a good bit of peer status may be accorded to the girl who is "going with someone." Other girls defer romantic relationships, sometimes expressing realism or even cynicism about boy–girls liaisons. Girls in eighth and ninth grade who think about relationships in particularly idealistic ways are especially vulnerable to sexual exploitation by older boys whose prevailing interest is in sexual experimentation. By ages thirteen and fourteen, the majority of boys have experienced nocturnal emissions and ejaculation. They are very much interested in knowing human sexuality firsthand, even though they may still be generally reluctant to act on that interest.

There is no better time for adults to help youngsters learn responsibility about human sexuality than during these years of early adolescence. Opportunities for youngsters to develop naturally and healthily are being circumvented by premature sexual activity and ignorance about the risks involved. Girls are especially vulnerable. It is estimated that a whopping "40 percent of American girls will become pregnant at least once while in their teens . . . and 85 percent of those pregnancies [will be] unwanted" (National Organization for Women, 1989). These figures point to an expanding national tragedy that is denying a full adolescent experience to large number of girls. School is the only public agency that can help redress this trend on the scale that is necessary, and I contend that one of our most urgent obligations is to help youngsters understand themselves as sexual beings and the attending risks and responsibilities.

Regardless of sex-related differences in their contexts—the generally more romantic idealism of girls and the more carnal interest of boys—all youngsters who are experiencing somatic changes are extremely curious about themselves, same-sex friends, and the opposite sex. In fact, I know of no group more interested in adolescent development and sexuality than young adolescents themselves. Hence, responsible adults must both understand this developmental period and be reliable adult advocates for kids experiencing these changes and conditions.

Early and Late Development

The overwhelming majority of children go through these somatic transitions more or less within a couple of years of each other. There are always children whose physical development occurs much earlier than that of age-mates, and there are also those whose growth spurt and subsequent physical development occur noticeably later. Children whose physical changes occur unusually early or late often contend with circumstances notably different from those of their more average peers. Early-maturing girls and late-maturing boys tend to be most at risk in terms of likelihood of adjustment problems (Brooks-Gunn & Reiter, 1990, p. 41). One study showed that early-maturing girls, as defined by age at menarche and dating, have greater dissatisfaction with their bodies and may be at greater risk for developing eating disorders such as anorexia and bulimia (Smolak, Levine & Gralen, 1993). In another study, Dubas found that late-maturing boys showed the lowest achievement levels, whereas late-maturing girls showed the highest achievement (1991).

There is also evidence that social advantages attend boys whose physical maturation is earlier or faster than that of peers (Jones & Mussen, 1957, 1958). Early-maturing boys tend to enjoy greater prestige among their peers, appear to feel positive about their physical development, and are relatively free from neurotic symptoms. Late-maturing boys, on the other hand, tend toward more attention-seeking behaviors believed to compensate for felt deficiencies about their delayed physical development.

Early development in girls works quite differently as a determinant of prestige (Faust, 1960). Girls in the sixth grade who mature earliest do not enjoy the prestige accorded their male counterparts. However, while prestige derives from attributes other than physical maturity at age eleven, a trend toward associating prestige with physical maturation begins in seventh grade and continues for approximately the next two years. The more mature girls receive progressively higher prestige ratings among their age peers.

Teachers must be especially aware that extreme differences in development may have differing academic and behavioral influences and consequences. It is prudent to always keep in mind the potential relationship between youngsters' rates of physical maturation and other aspects of their development: academic performance, behaviors, self-concept, and personal responsibility. This understanding is necessary in order to recognize group dynamics among students as well as to be alert to our own expectations of youngsters and those of our colleagues that may be too easily associated with the timing, rate, and extent of youngsters' physical development.

Health Issues

> In the 1990s, the state of adolescent health in America reached crisis proportions: large
> numbers of ten- to fifteen-year-olds suffer from depression that may lead to suicide; they
> jeopardize their future by abusing illegal drugs and alcohol, and by smoking; they en-
> gage in premature, unprotected sexual activity; they are victims or perpetrators of vio-
> lence; they lack proper nutrition and exercise. Their glaring need for health services is
> largely ignored. (Hechinger, 1992, p. 21)

During these transition years, youngsters begin to exercise more frequent and consequential personal choices in day-to-day matters, while at the same time our contemporary
culture presents too many choices that can damage personal health. Some of these new
choices pertain directly to taking care of themselves, such as deciding what to eat, how to
maintain personal hygiene, how to spend leisure time, and how to respond to risk-bearing
social pressures. Most youngsters have a degree of control over these matters that puts
them all at considerable risk. Those of us who work closely with them need to acknowledge this kind of newfound authority in their lives in order to help them understand their
physiological needs and the consequences of personal choices.

Nutrition. One very serious health issue for this group, which doesn't get the media attention given to drugs and sexual activity, is poor nutrition. Young adolescents who don't
abuse their bodies with poor eating habits or drugs generally enjoy good health. They are
experiencing a time of rapid physical growth, so eating habits that ensure balanced nourish-
ment are especially important. The popularity of junk foods with this age group is an especially urgent consideration for adults, one that invites a study of kids' dietary needs along
with an assessment of their personal eating habits. The nutritional maintenance needs of
adults are different from those of developing adolescents, and youngsters need to understand how to help themselves grow healthily by balancing their diets (see Wunderlich &
Kalita, 1984). A youngster's poor eating habits may be associated with disorientation and
difficulties with schoolwork and learning as well as with hyperactivity. It is also apparent
that malnutrition is the greatest single cause of failure to achieve full physical development.

The incidence of dieting among girls increases during the early adolescent years,
and teachers should monitor this practice carefully. Our culture celebrates thinness in
the female figure, and at this time of growth in body mass and more intense introspection, a girl's attention to her body image may be overdone, even becoming obsessive.
The eating disorders of anorexia nervosa and bulimia that seem to be associated with
poor self-esteem appear to begin in the early adolescent years. Teachers are in a
unique position to help distressed girls obtain the support and specialized care they
need.

Use of Controlled Substances. The inclination of many young adolescents to try things
out for themselves, to want and seek acceptance from peers even when risks are involved,
and to believe that "it won't hurt me" makes this age group especially vulnerable to experimentation with tobacco, alcohol, and drugs. Cigarette smoking has been tried by an overwhelming majority of adolescents by the time they are fourteen. Most of them have used
alcohol, and as many as half have at least experimented with drugs (Ames, Ilg, & Baker,

1988). The physical and emotional health risks that attend these activities are substantial, and educators simply cannot leave it up to parents, churches, and civic groups to address these vital issues. Again, formal study of these substances as well as inquiries into practices in one's immediate context are essential components of responsive school programs.

Exercise and Stamina. Extremes of lethargy and restlessness are common, especially among young adolescent boys. Parents note changes in kids' sleeping habits. Irregular metabolic rates and body growth affect youngsters' needs for exercise as well as their requirements for rest and recuperation. For many of them, the ability to remain seated for protracted periods of time is similarly variable. The need of young adolescents for movement—especially the freedom to move around the classroom—should be recognized as a legitimate response to the bodily changes that are occurring during this developmental period. Youngsters also appreciate some variety in classroom furniture to accommodate the need for various seating positions.

Increase in muscle mass renders them capable of more extended periods of vigorous exercise. Opportunities for such vigorous exercise—especially cardiovascular activities—should be part of every day. Some experts lament that contemporary children "have grown heavier, slower, weaker, less healthy and . . . are in terrible physical shape" (Weldon, 1989, p. 23). Physical fitness is just as much a responsibility for all middle level educators as academic and intellectual fitness.

Personal Hygiene. Another dimension of the introspection that takes place during these years is these children's practice of studying themselves in a mirror, sometimes for prolonged periods. Distinctive body odors and skin problems such as acne accompany the physical changes of early adolescence. Elkind's "myth of the imaginary audience" speaks to a youngster's preoccupation with "how I look." In general, this attentiveness to both hygiene and grooming typically begins gradually around the ages of ten and eleven, then accelerates at thirteen and fourteen. For example, one of our sons began rather abruptly at twelve to study his hair and to experiment with different ways of combing it. Sometimes he'd spend as much as a half hour trying out different looks. Prior to this change it was common for his mother or me to have to remind him to brush his hair before he left for school in the morning. Body image priorities are affected both by growing interest in the opposite sex and wanting to look good for them and by the desire to fit in with a particular group of peers.

Intellectual Domain

I was a fantastic student until 10, and then my mind began to wander.

Grace Paley (author)

School's just not for me. I feel stupid all the time 'cause I just don't get it. Especially math—UGH! And English, too. I can't figure out what all those rules have to do with being a good writer. I think I'm already a pretty good writer, and I like to write—stories, letters, a poem or two sometimes. I've always wanted to try to write a play, maybe with music. But Mrs. Blake says we have to cover all this stuff so we'll know it when we get to high school. I don't care about that. I just want to get out of here. What's the use of doing all that stuff I'm never going to use anyway?

I don't think I'm stupid really. Sometimes I think I'm pretty smart. Maybe I just have a poor background.

Lillian, age twelve

Difficult as it may be, we must never forget that human development takes place over many years. We need to understand what is going on in terms of intellectual changes in the ten- to fourteen-year-old. The greatest single deficiency of middle level school where I have worked over the years is the same deficiency evident in the anecdote about my short story unit that opened this chapter: ignorance of the changing intellectual nature of young adolescents. Middle level teachers especially need to ensure that the things we do and teach are educationally viable for these youngsters, that what we are expecting them to learn and do is compatible with their readiness. We can make wise pedagogical decisions only when we know as much as possible about how our students are changing intellectually.

Few of us were formally prepared to design curriculum and select instructional practices that specifically complement young adolescents' developmental conditions, so my criticism does not demean the sincerity of teachers' efforts. Many of the most wonderful people I have been privileged to know are middle grades teachers, so this comment is descriptive rather than personally critical. But unless and until we understand how our youngsters think and learn so that we are able to pattern our teaching in light of those conditions, schooling will continue to misconnect with Lillian and multitudes of more confused and probably alienated youngsters like her. Professionalism in teaching, as in medicine, requires that we understand our constituents so that our responses to their needs and conditions will be appropriate to their developmental readiness.

The intellectual changes of early adolescence are as profound as, but considerably more subtle than, the more outwardly visible physical changes taking place at the same time. The fact that youngsters are changing so much makes this a particularly intriguing age group with which to work. Their variability frees us from having to follow single approaches to teaching and learning, while at the same time it challenges us to help youngsters find their own intellectual gifts, talents, and dispositions. It is no longer responsible for us to think or act as if intelligence is merely two-dimensional, as is suggested by references to students being "smart" or "dumb" and "fast" or "slow." We must do all we can to understand and complement each youngster's intellectual talents and shortcomings.

Keeping in mind the caveats articulated at the beginning of this chapter, and remembering that children grow and change from infancy throughout the life span, I want to characterize the intellectual changes occurring during early adolescence as movement from the predominantly childlike ways of thinking typical of ages eight or nine toward the increasingly (but not yet predominantly) adult ways of thinking of typical sixteen- to seventeen-year-olds.

It is central for us to understand and remember that children don't yet think the way we do; they think like children. They have their own ideas, and for us to have a true intellectual relationship with them, we need to understand and respect how they think. Development is the sometimes gradual, sometimes more abrupt evolution toward increasingly adult ways of thinking, and we must not forget that this transition is irregular and protracted. It is also quite individualized. Advances may appear only fleetingly at first, but they become increasingly typical of the youngster's expressed thought and behavior over time, given a context that honors and cultivates natural intellectual expansion and growth.

Consider these thumbnail sketches of youngsters' intellectual development at their respective ages:

Ages Eight to Nine

Eight- to nine-year-olds are experiencing an intellectual transition that both accelerates and diversifies during early adolescence. A year or so earlier they might be described as "reality centered," with "reality" being whatever is happening to or with them at a given moment. Continuity of thought for them occurs moment to moment more than day to day. As this transition begins to accelerate at eight or nine, however, logic becomes increasingly evident in their reasoning. Although this emerging rationality still applies primarily to their immediate circumstances, they are nevertheless thinking in new ways. Now they are beginning to comprehend complexities and interrelationships that previously went unnoticed. The child's background of personal incidents and anecdotal stories is becoming increasingly a referent for current decisions.

Children at this age are still quite literal in how they comprehend literature as well as the stories they tell to each other, and they enjoy adventurous, enchanting fantasies. Drawing inferential meanings, however, isn't yet natural to them. While facts and fantasy may still get somewhat mixed up in their minds, they're beginning to organize events into increasingly coherent sequences. The way they classify and establish priorities is becoming comparatively more reasoned and deliberate. They also become better able to explain the meaning of a whole event. Although generating their own propositions is still very difficult (if possible at all), they usually accept the morals and meanings explained by adults.

Until intellectual processes become more qualitative, their prevailing orientation to knowledge is that questions have single right answers, although they may be argumentative about particular answers. As they mature they begin to recognize that multiple answers and explanations are possible. The most trusted source of answers is still adults, and they value the ability to please adults, but they're beginning to doubt adult infallibility. They are also becoming increasingly competitive both in studies and in play. Rules are recognized as necessary and are generally accepted without much question or challenge unless another child is suspected of cheating or adults treat them inconsistently. Then they become indignant about preserving fair play. They can acknowledge a larger related concept such as justice, but they are not yet able to explain it very well.

While in the past they have functioned in what might be regarded as intellectually conservative ways, they're now thinking more adventurously. Imagination is fueled by the realization of newly conceived possibilities. They're increasingly interested in speculations about "What if . . . ?" They develop genuine intellectual interests and preferences for particular activities and types of studies. All these recent, hitherto untested attributes signal a transition that when nourished and strengthened will evolve over the next few years into mature adult thought.

Ages Sixteen to Seventeen

Although these young people in middle adolescence have already accomplished substantial intellectual transformation in just a half dozen years, their development is not yet complete. They think much more conceptually and analytically, and they are much more adept at recognizing interrelationships and concepts, such as theme and metaphor in literature. Formally approached ideas and theories in academic work make sense, and they may even construct their own theories to explain complex but familiar phenomena such as the stock market or the chances that the Red Sox will win the pennant. Hypothetical questions are taken seriously and generally provoke exchanges of ideas and opinions based on both personal experience and a wider knowledge of pertinent issues. Formal debate requiring research, knowledgeable organization, and discernment of strategy accommodate their higher-order reasoning abilities. At the least, so-called bull sessions become important ways to exercise their expanded intellects. It is natural and appropriate that they challenge conventional wisdom on a variety of issues ranging from school rules to global issues.

While younger children's thinking tends to be focused on objects in hand and immediate events, these older students are able to think about objects in their relationships to more complex phenomena. For example, adolescents can comprehend a carburetor as an entity but also as a functional part of the interdependent system of an internal combustion engine. Furthermore, more highly developed thinkers can conceptualize objects and interrelationships abstractly, without having them in hand. They can carry out a mental analysis and articulate likely theories about the carburetor's malfunction. This ability to mentally work forward and backward along an established path of functions and relationships elevates thought to a new level of abstraction that is manifest through purposeful experimentation.

These older and more highly developed thinkers are now more fully capable of judging issues according to multiple criteria. Forming hypotheses and theories is an expression of their emerging ability to think propositionally. Moral standards, ethical codes, and philosophical postulates can be applied in assessing the state of the world. Politics, economics, and social relationships become more relevant as adolescents are more able to apply, analyze, and evaluate. Cynicism and skepticism may accompany these new abilities to clarify, calculate, and propose. Planning, organizing, budgeting, keeping records, interpreting trends—all of these commonplace skills necessary to adult life are increasingly internalized as adolescents go about their day-to-day lives and plan for a future that is increasingly a part of their thought.

Developmental Stage Theory

The most significant contributions to our understanding of early adolescence as a developmental stage come from the rich work of Jean Piaget, a Swiss psychologist who spent his life studying the thought processes of children (Inhelder & Piaget, 1958; Piaget, 1952, 1960). The preceding thumbnail sketches that reflect some of our understanding of child development are products of Piaget's monumental work with abundant contributions by others who augmented his research (Elkind, 1974; Flavell, 1963). Piaget's stage theory conceptualization is especially pertinent to our understanding of early adolescence because it is the several-year transition time between thinking that is indigenous to childhood and that of adolescence and subsequently adulthood.

The central dynamic in Piaget's theory is the interactive relationships between thinking and learning. Popular wisdom seems to assume that learning is limited to what children demonstrate in school in their classes and on whatever measures might be employed, such as teacher-made standardized tests. While it is understandable that these priorities affect how parents and even many teachers think about a youngster's knowledge, Piaget has given a far more comprehensive picture that we must employ in designing educational activities that promote genuine learning and development. The central dynamic in Piaget's conceptualization will be briefly described here to provide a context for understanding intellectual developmental changes in early adolescence, but teachers are implored to study this work and that of others already cited in order to grasp the full spectrum of this forceful work.

From infancy the child forms ideas about all kinds of connections that result from his interactions with objects and people in his environment. His perceptions of these interactions form concepts—intellectual constructs that embody parts, interrelationships, and meaning. Piaget named these concepts *schemas,* which we might think of as blueprints. As the child has more and more experience, his incorporation of some of that experience is called *assimilation.* As schemas are changed to reflect new adaptations, *accommodation* occurs. Development is a continuing process of assimilation and accommodation, resulting in schemas that are increasingly more elaborate, complex and highly organized. Particular schemas that Piaget identified through his clinical interview method correspond to developmental changes he identified as *stages of intellectual development.* Mental actions associated with the stages Piaget identified are *operations.*

Teachers at all levels need to understand their students in terms of developmental stages, but two stages and the transition between them are especially vital for teachers working with young adolescents. Without understanding readiness and needs related to these stages and the highly individualistic transition between them, matching academic expectations and instruction with development is left to chance. The preceding thumbnail sketch of eight- to nine-year-olds briefly describes children who, according to Piaget's stage designation, are beginning to function at the stage of concrete operational thought—generally occurring between the ages of approximately seven and eleven. Note the words *beginning, generally,* and *approximately.* While we can generalize from Piaget's work about changes in age groups, individual development remains idiosyncratic. Review the characterization of eight- to nine-year-olds and note also the beginnings of what for them are largely new concepts.

Now review the sketch of sixteen- to seventeen-year-olds. That characterization is intended to show that these youngsters have made substantial developmental strides in terms of their abilities to think and learn. That characterization reflects young people functioning at the stage of formal operational thought. Remember, movement toward this stage depends heavily upon experience. Thus, the kind of experiences and the quality of stimulation we provide during these transition years have a great deal to do with whether or not healthy development continues between these two stages. Review the description of sixteen- to seventeen-year-olds to identify differences between the two stages, and then imagine ways in which a school might facilitate healthy development that respects the fact that youngsters don't develop at the same pace.

Before we leave this brief overview of Piaget's work, a few selected principles especially germane to our consideration of early adolescence are included.

1. Young adolescents' schemas are different from those of adults. Even though they may increasingly resemble adults in appearance and verbalizations, they don't yet think the way adults think.

2. Age designations for the concrete and formal operational stages are approximate. Individual children move from one stage to another according to an idiosyncratic combination of physical maturity, firsthand experiences working with concrete things, and interactions with other people, especially other children and people outside the school. It is also common for them to function at one stage for some operations and at a different stage for others.

3. Early adolescent intellectual development is enhanced when youngsters actively explore their world by having firsthand interactions with people and objects in their environment: talking, working with adults and classmates, using objects such as tools, and organizing personal experience. They construct their own knowledge (schemas) through such activities.

4. Genuine learning is the learner's process of making and remaking concepts (assimilation and accommodation) through firsthand activities.

Some Additional Views of Early Adolescent Development

Many intriguing views of human learning are not developmentally grounded. Since our concern here is to examine a teacher's view of development, however, nondevelopmental views have not been included. The study of human development at all ages and stages continues. Through professional reading and formal study of the discipline, teachers can stay abreast of findings that pertain to our work with young adolescents.

Moral Development. Middle grades teachers should be especially attentive to the changing ways in which their students reach ethical determinations. Classic studies of moral development have been done by Lawrence Kohlberg, influenced if not precipitated by Piaget and augmented by Carol Gilligan, Thomas Lickona, and others (Gilligan, 1982; Gilligan, Lyons, & Hamner, 1990; Kohlberg, 1981, 1983; Lickona, 1983; Piaget, 1965). An especially useful book, which was written originally for parents but is also an excellent resource for teachers, is Thomas Lickona's *Raising Good Children* (1983). The author combines a clear exposition of the stages of moral development with pedagogy designed to guide children's assessment of the moral issues in their lives; some of those moral challenges are likely to appear in their immediate future.

Expanding on the attributes of concrete operational thought from Piaget's work, Kohlberg focused on the moral ideas and choices of ten-year-old boys through adolescence and continuing into their adulthood. His conceptualization delineates three levels and six stages of moral reasoning between middle childhood and full adulthood, providing a developmental framework that is vertical and horizontal. (See Figure 4.2)

Progression from lower to higher stages and levels derives from a complex of experiences similar to those affecting intellectual development in Piaget's construct. Beginning with the essential principle that children must be treated morally, teachers and especially parents can influence healthy growth first by recognizing and raising consciousness about moral issues in the immediate context and beyond. Then, using questioning and clarifying techniques and understanding others' perspectives through role playing, children come to recognize a hierarchical order (Hersh, Paolito, & Reimer, 1983; Raths, Harmin, & Simon, 1966). It is incumbent on teachers to help students recognize and seek the moral level or stage of reasoning that is higher than their own. To thus enhance moral development requires commitment to a great deal of talk. Listening and sharing points of view in a context that recognizes the legitimacy of differing views, and clarifying prevailing views while teaching higher values—this is the enterprise of moral growth.

Consider the extent of moral issues that exist in youngsters' lives during early adolescence: truth telling, stealing, teasing, cheating, bullying, juvenile crime, betrayal, treatment of the environment, care for people in need, drug and alcohol use, sex. In addition to the natural pressures that are part of the personal development process, contemporary

STAGE 0: **EGOCENTRIC REASONING** (preschool years— around age 4)	WHAT'S RIGHT: REASON TO BE GOOD:	I should get my own way. To get rewards and avoid punishments.
STAGE 1: **UNQUESTIONING OBEDIENCE** (around kindergarten age)	WHAT'S RIGHT: REASON TO BE GOOD:	I should do what I'm told. To stay out of trouble.
STAGE 2: **WHAT'S-IN-IT FOR-ME FAIRNESS** (early elementary grades)	WHAT'S RIGHT: REASON TO BE GOOD:	I should look out for myself but be fair to those who are fair to me. To stay out of trouble.
STAGE 3: **INTERPERSONAL CONFORMITY** (middle-to-upper elementary grades and early-to-mid teens)	WHAT'S RIGHT: REASON TO BE GOOD:	I should be a nice person and live up to the expectations of people I know and care about. So others will think well of me (social approval) and I can think well of myself (self-esteem).
STAGE 4: **RESPONSIBILITY TO "THE SYSTEM"** (high school years or late teens)	WHAT'S RIGHT: REASON TO BE GOOD:	I should fulfill my responsibilities to the social or value system I feel part of. To keep the system from falling apart and to maintain self-respect as somebody who meets my obligations.
STAGE 5: **PRINCIPLED CONSCIENCE** (young adulthood)	WHAT'S RIGHT: REASON TO BE GOOD:	I should show the greatest possible respect for the rights and dignity of every individual person and should support a system that protects human rights. The obligation of conscience to act in accordance with the principle of respect for all human beings.

Figure 4.2   The Stages of Moral Reasoning. (Ages indicate reasonable development expectations for a child of normal intelligence growing up in a supportive moral environment.)
Source: Adapted from *Raising Good Children*, by T. Lickona. Copyright 1983 by Bantam Books.

youngsters also live in a peer community rife with dissolving families, pressures associated with their own home lives, discipline and authority problems at school, and pressures to steal, cheat, and commit vandalism. And if this were not enough, there's the omnipresent pressure to experiment with tobacco, alcohol, and drugs.

The public should not be surprised at the effects of such aggregate forces on young adolescents. There is no student community more in need of responsive schooling that accommodates the moral growth dimensions of their development. Young adolescents are becoming increasingly able to conceptualize ethical and moral dilemmas; they are similarly becoming more idealistic about how to rectify social injustices and neglect. This emergence of philosophical, ethical reasoning invites education about good citizenship. These youngsters stand ready to take actions aimed at improving our society. These years present a prime opportunity for them to learn cooperation roles and strategies, sharing, and skills in mediating interpersonal differences so that losing disputes becomes superfluous. Their keen consciousness of fair play can be cultivated into realizations of the complexities of concepts of justice and responsibility. Savvy middle level educators recognize and cultivate their students' readiness to engage often complex moral and ethical issues, and they also help their students to act constructively on their indignation about injustices.

Individual Differences. A particularly trying challenge to middle level teachers is to become more discriminating in our understanding of individual differences among our students whose intellectual readiness is in flux. Part of this change is the emergence of what might be regarded as distinctive abilities, proclivities, and styles in learning. Given the intensity of young adolescents' striving for a positive personal identity, they become increasingly concerned about being good at thinking and learning. How common is it to hear a student declare, "I'm a good speller" or "I'm not good at math." Early adolescence is an especially ripe opportunity for us to learn *with* our students about their distinctive proclivities. In a continuing emphasis inquiry (Chapter 3), consider Armstrong's suggestion that we systematically observe how students spend their free time in school. He suggests that we ask ourselves "what do they do when nobody is telling them what to do? If you have a 'choice time' in class when students can choose from a number of activities, what activities do students pick?" (Armstrong, 1994, p. 28; see also "Checklist for Assessing Students' Multiple Intelligences," pp. 29–31)

The multiple intelligences theory proffered by Howard Gardner is especially useful and provocative for thinking about differences we routinely notice among our students' (as well as our own) predilections for learning in and from particular disciplines, activities, and the arts. Gardner defines intelligence as an "ability to solve genuine problems, or to create products, that are valued within one or more cultural settings" and then proceeds to outline eight distinct criteria for intelligence and seven human competencies to fulfill them. These intelligences constitute "frames of mind . . . relatively autonomous human intellectual competencies" (1985, p. x). His description of these intelligences (Linguistic, Musical, Logical-Mathematical, Spatial, Bodily-Kinesthetic, and Personal) sounds familiar to the experienced observer of adolescent development. Armstrong (1989, 1994) has recommended an array of activities and tools that cultivate the seven intelligences inherent in every person. Selected suggestions are excerpted below as appropriate for young adolescents.

Linguistic intelligence—books, tape recorders, typewriters, word processors, label markers, printing equipment, storytelling, talking (tape-recorded) books, writing materials, discussions, debates, public speaking. Logical-mathematical intelligence—strategy games such as chess, checkers, Go; logic puzzles such as Rubik's cube, science kits, computer programming software, nature equipment, brain teasers, Cuisenaire rods, detective games.

Spatial intelligence—films, slides, videos, diagrams, charts, maps, art materials, cameras, telescopes, graphic design software, three-dimensional building supplies, optical illusions, visualization activities, drafting materials.

Bodily-kinesthetic intelligence—playgrounds, obstacle courses, hiking, swimming, gymnasium activities, model building, wood carving, clay modeling, animals, carpentry, machines, drama, video games.

Musical intelligence—percussion instruments; metronomes; computerized sound systems; records and tapes; musical instruments; singing; sounds of nature; things to strum, tap, pluck, and blow into.

Interpersonal intelligence—clubs, committees, after-school programs, social events, cooperative learning, interactive software, group games, discussions, group projects, simulations, drama, competitive and noncompetitive sports, peer teaching.

Personal intelligence—self-paced instruction, individualized projects, solo games and sports, lofts and other spaces to retreat to, diaries and journals, meditation, self-esteem activities.

In a subsequent volume Gardner suggests that "it is in the years of middle childhood . . . that children most appropriately acquire necessary competencies . . . to produce works that will make sense and be judged meritorious [and perhaps creative] by the surrounding culture" (1989, p. 115). This "frames of mind" conceptualization of intelligence provides a rich, provocative reference for middle grades teachers to understand youngsters' development and their proclivities for particular kinds of activity. It also argues for organizational and instructional diversity.

Learners who demonstrate consistently recurring patterns in their individual approaches to learning are often described by teachers and researchers as being predisposed toward particular learning styles (Dunn & Griggs, 1989). Teachers are also familiar with groups of students who seem to learn particular types of knowledge in similar ways that may differ from the preferences of some other classmates. Understanding both idiosyncratic and shared learning styles is extremely useful for all teachers, for "they are the education-relevent expressions of the uniqueness of the individual" (Joyce & Weil, 1986, p. 435).

Given young adolescents' unfolding capacities for greater variety and depth of thought, knowledge of learning style theory especially enhances the middle level teacher's understanding of her charges. When the goal is to create education that is responsive to the developmental circumstances of changing students, the teacher's grasp of students' intellectual styles is essential. In order to help students learn how to learn, we must understand as much as possible about the circumstances under which they learn most effectively. With that knowledge, matching instruction to their styles becomes more feasible. Researchers have generated a promising variety of approaches to learning styles that merit further study (Dunn & Dunn, 1978; Dunn & Griggs, 1988; Gregorc, 1979; "On Mixing," 1989).

Another dimension of individual differences is captured in the research on brain hemisphericity (Edwards, 1979). The essence of this work shows that the two hemispheres of the brain differ in their levels of electrical activity according to the nature of the thought taking place at any moment in time. This energy is concentrated in the left hemisphere when the focus is predominantly analytical, verbal, abstract, linear, and logical. When the work is more concrete, nonverbal, and spatial, involving synthesis and more holistic perceptions, brain energy is focused in the right lobe. Of course, activity that stimulates both hemispheres is necessary to full learning, but individual preferences for activity that centers in one or the other hemisphere are often observable among young adolescents. Teachers should attend to youngsters' natural inclinations toward one type of thinking while preserving the necessary balance adequate for healthy continued development and learning.

A final issue related to individual differences among students that middle level teachers recognize in day-to-day practice has to do with their attention span. Conrad Toepfer and his graduate students conducted an inquiry (1984) that showed that the attention span of young adolescents drops below that found among children in the later elementary grades before lengthening again in the high school years. We know from our sometimes trying firsthand experience that some students are able to pay attention only momentarily to a lesson presented by a teacher, while others may be "with you" for much longer. Toepfer observed that the upper limits of attention span duration for most young adolescents listening to a lecture or teacher demonstration was seven to eight minutes, and he went on to suggest approximately five minutes as an optimal period of time to plan for this type of instruction. Although no causal relationship has been demonstrated between these fluctuations and this period of intellectual transition, it is especially important that middle level teachers aim for clear, well-organized, and succinct slices of direct instruction.

Part of the enormous intrigue of these few years of early adolescence is that individual change abounds. It occurs unpredictably, and it is impossible to quantify. What is very clear is that humans' steady growth from infancy into adulthood undergoes an extremely significant passage. Early adolescence is a developmental period that begs for opportunities for youngsters to engage in active exploration of their worlds with perceptive, responsive adults who value healthy intellectual development over the mindless traditions of lecture- and textbook-centered schooling appropriate to the more fully developed intellects of adult learners. This is an era of dynamic expansion, curiosity, and energy, not a time for passive receptivity and obedient regurgitation.

No matter how much enthusiasm one may have for standardized measures of IQ and academic achievement, they do not come nearly close enough to accounting for the changes and possibilities inherent in young adolescent intellectual development. The only exception to this generalization I will make is the individualized intelligence measures such as the Wechsler tests when they are administered by a trained professional. These wider, more inclusive assessments can provide very useful clues about possible intellectual dispositions. However, I must say again that middle level teachers must abandon the medieval practice of thinking and speaking of their students according to one-dimensional measures such as IQ, regardless of how such a score has been obtained.

Familial Domain

I am a rather optimistic, unemotional, and logical person. I believe in equality and giving your best. Unfortunately I also tend to be very sarcastic and have a harsh temper. My parents divorced when I was two years old, and I barely remember it. They are both now remarried, and I live with my mom. My mom and stepfather are strict, critical, kind, and can be aggravating. They force me to do my best and then say I'm pushing myself too hard. Sometimes parents aren't logical.

Kathie, age thirteen

The developmental changes experienced by young adolescents not only affect them personally but often precipitate changes in relationships within the immediate family—especially with parents. The passage of one family member through puberty may challenge the roles and relationships of everyone in the family (Hill, 1980; Hill & Holmbeck, 1987). Interactions with siblings and other relatives may also change as the youngster's role within the family shifts from more or less complete dependence and subservience toward increasing involvements and commitments outside the family. Ideas, ideals, and values that have previously been derived predominantly from parents become influenced by peers (Steinberg & Silverberg, 1986). It might be said that this period marks a transition from parents as the ultimate authorities in youngsters' lives to peers and the peer group as the primary influence. Additionally, the child's concept of family may become more inclusive than heretofore. This gradual reassignment of authority and deference to standards outside the immediate family can become confusing and upsetting to both generations. Teachers need to be aware that this phase is part of a natural process of personal and family evolution, and they may also help parents understand what is going on. Youngsters' desire to move toward more adultlike judging and decision making about themselves is an inevitable component of early adolescent transition, but it sometimes takes parents by surprise.

The familiar stereotype of the "thirteen-year-old going on twenty" exaggerates the case, however. While there are certainly cases in which a mother claims in frustration that she's "pulling out her hair," most of the changing interpersonal dynamics at home are not so dramatic. A relatively small proportion of cases are so tumultuous and impassioned that severe parent–child alienation occurs. Still, since the potential for unanimity between school and home can be such a valuable influence on family equilibrium, teachers need to be tuned in to the possibility of changing dynamics at home.

Multiple Life Changes

It is even more difficult to accurately depict a typical young adolescent's family structure than it is to correctly generalize about kids' development, for families are composed in so many ways that are different from the tradition of the two-parent nuclear family. It is not uncommon for up to half of the youngsters in a class to come from families that differ from that prototype. In fact, as little as 7 percent of today's population fits the traditional family profile of earlier times (Naisbitt, 1982). Single-parent and second-marriage families abound, and while many of these family units function very well, it is certain that children have had to work through stressful circumstances and may be continuing to struggle with them. Disillusionment with parents, emotional pain, frustration, and anger are commonplace. Confusions about adult relationships are often common. Many of our students have experienced very difficult times at home in their short lives.

Stresses deriving from family tensions show up in how children function at school. Particular behaviors associated with stress in young adolescents' school lives are "absent-mindedness, nervousness, weariness (lethargic, tired), moodiness, withdrawal, declining grades, physical complaints and misbehaving" (Allers, 1984, p. 5). Of course, these behaviors do not necessarily signal problems at home. Physical changes alone can be exhausting to a child, so we must not leap to the conclusion that because a youngster is weary, he or she is suffering from stress related to something amiss at home. From time to time I've had students who have fallen sound asleep at school. Sometimes that is a result of their having been unable to relax and rest at home. I've also known a few students who would stay at school as late as I'd allow, or who would daily go to a friend's home rather than return to their own stress-producing homes. When a family is undergoing transition, especially changes that are expressed emotionally, the already considerable challenge of dealing with one's own changes is exacerbated. Even with supportive family circumstances, however, the child's natural progress through the developmental process will still affect the relationship with parents and roles within the family. Working out changing relationships with parents, whatever the home circumstances may be, is still a necessary passage.

Parent–Child Relationships

As children become more savvy and analytical about influences and events in their lives, they inevitably come to question and challenge parental wisdom and authority. The virtual disappearance of culturally defined markers—"external signs of where (one) stands"—obfuscates the expectations and privileges associated with any particular time of the child's life (Elkind, 1984). Previous generations grew up in communities and neighborhoods and at a time when there was much wider agreement about what children were permitted to do at a particular age and what they must achieve in order to enjoy greater independence or responsibility. Elkind goes on to show that separation and divorce, "blended families," and the media have added immeasurably to confusions about family roles and values that can exacerbate the conflict between parents and emerging adolescents. While it does not appear that a total overhaul of parent–child relationships is called for, this is an appropriate time for "realignment and redefinition of family ties" (Steinberg, 1990, p. 255). I have found that early adolescence is an excellent time to engage students in curriculum units designed around formal studies of their own families, especially family stories (see Chapter 6).

> I'm still confused about my junior high years. I was worried all the time about what to do and what to wear and what to say. My mom would just say, "Be yourself." Then I'd really panic. How do you do that? If I couldn't tell what the hell was going on, how could I figure out what "being myself" meant? I'm still disappointed in [my mother] for letting me down then.

> *Kelly, age nineteen*

When children are at about the age of ten, they tend to get along with both parents reasonably well. They want to believe in their parents, and pleasing them is important, so relatively harmonious relationships are likely. However, as children begin to change more quickly at eleven and twelve, they may become increasingly negative about mother's criticism and resistant toward her rulings. Mothers generally tend to be closer to decision-making action than fathers. Yet, young adolescents may still perceive the father as an ultimate authority, and his pronouncements tend to be more intimidating—the final word. Because mothers tend to be more frequently in the position of having to decide whether or not to comply with kids' requests, they may likewise experience more conflict with their children than do fathers. Discipline that may have passed unchallenged in previous years may become more difficult.

Tensions are more likely to persist between parents and daughters than between parents and sons, although conflict between mothers and sons is not uncommon (Steinberg, 1981). A pattern of stress in relations between parents and daughters sometimes occurs following menarche (Hill & Holmbeck, 1987). Furthermore, there has been for a long time a generalized cultural expectation that boys are supposed to begin to assert their independence at this time, while girls are expected to remain more acquiescent. Historically, we have justified male independence as a rite of passage while "protecting" girls by keeping them close to home. As contemporary cultural expectations change to become less sexist, however, we must act on our realization that this growing independence is just as important for girls. Teachers are in a unique position to help parents understand and find ways to enhance this natural process without upsetting family relationships and routines.

Toward the ages of thirteen and fourteen, young adolescents may be concerned about yet another dimension of their parents—how parents appear to others. There emerges in these youngsters a new self-consciousness associated with parents' physical appearance, how they dress, the family car or house, and how parents behave around their teachers or friends. Again, mothers usually get the worst of it, as children seem to be more self-conscious of their mothers than their fathers. But regardless of how much care the parent invests in trying to be an asset to a child insofar as appearance is concerned, it is reassuring to remember that this is a natural transition and should not be taken too seriously if the quality of communication and parent–child relationship they actually share remains generally good. Tensions between "the way it used to be" and "how it is now" are transient issues in the introspective concerns of young adolescent children.

Whole Family Relationships

The ease of communication between parents and the young adolescent family member remains the primary issue affecting comfort within the family. Often there are other siblings, half siblings, or stepsiblings, however, and relationships among siblings always affect the dynamics of the family unit. Siblings may remain close, especially when their age differences are so great that they don't tend to compete as much with each other as do siblings who are closer in age. Adolescents of comparable ages may remain close in spite of occasional rivalry about schoolwork, sports, or parents' attention. Petty irritations about possessions, chores, "who did what to whom" allegations, teasing, and so on are organic to sibling relationships, especially when at least one of the children is passing through early adolescence and there are siblings within two or three years of the same age. One dimension of the emerging adolescent's efforts toward self-definition may be contentious relationships with siblings. But it is very disturbing when orneriness doesn't dissipate naturally and evolves into acrimony and violence by siblings toward each other.

Changes in family composition and parents' employment further add to the uncertainty about the child's place. Many if not most kids are dependent on parents or other adults to transport them, give them money, and schedule their lives while parents are working. Kids appear to be spending much of this time like airplanes circling in a vast holding pattern, waiting to make contact with the world of actualities around them. Lacking very much opportunity for taking on real responsibility in the world of work, having few established ways to provide useful service to the adult world, and having very little real authority over what they do and how they spend their time, these youngsters have in a real sense "arrived" but have not yet received "permission or instructions regarding landing." Tragically, too many kids exhaust their fuel circling, and they crash before reaching adulthood.

Research into interpersonal relationships within American families reveals that the average home is a place of greater violence than was previously believed (Strauss, Gelles, & Steinmetz, 1980). Parents act violently toward each other as well as toward their children. Most frequent, however, is turbulence among siblings. The classic scenario is one of tensions that for a time are manifested as squabbles until they erupt into outright physical fights. Chronic bitterness can grow into hatred that turns the home into a battleground. Teachers must not be naive about the probability that some of their students are suffering through such situations and being victimized by abusive parents and siblings as well as committing violence themselves.

Family rituals and traditions that require everyone's participation may become a source of tension. During early adolescence, youngsters are increasingly interested in being with their peers after school, on weekends, and during holidays. Traditional family outings such as a camping trip or bicycling or celebrating a holiday may be perceived as an imposition on their freedom, and even parents' most sensitive efforts to enlist the young adolescent's participation may turn into a dispute. The youngster may have no rational objection to the activity, but the fact that it is compulsory makes participation onerous.

Grandparents and other relatives outside the immediate family—even if they live at a distance from the primary family group—may become the focus of respect and confidence for a youngster in conflict with his or her immediate family group. Earlier in the evolution of American family structure, the extended family in which grandparents and sometimes other relatives lived under one roof and shared responsibilities was more commonplace than it is today. Under those circumstances, there were several adult family members among whom a child could choose in order to develop an easy affiliation. It is natural for young adolescents to develop such a closeness and special feeling of belonging with a particular relative who reciprocates the relationship. These important relatives may serve as the embodiment of family identity at times when conflicts between parent and child create animosity and confusion.

As children grow older, increasingly adept physically, and more able to share some of the responsibilities previously met by adults, parents naturally expect them to help share the burden of running the household. The more they change, the more is expected of them. Those expectations tend to be manifested by somewhat menial chores more often than by participation in the family decision making process about matters such as a trip or a major purchase such as a car. At this time when young adolescents are increasingly capable of more adultlike thinking, it is advisable to invite their ideas and their vote in reaching family decisions.

Authoritative Parenting

There is good evidence of a positive correlation between particular parenting practices and young adolescents' responses to school expectations and responsibilities. The preferred parenting mode is referred to as "authoritative parenting," a distinct complex of adult–child relationships (Baumrind, 1978). The young adolescent who begins to object to parents' decisions and challenge adult authority may in actuality be in a "pseudo-independent stance, rebelling in the service of emancipation. Parents then may assume mistakenly that the [child] is really capable and desirous of substantial autonomy and withdraw their own commitment" (Baumrind, 1978, p. 259).

The characterization of authoritative parenting is rich with implications for effective relationships between these same youngsters and teachers. Briefly summarized, authoritative relationships embody the following attributes (excerpted from Baumrind, 1978):

1. *Communication*—The emphasis is on talk, and discussions are open and candid. Decisions are negotiated, and democratic deliberations are valued by both generations. Adults use and emphasize rationality in assessing dilemmas and making decisions.

2. *Expectations*—Adults have clear and consistent expectations for behavior. Adults look for ways to affirm children's qualities, and the standards they set are realistic, clear, and consistent.

3. *Respect*—Adults never fall back on guilt-provoking or techniques of psychological intimidation to control youngsters. The power of authority derives from respect, reason, and interpersonal competence.

4. *Affection*—Interpersonal warmth and close relationships are the rule. Adults genuinely value relationships with young adolescents as they are, respecting and understanding children's circumstances.

Relationships characterized by these qualities breed social confidence and competence, which enable the youngster to feel secure in the home and at school. Furthermore, self-esteem becomes a more likely consequence of successes in interpersonal relationships among children and adults at school. The fact that authoritative parenting appears to promote school success should influence all adults who work with young adolescents to develop interpersonal relationships that emphasize the qualities listed above. Strategies for applying these qualities in a class or team where students have an authentic opportunity to practice democratic decision making are discussed in Chapter 7.

Middle level educators need to take the initiative toward knowing their students in their family contexts. Given the middle school concept that emphasizes teaming and teacher advisories, it is much more possible for a teacher to know and communicate with a manageable number of parents. By being on friendly speaking terms with parents we are often able to understand much more fully the developmental challenges as well as the kinds of support our students are experiencing.

Communal Domain

> Most of our problems and most of our fun is with friends. Sometimes I get closer to them and sometimes we get farther away. I'm not sure I understand it. I just know that relationships are something you can't control by rules.
>
> *Sara, age twelve*

It has been suggested that the paramount reason young adolescents come to school is not for the education we offer but because school is where the other kids are. In my years of being a teacher and researcher with ten- to fourteen-year-olds, I've come to recognize that both goals—companionship and learning—are powerful, complementary motivators. Although I have occasionally worked with youngsters who seem to function happily more or less on their own and who don't appear to have very much interest in interacting with classmates, an overwhelming majority of youngsters very much value having one or more close friends and being accepted in an informal peer group. Furthermore, these affiliations are themselves dynamic—alliances constantly break up, and new ones form. This is a time of ongoing social exploration.

Consider the amount of time youngsters spend talking with each other on the telephone, their delight in hanging out with friends at the mall or on the street, their rushing to be together as much as possible during the three or four minutes between classes. There's no question that they are crying out to be together in settings where they feel accepted and enjoyed by others. Meanwhile, the organization of large, impersonal schools works against this need by imposing schedules that have students changing classes and classmates every thirty or forty minutes. An eighth grader who felt alienated from her school, because the way it was organized kept her separated from many of her friends, said cynically, "I think they're just trying to keep us away from each other so we'll stay confused."

During these years of early adolescence, youngsters shift toward other kids for acceptance and confirmation—a gradual turn from primary dependence on approval by parents and teachers to a quest for what Charity James refers to as "belonging with" age-mates and significant adults beyond parents and teachers (James, 1974). A twenty-year-old drug abuser who had left school after the eighth grade and supported herself as a prostitute in a large city nearby explained to me, "I didn't really enjoy using drugs in junior high school, but the druggies were the ones who accepted me and didn't judge me. They were the people I belonged with." This tragic example of the extreme one young girl went to in order to resolve a desperate need for affiliation and affirmation in a large, impersonal school illustrates the great value that young adolescents place on belonging.

Many schools I have worked with report declines in student behavioral problems and office referrals after shifting from a departmental-home room organization to interdisciplinary teams and advisories, especially when group assignments take the students' preferences into consideration. The encouraging research analysis conducted by Paul George and Kathy Shewey indicated that when teaming and advisories were implemented effectively, student deportment improved considerably (1994). Given the urgency of youngsters' need for affiliation and personal belonging to a small community of peers, it simply makes good common sense for schools to organize themselves to accommodate those needs.

Affirmation resulting from mutually satisfying and productive collaborations, especially with classmates but also with selected adults, enhances the youngster's primary developmental task of identity formation. Peter Scales identifies "positive social interaction with adults and peers" as the very first developmental need of young adolescents. He goes on to say that they "desperately want to belong" and "although they may not often admit to it, they also have a similar need for caring relationships with adults who like and respect them" (1991, p. 13). And although the research is less clear about the extent to which youngsters' choose adult's values over peer values, there are strong indications that parents and other significant adults have a much greater influence on adolescent values than it has been popular to believe. Empirical experience has shown me that when student–adult relationships are authentic in terms of trust and respect, adult values are highly influential on adolescents.

The dynamics of interpersonal relationships for this age group should be considered from both macro and micro perspectives. Crowds and cliques are the two major types of group in the adolescent culture (Smart & Smart, 1973). The crowd offers group identity, and the clique provides a context whereby members meet each others' needs to "belong with." In the ideal school, middle level educators would recognize the naturalness of these social needs and organize the school to help complement them. Many exemplary schools are organized so that students and teachers compose 75- to 125-member teams that have team names, procedures, and schedules. Such teams also stand for specific values that are clearly articulated and taught through team activities (see Chapter 9). These schools also often provide even smaller groups—advisories—composed of eight to ten students and a teacher (see Chapter 10). It is not assumed that these intentional affiliations supplant youngsters' own selections of group membership, but they ensure that every youngster belongs with both a crowd and a smaller, more intimate group. Deliberate actions to satisfy kids' need to feel connected to a group can then enhance the school's constructive influence.

Young adolescents also want to do things that are useful to their community. Their newfound idealism primes them especially for rendering services to their community. They also need and want adult recognition for the useful things they do that are more adultlike than childlike, and the recognition they value is that which is authentic—not the patronizing, head-patting approval often displayed by well-intentioned grownups. These youngsters are ready and eager to act on their aspirations to make a genuine difference to others. Responsive educators create opportunities for them to do so. There are decided advantages of working with young adolescents on social issues. First is their growing ability to reason about social dilemmas, recognize ethical principles, and figure out ways to respond to need. Under the guidance of sensitive, thoughtful teachers they can use basic logic to think through a social problem, imagine multiple possible solutions, and create an action plan to address the issue. For example, a teacher in a middle level school near a convalescent home learned that most of the residents had few visitors, and some of them had no visitors at all. That perceptive teacher shared that information with some of her students, whose compassion and indignation led them to invent their own adopt-a-grandparent program. Some of the most moral judgments and actions I have ever witnessed have come from young adolescents whose idealism has been respected and nourished by responsive teachers.

As in the other domains, the typical youngster's interpersonal priorities evolve gradually from the beginning of early adolescence through the next several years. Selected issues vary somewhat as well between the sexes. By age ten, having a single best friend or being a member of a two- or three-member band has become important to both boys and girls. Parents note an increase in the amount of time kids spend with each other on the telephone. Teachers see kids who are constantly together in their free time—sometimes in conversation, at other times playing or working together. Close friendships provide affirmation, belonging, and the assurance that there is someone who can be trusted with innermost secrets. Although these friendships matter a great deal at the time they occur and when they are dissolving, they are often relatively brief in comparison with the more enduring alliances that develop a few years later (Ames, Ilg, & Baker, 1988).

As kids grow and develop, the spectrum of same-sex friends widens and the intensity lightens. Friendships with members of the opposite sex develop, but quasi-romantic overtones either felt or presumed by others tend to be confusing. Girls, who are often developmentally ahead of boys in their interest in romantic friendships, are especially attentive to the intrigue associated with "who you like" and "who likes you," with "like" expressing romantic rather than platonic attraction. By the advent of middle adolescence around ages fifteen and sixteen, however, many boys' interests have caught up, and being in love may become an informal condition of high status for both sexes. Issues of belonging become wrapped up with liking and being liked.

Regardless of adults' attitudes toward first loves, the youngster's thoughts are easily and naturally dominated by thoughts of the beloved. While grownups may dismiss this developmental event as mere puppy love, it is nonetheless a very intense feeling that often has profound effects on the day-to-day life of the novice. Adolescents may not be able to rationally conceptualize such love in adult terms, but they have very intense feelings about it. Sensitive teachers can understand that children whose family lives are in disarray may understandably become preoccupied, even obsessed, by the affirmation the beloved provides. Those of us responsible for these youngsters serve them best when we acknowledge and respect the magnitude and intensity of these developmental changes, all the while seeking ways to respond to and complement their new needs and inquisitiveness.

Youngsters who are consistently rejected by peers have an especially hard time as developing adolescents. The reasons for rejection are complex and not always clear to adults, although the phenomenon appears to begin in early childhood. By the time social isolates reach the middle grades, they are likely to accept their peers' social discrimination and suffer depression, low self-esteem, and delinquency. At this time when peer acceptance is prized, rejection brings misery that becomes disheartening to such a point that many youngsters drop out of school as soon as they reach the legal school-leaving age. Middle grades educators may have the final opportunity for helping disliked kids find ways to build relationships that will help them achieve acceptance by their peers.

Although there are no guaranteed techniques for resolving peer discrimination, the growing rationality and inclination to idealism of young adolescents present a promising opportunity for concerned responsive educators. Recognizing the urgency of assisting socially isolated youngsters to learn how to work constructively with classmates and to increase their chances of building friendships, many middle level educators regularly use a variety of tested grouping formats for introducing small group work. Using such groupings in several different cooperative learning contexts, and teaching students how to mediate interpersonal conflicts, are especially beneficial strategies.

SOME CLOSING COMMENTS

A great expanse of developmental territory has necessarily been skimmed in this chapter. As stated at the outset, it is not intended that a reading of this chapter will adequately substitute for more comprehensive and concentrated study of these several domains of early adolescent development. This overview is necessary, however, as a context for the reader's reflection on firsthand experience and insights gained from shadowing and inquiry. The recommendations found in the balance of this book rest largely upon my own continually growing understanding of child development in the middle years.

Above all, it is essential to remember that these are tender years during which children are beginning to confront some new realities and complexities of the actual world in ways that are different from anything they have previously known. They can be at once bold yet conservative, wise yet innocent, curious yet subdued. Their perceptions are expanding and becoming more refined, and a variety of intensified personal feelings filters their experience. Each individual's view on any matter is composed of an idiosyncratic complex of the past that is constantly being augmented by current adventures. The challenges of coping and survival they face are often enormous, and we must not underestimate their jeopardy. When we serve them best, we respect their inexperience and protect their frailty from harmful societal influences as well as well-intentioned but misguided schooling practices that have brought down far too many children of prior generations. By working with sensitivity and serious commitment to their healthy development, we may also find it possible to reconstruct the elements of those years in our own lives, too.

We must accept the reality that young adolescents today are growing up in a world that is often bewildering and self-contradictory. It is a world that seems to simultaneously expect both more and less of them than was the case in the past. Only a century ago, most young adolescents had specific roles and functions in society: many worked full shares as laborers on the family farm; they worked in mines and factories; they apprenticed to craftsmen. No reasonable person would wish to see today's children returned full time to such exploitive roles. On the other hand, perhaps our society has overreacted to traditional child abuses by giving youngsters little or nothing to do that is worthwhile to them. Have we unintentionally and mistakenly insulated children too much from the adult world, failing to salvage valuable opportunities for learning that are unavailable in classroom-bound schooling? In our eagerness to protect them from exploitation, have we created a no-person's land for our youngsters caught between childhood and young adulthood—our in-betweeners? It can fairly be said that the children of contemporary culture are growing up more sophisticated but less mature than their counterparts of earlier generations.

The only sensible way to design schooling for children ages ten to fourteen is, in the words of *The Music Man*'s Professor Harold Hill, "to know the territory." Middle level educators *must* know their territory, and that territory is early adolescent development. And knowing it in the abstract sense reflected in this chapter is, by itself, insufficient for responsive teaching. General knowledge must be illustrated and augmented by firsthand observations and investigations, such as those processes of shadowing and inquiry described in Chapters 2 and 3. As we genuinely learn who young adolescents are, we'll make far more enlightened decisions on how to go about designing their education.

Supporting Activities

Awareness of the subtleties of children's complex, multifaceted development grows incrementally over years of study and firsthand experience. Therefore, students preparing for middle level teaching must begin to expand their already existing knowledge by reading, observing, interacting with students, and then sharing that experience with colleagues. Learning to recognize the indications of transition from childhood toward adolescence is enhanced by coordinated reading, observation, and interaction with youngsters. Since the literature concerned with early adolescent development is so vast, I recommend that university students be organized into small teams (three to five members) to explore the literature collectively as well as to study firsthand either individuals or cliques.

Reading

Excellent sources cited in each of the domains covered in this chapter are listed in the references. Additional readings are available through the Educational Resources Information Center (ERIC).

Child Studies

Linking ideas derived from observation and interactions with kids to professional reading contributes to our understanding of young adolescents. Through shadow studies and inquiries, firsthand experience creates knowledge about youngsters in their school contexts.

Understanding is further enhanced by systematic child studies—documentation of one student or an existing clique. What linkages can be made between what you have read and what you observe and experience?

Using the five developmental domains presented in this chapter as background, describe either a young adolescent or each of the members of a coterie of kids you have shadowed and interviewed. Some additional issues you might consider are these:

1. *What amuses them?* What kids find funny may provide some insights about thinking, self-perceptions, and perceptions of other kids. Wit that plays on language such as puns, limericks, satire, parody, and double entendres reflects awareness of more advanced relationships in language than was present in the jokes that amused children at a previous, more literal stage. Take note also of kids who seem confused and say, "I don't get it."

2. *What do they like to do?* Aside from the social enjoyment of participating in games, what specific games appeal to them? What games do individuals play best? What are other favorite things to do? Observe students to see how they think when they're at their avowed best. What is "in" and "out?" Who or what are their ideals? Heroes?

3. *How do they respond to puzzles? Riddles? Mystery?* The emphasis here is on dealing with different kinds of problems. How do youngsters go about clarifying and trying to solve problems? What do their approaches suggest about individual proclivities? Getting the solution may be the purpose for them, but understanding how they try to do it is what informs us.

4. *What are the "uniforms" you see kids wearing?* By uniform I refer to kids' ways of dressing. How are informal groups defined by how they dress? What are the relationships between dress and group membership? Values? Kids' perceptions of each other?

5. *What are the operative language idioms?* Particular language usages come and go like other fads. What are the expressions being used? What conventional meanings do they convey? Can you identify the sources of these idioms? What differences are there between the children's idioms and those of your own generation? What differences in language use are there among small groups or cliques in the same school? Are there ethnic or racial differences?

Presentation

While it is appropriate to summarize a child study in writing, completed studies are best presented to colleagues or classmates along with any available documentary evidence to support the observations. This process is similar to that referred to in hospitals as "clinical staffing," whereby a group of physicians consult together in order to take advantage of each other's understanding of a syndrome or disease. The discussion that ensues in a child study sometimes raises questions or possibilities that further enrich the presenter's understanding of the study. The final piece of a child study is the presenter's list of questions that remain, uncertain assumptions, and sometimes proposed next steps.

REFERENCES

Allers, R. (1984). Helping middle level early adolescents from broken homes. *Schools in the middle: A report on trends and practices.* Reston, VA: National Association of Secondary School Principals.

Ames, L. B., Ilg, F. L., & Baker, S. M. (1988). *Your ten to fourteen-year-old.* (Gesell Institute of Human Development). New York: Delacorte.

Armstrong, T. (1989, Summer). *Mothering, 52,* 80.

Armstrong, T. (1994). *Multiple intelligences in the classroom.* Alexandria, VA: Association for Supervision and Curriculum Development.

Baumrind, D. (1978). Parental disciplinary patterns and social competence in children. *Youth and Society, 9,* 239–276.

Beane, J. A., & Lipka, R. P. (1980). Self-concept and self-esteem: A construct differentiation. *Child Study Journal, 10.*

Beane, J. A., & Lipka, R. P. (1986). *Self-concept, self-esteem, and the curriculum.* New York: Teachers College Press.

Beane, J. A., & Lipka, R. P. (1987). *When the kids come first: Enhancing self-esteem.* Columbus, OH: National Middle School Association.

Benson, P., Williams, D., & Johnson, A. (1988). *The quicksilver years: The hopes and fears of early adolescence.* (Search Institute). San Francisco: Harper & Row.

Brooks-Gunn, J. & Reiter, E. O. (1990). The role of pubertal processes. In S. S. Feldmann, & G. R. Elliott (Eds.), *At the threshold: The developing adolescent.* Cambridge, MA: Harvard University Press.

Dubas, J. S. (1991). The effects of pubertal development on achievement during adolescence. *American Journal of Education, 99*(4), 444–460.

Dunn, R., & Dunn, K. (1978). *Teaching students through their individual learning styles: A practical approach.* Reston, VA: Reston.

Dunn, R., & Griggs, S. A. (1988). *Learning styles: Quiet revolution in American secondary schools.* Reston, VA: National Association of Secondary School Principals.

Dunn, R., & Griggs, S. A. (1989). Learning styles: Key to improving schools and student achievement. *NASSP Curriculum Report, 18*(3).

Edwards, B. (1979). *Drawing on the right side of the brain.* New York: St. Martin's.

Elkind, D. (1974). *Children and adolescents: Interpretive essays on Jean Piaget.* New York: Oxford University Press.

Elkind, D. (1984). *All grown up & no place to go: Teenagers in crisis.* Reading, MA: Addison-Wesley.

Erikson, E. (1968). *Identity, youth, and crisis.* New York: Norton.

Faust, M. S. (1960). Developmental maturity as a determinant of prestige in adolescent girls. *Child Development, 31*(1), 173–186.

Filipovic, Zlata. (1994). *Zlata's diary: A child's life in Sarajevo.* New York: Viking (Penguin Group).

Flavell, J. H. (1963). *The developmental psychology of Jean Piaget.* Princeton, NJ: Van Nostrand Reinhold.

Gardner, H. (1985). *Frames of mind: The theory of multiple intelligences.* New York: Basic Books.

Gardner, H. (1989). *To open minds: Chinese clues to the dilemma of contemporary education.* New York: Basic Books.

George, P. S. & Shewey, K. (1994). *New evidence for the middle school.* Columbus, OH: National Middle School Association.

Gilligan, C. (1982). *In a different voice: Psychological theory and women's development.* Cambridge, MA: Harvard University Press.

Gilligan, C., Lyons, N. P., & Hamner, T. J. (Eds.). (1990). *Making connections: The relational worlds of adolescent girls at Emma Willard School.* Cambridge, MA: Harvard University Press.

Goodlad, J. I. (1984). *A place called school.* New York: McGraw-Hill.

Gregorc, A. F. (1979). Learning/teaching styles. *Student learning styles: Diagnosis and prescribing programs.* Reston, VA: National Association of Secondary School Principals.

Hamburg, D. A. (1993). The opportunities of early adolescence. *Teachers College Record 94*(3), 466–471.

Hechinger, F. (1992). *Fateful choices: Healthy youth for the 21st century.* New York: Carnegie Council on Adolescent Development.

Hersh, R. H., Paolito, D. P., & Reimer, J. (1983). *Promoting moral growth: From Piaget to Kohlberg.* New York: Longman.

Hill, J. P. (1980). The family. In M. Johnston (Ed.), *Toward adolescence: The middle school years* (pp. 32–55). 79th Yearbook of the National Society for the Study of Education. Chicago: University of Chicago Press.

Hill, J. P., & Holmbeck, G. N. (1987). Familial adaptation to biological change during adolescence. In R. M. Lerner & T. T. Foch (Eds.), *Biological-psychosocial interactions in early adolescence* (pp. 207–223). Hillsdale, NJ: Erlbaum.

Hunter, Latoya. (1992). *The diary of Latoya Hunter: My first year in junior high.* New York: Crown.

Inhelder, B., & Piaget, J. (1958). *The growth of logical thinking from childhood to adolescence.* New York: Basic Books.

James, C. (1974). *Beyond customs: An educator's journey.* New York: Agathon (Schocken).

Johnson, M. (Ed.). (1980). *Toward adolescence: The middle school years.* 79th Yearbook of the National Society for the Study of Education. Chicago: University of Chicago Press.

Jones, M. C., & Mussen, P. H. (1957). Self-conceptions, motivations, and interpersonal attitudes of late- and early-maturing boys. *Child Development, 28*(2), 243–256.

Jones, M. C., & Mussen, P. H. (1958). Self-conceptions, motivations, and interpersonal attitudes of early- and late-maturing girls. *Child Development, 29*(4), 491–501.

Joyce, B., & Weil, M. (1986). *Models of teaching.* Englewood Cliffs, NJ: Prentice-Hall.

Kagan, J., & Coles, R. (Eds.). (1972). *Twelve to sixteen: Early adolescence.* New York: Norton.

Katchadourian, H. (1977). *The biology of adolescence.* San Francisco: W. H. Freeman.

Keizer, G. (1988). *No place but here.* New York: Penguin.

Kohlberg, L. (1981). *The philosophy of moral development.* New York: Harper & Row.

Kohlberg, L. (1983). *The psychology of moral development.* New York: Harper & Row.

Kohlberg, L., & Gilligan, C. (1971). The adolescent as philosopher. *Daedalus, 100*(4), 1051–1086.

Kohlberg, L., & Mayer, R. (1972). Development as the aim of education. *Harvard Educational Review, 42*(4), 449–496.

Lawrence, G. (1980, May). Do programs reflect what research says about physical development? *Middle School Journal,* pp. 12–14.

Lerner, R. M., & Foch, T. T. (Eds.). (1987). *Biological-psychosocial interactions in early adolescence.* Hillsdale, NJ: Erlbaum.

Lickona, T. (1983). *Raising good children.* New York: Bantam.

Lipsitz, J. (1977). *Growing up forgotten: A review of research and programs concerning early adolescence.* (Report to the Ford Foundation). Lexington, MA: Heath.

Lipsitz, J. (1980). The age group. In *Toward adolescence: The middle school years.* National Society for the Study of Education (NSSE) Yearbook, pp. 7–31.

Naisbitt, J. (1982). *Megatrends.* New York: Warner.

National Organization for Women. (1989, December). *Fact sheet—Parental consent.* Washington, DC: Author.

On mixing and matching of teaching and learning styles. (1989, December). *Practical Applications of Research, 3*(2). (Newsletter of Phi Delta Kappan's Center on Evaluation, Development and Research).

Pearce, J. C. (1971). *The crack in the cosmic egg.* New York: Julian Press.

Peterson, A. C. (1987, September). Those gangly years. *Psychology Today,* pp. 28–34.

Piaget, J. (1952). *The origins of intelligence in children.* New York: International University Press.

Piaget, J. (1960). *The child's conception of the world.* Atlantic Highlands, NJ: Humanities Press.

Piaget, J. (1965). *The moral judgment of the child.* New York: Free Press. (Original work published 1932).

Pipher, Mary. (1994). *Reviving Ophelia: Saving the selves of adolescent girls.* New York: Putnam.

Raths, L. E., Harmin, M., & Simon, S. (1966). *Values and teaching.* Columbus, OH: Merrill.

Rieser, P., & Underwood, L. E. (1989). *Growing children: A parents' guide.* Bethesda, MD: Genetech (Human Growth Foundation).

Rogers, V., & Stevenson, C. (1988, February). How do we know what kids are learning in school? *Educational Leadership, 45*(5), 68–75.

Scales, Peter C. (1991). *A portrait of young adolescents in the 1990s.* Carrboro, N.C.: Center for Early Adolescence.

Simmons, R. G., & Blyth, D. A. (1987). *Moving into adolescence: The impact of pubertal change and school context.* New York: Aldine DeGruyter.

Smart, M. S., & Smart, R. C. (1973). *Adolescents: Development and relationships.* New York: Macmillan.

Smolak, L., Levine, M. P., & Gralen, S. (1993). The impact of puberty and dating on eating problems among middle school girls. *Journal of Youth and Adolescence, 22*(4), 355–368.

Steinberg, L. (1981). Transformations in family relations at puberty. *Developmental Psychology, 17*(6), 833–840.

Steinberg, L. (1990). Autonomy, conflict and harmony in the family relationship. In S. S. Feldmann & G. R. El-liott (Eds.), *At the threshold: The developing adolescent.* Cambridge, MA: Harvard University Press.

Steinberg, L., & Silverberg, S. (1986). The vicissitudes of autonomy in early adolescence. *Child Development, 57,* 841–851.

Strauss, M., Gelles, R., & Steinmetz, S. (1980). *Behind closed doors: Violence in the American family.* New York: Anchor Doubleday.

Takanishi, R. (Spring 1993). Changing views of adolescence in contemporary society. *Teachers College Record, 94*(3).

Toepfer, C. (1984). Speech at the Annual Conference of the National Middle School Association, Columbus, Ohio.

Van Hoose, J., & Strahan, D. (1988). *Young adolescent development and school practices: Promoting harmony.* Columbus, OH: National Middle School Association.

Weldon, G. (1989, December 6). Children need fitness education. *Education Week, 9*(14), 23.

Wheelock, A., & Dorman, G. (1988). *Before it's too late: Dropout prevention in the middle grades.* Boston: Massachusetts Advocacy Center.

Wunderlich, R. C., & Kalita, D. K. (1984). *Nourishing your child: A bioecologic approach.* New Canaan, CT: Keats.

PART TWO

About Responsive Teaching

INTRODUCTION TO PART TWO

A persistent, controversial question that never fails to elicit strong opinions runs through the movement to reform middle level education: *What should be the middle level curriculum?* Through the years of middle level reform as described in Chapter 1, emphasis was understandably focused first on how schools should be organized in order to become more responsive to young adolescents' needs. During those same years an unprecedented expansion of knowledge and technology made the curriculum question particularly difficult to resolve in the terms historically used to define *curriculum*. James Beane suggests that "the curriculum question has been the 'absent presence' in the middle school movement" (1990, p. 1).

Learned professional organizations promote curriculum designs that tend to emphasize content, concepts, and skills within their particular disciplines. In general, these designs reflect concern about establishing an academic foundation that will support future learnings in that discipline in the even more strictly content-focused high school curricula. Sanctioned state, district, and school curriculum guides tend to reflect the idiosyncratic subsets of those expansive scope and sequence organizational schemes proffered by professional associations. From time to time there is discussion about the propriety of a national curriculum that would presume to guide all teachers and students across the country. A national thrust in the 1990s appears to be directed toward defining what students should know and be able to do across the disciplines (O'Neil, 1990). In the final analysis, textbooks have probably had more say in responding to the question than any other single influence. To add to the complexity of this crucial question, every teacher and parent associated with young adolescents seems to have his or her own biases about what these youngsters should be taught. It is probably impossible to formulate educational answers to the curriculum question that are free of political or commercial influences, or both.

I am not different from anyone else in terms of personal biases about what should constitute middle level curricula. My years of experience with young adolescents have taught me that there are many, many more appropriate and viable curriculum possibilities than we have the necessary time and opportunity to present. In fact, the phenomenal expansion of knowledge in my lifetime leaves me awestruck by the challenge of identifying curricular priorities for all students, deciding what must be included and what must be left out.

In attempting to conceptualize this task, I have searched for a metaphor. As a beginning teacher I was admonished that the "tabula rasa" notion of a child's mind was refuted by research. Children did not enter school as so-called blank slates on which could be written society's agreed-upon knowledge. Yet, the behavioristic orientation toward teaching and learning that predominated in my own teacher preparation implied an established body of knowledge that children should progressively master according to a quasi-training process as they move through their twelve years of schooling. In fact, "training" became the working metaphor for that orientation toward schooling, and I am troubled today as I see how insistently so many teachers pursue such poor versions of that approach: lecture or demonstration followed by recitation followed by corrective instruction followed by testing, this cycle repeating endlessly in mindless repetition whether or not children are becoming more fully informed, competent, and empowered as learners.

The Introduction to Part One includes a letter to readers that points out the parallels between teaching well and sailing well. In keeping with that theme, I suggest that questions about what we teach, how we teach, what children learn, how they learn it, and what they believe about themselves as learners can be both understood and addressed by thinking of curriculum in terms of another metaphor: an estuary.

A healthy estuary is one of the richest ecosystems on our planet. Consider a portion of William Warner's characterization of an estuary from his vivid book about the Chesapeake Bay (1976, pp. 4–5):

> To qualify as an estuary, a body of water must be well-enclosed, provide easy entry and exit for open sea water and enjoy a vigorous infusion of fresh water from one or more rivers. . . . A good estuary with high biological productivity requires other things. Shallow water, for one, which the sun can penetrate to nourish body plankton and rooted aquatic plants. Extensive marshland is another.

So it is with the mix of curriculum that makes sense for young adolescent learners. Like the estuary, the middle level curriculum must be well enclosed: it must be limited to a vigorous infusion between the vast seas of human knowledge and the fresh waters of children's experience that flow as countless tributaries. Those fresh waters are agitated with individual children's ideas, curiosities, imagination, predispositions, and bewilderments, and their validity derives from the simple fact that they are the organic mental rhythms of all human beings. The middle level curriculum must be protected from a well-intentioned but nevertheless misplaced invasion of academic pressures to cover more curriculum earlier and faster that so often derives from some parents' assumptions about what constitutes preparation for high school.

An abundance of shallows is likewise absolutely essential in the middle level curriculum. Shallows are the myriad interests that children bring with them and that they encounter, which, although they are legitimate knowledge, are not ordinarily included in school curricula. For example, our son's interest in the Punic Wars and another son's preoccupation with motorcycles would not be likely inclusions in any prescribed middle level curriculum. Yet, in both cases the opportunity and encouragement by teachers were sufficient to help them grow and mature as learners, both at the moment and in their own time. It is such "shallows" that enable individual learnings to take life and become nourished through the warmth of affirmation and encouragement from adults and peers. These learnings are also the often impressionistic understandings that feed youngsters' subsequent exploration of more formal and traditionally respected academic knowledge.

A good mix of salt and fresh water is vital to estuarian life, just as a proportional mix of prescribed content balanced by individual interests is fundamental to a dynamic middle level school curriculum. Both horizontal and vertical circulation are necessary to maintain estuarian health. That omnidirectional characteristic has direct implications for our curriculum decisions, and we must be attentive and perceptive to maintain a good mix between studies prescribed by teachers and interests rising from individual students' experiences.

Horizontal circulation occurs in an estuary when "heavier salt water . . . slides under the lighter and fresher surface water" (Warner, 1976, p. 5). So it is with a good curricular mix. We learn about our students' interests by listening to them and using the shadowing and inquiry strategies already described. We subsequently challenge them with unique opportunities to explore those interests in ways that draw on existing academic knowledge. We also create and introduce new studies such as those described in the chapters that compose this section of the book. And through it all we take soundings and study samples in order to understand how well learning is being accomplished.

Vertical mixing occurs differently in an estuary. A deep channel runs the length of the estuary, usually in a north–south orientation, and at the bottom of the channel are accumulations of silt and sedimentation. Significant contrasts in depth between the channel and the shallows are necessary to achieve optimal mix. The long channel axis also encourages horizontal circulation, in effect creating two-layered gyrations in which the infusion of fresh water is constant and vigorous. Again, so it is with curriculum. The deep channel, with its rich sedimentation, represents the certain evidence of necessary academic and cultural literacy and wisdom that form civilization's central core of knowledge. It is important to bear in mind that the channel is also a *two-way* conduit in which silt is stirred and moved by the tides or currents of new insights and advances.

So how does the estuary metaphor help us answer the middle level curriculum question? First, I cannot conceive of being able to be a responsive teacher without having the authority to make many decisions about what students might learn. Likewise, I cannot imagine controlling or limiting students' choices to my purely external agenda. We must recognize and never forget that even when one teaches every student in a class exactly the same material, an individual student's learning will be idiosyncratic—a phenomenological truth we would do well to acknowledge and attempt to understand better. Therefore, we must constantly seek balanced circulation between the shallows and the channel. We must recognize that it is natural to adolescent learners to have a host of shifting interests, to be eager to explore, to seek and desire personal empowerment as a chooser and learner, and to aspire to success and the human dignity that attends expertise. We must also see to it that in the processes the connections between exploring interests and excellence in scholarship are maintained. And finally, we must be vigilant to stand back far enough and often enough to remain certain that we are supporting the natural processes of human learning and development. Perhaps our response to "what should be the middle level curriculum" lies in *how* it should be (Stevenson, 1991).

REFERENCES

Beane, J. A. (1990). *A middle school curriculum: From rhetoric to reality*. Columbus, OH: National Middle School Association.

O'Neil, J. (1990, September). New curriculum agenda emerges for 90s. *Curriculum update*. Alexandria, VA: Association for Supervision and Curriculum Development, p. 6.

Stevenson, C. (1991). You've gotta see the game to see the game. *Middle School Journal, 23*(2), 13–17.

Warner, W. W. (1976). *Beautiful swimmers: Watermen, crabs, and the Chesapeake Bay*. New York; Penguin.

Chapter 5

Developmentally Responsive Pedagogy

○ *What do young adolescents engaged in authentic learning look like?*

○ *How can teaching be responsive to their nature and needs?*

○ *What is the student's disposition toward future learning?*

"You've gotta see the game to see the game."

The venerable baseball player and manager Casey Stengel is reported to have told people who found baseball slow and boring "to look at the game in the game." He was referring, of course, to the individual skills, initiatives, and especially communications that will likely escape the notice of a novice observer of baseball. Casey's advice is equally apt for those who try to comprehend young adolescents' learning both within and outside of schools. Middle level teachers learn to pay close attention to the ways their students approach and find personal success in learning tasks. We've learned for sure that *authentically engaged* youngsters demonstrate personal initiative and a spirit of collaboration, imagination, resourcefulness, and accountability. In short, they exude a growing maturity and self-reliance as learners and as adolescent citizens.

In its profound and far-reaching proposals for restructuring middle level education, the Carnegie Task Force on Adolescent Development reminds us that our overarching goals must focus on the multifaceted development of students toward their becoming "effective human beings" (1989, pp. 15–16). During early adolescence, students should develop as

> *intellectually reflective* . . . able to analyze problems and issues, examine the component parts, and re-integrate them into a new way of stating the problem or issue . . . able to appreciate and absorb the perspectives of culture . . . different from his or her own.
>
> *understand[ing] work as both the means of economic survival and an important source of one's identity* . . . pursu[ing] course[s] of study and develop[ing] cognitively in a manner that maintains all career options.
>
> *demonstrating good citizenship* by helping to determine the nature and character of his or her own school community . . . understanding basic values . . . principles of

democracy . . . global citizenship . . . feel[ing] personal responsibility for and connection to the well-being of an interdependent world community.

act[ing] ethically . . . exhibit[ing] courage . . . recogniz[ing] . . . good and bad and that it is possible and important to tell the difference . . . developing and maintaining close relationships with certain other[s] . . . including friends and family.

physically and mentally fit . . . hav[ing] a self-image of competence and strength . . . based on the fact that the youth will be at least very good at something, because success is critical to a positive self-image.

This We Believe: Developmentally Responsive Middle Level Schools, the educational policy position of the National Middle School Association, further reminds us that in order for students to grow in these highly valued ways, their schooling "must be grounded in the diverse characteristics and needs of these young people" (National Middle School Association, 1995, p. 5). This benchmark document goes on to spell out explicit recommendations that middle level schools should provide (National Middle School Association, 1995, p. 11).

- Curriculum that is challenging, integrative, and exploratory
- Varied teaching and learning approaches
- Assessment and evaluation that promote learning
- Flexible organizational structures
- Programs and policies that foster health, wellness, and safety
- Comprehensive guidance and support services

This emphasis on development reminds us that our task as teachers persists through the several years of early adolescence, and we must consciously strive for continuity and coherence. Such commitment to development has long been a "foundational concept of the middle level education movement" that observes "mounting evidence and . . . traditions built on those data to provide responsive effective education for young adolescents" (National Association of Secondary School Principals, 1989). As described in the previous chapter, the several dimensions of ten- to fourteen-year-old development are highly individualistic and variable from one youngster to another. Yet, the Carnegie goal statement closes by sanctioning these goals "for *every* youth of the nation, not just for those [who are more advantaged than others]. Our 15-year-old is a thinking, productive, caring and healthy person who takes seriously the responsibility of good citizenship" (1989, p. 17).

This is, quite evidently, no small task. Teaching these students requires that we think about our work in terms of what brings out the best in every youngster. A prerequisite is our belief that all children are capable of achieving these goals, and our considerable task is to create circumstances in which the human qualities upon which these goals are based can come to fruition. Our efforts to create developmentally responsive pedagogy must be guided by commitment to ensure flexibility in curriculum design and selected methodologies for teaching and learning that will accommodate individual differences, yet sustain these goals for all youth throughout these years of schooling.

PREDICTABILITY WITH UNCERTAINTY

Regardless of external pressures on teachers to teach particular skills or to cover specific content, we must be continuously mindful of the urgent necessity of ensuring that expectations and activities are compatible with our students' developmental readiness. Nothing of any lasting value is gained when teachers require students to cover material simply to give it back correctly and in the same form on tests or as homework. Furthermore, everything is risked if not lost when teaching is beyond the comprehension of students—when they are confused, frustrated, or even alienated from learning. So-called knowledge acquired under such duress has dubious value. It tends to be superficial and transient. Expectations that don't correspond with student readiness and consequently carry a significant possibility of failure have no place in middle level education. Developmentally responsive pedagogy refers to educational experiences teachers plan and implement that are based on what students are able to do and through which they will learn. Externally defined curricula are not ignored; rather, they are assessed for their inherent propriety for a known student or group of students. In order for teachers to choose wisely and plan appropriately, then, they must know their students and must position themselves so as to continually learn more about them.

The previous chapter's overview of early adolescent development persistently reminds us of the considerable variability between and among individual children. Although we generally know what kinds of changes will occur, we cannot predict either when they will occur or how intensely they will affect individuals. Flexibility and adaptability become important characteristics of curriculum, and singular options are needed to accommodate individual learners. This chapter identifies values and a variety of learning strategies for young adolescents appropriate to all curricular studies.

FORMING PARTNERSHIPS

During the summer before his first year as principal, Dennis Littky met privately with every teacher and student (Kammeraad-Campbell, 1989). The school had been a disaster for years, and Littky recognized that alone he could not change things very much. He initiated these meetings because he wanted to understand as well as possible people's interests, attitudes, and priorities. He also knew that from these conferences most people could see what they could do to bring about needed change. He was correct, of course. Partnerships emerged that affected almost everything about the school, from how courses were planned to the physical appearance of the building. The potential for forming educational partnerships with early adolescent students is, in my judgment, one of the most compelling reasons for working with them. These youngsters are beginning to test the waters of independence in new ways. In the earlier elementary grades it was necessary for teachers to have most of the responsibility for a child's learning. Although primary children are challenging and enjoyable to teach, they have not yet experienced enough of the world and grown to a point where they can fully comprehend their options and make well-informed choices. Besides, these children are more geared to doing what they are told to do. Thoughtful second-guessing about the teacher's judgment hasn't yet become as common and appropriate as it will in adolescence.

It is fitting that early adolescence be seen as an opportunity for weaning from the more complete dependence on adults of the younger ages. Given that our goal for early adolescent students is for them to achieve a personal and scholarly self-sufficiency, as envisioned in the Carnegie Task Force recommendations cited earlier, it is these very years when we must gradually but deliberately help them become more responsible for themselves and their own learning. This is obviously not a sudden or abrupt process. It is a gradual transfer of responsibility that is accomplished over the several years spent in middle level schools. But it must begin by age ten and expand gradually as individuals are able to handle it well.

Keeping up with the developmental readiness of every student we encounter is an exceptionally challenging task. To succeed requires provisions by which students become responsible for keeping their teachers informed about themselves and what they are doing. In accepting such partnerships and this accompanying responsibility, students learn how to set personal goals, keep records, and evaluate their progress. They learn how to plan a project, document their work, and critique it according to appropriate criteria. They further learn the value of initiative, the importance of details, and the urgency of efficient use of time and resources. Being known as a worker, a producer, an expert on something is becoming *somebody*—achieving identity definition. By accepting a share of these responsibilities and creating a coherent record of their work, teachers can in turn recognize students' developmental advances. Specific strategies for this kind of partnership are detailed in Chapter 8.

Finally, authentic learning must ultimately be led and sustained by the learner. The teacher's role is vital, to be sure. The teacher can explain an equation or dissect a complex sentence or demonstrate batik, but without the learner's acceptance and compliance in a partnership, the teacher's best efforts will be superfluous. Learning occurs only when learners accept and reciprocate the partnership. Furthermore, this essential partnership flourishes only in a context of mutual trust. Mutual respect and trust is the basis of all effective learning (Smith, 1986).

PITCHING FOR SUCCESS

A popular aphorism of the middle level education movement is "pitch it where they can hit it." (I first heard this expression from Conrad Toepfer at the annual conference of the National Middle School Association in November 1985.) This particular saying merits more serious consideration than is usually afforded such clichés, for its meaning is fundamental and essential: Middle level educators must do everything possible to enhance the probability that every student will be successful.

Our students' cultural heritage traditionally recognizes athletic accomplishment and, to a lesser extent, outstanding scholarship. Young adolescents grow up aware that rewards and recognition come to professional sports stars, but they also learn that schools similarly emphasize winning as evidence that some students are better than others—a "survival of the fittest" ethic. In a responsive middle school, however, teachers understand how extremely important it is for *every* student to taste success and experience the personal affirmation that recognition from classmates and teachers brings. In such schools, personal achievements are celebrated not because an individual or team overcame the opposition but because achievement is worthy in itself. Opponents of this point of view are quick to argue that such recognition waters down the status of competition-based recognition. That is a welcome thought, for this is a time of life when recognition should call attention to the progress youngsters make measured against themselves. Such recognition ensures an optimism that sustains initiative and continued self-development.

In order for all students to experience successes that matter to them, schoolwork must accommodate individual differences of talent and development. Students are developmentally unequal. Some of them have remarkable intellectual, artistic, or physical abilities. All of them have potential for developing themselves in ways that are useful to themselves and others. Therefore, educators must ensure that for substantial portions of their school lives, students will be able to seek their successes along a variety of paths. Teachers' expectations must reflect an understanding of individual differences. Some portions of curriculum content must accommodate individual choices and abilities. Ways of presenting curriculum must complement the vicissitudes in youngsters' individual talents or dispositions for developing knowledge.

By these directives I am not suggesting that teachers abandon whole group instruction of common material. What I am arguing for is an educational program that provides a deliberate balance between the contrasting approaches of whole group instruction and accommodating individual differences. There is certainly a place for whole class instruction, but there is an equally vital place for study and learning based on youngsters' much more individualized interests and choices, as long as the learning activities are responsive to learners' developmental needs and circumstances.

A TRADITION OF UNRESPONSIVE PEDAGOGY

Please wake me up when the lecture is over.

I picked up this note off the floor after a social studies class I had visited in a traditional junior high school. It could have been written to me (or by me) except that I would not have exalted the teacher's rambling monologue by calling it a lecture. The students and I had just sat through forty minutes of hearing secondhand, often incorrect information about Japan taken from an out-of-date textbook. In the entire period, students had raised just two questions about the content—a certain sign of disinterest. But they did have eleven questions about the homework assignment and potential items on the test they would have in two days. Any further description of the mindlessness of that classroom is unnecessary, for we are all able to recognize mismatches between learners and a performance so tedious that it doesn't deserve being referred to as pedagogy.

From my experience as a middle grades teacher and my study of middle grades schooling that by all apparent measures works for students, a framework of pedagogical designs has emerged. This structure organizes a variety of experiences that are demonstrably responsive to the transitional nature of early adolescent learners as described in the previous chapters. I have grouped these designs under five headings, each of which should be incorporated in instructional designs.

RESPONSIVE DESIGNS I: FRAMEWORKS FOR CONSTRUCTIVE SOCIAL INTERACTIONS

And a youth said, "Speak to us of friendship." And he answered, saying: "Your friend is your needs answered." (Gibran, 1961)

The early adolescent quest for self-definition is variously but decidedly influenced by the quality of interactions and affiliations that youngsters experience beyond the primary family unit. Day-to-day exchanges generate data for every person about how others perceive and respond to them. Affirmations from other people, especially classmates and teachers, affect the young adolescent's self-concept and self-esteem (Beane & Lipka, 1980). Schooling that is responsive to these needs creates a variety of ways for youngsters to establish and maintain ongoing social connectedness with other students and at least one teacher. Such schools also provide numerous ways for students to gain recognition and status with peers. Meeting these personal human needs must be a primary goal of middle level schooling.

The importance of providing "small communities . . . stable, close, mutually supportive relationships with adults and peers" is also recognized by its inclusion in the previously cited recommendation of the Carnegie Task Force (1989). The comfortable sense of belonging implied here can be achieved through skillful application of selected grouping practices. Exemplary schools provide a host of organizational configurations designed to promote positive, supportive interpersonal relationships between classmates and partnerships with adults. Four distinct arrangements commonly used in middle level schools are briefly described here and elaborated in later chapters.

Interdisciplinary Team Organization

Interdisciplinary team organization (ITO) is a central organizational design for middle level schools. In order to create smaller communities for learning, a group of students and teachers who spend most of their school time together constitute a team. Teams are therefore subsets of the total school, and a school is usually composed of several teams. Four or five core teachers teach only the 100 to 125 students on the team, and they take primary responsibility for students' academic and social welfare. Considerable emphasis is placed on one's belonging to a team, and the best of teams reciprocate the belonging and healthy interdependence of an extended family. ITO is widely employed to organize middle level schools. Research reports and accounts of exemplary practice provide explicit recommendations about its use (Erb & Doda, 1989; George & Stevenson, 1989; Arnold & Stevenson, (in press).

A derivative of ITO that shows particular promise in terms of curriculum integration, learner-centered pedagogy, and partnerships between students and adults is being referred to as "partner teaming" (Stevenson, 1996). These teams are smaller than ITOs, and usually comprise 40 to 70 students and two or three teachers who are responsible for all or most of the core curriculum. Although most teams appear to be composed of students from only one grade level, increasing numbers include students from two or three grade levels. Given youngsters' wide developmental differences during these years, multiage grouping can not only ease grade level rivalries but ensure that students and teachers will work together for more than a single year, thereby having the opportunity to reap the potential benefits of longer-term relationships (George, Spreul, & Moorefield, 1986). Their overarching emphasis is on matching curriculum and pedagogy to students in a context that ensures safety, mutual support, and success (see Chapter 9).

There are several essential distinctions between teaming and the more familiar departmental organization found in traditional junior high schools, where teacher assignments are based on subject matter specialties. It is the team—the community of students and teachers—that is the dominant association for all of its members. Although teachers often maintain primary responsibility for particular subject matters, that orientation is balanced by a primary responsibility to the members of the team. In other words, a teacher who is specially prepared in science education will draw from that curricular expertise, but she shares responsibility for attending to the other academic needs of students on the team, Furthermore, she shares equally with teammates responsibility for all of the other personal and social needs that can be addressed through team organization.

Teams are known by many of the same images that are associated with athletic teams. The team identity with which its members can identify themselves is symbolized in a name, colors, mascot, logo, motto, pledge, causes the team serves, rituals, traditions, and sometimes distinctive curricular themes or interests. Team members often advertise their membership on the team with T-shirts, pins, buttons, pencils, book covers, and other paraphernalia that reflect the team colors, logo, and other identifying characteristics.

In the standards and values a team cultivates, it achieves educational goals beyond merely satisfying youngsters' need to belong. Consider AWESOME, for example, one of four middle grades teams in a K–8 school. This particular team is composed of three core teachers, a part-time member (a special educator), and 65 sixth and seventh grade students. Two of the teachers have secondary certification (math and social studies), and the remaining member is elementary certified. They have worked on strategies for attending to all of the required curriculum, and through their creation of several original interdisciplinary units they have succeeded in providing a very rich academic program. Nick, the math teacher, oversees the math curriculum, but all of them teach mathematics just as they all teach reading, writing, and the rest of the curriculum.

AWESOME's values and standards are derived from its name:

A = Academics	"We learn academics."
W = Work	"We are workers."
E = Effort	"We give our best effort."
S = Service	"We protect endangered wildlife."
O = Options	"We have Optional Orbitals (O2s)."
M = Mediation	"We mediate our problems."
E = Excellence	"AWESOME is Excellence."

These slogans are posted throughout the team's rooms in one wing of the school, and they are printed in white on green book covers that also show the team name and school. The seven explicitly stated values constitute the agenda for goal setting and discussions in team meetings. They are also goals by which the team can be appropriately evaluated.

When the team was originally formed, the teachers chose a team identity around some values they shared. They were optimistic that students would support activities yet to be created around these values. In addition to the core academic program, the team supports efforts to protect wildlife and the environment. In one year, for example, they acted on these values by writing articles for the school newsletter and local paper, making buttons and selling them in order to contribute the proceeds to national fundraising efforts, writing to elected representatives to lobby against the use of leg traps, and planning an animal conservation fair at school. To the fair they invited hunters and sport fishermen, conservation activists, a natural resource specialist who worked for their state government, a local furrier, and environmental science students from a nearby college. Students from other teams joined AWESOME members at the fair to hear presentations by the guests and to participate in an open forum discussion about ways to conserve wildlife.

Another program dimension that AWESOME teachers wanted to include was the opportunity to learn about things individuals wanted to know more about. Their goal was to encourage and support independent learning. Their charge to students was "Become an expert." The program was called "Optional Orbitals," or "O2s" for short. "Optional" referred to the fact that students chose their topics. "Orbital" referred to the concept that in doing these studies one was "in one's own orbit." O2s often grew out of the core curriculum (the launch), and upon completion they were always presented to the students' teammates (the touchdown). In the meantime, students worked on the orbit while they were also carrying out their core work. It was also common that one student's O2 would spark the interest of other students, and if they requested permission to collaborate, permission was usually granted. Some examples of O2s under way on one visit I made to the team were Disasters at Sea, Tie-Dyeing, Vermont Wildlife, New Kids on the Block (a popular musical group at the time), Contract Bridge, Farley Mowat: the Writer, the San Francisco 49ers, Jobs for Teenagers, and Fort Ticonderoga.

In order to inculcate specific problem solving skills and an attitude and atmosphere of fair-mindedness among their students, the AWESOME teachers elected to teach student mediation as a strategy for resolving interpersonal conflicts. Students who wanted to become mediators took part in a training program taught by one of the teachers who had studied mediation. Through this training course, students learned how to structure a mediation session, enforce order, listen to and reflect all points of view on the conflict, and lead the principals to devise a resolution. Once these mediators had been trained, complainants worked with two student mediators to work out their difficulties.

These three distinctive curricular features ensure that AWESOME is clearly defined to team members. Through these activities, the rest of the school also learns what it stands for. Teaming provides a context within which these teachers and students can forge interpersonal bonds based on shared beliefs and activities that meet the youngsters' need to belong to something good and worth while. Meanwhile, they are also steadily becoming the "thinking, productive, caring, healthy" people the Carnegie report exhorts teachers to encourage.

Teacher–Student Advisory Programs

Where responsive middle schools don't exist, the transition from elementary to secondary school is often marked by an abrupt and premature shift from a self-contained classroom with a single teacher to a multiperiod schedule in which students work with different teachers every forty or so minutes. This leap from such a nurturing context to the impersonality of constantly changing teachers and classmates thwarts the development of longer, meaningful daily exchanges with a small group of classmates and the dependability of a single adult advocate. For many children, especially those who need the security of knowing they belong to one small group, the shift is socially problematic.

Exemplary middle level schooling usually incorporates such teacher–mentor relationships. While they may be called by various names (AA, TA, home base), they are most commonly referred to simply as advisories. Procedures for planning and implementing advisory programs in middle level schools are grounded in an enduring orientation toward affective education (James, 1986). Ideally, all members of the school staff serve as advisors to groups of approximately ten to fifteen students. Groups are balanced between the sexes and between grades where multiage groupings are used. Occasionally, guidance personnel are exempted from responsibility for an advisory group, since they oversee the entire program.

The overarching purpose of the advisory is to ensure that every student belongs to a small peer group attended by an adult mentor. According to some reports, the typical advisory ratio is one teacher for every fifteen to twenty-five students (Erb & Doda, 1989). However, since an advisor is not expected to provide such specialized professional services as those of a guidance counselor or school psychologist, it is possible for all interested and available adults on the school staff to serve as mentors and advocates for a small group of students. This expanded number of advisors makes smaller advisor–advisee ratios possible. Sometimes schools also use noninstructional staff members, including the custodial staff, school nurse, and dietitian. Advisors usually become oriented to this work through readings, in-service sessions, and staff meetings. When students need specialized support or help beyond the qualifications of an advisor, they are referred to trained guidance personnel.

Typically, students begin their school days by reporting to their advisories for a fifteen- to twenty-five-minute period. Traditional home room functions such as attendance, lunch counts, announcements, permission slips, and so on are taken care of, but after those housekeeping details there is time for informal conversation about anything of interest to the members. Since these sessions occur every day, students and the advisor become better acquainted than is possible without the advisory. The adult advisor works to establish a mutually supporting group dynamic so that the advisees feel assured of belonging to and with their advisory.

Building on this foundation of daily meetings, advisories often create further get-togethers: having lunch together on a designated day, sitting together at special school events, taking responsibility for a bulletin board, sponsoring an activity such as a spelling bee, or carrying out a service project. Often advisories get together for special reasons outside of school—having a cookout, going to a movie, taking a hike or an overnight camping trip, or participating together in a special community event like Arbor Day or First Night or the town's birthday celebration. Throughout these assorted advisory activities, the goal is to foster growing bonds of interdependence and trust, ensuring that no student is left out of having an adult mentor and belonging to a family-like band of peers.

Another potential-laden feature of advisories is the opportunity to establish good home–school communication that can "reengage families in the education of young adolescents" (Carnegie Corporation, 1989). Advisors serve as mentors, so they do whatever is necessary and appropriate to help each of their advisees be successful. Consequently, they keep up with their advisees, continually checking with them in order to know their circumstances at school. Advisors sometimes function as go-betweens with fellow teachers when advisees are having academic difficulties. Since the advisors are the adults at school who know students best, it is they who can provide the vital home–school communication link. It is the advisors who conduct parent conferences, distribute report cards, and serve as the parents' initial link to the school. In a departmentalized setting where teachers often see a hundred or more different students a day, it is impossible for any teacher to establish working relationships with many parents. The advisory format assures that every family has an adult link to the school and to someone who is helping their child achieve success.

The purpose of these descriptions of teaming and advisories has been to orient the reader to these two distinctively middle school organizational features that are clearly responsive to young adolescents' needs. Additional guidance is contained in Chapters 9 and 10.

Cooperative Learning Groups

Pedagogy that reorganizes a large group of students into smaller units in order to solve problems, produce a group product, or carry out other specific activities has long been common in middle level classrooms. However, simple regrouping of students as a way to vary instruction doesn't guarantee cooperation. Inducing a cooperative learning climate that is responsive to the needs of young adolescents requires the same quality of careful planning and gradual introduction that are necessary for students to learn any new group process. Cooperative skills are acquired over time under the patient coaching and guidance of teachers who develop expert skills themselves. Furthermore, it is important to remember that cooperative activities supplement, but don't replace, other approaches to instruction (Slavin, 1990a).

Cooperative learning groups that function well enable all students to contribute interdependently to accomplish common goals, regardless of the particular talents and backgrounds of the individual members. In achieving common goals, they also fulfill individual academic and social needs. Each individual's achievement helps his or her associates succeed as well. Rather than "operate" individually, students "cooperate"—that is, they operate together for their mutual benefit. They "generate energy that results in improved learning, [and the shared responsibility and interaction produce more positive feelings toward tasks and] other students, generate better intergroup relations, and result in better self-images for students with histories of poor achievement" (Joyce & Weil, 1986, p. 216). The literature describing cooperative grouping techniques that can be effectively implemented at the middle level is extensive (Johnson, Johnson, & Holubec, 1986; Kagan, 1989; Sharan & Shachar, 1988; Slavin, 1986).

In materials that describe cooperative learning and in this book's treatment of the subject, references to teams and teaming are frequent. The reader is cautioned to remember that teaming in relation to cooperative learning groups should not be confused with teaming as it applies to interdisciplinary teams. Cooperative groups are small, usually containing two to six members, and their composition may change at weekly intervals, unlike the larger, more permanent interdisciplinary team.

The following discussion of cooperative grouping is focused on aspects of the technique that are particularly responsive to the need for constructive social interactions characteristic of early adolescent development. Details about organizing groups, teaching students how to function cooperatively, and guidelines for monitoring groups are treated in greater detail in Chapter 7.

Self-Esteem

There is wide consensus that effective use of cooperative learning "can and usually [does] have a positive effect on student achievement" (Slavin, 1990b). Thus, as youngsters are successful as learners, their estimation of themselves as students becomes more positive, engendering further academic efforts. As self-esteem increases, new efforts are launched and a spiral of growing competence and self-confidence emerges. Increased time on tasks also becomes evident (Slavin, 1986). Being a part of a group that not only is academically productive but also enhances social development constitutes the very best of circumstances for building individual self-esteem. Liking one's group mates while at the same time being liked by them is a reciprocity that benefits each member's identity formation. Youngsters in effective cooperative groups grow in terms of hope and healthy optimism, a positive view of themselves, and a sense of control over their destinies.

Heterogeneous Membership

Cooperative groups emphasize interdependence among students whose talents, abilities, and performance levels differ from one another. In groups composed of such a mixture of characteristics, each member is afforded opportunities to make original contributions in a way that recognizes individuality. Onerous grouping practices such as tracking, by which students are grouped according to test scores or other so-called ability measures, are antithetical to the philosophy and values associated with cooperation. In the spirit of mainstreaming, where students with particular learning difficulties work in a regular classroom, cooperative grouping techniques can be employed to convey acceptance of all students, regardless of their differences, depending on the nature of the task.

Belonging

Closely related to one's need for academic success is the need to believe that one is a full member of a group in which that membership is valued. In order for a cooperative group to be successful, its members must be successful first. Successes establish connections through which each student has a valued place in the group. Out of those successes grows a spirit of belonging and camaraderie. Sometimes a group will take a name such as "People Powers" or "Superkids" so that members can enjoy a collective identity. It is also not only possible but desirable to use cooperative groups in mainstreaming, whereby students who often have even more intense needs for peer approval are able to belong to and contribute to a collective effort.

Defined Roles and Responsibilities

Cooperative grouping strategies require clear roles and functions for group members. In some cases roles are expressly defined, and they may be rotated among members from time to time. This kind of clarity with regard to functions, combined with the obvious necessity of teamwork to achieve the group goal, assures that every participant understands what is going on, where he or she stands in relation to the goal, and what is needed to help the group succeed. When improvement is needed, the remedies are usually clear, and either student or teacher intervention can get them back on track. Members are able to know where they stand in their group process. Thus, they are able to work together while at the same time enjoying each other, learning and appreciating their differences, and developing deeper friendships as well as making new ones.

Even though several groups may be created and instructed in the rules and procedures of one type of cooperative grouping at the same time, how well they will actually function remains to be seen. Since the idiosyncrasies of group members and therefore the combination of personalities will be unique, results will not be identical. Certainly, some groups will struggle, have arguments about who is supposed to do what and how it is to be done, and so on. This development is to be welcomed, because the cooperative procedures described in Chapter 7 provide the solutions. Roles and functions are explicit; with patient, careful coaching, students in conflict learn how to work out differences. With experience they learn how to listen, reflect, reach consensus, and ultimately achieve their goals. It is essential from the beginning that teachers understand such interpersonal conflict as an opportunity, not as a failure.

Reward and Recognition

"We're done! We did it! I'm successful!" Group accomplishment assures individual attainment. Is there any imaginable outcome of middle level schooling that is more valuable to healthy personal development than a student's belief in himself or herself because of real successes accomplished by working harmoniously with a few classmates? Cooperative group accountability depends on each member's individual participation, contributions, and learning. Individuality and each member's improvement are valued and rewarded both within the group and by the success of the whole group. Rewards and recognition are shared because they are dependent on each person's contribution. True excellence in teamwork brings out the best in each individual, leading to the accomplishment of goals that sometimes seems to be greater than merely the sum of the individual parts.

I cannot overstate the value of a learning climate in which students are recognized for both their individual achievement and their collective accomplishments. When students not only have ample opportunity to work with each other but also are sensitively coached by expert teachers, the possibility that school will be perceived as a positive place grows by a large measure. Interpersonal relationships in general are improved. The best of both kinds of success are possible in middle level schools, and the ultimate goal of a cooperative community of students and teachers is certainly worth the sustained effort necessary. Students report that they like school and the subjects being studied more when they work in effective cooperative groups, and their daily school attendance also improves (Slavin, 1990b). Cooperative grouping arrangements hold enormous promise for educators who are trying to be directly responsive to early adolescent needs for identity-enhancing academic and social interpersonal relationships.

Service Projects

Young adolescents working together to do something that directly benefits others are able to see themselves in a new and developmentally valuable light. Their work is evidence of a growing capacity for taking on responsibility in more adult terms. Doing chores at home such as washing dishes or taking out the trash are useful and appropriate. But the concept of service described here is a totally different dimension to youngsters whose consciousness of an interdependent society is expanding and becoming more idealistic. When students begin to recognize conditions of need, imagine ways they can help, and agree to collaborate in exercising initiative, planning, and organizing, their individual identities grow healthily.

Ordinarily, students who participate in service projects do so through scouting or church groups. Sometimes community civic organizations sponsor projects that recruit adolescent help, such as Arbor Day or a community clean-up day. At best, however, only a few students have these experiences, and those who do generally do so because of their family values and involvements. Exemplary middle schools have recognized, however, the propriety of firsthand experiences in doing service for all students as a way to support identity formation needs and also to further the social and ethical climate at school. Community service projects are integral expressions of the school's philosophy at many outstanding middle schools such as Shoreham-Wading River Middle School in New York (Lipsitz, 1984, pp. 129–163) and Kennebunk Middle School in Maine.

Examples of service projects appropriate for middle grades students and details about organizing them are also included in Chapter 11. The discussion here focuses on the ways in which such experiences can help meet youngsters' identity needs associated with social interactions involving peers, younger children, adult community members, older adolescents, and each others' parents. Effective working relationships in a community service context produce satisfactions, recognition, and respect that are central to healthy identity formation.

Approximating Adulthood

As described in the previous chapter, early adolescence brings about an awakening to some of the possibilities of adulthood. In their earlier growing-up years, our students relied exclusively on parents for their needs, and they were comfortable with the expectation that parents take care of things. As they grow in curiosity, awareness of their surrounding world, and adult limitations, however, they become more able to imagine themselves being involved in ways that will improve that world. A major theme of numerous interviews I have conducted with young adolescents is a sense of personal destiny—a combination of an emerging ethical indignation with the desire to right wrongs and to protect the vulnerable and innocent. These expressions are akin to, but not precisely the same as, the notion of "personal fable," a sense of being special and unique that persists through adult life (Elkind, 1984). I submit that this emerging desire for the ideal and the students' readiness to sacrifice for a cause is justification for our being optimistic about future generations so long as we nurture and educate children well during these years when they are new to benevolent causes.

Firsthand Experiences

Service and doing are inextricably wound. Whether the service being rendered is reading to kindergarteners or planting flowers on the village green, the experience is hands-on: something actually done. Firsthand (or hands-on) activity is original and experiential; reading or hearing about someone else's activity is secondhand. Textbooks and other prepackaged learning materials are secondhand sources, regardless of how well conceived and developmentally appropriate they may be. Learning by doing requires actions that are developmentally appropriate for young adolescents. Not only do students learn cognitive concepts and the details of planning and carrying out an endeavor, they also acquire valuable learnings about themselves, their peers, and the beneficiaries of their service from firsthand experiences that cannot be simulated through secondhand means or sources.

Reciprocal Benefits

Generally the initial motivation for doing a service for others is to give help. A clothing drive for a family whose home has burned, and an adopt-a-grandparent project in a nursing home, are examples of ways young adolescents have given of themselves to others. Adults recognize such gifts, and they usually make a point of passing along compliments and appreciation that confirm the rightness of the good deeds and the do-ers. Being appreciated thus becomes, in turn, a gift to the givers—a gift of acknowledgment and ascent into adulthood. Fidel Castro proclaimed before the United Nations that Cuba was going to solve its monumental illiteracy problem, and the call went out for volunteers willing to leave their homes to go into the countryside for a year to work in the fields with campesinos by day while teaching them to read and write at night. Half the volunteers who answered that call were young adolescents, and the extent to which that experience benefited them in terms of identity development is evidence of the reciprocity of service (Kozol, 1980).

Preserving Innocence

When very young children give, they express their love. A corruption of childhood is the message that doing things for others must always be compensated. In our eagerness to convey the free enterprise ethic of financial remuneration for work, distinctions between giving and earning become blurred. The unintended moral becomes "everything has a price tag." Another version of the same message is often implied in the ways schools reward students. A contract promises that in exchange for specified products and sacrifices, students will receive some stated benefits or recognition. Certainly this kind of correspondence has its place, but I suggest that it also breeds a mercenary attitude, as represented by the expressions "What's in it for me?" and "How much is it worth to you?" These equations are sometimes augmented by well-intentioned parents who promise dollars for grades or set individual prices on household chores. By engaging in community service projects, students can be returned to an appreciation for an earlier motivation for serving others—that helping others is an act of love, and love is good.

Fulfilling a Prophecy

It is axiomatic that children who are told that they are bad, worthless, and incompetent will behave accordingly. Because the emphasis is on what they cannot do well, they are alienated from an inner nature that is lavish with potential for good. Adolescents who drop out of school do so because grouping and instructional practices, among other schooling strategies, have emphasized their inadequacies and failures (Wheelock & Dorman, 1988). Messages of failure ensure failure. On the other hand, when the emphasis is on things all youngsters can do successfully, such as rendering meaningful service to others, the potential for salvaging one's self-image as an able, worthwhile human being is possible. The identity formation process youngsters undergo in these years needs to be profoundly affected by experiences that teach them that their individual participation matters, that their service is appreciated, and that they can further contribute to making a better humanity.

Early adolescent involvement in providing service to others is one of the more recent developments in middle level schooling. For a very long time, educators have left this dimension of education up to families, churches, and civic groups such as scouting. More recently, however, we have come to recognize that when youngsters have successful experiences through school service projects, they see themselves in a new and more positive light as students. As curriculum experiences increasingly engage the community outside school grounds, opportunities for service that are complementary to academic priorities also become increasingly possible. Examples of linking service to curriculum are included in the next chapter.

Tracking—A Destructive Design for Healthy Development

The purpose of this chapter is to examine pedagogy that is developmentally responsive to the nature and needs of young adolescent students. Ordinarily I would not include examples of pedagogy that are harmful to them. The practice of tracking or homogeneous grouping—sorting class assignments for students by so-called ability measures—is, however, so fundamentally hazardous to healthy development that it must be addressed here. This particularly pernicious practice brings vast potential for sabotaging healthy, optimistic identity formation among young adolescents whose capacities and abilities are changing. Furthermore, tracking does not produce the achievement benefits assumed to derive from its application in middle level schools (Wheelock, 1992; George, 1988; Slavin, 1987). Yet, tracking is still so widely practiced in middle level schools that it cannot be ignored. Some of the ways tracking is harmful to the social interactions of young adolescents will be mentioned briefly here, and alternatives to tracking are presented in Chapter 7.

A False Definition of Ability

As the previous chapter has already shown, young adolescents undergo substantial intellectual and dispositional changes toward academic learning during these several years of transition. To claim any definitive measure of ability at a particular age is to deny the variability of timing, intensity, individual differences among children, and the multifaceted composition of their changes. Furthermore, as our knowledge of human intelligence grows we are becoming increasingly aware of many more dimensions of human intelligence than merely the verbal-quantitative dualism presumed by conventional paper-and-pencil measures. Grouping students according to so-called ability measures is no more justified than grouping them by shoe sizes.

Covering Is Not Learning

It is true that students who read quickly can cover more pages in a fixed amount of time than students who read more slowly, just as it is true that children who are fast runners can cover the length of a basketball floor more quickly than students who run slowly. Covering, however, must not be confused with or equated to learning, just as fast running must not be equated with being a successful basketball player. Teachers who defend tracking usually do so on the grounds that they can cover more material when fast students are together, and they can give more individual attention when slower students are together. With the possible exception of using the Joplin Plan for grouping for mathematics, this assumption is simply not upheld by the considerable research on the subject (Slavin, 1987). Teachers whose preoccupation with covering material supersedes their commitment to students' healthy identity formation don't belong in middle level education, regardless of how skillful they may be at imparting information.

Students' Perceptions of Themselves and Each Other

Informal teacher inquiries into what students think about tracking have suggested that young adolescents accept tracking—that they assume smart and dumb people should be grouped separately (Stevenson, 1986, p. 40). Understandably, these children aren't aware that their ability is not static, that their capacities for learning are changing, or that they can positively affect their own learning through the experiences they have: ". . . it is clear that intelligence is not fixed at birth. Human beings can become intelligent and can learn intelligent behavior . . ." (Wheelock, 1992, p. 13). The elitism or classism that grows out of designated ability groups is familiar to those of us who have attended tracked schools, especially if our membership was in the lower and thus less esteemed tracks. The possibility that even one youngster will accept a deficient label or classification for himself or any age-mate at this time of life is too great a risk to justify tracking.

A Contradictory Philosophy

As spelled out at length in Chapter 1 and again at the beginning of this chapter, the overarching purpose of middle level education is to provide schooling that brings out the best in our changing young adolescent students. Given our knowledge of how students are changing and how vulnerable so many of them are to unwanted labels, pedagogy must be conceived to enhance healthy, integrated growth. Grouping arrangements such as tracking refute the student-centered values of the best of contemporary middle level education. Among exemplary middle schools, tracking is infrequent (George, 1988).

In Closing

Even if educators could be certain that young adolescents' learning abilities were finitely measurable, ethical and legal questions would still challenge schools where students were tracked. Equality of opportunity and the right of schools to segregate students are legitimate grounds for opposing the practice. However, finite ability measures are not available, so the issue of tracking should be moot. Furthermore, the research does not show that students' learning is superior in tracked classes compared with those that have not been tracked. There is, then, no justification for tracking. Ignorance of the research data, appeasement for uninformed parents, or mindless loyalty to traditional practices—any one or all of these excuses are unacceptable as a basis for as consequential a matter as tracking. Middle level educators must become as intolerant of this venal form of student segregation as we are of racial apartheid.

Summary

The preceding pages have presented four organizational plans for addressing the young adolescent's needs for social interaction: interdisciplinary team organization, teacher-advisory programs, cooperative grouping, and service projects. These portrayals are of necessity brief and general. It is important to point out that each of these features constitutes a substantial area of study for teachers and teacher candidates, and middle level educators must experience them to understand them. From this introduction, the reader is advised to consult the readings listed at the end of this chapter, to visit schools where these practices are in place, to engage in further formal study of each design, and then to innovate in a school setting where there is commitment to providing the very best of schooling for this age group.

RESPONSIVE DESIGNS II: ENSURING FIRSTHAND LEARNING

Curiosity about countless elements in their immediate context as well as the world intensifies during early adolescence, and finding ways to support students' personal agendas while presenting traditional curricula poses a formidable challenge. School behaviors and attitudes often interpreted as apathy or boredom or rebelliousness are usually evidence that youngsters are not learning about things that they really care about at the time or that instructional methods are not compatible with how they learn best. It becomes important, therefore, to create learning designs that will satisfy both of these obligations in order to salvage students' interest and advance their development as learners.

A certain route for accommodating individual interests and giving direction to curiosity is to provide firsthand contacts where that is possible and practical. For example, eighth grade boys interested in automobiles can learn a great deal from observing in an auto service shop, interviewing mechanics, polling owners, and reading assorted automobile literature. The point of such work is not necessarily that the concepts and knowledge gained are critical to having a well-rounded education (although that point could be argued). The point is to support the natural human enterprise of learning, regardless of the subject matter so long as it is moral. By helping youngsters learn about matters that interest them, we affirm the legitimacy of their interests as well as learning as an organic process that includes active, firsthand contact with the subject matter. Using our expertise about how to guide learning in response to students' interests holds much promise.

When young adolescents begin to challenge conventional assumptions about the relevance of their school studies, they are in fact flexing their emerging abilities to think in more formal and adultlike ways, reexamining the context in which they live, critiquing the ways things appear to be, and imagining or theorizing alternative possibilities. These intellectual activities are essential to the development of cognitive maturity. As teachers we must welcome these changes as signs of intellectual growth. But our welcome will be hollow if we don't follow up with collaborations that enable them to pursue their ideas and questions further, even when their interests don't always overlap with our particular curricular agendas.

Direct, firsthand engagement of the actualities of the adult world produces information about how things are. A seventh grader who shadows a salesperson or an attorney sees, within the limitations of the shadower's ability to comprehend and the length of the observation, exactly how things are for that individual. That experience answers the youth's questions and provokes thinking about additional possibilities. The physical movement beyond the classroom that is necessary for such firsthand activities also helps accommodate the restlessness resulting from adolescent metabolic and hormonal changes.

Firsthand, then, simply means contact with primary sources. There must be active intellectual and physical engagement between the learner and the object or source. And that engagement must spring at least in part from the learner's curiosity. Whether a student is observing cell structure through a microscope, interviewing a military veteran about his or her war experience, or counting automobiles at an intersection for subsequent arithmetical data analysis, the emphasis is on purposeful intellectual and physical engagement with the source. More customary classroom expectations of sitting most of the day at a desk, listening to lectures or recitations, working in books or other materials of dubious interest to the student, and performing paper- and pencil-exercises must be augmented by firsthand contacts.

Middle school advocates appeal for an exploratory curriculum at this level of education (National Middle School Association, 1995; National Association of Secondary School Principals, 1985). Exploration is described as "a point of view or a process, not just as specific exploratory content" and the purposes of exploration are "to help young people to know themselves, their interests, aptitudes, and capabilities, and to satisfy their natural curiosity and questing" (Lounsbury & Vars, 1978, p. 83). The emphasis here on the learner as the origin of the exploration is critical. It is one thing for a teacher to create a unit that "explores" a topic such as the Treaty at Versailles. Given the unsophistication of middle grades students, the only reasonable thing the teacher can do is to explore the subject. But the use of *exploration* here embodies a vital difference: the emphasis on the student's interests, curiosity, and exploration.

The linkage between *firsthand* and *exploratory* is probably obvious. Having firsthand contact with a topic of interest is a natural aspiration for predominantly concrete learners whose nature it is to seek hands-on experience. The curriculum should be organized as much as possible and whenever possible so that it incorporates both exploratory and firsthand learning. Although it may be difficult and even impossible to achieve firsthand exploration of many topics of interest to young adolescents, teachers and others must continually look for ways to enhance personal connectedness.

Conditions of Firsthand Experience

Surrounding American youth is an abundance of possibilities that they encounter serendipitously. A casual conversation with the person who delivers mail may be nothing more than passing the time of day. On the other hand, questions rising from the youngster's curiosity and the ensuing dialogue constitute an exchange that is both exploratory and firsthand. As the dialogue expands, concepts may be formed, creating a larger, unified context of knowledge. Firsthand learning should not be left up to such chance interactions, however; it must be deliberately planned.

What Are the Curiosities? Questions? Already Existing Knowledge?

At age eleven, Erica unabashedly adores animals—all animals. She feels passionately that most people don't treat animals with the care and respect they deserve. Most of her free reading is about animals, especially cats. She's particularly interested in some purebred kittens for sale at Love for Sale, the pet store in a neighborhood shopping mall. Erica's perceptive teacher talked with her at length in order to get a clearer idea about just what Erica already knew about cats and what she was interested in finding out. The teacher questioned her and other students to get a better sense of what all of them knew about the operation of a retail business such as the pet store. This discussion inquiry produced lists of things already known, as well as questions Erica might consider in an exploratory study of both cats in general and Love for Sale. Determining what is already known or what an individual believes about a topic occurs simultaneously with the process of identifying questions worthy of investigation. This dialogue constitutes the initial step in learning how to go about learning.

Erica's teacher recognized that her basic attraction was directed much more toward the kittens than toward the store. But as their dialogue grew, Erica began to imagine herself seeking a job in the store in a few years, and she also contemplated becoming a veterinarian. As she recognized additional dimensions and possibilities, her curiosity grew naturally. It was also fitting that her teacher interjected some questions into her study. He knew that the store owner would have a business license and would also have to satisfy a local health code—ideas Erica had not yet considered. Consequently, he required that Erica find out what government requirements the owner has to meet. Soon Erica's initial interest in animals and her attraction to a litter of kittens had evolved and expanded to broadly encompass the pet industry as well as career possibilities in it.

How Will the Exploration Be Organized?

By this time, Erica was eager to get started. Armed with assumptions and questions, she wanted to plunge headlong into her exploratory project focusing on the pet industry. No organizational pattern to guide her inquiry had emerged, nor was she concerned about having a particular structure. Her priority was to get on with it. For an eager eleven-year-old, that is just how it should be. Rationalistic organizational schemes for exploratory studies that are logically organized into progressive steps stipulate detailed planning and a preferred sequence of events. Yet, that kind of sequence doesn't necessarily match the readiness of young adolescent learners, who first need some direct involvement with the object of the study.

The ultimate organization of the knowledge gained unfolds in the process of the study. Learning occurs incrementally, resulting from a variety of experiences. An assortment of planned questions and activities is necessary to get started, but it is also important to allow for the inevitable serendipitous experiences that will occur along the way. What is extremely important here, however, is that the learner creates the organization as she goes. Erica, for example, got started by talking on the telephone with the owner. From that conversation came an invitation to visit the store, where her questions led to a second invitation, this one to spend a few afternoons helping out with animal care, cleaning cages, stocking shelf supplies, and preparing the shop for closing. The events occurred randomly, and Erica built schemas of understanding from a variety of experiences, all of which related to the animals and the shop's operation.

It was up to Erica to judge what was most significant about her study. She was excited by new concepts. The relatively high utility costs of a pet store necessitated by twenty-four-hour climate control for tropical animals was an insight. Learning that animals had a prime marketing time was another new insight. Her growing maturity as a learner depended on her coming to grips with organizing and classifying her insights in order to present her experience coherently to others. This process of assimilating experience, judging and ordering it, and subsequently sharing it with others assures that the learner—in this case Erica—becomes the authority of record about the study. This kind of ownership is a likely outcome of firsthand exploratory studies.

Erica's teacher's primary responsibility was to serve as her counsel and coach. Confusion, questions, or ideas that came to her were tried out with the teacher, but the initiative had to be Erica's. When she found herself bewildered about how to go about putting the whole experience together, her teacher coached her through the confusion by helping her clarify her priorities. In order for the eventual representation of the experience to reflect her knowledge, however, the ultimate decisions had to be hers. It was she, after all, who was there, who made choices when they were called for, and who was ultimately the person most accountable for her own learning. It is sometimes very difficult for well-motivated teachers to figure out when to keep hands off to the extent that Erica's teacher did in this example. However, if students don't do the things Erica did and go through the sorting process she confronted, they don't learn how to do these things. And it is essential to remember that the greatest value of such work is the student's learning how to work through such a process, exercising personal initiative, and organizing the experience to share with others. Students who have very little of this kind of involvement in their work are inclined to reflect their deprivation in blank looks of indifference and queries such as "Is this what you want?"

How Will Learning Be Represented?

Representation is a vital part of firsthand learning experience. Just as the original curiosity and the day-to-day activities belonged to Erica, so also must the representation of the new knowledge be hers. She might choose to prepare an oral presentation for the class or produce a videotape or post her work on a bulletin board or arrange a display in the library or write a report. She also might choose to use more than one of these devices. The crucial factor is that the choice must be hers. The essence of representation is accomplished when she studies her work, identifies elements that she believes will interest and inform others, and works out a way to portray it. The student judges what is worth knowing and how to portray it best. Deciding not to share at all, however, is not an option.

Teachers and students are both familiar with established school procedures of judging learning according to such measures as test performance, homework, and projects. Grades of A to F and arithmetical averages are likewise common. According to these traditions, teachers establish the criteria by which work is to be evaluated. The concept of representation is quite different from these traditional methods, however, in that emphasis is on a personal interpretation of an experience unique to the individual. Firsthand exploratory learning creates knowledge structures that are idiosyncratic to the learner, and although teachers are certainly free to spell out evaluative criteria, the emphasis upon the individual's learning as he or she perceived and internalized that experience should be maintained.

Erica's study was individual, and her representation of it was therefore unique. A local radio station that was popular with Erica and her classmates often sent a mobile unit to broadcast for a couple of hours from businesses that were having sales or from community events such as a fair. It occurred to Erica that by creating a fictional tape recording of a mobile unit visit to Love for Sale, she could represent her newly acquired knowledge through staged interviews with the owner and employees. With her teacher's help, she prepared a script for her collaborators and produced a twenty-two-minute radio show that also included several ten- to fifteen-second musical interludes. Classmates were invited to listen to the tape whenever they wished, and she also produced a book to further inform interested people. The book included a floor plan and illustrations she had drawn of Love for Sale, a directory of other pet stores and breeders in the area, prose descriptions about how to care for common household pets, and pamphlets she had collected about nutrition and grooming.

Some Options for Learning

A certain way to find out how young adolescents learn best is to ask them. One team I visited shared their results from a recent inquiry into the components of meaningful learning. Here are their results:

Meaningful learning . . .
is hands-on.
happens in small groups.
is active.
is practical.
is individualized.
happens in and out of school.
is challenging.
is fun.
provides feedback.
is purposeful.
is goal-oriented.

Alpha Team 1994
Shelburne Middle School, Vermont

In addition to basic literacy, planning and problem solving skills, there is a wide variety of activities that help promote learning connections for young adolescents. An alphabetical listing of some strategies follows:

act	construct	graph
adapt/adjust	contrast	group/classify
analyze	cook	hypothesize
annotate	cooperate	identify
apprentice	copy	imagine
apply	count	implement
arrange	create	improvise
assemble	critique	infer
assess	debate	integrate
budget	defend	interpret
calculate	demonstrate	interview
care for	describe	invent
categorize/classify	design/test	judge
celebrate	discuss	lead
choose	document	manipulate
collaborate	draw	map
collect (data)	edit	match
compare	evaluate	measure
compliment	experiment	memorize
compromise	explain	model
conceptualize	find attributes	modify
connect	find patterns	narrate
consult	follow directions	negotiate

observe	record	solve
organize	reflect	sort
paint	reorganize	speculate
paraphrase	report	summarize
parody	resolve	survey
perform	respond	synthesize
persuade	retell	talk
photograph	review	tape record
plan	revise	teach
posit	role play	telephone
practice	score	test
predict	sculpt	theorize
present	self-assess	trace
program	self-discipline	track
publish	sequence	videotape
question	set goals	visit
rank order	share	volunteer
reason	simulate	vote
recognize	simplify	weigh

Summary

For many years, middle level *schooling* has taken place in classrooms while an enormous potential for middle level *education* outside schools has gone uncultivated. Given the tradition of departmental organization and a preoccupation with covering externally prescribed curriculum, that heritage is not surprising. More recently, however, we have become increasingly aware of something we've always known but have allowed to slip away: that what appears to be less can in fact be more. Our challenge is to create balance between firsthand, exploratory opportunities and studies that are best accomplished using preconceived materials and direct instruction. Ultimately, it is what students believe about themselves as learners that matters most. Through authentic work on this project, Erica grew as both an emerging adolescent person and a more savvy, skillful seventh grade scholar.

RESPONSIVE DESIGNS III: ESTABLISHING MORE SYSTEMATIC PATTERNS OF THINKING

Gordon, almost eleven, had been assigned a project about patterns a few days earlier. Now, on the day before the project was due, his teacher was absent for the day. Although she had already provided the class detailed guidelines for their projects, the only way Gordon could define his assignment to the substitute teacher was "It has to be two hundred words." Her questions to him about other guidelines were met with shrugs and "I dunno." Their ensuing conversation demonstrated that while Gordon understood the concept of patterns as far as being able to recognize them in his plaid shirt and in the floor tiles, he had absolutely no sense of how to conceptualize a project about them. In brief, then, his concept of the project was stuck on "patterns" and "two hundred words." Gordon is not

bicycle	soccer	model airplanes
tire treads spokes handlebar grips	black & white pentagons pitch give and go corner kicks	ribs wings struts propeller

Figure 5.1 Gordon's Patterns.

intellectually deficient for his age; his reasoning is simply literal and concrete, which is normal for this time in his development.

In order to shift Gordon's focus from his frustrating struggle trying to "figure out what she wants," the visiting teacher engaged him in conversation about things he liked to do when he wasn't in school. He looked at her with distress. "But I have to turn in this project tomorrow." She smiled and urged him to think about her questions. "Tell me some of your favorite things to do outside of school." Gradually, still looking at her uncertainly, Gordon indicated that some of his favorites were bicycling, soccer, and making airplane models. On a scrap of paper, the substitute teacher penciled a matrix, labeling three vertical columns with those activities (Figure 5.1). "Now, Gordon, tell me about your bicycle. Do any of the parts have patterns?" After a brief, puzzled pause, he said, "The tires. The tires have treads." After another pause he added, "And the spokes. And the handlebar grips—they have little places for your fingers." Upon each response she wrote his words under the "Bicycle" column of the matrix.

"Now, tell me about soccer. Can you think of any patterns in soccer?"

"Yes, the ball had little black and white shapes on it."

"Pentagons?" she asked.

"Yes, that's it—pentagons," Gordon agreed. She wrote "black and white pentagons" under the soccer column.

"Any other patterns in soccer?" she asked.

"The pitch?" Gordon thought. "Is the pitch a pattern?"

"Can you draw it?" she asked. Gordon quietly drew a rectangle, adding a midfield stripe, penalty areas, and goals.

Jerry, Gordon's classmate, who had been watching their interaction, joined them and offered, "What about soccer plays, like the give-and-go?"

Gordon stared for a moment, then his face brightened as he added, "Yeah, and corner kicks." At this point the boys' ideas had gone beyond the visitor's knowledge of soccer, but she felt certain that strategies in soccer, as in other team sports, included plays that qualified as patterns. She added "plays" to the column and suggested that they shift the subject to Gordon's third favorite activity, making models.

By now Jerry was an excited participant. He asked if he might add some of his favorites to the project. "If you do," Gordon pointed out, "it'll mean four hundred words."

This anecdote captures an intellectual transition that is critical to successful development in early adolescence: establishing a meaningful order for selections of the abundant knowledge children already have. In this example, the substitute teacher saw that Gordon was mentally blocked and had no idea how to conceptualize his task. She was able to shift his concentration away from the impasse he could not penetrate alone and toward a way to organize some things he knew. Gordon's conceptual dilemma is extremely common to youngsters at his time of life. This example of a teacher exposing a student to a concept slightly beyond but within reach of his current functioning exemplifies responsive teaching in terms of helping students acquire more systematic ways of thinking.

A delight of being around and working with very young children at home and in primary schools is their rapidly expanding awareness of the world around them, their endless queries of "Why?" and the fascinating, often amusing ways they reason. Spontaneity and randomness abound. Vivian Paley's account of young children's thinking captures both the richness and the charm of their intellectual activity as they work to explain how things work (Paley, 1981). As children gain experience and develop as thinkers, they are increasingly able to think serially, as is evidenced by the stories they tell about an event involving the teller, or the story line they retrace from a movie or book. The expansion and refinement of their consciousness flows like an ever-widening stream that increases in velocity and power as it is fed by tributaries of new experience.

A comparable delight of working with young adolescents is the emergence of their access to new ways of thinking as exemplified in Gordon's anecdote. As the previous chapter describes, conceptualizations begin to take on greater complexities that indicate growing intellectual sophistication. Over these few years, youngsters become increasingly able to form more intricate explanations and theories to explain events and relationships. They also begin to challenge assumptions they had previously ignored or taken for granted. The tentative, often awkward intellectual refinement they are exhibiting signals noteworthy developmental changes, all occurring according to individual schedules. If the rapidly developing thought of young children revealed through their language is the first age of reason, then the early adolescent years when intellectual thought becomes more differentiated and refined must surely be the second age of reason.

Parents, teachers, and other adults who recognize the importance of understanding children's thought make deliberate, studied observations of youth at work and play in order to recognize and nurture these intellectual changes. Observations of how a youngster handles selected learning tasks can tell us quite a lot about his intellectual development and readiness for more or less complex curricular challenges. Piaget's conservation tasks are widely used by teachers of young children to ascertain a student's readiness for a variety of educational challenges (Labinowicz, 1980). For example, children who "conserve" are generally ready for more conceptually challenging experiences than their age-mates who are not yet "conserving." Responsive teachers subsequently stimulate growth by presenting students with challenges they can manage. A key element in the responsive middle level teacher's approach to teaching is to employ an array of tasks that, while valuable learning in themselves, also provide insights about the nature of the youngster's intellectual functioning.

Evidence of students' intellectual changes are often less apparent to teachers of twelve-year-olds than to those who work with six-year-olds, however. Part of the difficulty lies in differing expectations about what is appropriate for learners to do. Young children acquire language and reveal their thought through their talk, so savvy teachers encourage talking. By the middle grades, however, the tradition has become one that discourages talking except for recitations—hardly the kind of language use that challenges thinking and supports exchanges of ideas, debate, and interpretation—the mental exercises that provoke more complex conceptualizations among adolescents. Teachers who are responsive to the nature of young adolescent learners cultivate their more systematic thought through the same qualities of talk used by laboratory scientists, city planners, and even teachers as they go about tackling intellectually challenging projects.

Another difficulty of recognizing intellectual changes lies simply in the amount of time a teacher has with individual students. Traditional junior high school organization runs large numbers of students and teachers through high-school-like schedules that thwart if not prohibit the sustained observations that help teachers get to know and understand the intellectual development of their individual students. One of the compelling rationales for teaming in middle level schools is that the numbers of different students that teachers see each day are reduced, and time is scheduled for teachers to exchange insights about the development of the students they work with in common.

Recognizing changes in mental functioning is quite possible, however, when teachers understand the intellectual transitions that occur during early adolescence and when they have enough sustained access to students to observe their minds at work. Teachers' central responsibility must be to facilitate youngsters' intellectual growth and refinement through activities that enhance their capacity to think successfully and productively.

Stretching to Learn

Learning theory is a fascinating and appropriate study for all educators, and a specialized study of theory pertaining to young adolescents is especially fruitful in designing teaching that is responsive to their conditions of development. A review of relevant theory is much too broad, however, to be adequately and equitably summarized in this book. The strategies outlined in the following pages appeared to serve me and my middle grade students well as we worked to nurture learning through activities that required and reflected increasingly systematic thought.

Understanding the mental transitions my students were making, I continually explained to them that they were changing and that every individual's personal task, myself included, was "to stretch yourself." I further reminded them that every individual was unique and that each person needed to find a personally comfortable rhythm of learning—a comfort zone where activities were satisfying and felt natural. Then the challenge was to stretch oneself to undertake deliberately a task believed to be just a bit ahead of one's comfort zone.

In their outstanding longitudinal study of adolescent transition, Simmons and Blyth (1987) reflect on lessons from their study and speculate about a similar idea they chose to describe as an arena of comfort.

> If change comes too suddenly—that is, if there is too much discontinuity with prior experience—or if change is too early given the children's cognitive and emotional states, or

if it occurs in too many areas of life at once, then presumably individuals will experience great discomfort. They will experience discomfort with self and discomfort with the world. Such children will not feel at one with themselves nor at home in their social environments. Individuals should do better both in terms of self-esteem and behavioral coping if there is some arena of comfort in their lives. (Simmons & Blyth, 1987, p. 351)

The notion of having a comfort zone and then gradually, deliberately stretching oneself to enlarge that zone made sense and was generally well received by my students. "Stretching" became part of our vernacular, and, as will be described further in Chapter 8, it became a major criterion for self-evaluation. One student wrote whimsically about this concept as part of a report on a study of an island community in New England we did together.

> He worked them hard,
>
> he did, all right.
>
> He made them S-T-R-E-T-C-H
>
> with all their might.
>
> He wanted an A–1 job
>
> from them all,
>
> so with mighty efforts
>
> they cleared the walls.
>
> But what a shock that man got,
>
> When, after such stretching,
>
> They suddenly S-N-A-P-P-E-D.

In order to help my students find their comfort zones and stretch themselves, I focused on developmental tasks that everyone could handle at some level. As they stretched and grew, their progress was evidenced by the way they handled these tasks. I likewise learned a great deal about each student and his or her comfort zone and about how to guide their future activities. Some patterns of thought that require degrees and dimensions of systematic reasoning follow.

Description

The following description of a neighborhood market shows the random structure appropriate for an eight-year-old author:

> The market has a lot of customers every morning. Some parts of the store sell cake and cupcakes and other things like that. The things are all put in order so people can find them. He sells most of the things you would probably want. The market doesn't smell at all. He sells a lot of variety of everything he has and sells. It is crowded most of the time. His cellar doesn't leak. He has prices that are fine for the kind of food he sells. It's a good little market. He has good everything.

Louis, age eight

Louis's description leads the reader through the flow of observations—some of them seemingly unrelated—characterizing his young child's view. He saw and noted details, and he made some general personal observations. While this is good description for an eight-year-old, his more experienced and careful observations as a twelve-year-old reflect greater intricacies and interconnectedness in his observations of swans:

> Last evening I walked down to the pond where I saw a family of Mute Swans. The mother and father were swimming about two feet apart with three little signets [cygnets] between them. They swam around the eastern end of the pond for a few minutes before they went back to their nest. The mother stood up over the nest while the father swam in the pond feeding. The nest was hidden by the tan cattails but with the mother standing and being white with an orange and black bill I could tell where the nest was. The signets are all downy and fluffy, and they were a brownish color with black interspersed. The male swan is the same color as the female. Mute swans are just that, having no call, but they are very graceful in their movements.

Louis, age twelve

While Louis's second description isn't edited as precisely as he will render later in adolescence, the differences between these two samples reflect additional experience and greater intellectual maturity. In the first piece, he was a novice at observing and describing; over four years his skill grew conspicuously. On both occasions he used written words to describe a firsthand experience. What the pieces show or neglect to show and what isn't clearly articulated provide clues to his development.

Teachers who appreciate description as an indicator of systematic thinking provide lots of opportunities for students to describe and report firsthand experiences. By describing as well as explaining what they see, they are increasingly able to step outside the experience in order to relate it to others. And although writing is an essential medium for developing more refined skills of description, speaking is equally important. The art of rhetoric also grows with experience in reading one's work to others (and therefore hearing) and in making presentations. Illustrations, diagrams, and sketches may add to the richness of detail and clarity of description.

Classification

In its simplest form, classification is naming and sorting things according to some prescribed attributes. Categories may be simple or complex, depending on the categorizer's thought. Young children sort cookies according to "one for me and one for you." Sometimes they evolve simple equivalencies: "I'll give you two raisin cookies, and I'll take only one chocolate chip." More complex thinkers may also sort simply, but they become increasingly able to conceptualize complex categorizations that account for multiple attributes. They also recognize that categories may overlap. Introducing modestly advanced ways of classifying is one of our most important opportunities for responsive teaching to help our students advance to more systematic reasoning.

It is common for young adolescents to collect such things as pins, baseball cards, stamps, and so on. The organizational schemes for these collections are often simultaneously simple and complex. One eleven-year-old explained that her stuffed animals were arranged in her room from oldest to youngest (newest), but the ones she positioned standing up were her favorites and those with green ribbons were endangered species. She had worked out her own organizational and valuing strategy that might not be the same as any other person's scheme. The implication here is that young adolescents need lots of opportunities requiring them to organize their experience into systems of classification, and hierarchies may be helpful in establishing priorities. I urge teachers to encourage collecting as a certain way to cultivate thinking about classification possibilities.

One sixth to seventh grade team conducted a study of the garbage problem in its community (Stevenson & Carr, 1992). As a strategy for estimating their community's garbage production, each family sorted its garbage for a week according to several categories: paper, glass, metal, food, and so on. While other classification schemes are possible, this particular one served their need. By collecting and weighing each family's garbage production, they were able to make projections about how much of each type of garbage was produced in their town. They also regrouped their categories according to feasibility of recycling, burning, burying, and so on. This kind of classification and reclassification stimulates higher-order reasoning that is right for these youngsters.

Memory

One of the most interesting and puzzling areas of difference among young adolescents is memory. Some students seem to function quite efficiently when memorizing poems or lists of data, such as the parts of a flower or state capitals. Others struggle, sometimes painfully, to recall the same material. Traditional school practices have exaggerated the importance of memory to the neglect of other intellectual functions. My concern as a teacher of students of such diverse intellectual talents was that memory not be equated with intelligence or become the overriding criterion of good scholarship. Some noteworthy aspects of memory have emerged from my day-to-day experience of teaching these youngsters:

Narrative Memory. Most youngsters recall stories generally well, especially those that include intrigue, drama, and surprise endings. Narrative form is particularly accessible to concrete learning, in which the story in its literal form takes precedence. Concept maps are useful ways to organize related information to tell a story. Young adolescents need frequent opportunities to organize information in narrative form for understanding as well as eventual recall.

Utilitarian Memory. When something works once, then works again and again, it is incorporated as reliable and useful—that is, utilitarian. For example, a youngster building a box learns that correctly applying a carpenter's square to corners will always let him know whether or not the corner will work. This useful function becomes part of that person's repertoire of responses to situations this application fits.

Memory Maps. A memory map is a drawn device that combines elements of the narrative and utilitarian. In its simplest form, the central concepts of a topic being studied serve as focal points for remembering related details. Consider the excerpt from a memory map constructed by thirteen-year-old Kathy to explain and remember the physics of airplane flight (Figure 5.2).

The two central concepts linked in this example about the physics of flight are thrust and lift. The former concept refers to the force that pushes an airplane forward; it may be generated by propellers or a jet engine. Gliders as well as powered planes require a degree

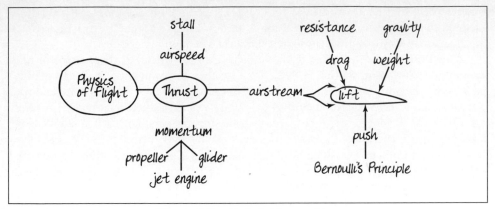

Figure 5.2   Kathy's Memory Map.

of momentum in order to remain airborne, and when the momentum falls below a minimal airspeed, the plane stalls. Drag and weight are factors caused by the resistance of air and gravity, which work against lift, the second organizing concept in this excerpt. The student has cleverly drawn a cross section of an airplane wing as a reminder of Bernoulli's Principle, the explanation of how the airstream flowing over the top of the wing faster than the airstream underneath causes pressure differences that push the wing and therefore the plane up. Kathy constructed this map to read like a book, left to right. She is able to explain the individual elements as she goes. Memory maps appeal to students who more easily comprehend conceptual relationships through their own graphic portrayals. They also help the teacher assess and understand a youngster's knowledge.

Habit. Practice at memorizing has long been teachers' final resort to enforce learning. Students have likewise devised assorted mnemonic devices to be able to recall specific information. Perhaps overreliance on these activities has given education a bad name with many students and teachers when, in fact, practicing to a point of habit is just what is needed for many algorithmic functions. The most important function here is the recognition by both student and teacher of just what knowledge is appropriate and worthwhile to practice until it is fully committed to memory. Memorizing lists of dates in history is pointless in early adolescence, but knowing mathematical tables by heart is very important.

Idiosyncrasy. A major problem with learning systems that emphasize recall is their failure to accommodate knowledge that is uniquely individual, sometimes serendipitous, and often inexplicable. Yet, it is just those unique memories that are so often memory's keys and glue—the elements that stimulate the recall and hold it together. Credibility for the idiosyncratic character of learning is tremendously important in early adolescence.

From careful listening and observation of students' accounts we can gain some clues about how they construct, organize, and draw upon their knowledge. This framework evolved over the course of my sixteen years as a middle grades teacher, not from any theoretical framework I read about. Yet, it helped me respond to students in accordance with what appeared to be their favored mechanism.

I recognized that all of my students relied on narrative memory, so I showed them how to "story" things. By "storying" I refer to teaching them how to organize events or ideas so that there is a coherent flow involving a beginning, a conflict or connection, and a resolution. This simple device produces something that makes sense to the person doing the storying and is more easily internalized than more arbitrary items. Utilitarian memory works similarly in that the conflict or connection is something that works, and the ending refers to ways that "working" can be applied.

Synthesis

Youngsters need lots of experience pulling together pieces and parts of an experience in order to construct a coherent whole that can be explained to others. For example, the student who studies a local branch bank is exposed to a host of operations that include such aspects as the responsibilities of the manager, where the money comes from, where the checks go, how money is counted and accounted for by the tellers, and even the system used for attending to the maintenance needs of the building. Whether or not the child follows a teacher-established outline in reporting on the elements of his study is not the crucial issue here. After all, there is no single way to organize and present such an experience. What is important is that the child decides how the bank works and what is likely to be most interesting to others and noteworthy by his own standards. This example of synthesizing elements of an experience into a coherent whole challenges systematic thinking in ways that are appropriate and manageable during this transitional time of life. The essence of synthesis lies in the child's pulling together whatever he selects from his study to present to others. Perceptive teachers can realize a great deal about the maturity of a youngster's thinking by how such a task is rendered.

Analysis

In this context, analysis refers to the student dissecting the whole into parts or categories that make sense to him. This classification reflects the youngster's ideas about how the experience should be organized. He then forms some conclusions (analysis) of what is deemed worth knowing about the separate parts. This use of analysis is not necessarily the opposite of synthesis, however. In the example of a study of a bank, analysis would be reflected in a map of what the child deems to be central concepts or ideas that can be listed: bank jobs, how money comes and goes, types of business that customers transact at banks, how a bank makes a profit, and so on. For the child engaged in the considerable task of creating a structure for organizing his learning, no particular headings are essential unless the teacher has opted to establish categories by which the learning must be first synthesized, then subsequently analyzed. It is through the depth and range of interpretations that we gain insight into the youngster's application of analysis.

Inductive Logic

One of the most familiar forms of reasoning that reflects the natural egocentricity of childhood is revealed in a claim such as "I learn math without homework; therefore, there should be no math homework." The statement reflects the assumption that "what is good for me is good for everyone else." For example, there is an inclination to generalize that what works in a specific situation denotes a principle that can be applied universally. It is essential to appreciate and understand the naturalness of this kind of thinking throughout childhood, but it is especially important in early adolescence when youngsters are becoming aware of and concerned about principles and developing theories to explain how and why things work. When witnessing such thinking, the perceptive adult encourages the individual to elaborate the newfound principle, to develop its implications, and to test it against other students' perceptions.

Deductive Logic. Children enjoy finishing the statement "There ought to be a law . . ." For example, Vermont children learn that the practice of applying road salt to icy roads in the winter results in an exaggerated sodium accumulation that often kills vegetation along the road shoulders. An imaginable offering to the statement completion might be "There ought to be a law that road salt cannot be used in Vermont." In their subsequent discovery and realization of the deductively derived consequences of the proposition, an awareness of and appreciation for systematic reasoning emerges. They come to understand in this example that extreme travel hazards attend frozen roads, that more frequent use of scrapers ruins the road surface and results in escalating maintenance costs that raise taxes, which create special hardships for the poor, and so on. In exercising deductive logic, youngsters identify a principle, then pursue the consequences of its application. Through this type of syllogistic reasoning, they come to recognize consequences and thus previously unimagined implications. Such deductive thinking is necessary if one's conclusions are to be well considered and just.

Combinatorial Logic

Sure evidence of intellectual maturing is visible when a youngster applies more than one system of reasoning to the same problem. The application of interconnected concepts further confirms maturing dimensions of thought. Efforts to systematically arrive at solutions to puzzles, riddles, and logic problems signal their evolving intellectual refinement as they go about figuring things out. This reasoning is especially evident in many problem-solving activities. For example, students confronted with constructing a small boat that will sail in a tank downwind before a window fan encounter problems of balance, steerage, and resistance. Perhaps the child begins by concentrating on balancing a small boat cut from a piece of wood. Once the balance problem is settled by experimentation with weights (ballast) on the boat, the child tackles steerage. In making modifications to make the boat go straight (rudder, keel), balance may be changed. Now he must think about at least two functions: what makes it balance, and what makes it go straight. Then he notices a classmate's boat made from the top of a styrofoam egg carton: it sits on top of the water and moves very quickly before the fan. Now he confronts a new possibility—that his wooden boat is slowed by sitting too low in the water (resistance). His subsequent thinking will combine what he has learned about balancing, steering, and reducing drag as much as possible. This combinatorial reasoning and the puzzles or problems to which it is applied are especially important to youngsters who are in the middle grades. That "life grows increasingly complex with our ability to comprehend its complexity" is a truism especially pertinent for emerging adolescents.

Hypothetical Thought

The process of creating theories that in the theorist's mind explain circumstances is a hallmark of accelerating intellectual change. Hypothetical thought is the process of stating assumptions (beliefs) about causalities. Expressing such propositions is common; exploring them to examine their veracity is much less common. Youngsters in early adolescence appear to be especially inclined toward explaining social behaviors in terms of hypotheses: "Marge sits with Susie and Gail because . . ." This inclination toward asserting causal relationships also helps them make at least tentative sense about other conditions: "Lake Champlain's water is polluted by farmers." Central to this kind of reasoning is the teacher's ability to help frame and articulate the hypotheses so they can be pursued by collecting necessary information and data around which reasoned speculation can occur. The teacher's leadership in examining untried assumptions is critical.

Representational Thought

Today's American youth are bombarded with the icons of their time: the golden arches, a polo player stitched on a garment, pierced ears and earrings on girls and boys. Each of these icons is a representation of an information complex that includes values, images, personalities, and points of view. Young adolescents' increasing abilities to reason differentially cause them to associate particular cultural elements with symbols. They use improvisation, often referred to more generically as creativity.

> Improvisation depends a great deal on bouncing ideas off each other, and thereby provoking the unknown into tangible ideas, which in turn become the source of further improvising. A great deal depends on taking advantage of accidents, on making use of material not planned for. Much careful listening is required, along with faith that something can always be created from something else. Improvising, then, is a kind of stretching of ideas and thoughts . . . a wonderful dance of the possible. (Lewis, 1987, p. 5)

Another dimension of youngsters' growing facility for representational thought is their increasing awareness of meaning conveyed through satire, innuendo, and caricature. The enduring popularity of *MAD* magazine among young adolescent readers is evidence of this growing prowess. Early adolescence is a ripe time for teachers to cultivate this emerging aptitude by helping students create representations of their knowledge, ideas, and ideologies.

Planning and Organizing

A common response to "What's your biggest frustration at school?" is a reference to the shortage of time to do all the things students need or want to do. Regardless of how efficiently they actually use time, young adolescents say they feel pressured to do things quickly. Teachers can help students function effectively in the face of real and imagined pressure by making sure work expectations are reasonable. We can also help them begin to learn how to plan and organize. Youngsters have an enormous potential for developing the ability to conceive a task in terms of its whole composition as well as the details. The earlier example of Gordon's project about patterns reflects a beginning; Gordon had no conceptualizations of a project beyond the requirement that it had to be two hundred words. With the substitute teacher's assistance, however, he learned a way to organize his ideas so that his subsequent work would be more efficient and directly related to his project. One of the most valuable services teachers can provide to young adolescent learners is guidance in their planning. Whether a student is struggling as Gordon was, or has become much more organized and purposeful as Kathy evidenced by her memory map about the physics of flight, every student will benefit from learning to conceptualize and identify tasks that are goal-directed. Once the task is clearly understood, the work that must be done will become more efficient. Additionally, a desirable criterion for forming cooperative groups is the maturity of youngsters' skills in planning and organizing. Less skilled group members will learn from their more proficient peers. More will be offered on this subject in Chapter 7.

Inquiry

Chapter 3 addresses adults' use of inquiry to learn about the culture of young adolescent students. However, inquiry is also a very useful tool for students to learn some of the things they need and want to know. My ten- to fourteen-year-olds were generally eager to poll classmates or parents about an issue that interested them.

A dozen or so of my students carried out an inquiry into the television-viewing habits of families in our school. Their elaborate investigation involved collecting data from students in each grade. We were able to get what we believed was an accurate profile of this aspect of family life in our community. Subsequently, we published a report of our study that was available to parents and other interested people.

Gathering information in this manner not only helps youngsters make sense of things but involves them in a process that models systematic reasoning: brainstorming ideas, setting priorities, formulating items, creating a way to collect information, interpreting the results, and finally presenting what was learned. Inquiry also requires a variety of activities—an additional benefit to young adolescents who are restless and who value firsthand involvement.

Judging and Choosing

As children mature into adolescence they become increasingly more capable of examining options analytically and objectively than they were in earlier years. Some of the questions they assess and choices they make are also quite formidable, especially those having to do with participation in sex and drug, alcohol, or tobacco use. Pedagogy should therefore attend to the processes of judging and choosing throughout the curricular program. These youngsters are becoming increasingly able to examine their choices in terms of risks and consequences. Whatever is best or preferred should involve the student in identifying and comparing elements in a choice. This kind of decision making also entails classifying and categorizing possibilities and imaginable consequences. Negotiating rules is an excellent way to involve students in such thought; it also makes the democratic process real rather than simulated. Whether the matter at hand is a ruling about an issue on the team, the choice of an academic project, or a private decision about whether or not to drink a beer, the importance of clarifying risks, consequences, and personal standards in judging and choosing cannot be overemphasized in the middle grades.

Studied Speculation

A group of twelve-year-olds interviewed a man about the merits of a particular site for a proposed new landfill. Although he did not directly reveal that the land in question was owned by his brother-in-law, his vague and occasionally self-contradictory responses to some of their questions were initially confusing and created some suspicion. Two students inferred that there was more to the matter than they had been able to identify in the interview. While discussing the interview protocol afterward, they swapped theories to explain their enigma. Subsequently, they resolved to interview some additional community people for other ideas about the appropriateness of the site. It was through just such a follow-up session that they learned about the kinship and realized that their initial attentiveness, speculations, and ensuing persistence had brought them new understandings. A natural tension exists between what youngsters perceive others as believing and their own private hunches. Personal theories, multiple explanations, and alternative solutions to problems are exercises essential to the intellectual vitality of young adolescents. Responsive teachers model the studied speculation students must exercise if they are to grow into ethically responsible adults.

Transcendent Judgment

Young adolescents are very conscious about right and wrong. Theirs is also a time of life during which youngsters like to imagine a more ideal, more nearly perfect world. Most of their beliefs derive from their families and particularly their close friends. They also recognize that there are higher truths in our society than those evident in their immediate living context. In my countless interviews as a teacher, I rarely experienced a young adolescent who seemed to have no consciousness of a higher moral order. Especially reassuring and encouraging are expressions that convey their realization of an ideal that transcends their actuality. Conflict between the way things are and what they might be encourages personal reflection and can lead to more responsible decision making. Discrimination in social relationships particularly exemplifies this dilemma. The equality of humankind is an ideology young adolescents endorse; yet, they are conscious of their own day-to-day discriminations. These new abilities to recognize the actual and the imaginable invite both discourse and carefully planned actions such as community or school service projects. Subsequent personal initiatives toward remedying some of society's deficiencies are the essential steps that build character.

Some Reminders and Observations

As in all dimensions of early adolescent change, children vary considerably from one to another in terms of their readiness and propensity for systematic thought. Some may even appear to reject outright any rational approaches to problem solving. Given the unprecedented complexity of contemporary life, however, it is imperative that adolescents learn how to work successfully through logic systems. It is equally urgent that they learn how to conceptualize, plan, and carry out a structure for time and work, such as setting a personal schedule. A tragedy of our times is the enormous number of adolescents and adults who are wandering through their lives without a clear purpose and an organized way of pursuing personal goals in an era when personal skill with such organization is more critical than it has ever been.

Some benchmarks of changing thought are evident in subtle shifts in the child's thinking about what is funny. Slapstick humor and simple silliness continue to tickle most developing adolescents, but there is also increasing evidence of an appreciation for what appears to be more sophisticated sources of amusement. Language manipulations such as puns, and stories embodying double meanings, begin to make more sense to young adolescents than they did at an earlier time, and in this newfound meaning, more adultlike amusement occurs. It is not unusual to observe within a school or neighborhood culture that such humor forms become the craze for a time. Tom Swift jokes and limericks were the rage for a while, much like similar spates of enthusiasm for yo-yos and hula hoops.

Another familiar indicator of the youngsters' evolving potential for more systematically patterned thought is their expression of reflective ideas about ethical matters. Interest in issues of right and wrong that transcend merely "what he did to me" indicate that the child is assessing elements in his or her expanding awareness. One week's leading news story concerned the international cooperation being invested in saving two California gray whales trapped in an Alaskan ice pack. Conversations with elementary school children revealed their belief that above all these two animals should be saved—regardless of difficulty and expense. Saving the animals was all that mattered. Twelve- and thirteen-year-olds offered somewhat different points of view on the issue, however. While they, too, wished to see the whales saved, they could also understand the issues and justify not making the effort to save them, invoking their awareness about the balance of nature and questioning the propriety of using millions of dollars to save only two of an estimated population of 15,000 whales of this species. The children also related and weighed the relevance of tangential issues, such as raising the public consciousness about endangered animals and the model of cooperation between the United States and USSR to rescue a species historically exploited by Soviet commerce. Such shifts in thinking are evident only when adults create contexts that enhance the expressions of kids' points of view, and sessions in which the adult is also a learner.

Yet another sign of change is the individual youngster's desire to be reflective about his life to date, taking stock of what is or has been prominent in his life or in the lives of family members or friends. Young children love to hear their parents' stories of adventures the parent recalls from his or her own childhood. But in the emerging adolescent, the activity shifts subtly from only enjoying such stories to retelling them in his own words, emphasizing elements that bear the more personal values and meanings he associates with the anecdote. Appreciative and respectful teachers of young adolescents relish such storytelling as evidence that the youngster is ruminating in more adult ways about valued elements in his life. It is a form of personal recapitulation that heralds the coming woman and man.

One final reminder appropriate to mention here is how very necessary talk is to learning throughout childhood but especially during the early adolescent years. It is no surprise to parents and teachers that these youngsters like to talk. Some of them spend much of their time at school and later on the telephone at home talking with their friends. But the talk I am referring to here is not directionless banter. I'm speaking of the talk that is necessary for students to explain their understandings, ideas, theories, and interpretations as well as to question, clarify, compare, and collaborate. They must be able to talk as an essential tool for systematically working through issues. And as relative beginners in higher-order thinking, they will be predictably inconsistent, ragged, and easily distracted from their tasks. To paraphrase Edgar Dale, such purposeful discourse "doesn't always flow—sometimes it leaks, spurts, and dribbles" (1984, p. 16). A significant part of our responsibility as responsive teachers is to help youngsters learn how to use systematic, goal-directed talk in order to accomplish the collaborations that will serve everyone best.

There is, then, a sweeping but gradual movement in the ways youngsters think and process their experiences during these several years. Failure to move successfully from childlike to more adultlike thought in early adolescence has far-reaching and possibly long-lasting results. Prudent teachers, parents, and other adult leaders attend conscientiously to their responsibility to cultivate youngsters' experience of thought in order that they may think in ways that will allow them to solve the problems they face now and in the future.

RESPONSIVE DESIGNS IV: NURTURING RESPONSIBILITY AND ACCOUNTABILITY

The justification for ensuring education for all of our citizens through public funds is largely an expression of belief in the importance of every person's life. Implicit throughout all of the middle level education policy statements recounted in Chapter 1 is a common goal to develop increasingly competent, confident, self-sufficient learners. I know of no better time to help them learn how to take an increasing portion of the responsibility for their own education than during these middle years. They are eager to explore, and they crave recognition. With responsive designs in place, we can help them not only learn more from established curriculum but also learn about matters of personal interest that may not be included in a school's program of studies.

Every teacher should know what it is like to be personally empowered and to be recognized by others as a unique, valuable human being. Our heritage of personal empowerment, equality under the law, and freedom of ideas are basic values on which the American way of life rests. This birthright should be at the heart of responsive middle grades schooling, because our students are becoming aware of how it is to need and feel personal empowerment. Whether or not educators choose to acknowledge it, young adolescents are quickly gaining autonomy of thought and action.

The term *empowerment* usually makes school people nervous, especially when it is employed in reference to empowering students. Traditional lines drawn between students and teachers, "us and them," have impressed educators with the necessity of maintaining firm control. Control has been simplistically interpreted as imposed authority, complete with consequences and penalties for violations of that authority. Adults make the rules, kids must live by them, and so-called student government is far more a simulation of democracy than a reality. Some strategies for shifting to students some of this responsibility and therefore authority are discussed in Chapter 9.

These traditional dividing lines are relevant to this discussion, however, in that pedagogy and curriculum have likewise become imposed. Adults again are in charge. We presume to know what is best, what is worth knowing and learning, and how it should be taught. And again, students must postpone their emergence as decision makers and self-directed learners. The responsive designs described here offer some strategies through which youngsters can begin to exercise their birthright regarding the freedom of ideas.

As young adolescents begin to establish themselves and their points of view in ways that differ from those of the adults around them, a potential for tension emerges. Yet, at the same time we have a unique opportunity to be constructively responsive to their needs for independence and responsibility. The partnership theme introduced earlier in this chapter comes to the forefront as we consider some pedagogical designs that will nurture youngsters' emerging individual identities in ways that will enable them to grow in terms of initiative, responsibility, and accountability—essential elements of self-sufficiency in terms of both citizenship and scholarship.

By partnership I refer primarily to participation by the teacher and each student in shared decision making about curriculum. Sometimes actual contracts are written out to state explicitly who does what. An example of such a contract appears in Chapter 7. For the present discussion, however, I am referring to a more generic concept of partnership in which the more traditional formal lines between student and teacher can become blurred in a mutual quest for learning. After all, it is in losing oneself in learning that one, of necessity, becomes the instrument of learning. And it is through instrumentality that one becomes self-sufficient.

Accountability

By the time students reach the middle grades, they have figured out for themselves how school works. They know (or believe they know) what they can and cannot do, particular teachers' soft spots and limits, how far to push the rules, who can be counted on for help, and so on. Disturbing by-products of such sophistication are traces of an accompanying cynicism that becomes more full-blown in later adolescence, when a compromise that smacks of minimalism seems to permeate high schools (Sizer, 1984). Given their increasing sophistication about the dynamics of schooling, it follows that young adolescents are capable of becoming much more accountable for themselves and their learning than teachers usually acknowledge.

In order for students to become more accountable, our pedagogical practices must establish structures and provide guidance so students can learn to contemplate their education more holistically and maintain records of their work: decisions, choices, activities, and time. Chapter 7 includes some examples of ways students can go about planning, assessing, and evaluating their learning so that responsibility for educational progress is right where it belongs—shared between teacher and student.

Choices

Every day every student repeatedly makes the same fundamental choice: to try to learn or not to. Regardless of how provocative or dreary, noteworthy or insignificant a topic or class may be, the student remains the one in control of whether or not any learning is going to take place. As kids become increasingly savvy about what it takes to satisfy teachers or to get by, they become increasingly distracted from what has been obliquely referred to for generations as "the joy of learning" that is so evident in the behaviors of younger children. When learning is good—that is, meaningful and satisfying to the learner—an individual has opted to commit whatever energy the task requires and make whatever sacrifices the learning necessitates. In short, the learner has chosen to learn. Our task as their teachers is to try to influence them to choose to learn.

"You can't make a silk purse out of a sow's ear" is an ageless expression we all know. I use it in this context to refer to the extreme difficulty if not impossibility of turning particular curricular content into something kids will recognize as worth learning. Each of us has been a student in the middle grades, and we may be able to recall curriculum that was difficult or nearly impossible to justify learning. My own favorite example of this kind of pointlessness is the social studies unit about climate in desert regions of the world being taught in February in a Vermont sixth grade. Most of the children dutifully but mindlessly carried out their teacher's instructions. When I interviewed several of them after the unit was finished to find out their understanding of why they had studied that topic, they could offer no explanation beyond "because the teacher said so" and "because it's in the book." The teacher's answer to the same question offered startlingly little additional insight about the rationale for the study. It was in the book, so they "did it" as if "doing it" would generate learning. As nice and well intentioned as that teacher may have been, she failed her students by perpetuating a mindless ritual in lieu of providing education. And the children did what they were told, oblivious to the meaning of it all.

A rationale often used in an attempt to justify curriculum to students is "You need to learn it because you'll need it in high school." To many youngsters, that excuse is hollow and unconvincing. High school requirements are rarely their immediate concern. Distrust toward teachers is justified most of the time this argument is made, because any interdependence between curriculum at the middle level and that in high school is extremely unclear. I suspect that beyond the acquisition of the tools of learning, the standardized middle grades curriculum is only marginally relevant to the secondary grades, regardless of how clearly plans of study are laid out in curriculum guides. A great deal of the curriculum material recommended for the middle grades has dubious value as far as I can judge, and I know from interviewing students that much of it is outright counterfeit if not simply corny to kids (Rogers & Stevenson, 1988).

Given these conditions and the need for young adolescents to learn how to choose responsibly, a framework that not just allows but requires student participation in deciding some of what is to be learned makes good sense. Over the last several years I taught on a multiage team composed of ten- to fourteen-year-olds (sixth, seventh, and eighth graders); my teammates and I evolved a system we referred to informally as the "Rule of Three." This system became the basis for determining what the curriculum would be for individual students on our team. We organized the school year into modules of three to four weeks each that were usually separated by a holiday or long weekend. During those modules each teacher would teach several minicourses and one interdisciplinary unit, and we would take responsibility for several math groups and book groups. At the beginning of a module, each student followed the "Rule of Three" to set personal academic goals based on choices from (1) the classes and projects we were offering, (2) each student's own personal assessment of "what I need to learn better," and (3) "topics/studies I want to explore," referred to as Orbital Studies. As students drafted personal goals, they met with a teacher-member of the team to review the choices, discuss modifications the teacher might recommend, and obtain the teacher's agreement to a final plan.

Specific academic goals might still be mandated by the teacher when necessary. Teachers know some things that students need to know or be able to do, so the entreaty becomes "Trust me." For example, a student who didn't like to write might want to omit writing, but the teacher would remind him of the necessity of writing well and make certain it was included in his plan. Because decision making was earnestly shared and rationales were explained, our students generally trusted us and our judgment in such cases.

During the three years youngsters were with us, they grew immensely in their ability to conceptualize a realistic and responsible plan. They also developed the academic competencies they needed to function successfully in secondary school (Stevenson, 1979). Further examples and details pertinent to student involvement in curricular choices are elaborated in Chapter 7.

Orbital Studies

During my many years as both a student and a teacher, I have learned a constant truth of human nature: everyone wants to be an expert at something. By *expert* I have in mind our personal need to believe that we have at least one area of specialized abilities and talents that are a basis for both personal pride and recognition from others around us. As a young adolescent I knew that I could outrun most other kids my age, that I was a fast reader, and that I could build things and fix things. Like anyone else, I especially relied upon knowledge of these personal competencies on occasions when I confronted the actualities that others were better spellers or stronger swimmers or understood algebra. Having a demonstrated basis for self-confidence is essential to everyone, but it is especially critical to young adolescents. We must heed the admonition that every youngster "must be at least very good at something, because success is critical to a positive self-image" (Carnegie Corporation, 1989, p. 49).

I first encountered a curriculum rationale for including studies by which students could explore their special interests and develop expertise in the Fourfold Curriculum design (James, 1974). From that introduction my teammates and I introduced "Orbital Studies," an option for students to learn about anything of interest to them that we could help them learn. We made it clear from the beginning that their interests might lead into areas about which we had little or no knowledge. However, part of our expertise lay in knowing how to go about finding out and learning. Thus we presented Orbitals as a proposal for partnerships between individual students and teachers, some of whom were almost certain to be adults outside the faculty. To our surprise, our students welcomed the idea, and while they were interested in lots of different things, they had difficulty choosing topics they wanted to explore formally. We discovered that they were apprehensive about such an unknown experience. Until they saw concrete examples of other students' Orbitals, they remained reluctant to choose.

We were also taken somewhat off guard by our students' initial reluctance to take on Orbitals alone. Even thought our original idea was that students would work individually, when a few pairs of students presented joint proposals, we approved and supported them. For example, two seventh grade girls wanted to investigate extrasensory perception. Although none of us teaching on the team knew much about ESP, we began with the library and the telephone book to track down materials and local people who might be knowledgeable. Another girl duo proposed to learn about cats, and an abundance of resources made it possible for them to begin immediately. A trio of boys wanted to learn about electronics, and a review of our parent files located an electronics engineer father who, after meeting with the boys one morning before school, agreed to come to school early two mornings a week to teach them basic circuitry. Finally, we received our first solo overture from Steven, a somewhat sullen loner who had yet to make anything nearly resembling a serious intellectual commitment to our program. He proposed to build a kayak, and the highly successful project that grew from his first Orbital spawned a dozen more kayaks over the next two years, several of which were tutored by Steven, now a recognized expert.

It is difficult now for me to imagine how a responsive middle level program can function without Orbitals or some other arrangement that enables students to develop individual specialties. The extremely valuable processes of choosing, making commitments of time and energy, and ultimately being responsible and accountable for one's learning may be possible to accomplish in a teacher-defined curriculum, but once established, these processes grow naturally in a context where students choose some of the things they will learn. Critics will argue against such a scheme on the grounds that there is no way to ensure that all students will cover the same material. "Covering the same material" all of the time is hardly a valid goal for young adolescents who are, we must remember, always the ones who ultimately determine *what is learned*.

Producing Knowledge

Traditional schooling practice appears to be based on an assumption that young adolescents must be consumers, not producers, of knowledge. For many areas of the curriculum, this is a valid supposition. Part of our responsibility as teachers is to select wisely for our students from the abundance of curricular material on the market. But it is also appropriate for young adolescent youngsters to be producers of knowledge. Knowledge consumption and knowledge production are mutually beneficial enterprises. A by-product of Orbitals, for example, is the development of new knowledge and expertise that can be instrumental in guiding the learning of others, as was the case with Steven's kayak Orbital. Another boy's study of his family history produced a family tree that constituted knowledge for his family members' edification that had not been previously gathered.

Students can also produce knowledge through group studies such as the interdisciplinary units more fully explained in Chapter 7. The emphasis throughout is on balancing what is already known and can be learned through study with what is unknown and must be found out. In its purest form, scholarship is a consolidation of existing knowledge, questions, and new knowledge. In this sense, young adolescents can enjoy and grow from scholarship in the same ways that university professors are scholars. Only the sophistication that produces more exacting knowledge differs. For example, an interdisciplinary study of a city park and the adjacent businesses blended existing knowledge available through public records and the local public library with the knowledge gained through firsthand research investigations that included observations and interviews (Erb and Rathbone, 1991).

The ways in which the knowledge that has been produced gets shared is a final urgent consideration. Arguably, schools most commonly expect students to demonstrate their knowledge through one or more forms of writing, usually reports or tests. But better uses of writing are applied through student publications of books, newsletters, magazines, and journals. Project displays and bulletin boards also require writing. Ultimately, the preferred way of demonstrating accountability for producing knowledge is through presentation—publication, lecture, demonstration, dramatic performance, and other ways students can share their knowledge by teaching others.

Taking Positions

Navigators study pertinent data in order to fix their position on the sea or in space. Acquiring a navigator's attitude is also appropriate for young adolescents. As previous sections of this book explained, part of the change process of these years is the emergence of their new consciousness about issues in their immediate context as well as the larger world. Examining one's inclinations through introspection, learning others' points of view, and then taking a personal position gives expression to their growing need for self-definition. After all, no age group is at greater risk of exploitation by those who peddle harmful substances than young adolescents, who are often naive about personal risks and who often distrust the admonitions of well-intentioned adults to "just say no." In my experience, studying ordinarily controversial issues such as euthanasia or drug legalization in candid ways that honor youngsters' thoughtful exchanges results in responsible, conservative positions. This outcome establishes a healthy, wholesome basis for the identity formation dynamics of their time of life.

Service

The propriety of young adolescents rendering services to their school and greater community has already been addressed, and more precise approaches to service activities are included in subsequent chapters. However, the relevance of service to pedagogy that is responsive to youngsters' developmental needs for responsibility and accountability is worthy of further brief mention here. During these several formative years, young adolescents are developmentally ready to begin to engage the adult world on terms that approximate exemplary adult citizenship.

Two issues merit special reminders here. First, young adolescents are now physically and intellectually capable of doing many things that are useful to other people: tutoring/reading to younger children, decorating and caring for the school buildings and grounds, using telephone chains to promote community participation in such activities as civic events and voting, sending letters and cards to the elderly or prisoners, assisting after school with day care, visiting convalescent home residents, and doing community cleanup projects. These are just a few examples. Additional possibilities for collaborations may exist through adult service organizations such as Kiwanis, Rotary, and local churches. The point is that kids can be useful to others.

The second reminder relating to responsibility and accountability is that in doing such work, youngsters experience firsthand what it means to be useful in more adult terms. There is truth in the axiom that "as the twig is bent, so shall it grow." Middle level educators must capitalize on this opportunity to bend the twig toward values about helping others that become connected with the simultaneous emergence of idealism and the potential destiny of a better society. Responsibility and accountability are goals for our students that transcend the usual context teachers are concerned about, such as doing homework and observing school rules. Our students need the experience of making service forays into the world of actualities they will soon enter as full citizens. As middle level educators we must keep the goal of excellence in citizenship at the forefront of whatever educational programs we devise.

Self-Assessment and Self-Evaluation

How do students judge their educational progress? How do they know how they are doing? Distinctions between these two processes are developed in greater detail in Chapter 8, but a major component of learning to be responsible and accountable has to do with systematically keeping up with one's progress. A common response to my entreaty "What are you learning that is important?" is an awkward expression usually followed by some version of "I don't know" or "I'm not sure." When I press the matter, students usually mention things they're doing at that time in one of their classes. I wonder if they're like workers on an assembly line who have some consciousness of what they're doing at the moment but who have little or no idea what they're assembling.

Part of their difficulty can be explained, of course, in terms of intellectual development that doesn't yet enable them to conceptualize the whole thing. But there is more at work here. Teachers plan units or courses so that in their minds the curriculum is appropriately sequenced and tied together with attention to the need for coherence. Often students receive handouts at the beginning to show them where they're going. However useful these outlines may be, they remain the work of teachers who understand what they're doing. Middle level teachers need to cultivate the emerging, tentative capacities for young adolescents to do the same. It is through learning how to assess one's education that the skills of accountability and the disposition toward being responsible can be cultivated.

By *self-assessment* I refer to a process for inventorying what one is doing, what has been learned, which tasks have been completed, and which ones have been postponed or abandoned. No external standards or criteria are necessary or appropriate to self-assessment. The most direct parallel is a weather report where the basic function is simply to describe what is going on at the moment, then make a forecast. Self-evaluation differs only in that the "weather report" is judged in terms of a standard. When students set academic goals, they evaluate their accomplishment in light of their goals. When academic standards are set by teachers, kids' work is evaluated according to the teacher's expectations. Both of these enterprises should have a central place in middle level education, although self-assessment is usually overlooked as a result of preoccupations with evaluation.

RESPONSIVE DESIGNS V: AMBIANCE

Earlier in this chapter I commented about young adolescents' enlarging capacities and readiness for forming educational partnerships with their teachers. When the school climate is tense and adversarial, those conditions play out in students' behavior toward adults and each other. On the other hand, when schools work best there is a self-evident state of partnership by which students participate in meaningful ways in defining the ambiance of their classrooms and school. For example, learning how to make enlightened, responsible decisions is a central part of being an educated person. As students develop they become increasingly able to comprehend possibilities, and they can also recognize the worth of democratic processes through participation in making important decisions. One dimension of this process is their exercising some personal curricular choices through options such as Orbital Studies. In this particular discussion, however, I want to focus on cultivating partnerships in determining the ambiance of the school and classroom context—that is, the interpersonal and physical climate.

It is important to be wary from the beginning about any claims that any specific manipulations of the environment will cause more or better learning. As everyone who has been to school realizes, the factors involved in human learning are too individual and variable to make definitive claims about causality. Yet, we also recognize features of responsive, nurturing environments that stand out and that are not present in settings that are indifferent to students or even oppressive. This discussion focuses on aspects of the school ambiance that are responsive to youngsters' readiness for decision making and are therefore supportive of them and their needs.

Goodlad uses *ambiance* to describe four elements of classroom life in the schools he and his associates studied (1984, p. 108). I use the term here to refer to the essence of the whole school. What is the interpersonal climate? the intellectual climate? the ethical climate? the physical context? In the healthiest of settings, the responses to those queries are products of partnerships that exist between the adults and students. Both generations listen to each other, make necessary compromises, and accomplish joint ventures. This is not to say, however, that all decisions must be negotiated. Educators are ultimately responsible for what happens in schools, and many issues cannot be negotiable. Students understand this truth, of course, and although they may push the limits on selected issues, they still know there are limits. Sometimes they push to find out where those limits are. It is prudent, therefore, to seek collaboration in areas where collaboration is possible and appropriate.

Where the ambiance of a school is depressed, partnerships were never formed or have failed and urgently need to be resurrected. Although there may be more hopeful, positive classes or activities here and there, a single individual working alone cannot overhaul the ambiance of a school, no matter how gifted and energetic that person may be. This truth is evident throughout the remarkable story of Thayer Junior-Senior High School's metamorphosis (Kammeraad-Campbell, 1989). Although the book is ostensibly about Dennis Littky, the embattled but persevering principal, a fundamental moral is provided by the partnerships he initiated with and among teachers, students, and community members. Littky's partnership style inspired others to collaborate, and although he was and continued to be the foremost inspiration, scores of collaborations were integral to the remarkable overhaul of that school. The agenda for partnerships I want to emphasize here is comparable in its triple focus: the intellectual context, the physical context, and the interpersonal climate.

Intellectual Context

"What is intellectual about the ambiance?"

At first this may appear to be a trite question to ask about a school's climate, but the majority of the schools Goodlad studied (1984) and many of those I have visited cannot be fairly characterized as intellectual. I'm accustomed to seeing students at work on academic assignments and listening to the teachers' presentations, but those activities do not necessarily equate with an intellectually responsive ambiance in which people of all ages seek dialogue about ideas, listen thoughtfully to each other, compare interpretations, speculate about possibilities, reflect upon previous learnings, formulate questions, and theorize. I look at a school's ambiance in terms of the questions listed at the close of Chapter 2 and in Chapter 3. Many of those questions explore academic issues as a subset of intellectual ambiance.

Ambiance that is reflective of responsive pedagogy is unmistakable. It is evident, first of all, in how students interact with each other and adults. They talk with each other, not just at each other. Their discussions range from familiar adolescent interests in music and sports to exchanges about favorite literature and how to repair a bicycle. I recently observed sixteen four-member cooperative groups of seventh graders working to solve a problem set by their teacher—to construct a robotic arm that would pick up an egg, move it a distance of one foot, and deposit it in an egg carton. Students were using all sorts of found materials to explore solutions for this engaging problem, and during the hour I observed I witnessed *authentic* twelve-year-olds' intellectual dialogue. Their interactions were young adolescent equivalents to those of a team of professional engineers working on a problem. The connection between pedagogy and ambiance there was unmistakable.

The physical environment also features the products of their intellectual engagements: representations of academic concepts, projects, displays, constructions. Evidence of representational thought are in graphic and three-dimensional art works, music, drama, and dance. Maeroff's (1990) description of Shoreham-Wading River Middle School portrays the rich variety of physical features, program offerings, and interpersonal exchanges that reflect the responsive intent and ambiance of adults that is reciprocated by their students in an ultimate example of partnership.

Physical Context

"Whose place is this?"

Goodlad's often-cited comprehensive study of American schools includes a reflection that is important to this discussion.

> While I believe that schools provide unique opportunities to create pleasing places to live and work, I am less distressed by their aesthetic deficiencies than by the apparent absence of participation by parents, teachers and students in their improvement. Here is an opportunity for young and old to share (1984, p. 240).

There is widespread opportunity for teachers, students, parents, and others to collaborate in making the physical composition and appearance of school spaces pleasing and conducive to excellence. Room decorations and displays, for example, ought to reflect a negotiated plan that has been conceived and carried out by partnerships of students and adults. Moral support, guidance, and counsel can be met by teachers who recognize the importance of the physical environment and the product of collaboration. Supplies usually must come from other adults. Ideas and labor reside in copious amounts in our students.

Decisions about decorations, the composition of bulletin boards, and student work that should be displayed ought to be shared by students and teachers. Likewise, taking care of the space ought to be equitably shared. In order for youngsters to feel personally connected to the spaces they inhabit and for which we hold them accountable, they must have full, active voices in the planning. Where these collaborations occur, ownership shifts from "Mr. Smith's Room" or "Room 10" to "our room."

Another considerable advantage of interdisciplinary teaming is the identity that can be given to physical spaces by a team of teachers and students. Teams usually occupy several adjacent rooms or a wing of the school. The team's name and other identifying characteristics such as logo and colors are often carried through the decoration of those spaces.

A sign painted in team colors and prominently displaying the team's logo, such as "Welcome to the Swamp—Home of the Gators," clearly identifies the place. Additional team slogans, mottoes, rules, displays of team members' work, and artifacts from past team activities further establish that the space, the program, and the people in the designated area belong to each other. Further connections between program and students are evident through additional tangibles that display the team name and colors: book covers, pencils, T-shirts, stickers, buttons, pins, and so on.

Interpersonal Context

"What kind of people live here?"

Imagine an eleven-year-old boy who is new to your school. What are his concerns? What are his priorities? How will he go about judging his new school? There's no mystery about the kind of interpersonal ambiance that makes an individual feel welcome and put at ease. An atmosphere that exudes hospitality and good will enables any newcomer to feel safe, and safety is a primary concern not just to students but also to their parents. Too often educators rationalize that a negative school or classroom ambiance is simply a reflection of the community or the kinds of homes students come from. Such conclusion is far too superficial. An overwhelming majority of all our students want a safe, cheerful, productive climate. Once adults and youngsters concur about their priorities, remarkable climate shifts come about.

The ambiance of developmentally responsive environments is especially reflected in students' dialogue and how they go about participating in activities. No particular expertise is required to judge whether or not the environment welcomes individuality, celebrates students' accomplishments, and emphasizes collaboration. Where students are pitted against each other academically through archaic and inappropriate practices such as grading on a curve, no one should be surprised that students become antagonistic toward each other and competitive in the same ways that many animals compete with each other to work out dominance and submission. The value of mutual respect is cultivated and learned though all day-to-day activities, not just through the abstraction of teachers' lectures.

In their study of adolescent students who did well in school, Beane and Lipka (1980) learned that the freedom to get up and move around their classrooms that students enjoyed was a high priority they associated with their successes. The most comfortable middle grades classrooms I've ever visited and taught in were ones where students moved about as their work required. The emphasis was much more upon learning by doing than by listening. The traditional picture of students sitting in rows of desks working on paper-and-pencil tasks or in textbooks or listening for more than fifteen minutes at a time to a teacher's lecture is a contrivance of schooling that obviates true learning. In reflecting on a day of observing in a junior high school, Goodlad remarked that he "witnessed no marked variations in these [same] pedagogical procedures" (1984, p. 93). Responsive pedagogy accommodates freedom of movement and the variety of ways students learn, and those conditions contribute to a productive interpersonal climate.

Although student management and mediation techniques are presented in greater detail in Chapter 7, it is also appropriate here to point out the connections between ambiance and how disciplinary matters are handled. Where interpersonal conflicts are resolved (1) by fellow students who have mastered the steps involved in mediating disagreements or (2) by clearly, consistently administered consequences that emphasize student decision making, students can more easily learn the benefits to themselves and others of living responsibly. Consequences for misdeeds can also be achieved through effective use of team meetings, essentially eliminating the tensions both students and teachers associate with traditional adult-centered policing. The more students assume responsibility for their learning and their citizenship, the more positive and welcoming is the ambiance of every team, classroom, or school.

Summary

The intellectual, physical, and interpersonal variables of any context constitute its ambiance. No single prescription of these ingredients will ensure more or greater learning; yet, it seems virtually certain that there are correlates between how students perceive their schooling and their subsequent achievement (Johnston, 1983). Teachers will serve themselves and their students well by employing pedagogy that is developmentally responsive and appropriate to their constituents—that is, their students.

Supporting Activities

1. *Frameworks for Constructive Social Interactions.* The most certain way to learn how well the instructional programs satisfy students' desire to work and learn together is to ask them. Use some of the approaches to inquiry described in Chapter 3 to find out what works well in terms of students' perceptions of their own learning. Direct the inquiry to specific program features of interest, such as teaming, teacher advisories, cooperative grouping, service projects, or tracking.

2. *Ensuring Firsthand Learning and Systematic Patterns of Thought.* Invite several young adolescents to join you in learning about an accessible resource such as a radio or television station, a business, or an environmental feature such as a pond or mountain. From the beginning of the project, be sure to engage the students in identifying what they already know, what questions might be explored, how to carry out the project, and how to communicate to others what was learned. Although the investigation itself is likely to become a focus, use the project to observe and record the students' intellectual and personal responses. Develop a brief profile of the patterns of thinking for at least one of the students. Share the profile(s) with teachers, soliciting their ideas.

3. *Nurturing Responsibility and Accountability.* Interview as many students as possible to find out what they'd like to learn about. Don't be surprised at first if they have difficulty with the question. Give them time to think over possibilities, to talk with each other, and to look through books and other materials for ideas. Then ask them to join you in building a list of interesting projects, questions, and topics from which they could choose to learn about as a group or explore individually. As another inquiry, ask for ideas they believe would improve their school or community.

4. *Ambiance.* What do young adolescents have to say about the learning climate in their school? interpersonal relationships? the physical environment? Where they are critical or express dissatisfactions, solicit their suggestions for improvement.

5. *Personal Reflection and Analysis.* Reflect upon what you regard as significant learning experiences from your own early adolescent years, such as learning to play a musical

instrument, carrying out a project, or learning something challenging from someone outside of school. Analyze that experience according to the things you did to learn, the ways you went about doing the necessary work, and what you regard as the product of your learning. What relationships can you make between those experiences and the content of this chapter? Share your results, and look for idiosyncrasies about each other's personal learning inclinations.

REFERENCES

Arnold, J., & Stevenson, C. (1998). *Teachers' Handbook on Teaming.* Fort Worth: Harcourt Brace (in press).

Beane, J. A., & Lipka, R. P. (1980). *Self-concept, self-esteem, and the curriculum.* New York: Teachers College Press.

Carnegie Corporation. (1989). *Turning points: Preparing American youth for the 21st century.* Washington, DC: Carnegie Council on Adolescent Development.

Dale, E. (1984). *The educator's quotebook.* Bloomington, IN: Phi Delta Kappa.

Elkind, D. (1984). *All grown up & no place to go: Teenagers in crisis.* Reading, MA: Addison-Wesley.

Erb, C. A., & Rathbone, C. (1991, April). The city hall park study. *Arithmetic Teacher, 38*(8), 44–47.

Erb, T. O. & Doda, N. M. (1989). *Team organization: Promise—practices and possibilities.* Washington, DC: National Education Association (Analysis and Action Series).

George, P. S. (1988). Tracking and ability grouping: Which way for the middle school? *Middle School Journal, 20,* 21–28.

George, P. S., Spreul, M., & Moorefield, J. (1986). Long-term student/teacher relationships. Columbus, OH: National Middle School Association.

George, P. S., & Stevenson, C. (1989). The "very best teams" in "the very best schools" as described by middle school principals. *TEAM, 3*(5), 6–14.

Gibran, K. (1961). *The prophet.* New York: Knopf.

Goodlad, J. I. (1984). *A place called school.* New York: McGraw-Hill.

James, C. (1974). *Beyond customs: An educator's journey.* New York: Agathon.

James, M. (1986). *Adviser-advisee programs: why, what and how.* Columbus, OH: National Middle School Association.

Johnson, D. W., Johnson, R. T., and Holubec, E. J. (1986). *Circles of learning: Cooperation in the classroom.* Edina, MN: Interaction.

Johnston, J. H. (1983). *Student perceptions of classroom climate and achievement in science. Schools in the middle: A report on trends and practices.* Reston, VA: National Association of Secondary School Principals, p. 5.

Joyce, B., & Weil, M. (1986). *Models of teaching.* Englewood Cliffs, NJ: Prentice-Hall.

Kagan, S. (1989). *Cooperative learning resources for teachers.* San Juan Capistrano, CA: Resources for Teachers.

Kammeraad-Campbell, S. (1989). *Doc: The story of Dennis Littky and his fight for a better school.* Chicago: Contemporary Books.

Kozol, J. (1980). *Children of the revolution.* New York: Delta.

Labinowicz, E. (1980). *The Piaget primer.* Reading, MA: Addison-Wesley.

Lewis, R. (1987). The butterfly in my pocket: On teaching the imaginative experience. (Issues for Educators—monograph series, Vol. 2, No. 1). New York: Queens College School of Education.

Lipsitz, J. (1984). *Successful school for young adolescents.* New Brunswick, NJ: Transaction.

Lounsbury, J. H., & Vars, G. E. (1978). *A curriculum for the middle school years.* New York: Harper & Row.

Maeroff, G. I. (1990). A close look at a good middle school. *Phi Delta Kappan, 71*(7), 504–511.

National Association of Secondary School Principals. (1985). *An agenda for excellence at the middle level.* Reston, VA: Author.

National Association of Secondary School Principals. (1989). *Middle level education's responsibility for intellectual development.* Reston, VA: Author.

National Middle School Association. (1995). *This we believe: developmentally responsive middle level schools.* Columbus, OH: Author.

Paley, V. (1981). *Wally's stories.* Cambridge, MA: Harvard University Press.

Rogers, V. R., & Stevenson, C. (1988). How do we know what kids are learning in school? *Educational Leadership, 45*(5), 68–75.

Sharan, S., & Shachar, Y. (1988). *Language and learning in the cooperative classroom.* New York: Springer.

Simmons, R. G., & Blyth, D. A. (1987). *Moving into adolescence: The impact of pubertal change and school context.* New York: Aldine De Gruyter.

Sizer, T. (1984). *Horace's compromise: The dilemma of the American high school.* Boston: Houghton Mifflin.

Slavin, R. E. (1986). *Using student team learning.* Baltimore, MD: Center for Research on Elementary and Middle Schools, John Hopkins University.

Slavin, R. E. (1987). Ability grouping and student achievement in elementary schools: A best evidence synthesis. *Review of Educational Research, 57,* 293–336.

Slavin, R. E. (1990a). Here to stay—or gone tomorrow? (Guest Editorial). *Educational Leadership,* 47(4), p. 3.

Slavin, R. E. (1990b). Research on cooperative learning: Consensus and controversy. *Educational Leadership,* 47(4), 52–54.

Smith, F. (1986). *Insult to intelligence.* New York: Arbor.

Stevenson, C. (1979). *A phenomenological study of perceptions about open education among graduates of Fayerweather Street School.* Unpublished dissertation, University of Connecticut.

Stevenson, C. (1986). *Teachers as inquirers.* Columbus, OH: National Middle School Association.

Stevenson, C. (1996). Partner Teaming. *VAMLE Focus, 1*(5).

Stevenson, C., & Carr, J. F. (1992). *Dancing through walls: Integrated studies in the middle grades.* New York: Teachers College Press.

Wheelock, A. (1992). *Crossing the tracks: How untracking can save America's schools.* Boston: Massachusetts Advocacy Center.

Wheelock, A., & Dorman, G. (1988). *Before it's too late: Dropout prevention in the middle grades.* Boston: Massachusetts Advocacy Center.

Chapter 6
Choosing Curriculum

○ *What are the curriculum possibilities in our context?*

○ *What do young adolescents need to know and be able to do?*

○ *Which curriculum complements their developmental readiness?*

○ *Which curriculum invites exploration? Requires disciplined study?*

○ *What are students' personal curricular interests and curiosities?*

○ *Which talents and abilities can be developed as curriculum?*

○ *What is essential for success in high school?*

I think a major problem . . . is not that kids are too brash and nervy but that we are not brash and nervy enough . . . We vainly hope to make a treadmill look like a sacred quest; we ask kids to be excited in a void of ideas, because only in talking about nothing can we be sure not to arouse any controversy. We don't even talk with them about patriotism anymore. We ask kids to take a stand in all the places where we have been taking a nap. Then, when we have few takers, we complain about the apathy of youth.

(Keizer, 1989, p. 11)

Any educational paradigm is challenged (if not brought to its knees) by the young adolescent student who doesn't have a Ph.D. in educational psychology, who hasn't achieved expertise in academics or sports, and who simply says, "This is boring. I won't do it." One of the refreshing and challenging actualities in the emergence of early adolescent individuality is a growing willingness to exercise such independent judgment in the face of what they have historically acknowledged as nonnegotiable adult authority about their learning. Whether a student simply goes through the motions of doing (assigned) work or expresses refusal most directly, as in the example, the result is the same. Difficult as it may be to get away from a traditional posture of explaining "because I said so," middle level educators MUST find ground for forming partnerships with their students if meaningful learning is to occur. Most kids are generally agreeable and adapt quickly and easily to collaboration. Some of them are more wary and require adults to demonstrate over time their trustworthiness for partnership. We can be sure that young adolescents need learning experiences that are satisfying if not thrilling. To paraphrase a contemporary aphorism, "If we create it, they will come." If we provide, they will seek more of the same. Further, they won't be so inclined toward the superficial or even dangerous involvements that seem inevitable when they are left to their own devices.

Every middle grades teacher, regardless of the setting, has an opportunity to show young adolescent students the joy and power of authentic learning. Being a positive influence on another person's education is, of course, much more than simply directing and supervising him or her through externally prescribed curriculum content. In the selection of every topic, design of every unit, and organization of every study, teachers make profound curricular decisions. The choices teachers make about what to teach and how to teach it are eminently important, for they define the limits of what may be learned. In classrooms where such decisions are abrogated to curriculum guides or textbooks, the scope of learning possibilities is unnecessarily and inappropriately confined.

Teachers' decisions and choices about curriculum must be informed from the very beginning by a general understanding of child development that is augmented by specific knowledge of the readiness and interests of the specific children being served. The questions opening this chapter are raised to guide the reader toward choices that will insure youngsters the opportunity to grow toward a learning lifestyle that transcends the assembly-line model descriptive of too many schools. This chapter reviews types of curriculum and instruction that are responsive to the varying developmental needs and interests of young adolescent learners.

While in the broadest sense curriculum consists of all aspects of a planned school program, including academics, the arts, athletics, and social values, in this chapter it refers to the focused studying and learning that students do in order to become better informed, more competent, and more confident learners. In their vernacular, it is "the stuff" they do—what they learn or are supposed to learn.

John Goodlad's work (1979) offers a useful framework to help us conceptualize curriculum and contemplate choices. He points out some fundamental differences between curriculum that has been sanctioned and published and what is actually taught and learned. His arrangement organizes curriculum according to five domains (pp. 58–64):

Ideological Curriculum—curriculum written by experts in a field, usually university professors and researchers, published as textbooks and/or curriculum guides from national associations.

Formal Curriculum—the plan of study formally sanctioned by school boards at either the state or the local system level.

Perceived Curriculum—the extant curriculum as believed by teachers, parents, and community people; there are numerous varying beliefs and assumptions within this domain.

Operational Curriculum—what actually occurs as documented by trained observers; what teachers perceive the curriculum to be may be quite different from what they are actually teaching.

Experienced Curriculum—what the students actually experience.

Responsible decisions about which curriculum to use require that teachers be well acquainted with the Ideological and the Formal. Certainly, one needs to be informed by relevant research and expert opinion. On the other hand, in order to be responsive to a given group of students, it is also necessary to remember that experts and policy makers are making general recommendations for all schools. Deciding the extent to which elements of the Ideological and Formal curricula are appropriate for a given class or team of students must always be an individual teacher's or team's professional decision. Where communication and public relations are a concern, especially with parents, teachers need to see to it that the Perceived Curricula is as close to actuality as possible. Suggested strategies for building effective communications with parents are included in Chapter 11.

The focal point of the discussion of curriculum in this chapter is the nexus involving the Perceived, the Operational, and the Experiential. The ultimate goal should be to bring about congruence between what the teacher is attempting to accomplish, what is actually going on, and what students believe they are experiencing and learning. Simple teacher-made assessment devices can help us identify and understand the extent of this congruence (Rogers & Stevenson, 1988). Strategies for creating such a two-way flow of information that are especially relevant to the Experiential Curriculum are included in Chapter 8. After all, regardless of how the other four domains are defined, it is the Experiential Curriculum that is ultimately most important. That domain is about the learning that actually occurs—the concepts, skills, and values that have become meaningful and therefore relevant to the learners.

RELEVANCE: AN ESSENTIAL CONSIDERATION

> The problem with this school is that they want you to know all of this stuff except that I'm never going to use it. It's a big waste if I'm never going to use it.
>
> *Caitlin, age thirteen*

Caitlin's complaint notwithstanding, the curriculum possibilities for working productively with young adolescents are vast and inviting, so long as curricular decisions preserve balance between what we are certain our youngsters MUST know and be able to do and what they WANT to know more about and be able to do. Preserving this balance is the key to making curriculum choices that will both serve their academic and intellectual needs and resolve the omnipresent issue of relevance bemoaned by Caitlin.

Experienced teachers know the challenge of trying to create ways to present curriculum that they recognize as irrelevant or inherently uninteresting if not outright boring to young adolescents. I recently observed a teacher struggling heroically to interest and inform his seventh graders about climate in Africa's desert regions. The subject matter was valid, of course, but in March in Vermont, the youngsters simply didn't care. Their indifference was also valid. Sometimes we obligatorily cover the material as quickly as possible, as the teacher in this anecdote did with the unverified advice to "learn it now, you'll need it later" or "when you get to high school, you'll thank me." Sometimes we resort to manipulations such as threats of reprisals for failure to do the prescribed work or promises of special rewards. On other occasions we simply defer to expediency by skipping topics or units we recognize as a poor fit for our students.

Curriculum choices should also be guided not just by deliberations about the inherent relevance of topics but also by our own abilities to create relevance. Through our own reactions to studies and choices of pedagogy, we communicate our personal estimation of how relevant or useful or interesting a study may be. Young adolescents can be swept up in studies they might normally reject so long as the teaching model is persuasive. Nancie Atwell writes,

> Adolescents are ripe to be hooked. With good teaching, this is an age when kids who are going to, become excited and interested. When teachers demonstrate interest and excite-

ment in our fields, we invite students to believe that learning is valuable. We answer the question, "Why do we have to do this?" with our own conviction and passion, modeling the power we derive from our knowledge and experience. (1987, p. 48)

Not all curriculum can be sold to all students, however, regardless of the teacher's performance. Young adolescents decide for themselves much as adults do, so we must also critique curriculum for its inherent value to our students just as thoughtfully as we assess its marketability.

As someone said, "when the horse is dead—dismount."

Middle grades teachers are especially well advised to pay close attention to the Experiential Curriculum of Goodlad's typology. Young adolescents are inclined to respond to here-and-now issues, to learning through doing, and to participating in group activities and other present-centered bases for deciding whether or not to make a commitment to learning. Unless and until students make personal commitments to the necessary work, authentic learning won't occur. The teacher's challenge in curriculum selection necessitates a second twofold judgment about relevance: What is inherently relevant about the topic? How can the topic be presented to enhance relevance?

CURRICULUM AS OPPORTUNITY

Whether they teach in a bona fide middle school, a self-contained elementary school, or a departmentalized junior high school, most teachers employ a great deal of individual choice about what and how they teach. Despite the abundance of sanctioned curriculum guides, Goodlad (1984) found substantial ranges of variability among teachers at the same levels with regard to the specific curriculum content they taught. While this finding might distress or confuse those who support uniform, standardized plans of study such as that implied by a national curriculum, it does not come as a surprise to experienced teachers. Middle grades teachers know well the challenges of attempting to balance externally defined expectations with more inductively derived studies and projects in which students have exercised some personal choices about what they learn. They appreciate the uniqueness of authentic learning experiences that are not always replicable. The dynamics within each group of students is a consequence of countless variables. Just as no two individuals are exactly alike, no two groups or classes or semesters are exactly alike. Every teaching unit presents new, original learning circumstances for students and for their teachers.

In exercising choices about curriculum, individual teachers working alone as well as those serving on collaborative teams are able to provide schooling that balances externally defined needs with personal interests. There is probably no better-known contemporary example of excellence in achieving such balance than Eliot Wigginton's (1985) Foxfire work in the southern Appalachians of northern Georgia. Wigginton details how he transcended the apathy his ninth grade students felt toward the established English curriculum by responding to their interest in their own southern Appalachian culture. By helping them create a magazine about their own community and culture, he addressed his responsibilities for his students' academic growth while affirming them and their heritage. Over the years the energy that produced that original magazine has produced a museum, a series of books, and scores of other publications.

Every curriculum unit and study involving middle level students presents opportunities, some of which may be known and predictable, and others that will emerge in the course of the study so long as the design ensures that balance will be preserved between external expectations and students' felt needs and interests. Consequently, the prudent teacher approaches curriculum choice and planning with an understanding and appreciation of curriculum as opportunity.

CURRICULUM AS EXPLORATION

Middle level education IS exploration!

(Melton, 1990)

The concept of exploration helps us clarify some fundamental differences between the externally defined, largely prescriptive nature of curriculum associated with junior high school programs versus the middle school emphasis on curriculum that is responsive to the developmental nature and interests of young adolescents. Let's consider a subject area that highlights this fundamental difference of perspective: second languages. Schools of all types that include the middle grades often provide instruction in a second language, usually French or Spanish. These studies are usually presented in a course format, often on an elective basis. Course content is most often defined in terms of what students need in order to be prepared for further study in high school. Sometimes the policy is that students who take one of these languages in the seventh and eighth grades receive one high school unit for that work and are subsequently placed in an advanced section in high school. In brief, the second language at the middle level is prescribed by the requirements and expectations of the high school program.

The exploratory second language curriculum is conceptualized quite differently from the model above. The middle grades are envisioned as an opportunity to explore other languages in the context of their cultures, building a richer awareness of our multicultural society and world. Such studies would last from as much as one semester or term to just a few weeks, depending on the resources of a given school. For example, conversational French would be learned as a central component in the study of several cultures whose languages are or derive from French. Spanish would be explored in the same way, emphasizing not just the Castilian origins but also derivatives spoken in Spain and in the Western Hemisphere. Other languages of European origin such as German and Italian could also be studied in the context of those cultures. Eastern languages, especially Japanese, Chinese, and Arabic, should be explored, especially in light of our changing world economy and the increasing presence of world cultures in our communities. These are simply examples, and I do not mean to limit this discussion to only the aforementioned languages and cultures. The resources of each school and community will determine such offerings. My point is that these middle years present what is likely to be the sole opportunity for youngsters to explore a variety of languages, to recognize their similarities and differences, and to recognize connections among cultures according to language. Subsequent decisions about specializing in the study of a single language are then better informed and delayed until secondary school, where specialization is more appropriate.

Applying the concept of exploration to decisions about middle level curriculum is one example of schooling that is responsive to the developmental nature of young adolescents and that accommodates their shifting interests. My students' parents often complained that their children had too many interests, kept changing their minds about what to do, and dismissed matters of substance too easily. Those are not unfamiliar characterizations of young adolescent children, of course, for it is natural in these transitional years for youngsters to develop a variety of interests. Once this realization evolved into my acceptance of their basic nature, I was able to understand their interests as evidence of authentic curiosity and potential for mind-building calisthenics. Now as I think about young adolescent needs, I think in terms of their need to act on their curiosities and acquire expertise. And when occasional students express very little curiosity, I know my task is to expose them to some of an infinite number of possibilities, always being alert to the flicker of interest that can be nurtured into the fire of motivation, understanding, and expertise.

The widely diverse interests and lifestyles of the four children in my own family reflect the idiosyncrasies common to a group of young adolescents. The list of their individual specialties during their early adolescent years is lengthy. While they shared a few family activities and sports interests, especially skating and skiing, their primary schticks were essentially idiosyncratic, even though their age range is only six years. One of them loved mechanical things; another preferred to draw and paint, another liked to write. One enjoyed an extensive circle of friends; another was content with a single chum. One was intrigued with mysticism and practiced meditation; another was quite literal and fundamental in terms of spiritual beliefs. One loved and read classical literature, another was immersed in medieval fantasies, another devoured war and sports stories, and one resisted reading anything at all beyond "how to" directions. In spite of common family experiences during these years, their individual personalities, interests, and ways of expressing their inner natures were distinctly individual. Musical tastes included hard rock, opera, reggae, disco, and country and western. Dress choices ranged from calculated fashions to preppy to hippy, and one of our boys was so unaware of clothing that he couldn't tell you at bedtime what he'd been wearing all day. As young adults now, they continue to be unique, and yet they appreciate each other. Helping them explore their interests and develop their individual natures was probably the best response their teachers and parents offered to help them continue to grow.

Curriculum that encourages and helps young adolescents explore their interests is often criticized as being "a mile wide and an inch deep." This description raises an important issue, for simply passing through cafeteria-style options without making considered selections is as unworthy of learners' potential as insisting that they all consume the same things at the same time. Yet, the critics' river metaphor is appropriate. Interests and therefore possibilities for learning are constantly flowing through the consciousness of students. With our insistence and assistance, youngsters must explore that stream, contemplating even momentarily as much of it as they are disposed to, making their own choices about where to dig deep into the stream bed in order to acquire the experience and knowledge upon which expertise is built. The foundational perceptions of themselves as learners as well as the knowledge and competence youngsters acquire in these years are constructed in this manner, and their teachers have a splendid opportunity to see that some of the exploration produces academic and personal substance that will serve them well into and throughout a lifetime of learning.

CURRICULUM AS EMPOWERMENT

A generally accepted rationale for curriculum is that it is the means by which schools perpetuate our culture. Scope and sequence plans are carefully scrutinized to ensure that content is consistent with prevailing views of history, literature, mathematics, science and so on. In the traditional paradigm of schooling, educators often become so wrapped up in this promotional function that students' own interests and growing-up issues are neglected.

What if a primary purpose of curriculum becomes the development of the collective interests and idiosyncratic abilities and talents of a particular group of students? It seems to have been taken for granted for a long time that as long as students achieve academically and athletically, schooling works. Yet, indifference and even cynicism among adolescents appears to be expanding. What if the students themselves were to become a curricular focus in the middle years? John Arnold posits that middle level curriculum should be based on "a positive view of young adolescents, [giving] them considerable control over their own learning, [engaging] them in meaningful tasks and [encouraging] them to contribute to the well-being of others . . . helping [students] understand how society shapes their development and at times exploits them" (Fall 1993, p. 9).

I recently received a telephone call from a twelve-year-old member of the Alpha Team in my neighborhood middle school. Finding my name as community resource person for the team, Erin explained that they were studying adolescence and asked if I could visit as a resource person. We made a date, and I showed up to spend the morning with them a few days later. Following the team's morning meeting, I joined Erin and seven of her classmates. After finding a comfortable place to work together, Erin explained that the whole team working together had generated several hundred ideas and questions about adolescence. They subsequently classified the items into six groups, and the students chose which group they would ask for help in investigating. She went on to explain, "We know we are changing in lots of ways. What we'd like your help on is explaining how we are changing *spiritually*."

Indeed. These children's collective realizations about their own state of transition reminded me once again not to underestimate their readiness and eagerness to more fully understand what was transpiring in their lives. Since I had little to offer in response to their query, I countered with "How do you think you are changing spiritually?" For almost an hour they talked about how they think about "lots of things" they hadn't thought about before. Our time together was at least as informative for me as it was for them. It also rang with the elements of personal efficacy previously described in Chapter 4. Once again the wisdom of John Dewey (1938) rings true: That the very best preparation for the future is to live (and learn) fully in the present.

SOME ESSENTIAL STIPULATIONS

One function of this chapter is to review a selection of types of curriculum appropriate for young adolescent learners. Before those options are detailed, however, some caveats are necessary.

Caveat 1

Seek Balance between Students' Needs and External Requirements

The easiest but most unresponsive way to make curricular decisions is simply to follow a textbook outline, scope and sequence, or curriculum guide, covering the content specified. Much of the curriculum discussion I hear among teachers is about how to organize material, design appropriate sequences, and so on. It is relatively simple to compare and critique textbook treatments of common subject matter or the relative merits of a kit or other learning package. I describe this way of choosing easiest because decisions are focused upon curricular content—material that can be organized and reorganized easily. However, decisions made in this manner don't take into consideration the students' needs and interests. Whether or not the resulting curriculum is responsive to students' conditions is usually left to chance.

More complex, but essential to maintaining the balance advocated here, is an equal emphasis on supporting students' intellectual interests, even when they do not fall within the scope of the recommended curriculum guide. False distinctions between what is academic and nonacademic further distract teachers from recognizing and responding to students' legitimate, intellectually worthy interests. Middle grade teachers must resist the temptation to judge the worth of students' interests on the basis of whether or not those interests complement an externally prescribed course of study. Learning for the sake of learning should constitute the first priority in middle level curriculum.

Caveat 2

Covering Is Not the Same as Teaching or Learning

Perhaps it is the explosion of knowledge over the last few decades and the proliferation of easily accessible materials that have enjoined teachers and students to hurry through as much material as they can cover. The urgency to get through a series of textbooks, to teach sophisticated material at younger ages, and to cram as many different things as possible into the school day promote a superficiality that falls far short of true education. And yet, "if we really believe in lifelong learning, why are we trying to do it all now?" (Combs, 1987). Sometimes I wonder whether we have confused unity with uniformity. We must be alert to the temptation to interpret "what students must know" as "what we must cover," gearing our classes to covering a given amount of material each day and expecting the same results from all students even though we know them to be remarkably diverse. A central flaw in too many curriculum decisions is an unquestioned assumption that all students in a class must cover the same content in the same way at the same time. Likewise, narrow approaches to evaluating progress, such as the predominance of teacher-made and standardized tests, have diverted us from the realization that genuine learning involves meaning that in turn inspires commitment from learners. Perhaps we should indeed think of middle level curriculum at its best as a mile wide and inch deep and expect that every individual will take selected studies to substantial depths in order to understand, appreciate, and construct the structures and interrelationships that constitute enduring knowledge.

Caveat 3

Seek Balance between Exploration and Mastery

All learning, especially that of young adolescents, is and must be recognized as exploratory. In order for learning to occur, new experience and exploration are necessary. Through exploration, interests become focused on components of the experience. As young adolescent learners become aware of and interested in new things, their capacity for exploring their curiosities to achieve a degree of mastery is at a new high. At the same time, their need to be both proficient and known for their proficiency renders them very responsive to teachers' efforts to help them master skills and successfully accomplish challenges they either choose or acknowledge that they need. Much of the curriculum at this level should be exploratory, and acquiring new understandings and competencies should be a primary goal for every student. Exploration and mastery are two sides of the same coin, and their interdependence is recognized and cultivated by responsive middle level teachers.

Caveat 4

Every Student Must Have Many, Many Successes

Make no mistake about it—every single student absolutely must have multiple successes during these years if his or her education is to be worthwhile. In recognition of this truth, the Carnegie Task Force strongly recommends that "middle grade schools [be organized to ensure success] for all students" (1989, p. 49). As Chapter 4 described, youngsters hunger for expertise and recognition as productive, respected, laudable people. Kids who constantly fail at school come to see themselves as failures, and eventually they become dropouts (Wheelock & Dorman, 1988). Any curriculum that is not conceptualized and organized to see that all students achieve legitimate successes also fails by being unresponsive to student conditions and needs. Quite obviously, traditional teacher-dominated, textbook-centered instruction, in which expectations are the same for all students and they are evaluated and graded on a curve, ensure that all students will not have many successes. Such methods are fundamentally unsuited for changeable, vulnerable youngsters such as typical young adolescents. Those methods derive from traditional schooling preoccupied with covering content—narrow methodologies that may be effective for older learners but are woefully inadequate for the huge majority of children in the middle grades.

Ultimately, students' legitimate successes—whatever they may be—are the most valuable components of any curriculum at this level. Youngsters' beliefs in themselves as capable learners must be our most venerated goal. I am not suggesting that traditional curriculum should be discarded, however. I am urging that it be carefully examined and assessed for the essentials. Then those essentials must be presented in ways that will enable youngsters to learn them successfully. The subsequent discussion of types of curriculum suggests a variety of ways to organize and approach those curriculum components judged to be essential for young adolescents.

Caveat 5

Young Adolescents Desire and Respond to Intellectual Rigor

One especially misleading dimension of the young adolescent stereotype is that these children avoid intellectual challenge and rigor. In the early 1980s several studies of changes in the brain mass suggested that between the approximate ages of twelve and fourteen, brain development is at a plateau between growth spurts (Epstein, 1978). The popularized interpretation of this brain periodization theory rationalized that curriculum at the middle level should provide horizontal enrichment, and presentation of more formal conceptual material should be delayed until the next growth spurt. Many teachers further rationalized that their students were disinterested in the curriculum being presented because their brains were resting. This easy excuse for the failure of irrelevant and ill-fitting curriculum contributed to the fabrication of the aforementioned stereotype.

In truth, the opportunity to explore fresh experiences and attempt new challenges has enormous appeal to young adolescents, who need very much to believe in themselves. Youngsters who have little self-confidence can be swept up by the momentum of friends and classmates being motivated toward previously unexplored experience. Among the sources of greatest satisfaction during my years as a middle grades teacher have been occasions when reticent, uncertain students became caught up in the momentum of a project being shared with classmates. Joy in learning was self-evident in their comments and behaviors. Observable changes emerged in how these previously unsteady youngsters went about their subsequent work and in their readiness to apply themselves to future challenges. Such fundamental human growth is not often evident in the routine pursuit of traditional curriculum, however. Authentic growth occurs when the learner makes the commitment that accompanies individual choices about what to learn. Because these youngsters are changing so much so rapidly but irregularly, opportunity to exercise choices within a variety of types of curriculum is essential.

In my experience, young adolescents prefer high expectations so long as they are achievable and especially when they are able to collaborate. They take more responsibility for themselves and each other, and they especially appreciate having their teachers work alongside them. It is all right to have high expectations for students so long as toughness does not become confused with "being mean" and teachers persist in showing them how to meet their responsibilities. It is when they are given arbitrary assignments without concrete support that students withdraw.

The Academic Core

The 3 Rs have long been the learning essentials for students of all ages, and young adolescents must especially be able to read, write, and use mathematics and technology successfully. These are the tools not only for scholarship but for continuing self-development into adulthood. Contemporary adolescents live in a world of unprecedented complexity, and to be unable to learn on one's own becomes a hazardous form of intellectual paralysis. And becoming self-sufficient is not a simple matter. While one might be tempted to assume that working on academic skills in workbooks, kits, and worksheets will develop and refine these tools of scholarship, those of us who work with young adolescents know better. Fill-in-the-blank activities require decoding abilities, but they are lame substitutes for reading. Frank Smith (1986) refers to such isolated published or teacher-made worksheets as "decontextualized trivialities."

The good news is that in spite of any outward cynicism or denial, kids know they need to be competent learners. As they become more perceptive about the complexities of their interests and career possibilities, they also recognize their need for competence in the academic core. It is also important that our communications with them on these issues be honest and straightforward. Gimmicks and gimcracks such as "How to smuggle (math, science, etc.) into the curriculum" have no place in an educational program that we want youngsters to trust and commit themselves to. Kids respect intellectual and academic rigor so long as it is within their reach, and cutesy versions reek of manipulations that will surely turn them away. Every unit of study and every lesson plan should be examined for its intellectual and academic substance.

Authentic learning occurs in a context that requires an individual learner's integration of multiple intellectual and academic functions. Young adolescents become skilled by reading, writing, calculating, and solving problems in contexts that have real meaning for them and where they learn and develop scholarly abilities through meaningful applications, not through paper-and-pencil busywork abstracted from a meaningful context. The overarching goal of the core academic curriculum must be to ensure that students become skilled through meaningful applications, not just to "have skills" as is implied by isolated performance tasks.

Reading

The urgency for a student to be both able to read and disposed to read cannot be overstated. No matter what technological advances may attract our attention and resources away from it, reading remains the primary process for students to access the wisdom and insights of others beyond their own immediate setting and time. Everyone, regardless of location or financial resources, can have easy access to an abundance of reading materials. It is fundamentally important that young adolescents not only develop as technically proficient readers but also become disposed toward reading as the primary avenue to needed information and the satisfactions of finding personal meaning. Reading also provides immediate access to an experience with art, because literature is a medium through which artists communicate to those who read their ideas, reflections, interpretations, and feelings. Learning from print material has always been vital to learning, but it was never more indispensable than it is in today's age of microcomputers.

In spite of the centrality of reading to learning, however, the extent to which it is taught in middle level schools is unclear. Furthermore, its place in young adolescents' family lives is even less clear. Apparently, the curriculum of many middle level schools excludes reading instruction except for students whose performance is deficient (Irvin & Connors, 1989). Yet, I know from my years as a teacher how much my students valued and learned from reading, was evidenced by their participation in book groups, their exchanges of recommended materials with each other, and their delight in a host of periodicals, the most popular of which was usually *MAD*. What should be self-evident is that all middle grades teachers must be reading teachers, whether they are skilled in analysis of problems and instruction or whether they simply promote and share reading in whatever their teaching assignments may be.

There is a lively, ongoing debate between proponents of a phonics approach to reading instruction and those who favor the whole language approach in which "a person is using all aspects of verbal or written communication at his or her disposal to think— sometimes literally, sometimes inferentially, sometimes aesthetically, but always evaluatively and critically" (Jacobs, 1989, p. 34). The argument is focused on the primary grades, where teachers working in self-contained classrooms are usually responsible for all of the core academic instruction (Weaver, 1990). Yet, the issue also has relevance for the middle grades, where teaching responsibilities are typically defined in terms of specific subject matter areas such as social studies or science. This change in role definition does not alter the reality that many young adolescent students continue to need direct instructional support in reading. Consequently, middle grades teachers need to be skilled in using specific strategies to enhance their students' literacy.

There are two literacy responsibilities every middle level teacher must fulfill. First, we must teach the value that "reading is good" by living it. Living it includes sharing the materials we read for our own interest and enlightenment, cultivating and listening to students' reactions to what they read, and continually making connections between literature and our students' known interests. By promoting exchanges of reading materials, book groups, and book talks, a constant exchange of literature becomes commonplace, as it should be. Second, we must all show students how to read and use the instructional materials we choose for our classes. It is regrettable that virtually 90 percent of the instructional materials used in classrooms are textbooks (Educational Products Information Exchange, 1977). These books become more difficult to read in the middle grades, and there tend to be more of them (Irvin, 1990). Furthermore, as a consequence of the political processes that control what is in textbooks and how they are written, they are notoriously boring and poorly written—qualities one researcher refers to as "inconsiderate text" (Armbruster, 1984). It is therefore incumbent on middle level teachers who use textbooks to show students how to analyze and overcome stylistic deficiencies in order to gain the understanding they need. Teachers relying upon textbooks must know how to employ combinations of such strategies as concept maps, outlines, and cooperative group techniques.

Writing

Writing is to talking as reading is to listening, and all four are integral to learning. Furthermore, of these vital intellectual functions, writing has historically been the most troublesome to children. I believe that one of the chief reasons so many people struggle to write is that unwitting teachers have prematurely forced students to conform their writing to intimidating structures. For example, I recently spent a day as a participant-observer in a fifth grade class where, under the rubric of writing, the teacher was attempting to teach the parts of a sentence using diagramming techniques. The lesson was further confused by references to parts of speech, especially verbs and nouns. There was nothing wrong with the subject matter, of course. What was wrong was that the material was conceptually beyond the comprehension of ten-year-olds. The teacher meant well, and she had prepared diligently, but the lesson was a disaster. What's more, the children were unavoidably left confused about the relationships between using writing as a medium of communication and the language abstractions they confronted in that class.

All middle level teachers must share responsibility for teaching and learning reading and writing, for our students' development as readers and writers must be nurtured through the middle grades. There are excellent accounts of inventive strategies for stimulating writing and effective techniques for refining skills (Calkins, 1986; Fulwiler, 1987; Atwell, 1990). The most helpful of all the accounts written for middle grades teachers that I have seen is Nancie Atwell's (1987) description of her workshop approach. This is an exceptionally rich resource that should be studied by all middle level teachers, regardless of their subject matter responsibilities. Not only does the workshop format enable the process of writing; the products generate insights about the personality and character of students in ways that are compatible with strategies described in Chapters 2 and 3 of this book. All middle level teachers can help their students become more comfortable about writing by attending to three conditions I will briefly describe: writing in contexts, choice in writing, and sharing.

With the same purposes and in the same spirit that the case has already been made for contextual reading, writing must also rise from experience that is meaningful to writers. To begin, students must have experience that goes beyond the confines of textbooks and classrooms. Experience provides a context for writing. Whether one is telling about an interview with another person or a field trip just completed or an event that occurred outside the school, in every case the individual has had a firsthand experience that provides something to write about. Ideas and reflections rise naturally from such experience, and just as a talker relates experience through conversation, the writer has something to write. Choices about curriculum topics and decisions about pedagogy should ensure that where writing is expected, opportunities for experience have been designed into the unit.

Whatever an experience may be, each student's perceptions and subsequent reflections about it are unique to that individual. Since the experiential base for every individual is personal and idiosyncratic, it should follow that each writer must also have reasonable freedom of choice in the selection of topics and types of writing. Prewriting, brainstorming, conferencing, and drafting are teachable techniques that can be utilized with every piece of writing undertaken, but individual writers must find their own most comfortable medium and voice. One qualification to this general guideline is writing that is done for purposes of documenting, assessing, and evaluating one's schoolwork. Guidelines for those devices for accounting for learning are included in Chapter 8.

In the spirit of the axiom that we must practice what we preach, it is important for teachers to write and share their writing just as students are expected to do. Teachers struggle to write clearly, and when they share that struggle but also their persistence, they model what a writer does to get it just so.

> I write with my students. I show them my drafts. I ask for their responses in writing conferences. I tell them writing is a new habit, one that shaped my life. I tear my hair out over writing, but I keep on writing because I can't stop. (Atwell, 1987, p. 48)

Writing for the sake of getting down what happened isn't particularly difficult for young adolescents, once the process has been demystified. But shaping it into a sentence, a paragraph, or a manuscript that is literary is where the work comes. In order to help our youngsters express their intelligence through writing, we must again engage them in a partnership that ensures them an experiential context, honors their choices, and honestly models the processes and character of a writer.

Mathematics

Every middle level teacher is likewise responsible for cultivating young adolescents' skills in the third R, "rithmetic." Just as reading and writing are intellectual processes constantly at work in every form of scholarship, mathematics must be employed as a way of organizing, analyzing, and interpreting experience that is best understood and expressed in terms of mathematics. Furthermore, the personal mathematical competencies of every middle grades teacher must be at a minimum equivalent to the mathematics expectations held for students. Whether students use geometric shapes in an art project, comparing weather data in a science activity, or interpreting baseball statistics for a written composition, every middle grades teacher must be competent to help them understand and apply mathematics.

There's one particularly knotty issue for middle level educators concerning mathematics: Should algebra be taught in the eighth grade? It is impractical to fully address this question here, but at least three issues ought to be weighed carefully in contemplating the question. First, eighth graders are usually thirteen to fourteen years old, and Piagetian tests administered to large numbers of these students seem to indicate that only approximately one fourth to one third of youngsters were reasoning at the stage of formal operations by age fourteen (Sayre & Hall, 1975; Shayer & Arlin, 1982). The ability to learn algebra well, as it is traditionally organized and taught, requires that a student be developmentally capable of formal reasoning. The match between mathematics subject matter and pedagogy, on one hand, and the developmental readiness of students, on the other, is vital to resolving the algebra question.

The second issue has to do with the impact of algebra sections on the rest of the school's programs, especially the schedule and other curricular plans. Algebra is usually offered according to a high school format: a year or semester course that meets daily for students grouped according to some measure of academic achievement. When one or two classes are thus organized, the organization of the curriculum for the remaining students and teachers tends to follow accordingly along the lines of a junior high school. If algebra is included in the curriculum, care must be exercised to see that it does not affect other more essential organizational components such as teaming and block scheduling, or curricular designs such as those described in the balance of this chapter.

The third issue in regard to this question concerns the need for an exploratory curriculum at the middle level in mathematics as well as in other subject areas. Algebra at the middle level is generally presented in a sequence much like that for second languages, with an emphasis on preparation and mastery, not exploration. The first year of algebra is usually followed by a second year in the ninth grade, followed by geometry, calculus, and so on through the high school years. This is a deductive structure, emanating from a sequential mathematics hierarchy that emphasizes specialization. While this design may be passionately defended by traditional mathematics educators, decisions must take into consideration vital additional issues germane to responsive middle level education.

Aside from the algebra question, expert mathematics educators and middle level educators appear to agree about the development of students' mathematics proficiency through its application in multidisciplinary contexts. Specific standards are recommended for grades five through eight by the National Council of Teachers of Mathematics (1989). Those standards emphasize the application of mathematics reasoning through problem solving, conceptual development, investigation and inquiry, exploration, and computations involving both formal and concrete experiences. These applications are within the reach of all teachers, not just mathematics specialists. The NCTM standards go on to be explicit about the place of number systems, relationships, and theory in establishing a sound foundation for the more specialized curriculum of the secondary school.

An expert study by the Mathematical Sciences Education Board (MSEB) also argues that at the middle school level, curriculum should emphasize "the practical power of mathematics" in which "problem solving [is] emphasized throughout all grades" showing that mathematics is "a discipline of reasoning that enables [students] to attack and solve problems of increasing difficulty and complexity" and where the "focus [is] on problems rather than just on exercises" (1990, p. 44). Again, every middle level educator is called upon to emphasize the appropriate mathematics inherent in every topic of study, just as the other basic literacy tools of reading and writing must be emphasized.

A Note of Explanation

In the preceding discussion of academic core, I have chosen to concentrate on foundation tools that are necessary for young adolescents to explore innumerable possibilities for their further learning. However, in confining that discussion to the 3 Rs, my intention has not been to devalue, in any way, other discrete learning tools or skills. Neither have I meant to devalue other excellent curriculum resources available through learned associations such as the National Science Teachers Association (NSTA), National Council for the Social Studies (NCSS), National Council for Teachers of Mathematics (NCTM), National Council for Teachers of English (NCTE), and others. These national associations are excellent resources for identifying the Ideological Curriculum (Goodlad, 1979).

NATIONAL MIDDLE SCHOOL ASSOCIATION

In the early 1990s the National Middle School Association formed a task force of distinguished middle level educators to develop a formal position paper, "Middle Level Curriculum: A Work in Progress." This resulting document argues for curriculum that complements young adolescents' developmental nature and needs, that helps them recognize connectedness in knowledge and in life, and that emphasizes learning through a variety of experiences. It goes on to address values of collaboration, diversity, and responsibility. The document is explicit in its rejection of a purely departmental or separate subject orientation, tracking, reliance on textbooks and workbooks, and pedagogy based on lecturing and note memorization. This forward-looking document is consistent with much of the case being made in this chapter, and it is available at no charge from NMSA.

CURRICULUM AS PARTNERSHIPS

There's an adage about a young man's search for the elephant cages at the circus. He finds the lion and monkey cages, but when he finally locates the elephant he sees that there are no cages. The elephants are controlled simply by a short rope connecting one forefoot to a stake driven into the ground. There these prodigious, powerful animals obediently stand, swaying silently back and forth. They seem unaware that with the slightest tug the stakes would pop out of the ground, and they could then go wherever they pleased. They seem ignorant of their enormous strength and power. The young man asks the trainer why the elephants are so submissive. The explanation is that they are tethered to a stake when they are young and not yet strong enough to break the rope or pull up the stake. They accept their limitation and continue their lives in mindless submission to the rope and stake. The moral is that elephants have "learned helplessness" (Flood, 1989).

The "rope and stake" that have limited the fuller exercise of young adolescents' intellectual and academic power has been teachers' traditional preoccupation with themselves as the sole choosers of curriculum, dispensers of knowledge, and controllers of learning. Failure to recognize the propriety of partnerships with students in curriculum selection has thwarted fuller development of the readiness of young adolescents for challenges and rigor of which they are capable and for which they are ready. Unlike elephants, however, young adolescents are not restricted by ropes and stakes when teachers create a variety of curriculum options, support their students' personal choices, and help them assess and evaluate their learning.

Teachers are more accustomed to thinking of middle level curriculum in terms of courses than in terms of a program of studies, "the complete set of educational experiences offered" (Glatthorn, 1990). While it may be understandable that we tend to think first in terms of courses, other effective curricular configurations for learning may prove more responsive to young adolescents' needs. The curriculum unit, "an organized set of learning experiences . . . typically lasting from one to three weeks," will be a referent of discussion in this chapter because the unit format is most responsive to young adolescents' needs and the various types of curriculum suitable to them.

No thinking person would suggest that teachers should relinquish responsibility for designing curriculum. On the other hand, no one who is knowledgeable about young adolescents would deny the propriety, if not the necessity, for students to also participate in choosing some of their studies and in planning their design. As students gain experience and become increasingly adept at planning, they can more fully grasp the planning framework presented later in this chapter. But again, the principle of concern for now is partnership. It is incumbent on the teacher or team of teachers to create an educational context in which students experience a variety of types of curriculum and teaching styles whereby they can find the methods and approaches to learning that best enable them to move toward increasing academic and personal self-sufficiency and self-confidence. One of my friends who is a very successful middle level teacher says, "I always ask myself if I am doing things that my students could do. We try to share as much of the planning and the actual work as they can handle." The following pages describe a dozen types of curriculum that accommodate youngsters' varying interests, degrees of scholarly development, and learning dispositions.

CURRICULUM INTEGRATION

No topic in recent years has generated more discussion about curriculum theory, practice, and outcomes than "curriculum integration." In spite of forward-looking earlier works (Lounsbury and Vars, 1978; Vars, 1987), it was James Beane's work (1990) that has proved to be especially effective and helpful in focusing professional attention on the deeper, more far-reaching implications of integration than had previously been given credence. The idea of doing units of study that draw from knowledge bases in traditionally organized separate subject areas has been common for some time. The added dimension of integration that Beane emphasized in the middle level curriculum in Figure 6.1 was "the intersection of personal concerns and social issues" where "we may discover a promising way of conceptualizing a general education that serves the dual purpose of addressing the personal issues, needs and problems of early adolescents and the concerns of the larger world, including the particular society in which they live" (p. 40). From this perspective, Beane posits "themes that ought to drive the curriculum of the middle level school as a general education program."

Such a framework is extremely valuable to teachers committed to curriculum constructed in partnership with their students, where students participate in determining the substance and scope of any study. Consider the following formats for curriculum integration.

EARLY ADOLESCENT CONCERNS	CURRICULUM THEMES	SOCIAL CONCERNS
Understanding personal changes	TRANSITIONS	Living in a changing world
Developing a personal identity	IDENTITIES	Cultural diversity
Finding a place in the group	INTERDEPENDENCE	Global interpendence
Personal fitness	WELLNESS	Environmental protection
Social status	SOCIAL STRUCTURES	Class systems
Dealing with adults	INDEPENDENCE	Human rights
Peer conflict and gangs	CONFLICT RESOLUTION	Global conflict
Commercial pressures	COMMERCIALISM	Effects of media
Questioning authority	JUSTICE	Laws and social customs
Personal friendships	CARING	Social welfare
Living in the school	INSTITUTIONS	Social institutions

Figure 6.1   Intersections of Personal and Social Concerns.

Integrated-Interdisciplinary Units (IIUs)

Most if not all topics of interest to young adolescents can be organized and pursued from multiple points of view. A study of the American Revolution, for example, can be legitimately examined through virtually every discipline represented in the middle level curriculum: American history, American literature, civics, economics, music, studio arts. Although a traditionalist might regard this topic as social studies, it can also embody as much of the mathematics, science, and technology of the era as teachers and students desire to include. The study should also be driven by the ideas and questions students have about independence in general and the American struggle for independence in particular. Tables of data about population distribution, industry and transportation, and the colonial economy lend themselves to mathematical analyses and calculations appropriate to early adolescent learners. Basic principles in the physical sciences affected domestic life as well as the industrial and military technologies of the era. Young adolescent youngsters' need for holistic, integrated understanding invites interdisciplinary treatments of curriculum that has been judged valuable if not essential to their education. Their knowledge should be, after all, a complex that is independent of the framework for a single-discipline focus.

Topics suited to integrated-interdisciplinary approaches abound. John Arnold's (1990) outstanding account of eighty inventive curriculum creations should stir the hearts and imaginations of every middle level teacher. This book shows teachers and students pursuing topics and issues in the immediate surroundings of their homes and their communities, across the United States and beyond. Some of the studies were simulations; others were experienced firsthand. Some of the studies addressed real problems, and some of them resulted in students providing services needed by others. In every example described in this excellent book, teachers created original units that reflected their holistic thought about not only what was academically responsible to do but also what was responsive to their particular students' abilities, needs, interests, and general development readiness.

The likelihood of being able to preserve balance between externally defined and deductively administered curriculum with teachers' own more original, inductively derived units is also enhanced within interdisciplinary teams. Consider a unit about "The Roaring Twenties," originally designed for eighth graders by social studies and math teachers (Brodsky, 1987). Upon seeing how well the unit worked in its initial offering, the remaining teachers contributed their expertise "to make the unit even more diversified and comprehensive" (p. 7). Two or three people planning cooperatively will produce designs that are more comprehensive and diversified than is likely to result from a single teacher working alone. When departures from externally defined curriculum are made for the first time, teachers feel safer about taking such risks when their teammates collaborate.

Once the teacher–curriculum designers have become freed from the compulsion to merely cover an externally defined curriculum, whether in a textbook or a curriculum guide, they are able to conceive a greater variety of possibilities for teaching and learning activities and for assessing the individual and collective interests and capacities of the students who will undertake the study. Units can then be more nearly tailor-made to the interests and priorities of a given team or school. Although most topics of study at the middle level can be designed as integrated-interdisciplinary units (IIUs) by teachers working alone with a single group of students, it is through teaming that the possibilities for optimal matches can be accomplished. Learnings regarded as most essential to single disciplines can be worked into the fabric of a study by teachers who are especially knowledgeable about those particular disciplines.

Let's consider an example of an IIU approach to the study of "Our Town." This particular topic is especially appropriate as an example because it can be studied in every school, whether it is in a rural village or a large city. Using the pedagogical suggestions described in the previous chapter, a study of one's community can reflect individual disciplines by pursuing these student and teacher-generated questions:

MATHEMATICS
What is the economy?
How is the population distributed over age groups and occupations?
What is the local budget? How is it organized?

English/Language Arts
What do the eldest residents recall?
What do records and archives tell about the town's story?
What do the print resources of comparable towns reveal?

Science
What are the influences of climate, agriculture, and technology?
How are energy needs met?
What are the environmental challenges, and how can they be met?

Social Studies
What are the students' family histories vis-à-vis the town?
How is the town organized (mapped and zoned)?
Who governs, and how are citizens' views represented?

By no means do these twelve questions represent all or even most of the learning possibilities for the topic "Our Town." In fact, it is appropriate that the unit concentrate on questions that teachers and students judge together to be pertinent for their particular community. Many questions would be common to studies in the diverse communities where I have lived, such as New York City; Shelburne, Vermont; and Manhattan Beach, California. On the other hand, each of those communities has its own history and character that would generate possibilities uniquely pertinent to that community. Once this initial assortment of queries has been articulated, planning moves in turn to each of three subsequent stages.

Figure 6.2 identifies each of the individual disciplines or subject matter areas that are likely to be included in a middle level curriculum. The graphic guides the reflective process of assessing the topic for discipline-specific connections. One might ask, "What connections exist between the topic and _____?"

In order to connect students' questions with the sanctioned curriculum, teachers must also know the essentials of the external requirements. They must also know either the subject matter of their community or how to find it out. If writing a business letter is identified as an essential curricular component, then connecting the English curriculum to

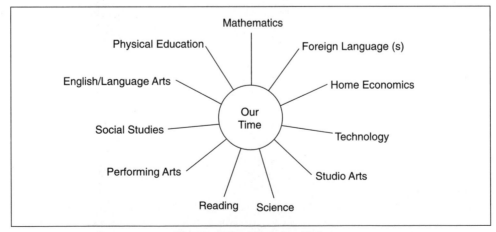

Figure 6.2   Discipline Web.

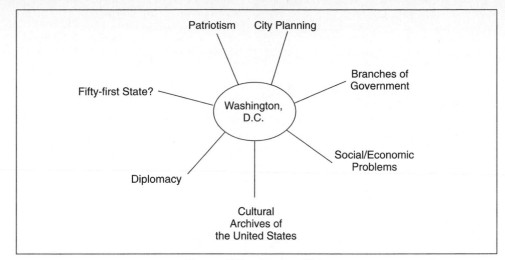

Figure 6.3   Concept Web.

the topic will involve students in writing formal business letters to community members. If calculating percentages is an essential component of the math curriculum, the connection can be made by conducting surveys of community members and expressing the data in terms of percentages depicted numerically and graphically.

Figure 6.3 identifies concepts that might be essential to an accurate study and a correct understanding of a particular community. These concepts will vary from one place to another, but again, there are also universal concepts such as transportation, health services, and economic interdependence. I've used our nation's capital city as the example of "Our Town" in defining some essential concepts, because that is perhaps the city best known to all Americans, whether or not they have actually lived there.

Figure 6.4 stipulates teaching and learning activities drawn from Chapter 5 that are responsive to some of the ways young adolescent learners go about learning. Note that in selecting these modalities, the teacher incorporates what is known about his or her students as individuals and as a group. This background is independent of external curriculum or the specific subject matter. This is what students and teachers will do as collaborating learners. Again, in the vernacular of young adolescent students, this is "the stuff we did to learn the stuff."

The ultimate unit design and individual lesson plans for "Our Town" as well as any other IIU blend elements of all three webs into a plan calculated to achieve responsible representation of disciplines and respectable treatment of subject matter. The question of whether or not the unit is interdisciplinary is settled on these two criteria. What is fundamental in determining the unit's true degree of success, however, is how well the students carry out and learn from the things they do—the integration of subject matter with subjects, that is, the students with the content.

As I work with teachers designing, teaching, and evaluating such studies, I've been accustomed to their becoming very excited about their work (Stevenson & Carr, 1992). I think their pleasure is a combination of the satisfaction of creating something original that has aroused their students' interest and enthusiasm, combined with relief that its curricular viability is educationally sound. The best of both the art and the science of teaching is

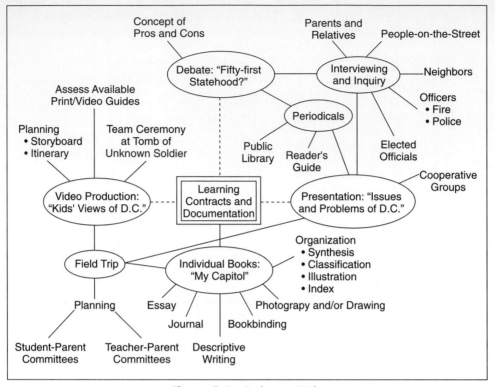

Figure 6.4   Pedagogy Web.

in place. Certainly, having once worked through a successful unit, responsive middle level teachers are no longer content to follow only traditional paths of pedagogy. Yet, IIUs must be remembered for what they are—means to an end.

> "Teaching young adolescents, it has to be recognized, is . . . presiding over human growth and development. It is guiding the critical and now accelerated maturation process. (Lounsbury, 1990, p. 41)

No matter how impressive any curricular studies may be, including the work previously cited, the ultimate measure of worth we must not lose sight of is the extent to which youngsters develop as confident learners who are competent, ethical, and responsible.

Exploratory Studies

As I stated at the outset, most of the curriculum at the middle level should be exploratory. Programs should reflect the curriculum designer's appreciation of the propriety of students at this level exploring their world in order to learn more about the possibilities for eventual specialization. This is a period in the twelve years of schooling when the emphasis must be upon investigating the surrounding world with as much partnership as is practical.

There is a specific contextual background meaning for *exploratory,* however, that relates to the evolution of middle schools from junior high schools and their secondary school antecedents. The traditional curriculum dichotomy of academic and nonacademic mentioned earlier led to distinctions between what is generally referred to as basic academic work and other studies such as music, the studio arts, home economics, and industrial arts. Additional courses from which students could choose might include general business, keyboarding, band or chorus, second languages, and algebra (Lounsbury & Vars, 1978; Alexander & George, 1981). The further distinction of Unified Arts is usually a course that includes minicourses in such techniques as printmaking, ceramics, photography, and so on (Wiles & Bondi, 1981). Note that in all of these examples the framework of curriculum organizations is courses—a descendant of the traditional content organization found in secondary schools and higher education. While these exploratory and elective courses add valuable balance to curricular offerings, I am using *exploratory* as a larger concept than just a categorization of types of courses.

From the perspective of the teacher–curriculum designer for whom this section is written, *exploratory studies* refers to projects in which pairs or small groups of students actually "explore" a topic that interests them and embodies legitimate intellectual substance and significance. For example, two of my students, Kevin and Eric, had been interested for a while in endangered species. While these twelve-year-olds knew something about the issue from prior experience, their knowledge was essentially superficial. That topic was not part of the defined curriculum in our school. Nevertheless, their curiosity led to an exploratory study in which their other teachers and I provided guidance and helped them identify possible resources related to endangered species in Massachusetts, the state where we lived.

Primarily by using school and public library resources, writing, and telephoning, Kevin and Eric pulled together a great deal of material about endangered animals all over the world. In the course of studying that material, they were especially drawn to waterfowl and sea animals in our state. As this exploration shifted directions, they elected to concentrate specifically on the plight of whales. Their research spanned the history of the eighteenth- and nineteenth-century whaling industry in Massachusetts to the then-current diplomatic tensions between the United States and Japan, where whaling was still permitted. The boys became so fully committed to action on the whaling issue that they made "Save the Whales" buttons and silk-screened bumper stickers to sell on weekends in local shopping areas. The income repaid the overhead, and they divided the balance between the Cousteau Society and the Fund for Animals. The boys' reputation spread throughout the community, so they produced a videotape to be circulated to other schools and the public library. They urged their peers to write letters of concern to local newspapers and letters of protest to the Japanese government. Later, Kevin and Eric were asked to testify before a state legislative committee formed to protect the whale population off the Massachusetts coast. Their initial exploration of a matter of substance led to knowledge, expertise, and activism—marks of people who are educated, responsible citizens, regardless of their ages.

Not every exploratory study is expected to develop to these proportions, of course. However, to be worthwhile they must lead to learning that both informs and empowers the explorers. Whether students are finding out about local architecture or learning about a local manufacturing industry, they are taking the initiative to explore territories of knowledge heretofore unknown to them. The teacher's role is predominantly to guide, to help locate resources, and to listen and reflect upon the process with the students. Regardless of the content and skills learned—and they will be substantial—it is learning how to find out that one begins to become a scholar. And a wonderful by-product of such exploration is the discovery that there are numerous good people who will help them achieve both good scholarship and active citizenship.

Theme

In contrast to "themes" as identified earlier by James Beane, here a curricular theme refers to teaching and learning activities that last from a couple of days to a week and that are usually associated with a particular event. Such a theme can be a persuasive, effective way to make educational connections between the school and events in the surrounding community. Consider the following original examples created by teams of teachers.

For four days in March of each year, the Atlantic Coast Conference college basketball tournament dominates public interest and the media in North Carolina. Four of the member schools in that conference are in the state, and people of all ages cheer for their favorites. "ACC Week," as it is known there, also affects people who are not otherwise basketball fans. Originally merely a basketball tournament, the occasion has become a cultural event. Responsive middle grades educators in the area have used their students' interest in the tournament as the impetus for having their own ACC Week observances. Statistics and calculations that are part of basketball record keeping are taught in mathematics, sports writing is studied in language arts, representations of favorite schools and teams are produced in arts classes, and so on. A cultural event in the larger community becomes a curricular theme in the school, bringing adults and students together in a shared celebration that is a natural vehicle for innovative curriculum design.

Anyone who has been a part of a theatrical group or a successful athletic team can appreciate the interpersonal effects of collaboration around a theme. In anticipation of the arrival of the Big Apple Circus in its community, the Alpha Team in the middle school studied the rich history of circuses and produced its own "Big Alpha Circus," a mock circus that was performed for parents and students on other teams (Stevenson & Carr, 1992). Another team addressed the issues of peer pressure and prejudice with a theme of the school year that addressed these community issues (Arnold, 1990). In her account of using Beethoven's Sixth Symphony as a six-week curricular theme, Sybil Marshall shows how interpersonal relationships among group members develop from shared responsibility for such a curricular focus (Marshall, 1968). Young adolescents' eagerness for innovation can be expressed naturally through such prudently selected and well-developed themes.

Selecting and developing a theme is one of those important occasions when an individual teacher or a team or an entire faculty elect to be creators of original curriculum. There are no rules or recipes that will guarantee success. I have been a part of innovative themes that aroused fairly modest interest and participation: a week's "Bags in America" theme in which many different types of sacks and bags were collected, sorted, and displayed in a schoolwide "bag museum" that showed these artifacts as purveyors of fashion, function, and idiom. I have also been a part of themes so well received by teachers and students that for a few days our school was transformed: the Winter Olympics, when a classroom study of the backgrounds of participating nations, their athletes, and the events was augmented by our own winter events, some of which were modeled after official events and some of which we created in fun. Regardless of how widespread was involvement in these themes, the students and teachers who participated found them to be context for learning that was responsive to the learning dispositions and needs of young adolescents.

Minicourses

When the middle level curriculum is entirely defined externally, problems of incompatibility and overkill occur. By this I refer to the incompatibility between the shifting nature of students' interests and semester- or year-long course designs. A limited number of such protracted studies consume available time and intellectual energy, routing students through a great deal more material than they need or care to know. While year-long or semester-long courses can be very appropriate structures for older adolescent and young adult learners, they quickly become ponderous for younger students, too many of whom become increasingly alienated from learning. Meanwhile, there is no end to the number of worthwhile topics appropriate for young adolescents to study in a brief course format. And where middle grades teachers are committed to being responsive to their students' existing interests and curiosities, minicourses are a legitimate way to address that curriculum.

My teammate for five years, Willy Claflin, and I discovered that minicourses were one of the two most effective and popular curriculum offerings we devised in terms of promoting the goal of helping our students take on increasing responsibility for their own education. Because Willy and I were a team, we were able to schedule the school day so that we'd have at least two large uninterrupted time blocks of two to three hours. We would each teach four or five minicourses of two or three weeks' length during these periods, and our students would most often choose the ones they took. Occasionally we required a youngster to participate because the subject matter was appropriate or because we felt a need to work with that student in a minicourse setting.

Suggestions for minicourses often came from the kids, and we would always create a few from our interests and knowledge of possibilities. Since we were sometimes learning along with our students we shared with them the actual work of pulling resources together. When a minicourse was particularly well reviewed by one group, others would ask that it be repeated. Occasionally minicourses met daily, but usually they met two or three times a week.

I have no idea how many minicourses Willy and I took responsibility for over those years, but some stand out in memory. I once knew nothing about opera, but a "German Operas" minicourse suggested by a couple of students introduced us to that fascinating art form. I likewise knew very little about internal combustion engines until a minicourse on two-cycle engines led us to a neighborhood repair shop, where we learned how to disassemble, reassemble, and adjust a Briggs and Stratton lawn mower engine. The book we created from that study became the "textbook" for the two additional offerings of that minicourse that followed consecutively. Some students' interest in transcendental meditation led us into learning about unfamiliar religions and lifestyles. One of my most popular offerings was "American Humor," whereby we read and laughed with some of our society's greatest humorists, including Mark Twain, James Thurber, and Will Rogers; several students participated in that minicourse more than once, because I continually changed some of the readings. Another minicourse, "Radio and Television," led to requests for one about electronics. One of the parents was an electronics engineer, and he agreed to teach basic electronics to a group of ten. Using simple components provided by his company, those students learned basic circuitry. Having seen what they had missed by not selecting the original minicourse, other students lined up for subsequent offerings. Happily, two boys in the original group learned the topic so thoroughly that they were able to lead additional groups. Willy offered "Song Writing" several times, resulting over the years in his becoming a published songwriter.

Critics of this kind of curriculum plan argue that such offerings are the *Reader's Digest* version of curriculum. I don't quarrel with that claim, because these are indeed condensed versions. However, the implication that this curriculum trivializes learning is without foundation. Our youngsters clearly appreciated the opportunity to study a topic of interest for a brief time, and I believe they generally worked harder and learned more because of their responsibility in designing and carrying out the studies. They also appreciated moving on as new interests occurred or as they reached a saturation point with a minicourse. It was Willy's and my responsibility to see that the studies were appropriate, worthwhile, and just the right length.

Inquiry

Inquiry is one of the scholarly behaviors most appropriate for teachers to model. Chapter 3 describes inquiries that can be used by teachers to learn about their students. Many of those same techniques can also be used by students to inquire into topics that interest them. Jim Burns, a middle grades teacher doing inquiries with his students, observed that "the secret to a powerful inquiry lies in not knowing the answer. I don't mean just the student, I mean NO ONE, including the teacher, knows the answer" (Burns, Shinas & Jeffreyes, 1994, p. 19). Another accomplished middle grades teacher, Ross Burkhardt, has used curriculum inquiry extensively and has published accounts of his and his students' work: "The process of inquiry is one of open-ended, interdisciplinary, flexible research into topics selected by students . . . [giving them] some measure of ownership of their learning" (1995, p. 6). Inquiry possibilities are limitless, but I have found that young adolescents' favorite ones most often have to do with other people they know—primarily each other, and sometimes their parents.

The most far-reaching inquiry I ever participated in with students was a study of television viewing habits in our school (Stevenson, 1986). By inviting every student to keep anonymous records of television watching for a week in his or her family, we obtained legitimate data about a matter pertinent to all of us. Once our calculations were complete, we published a summary report for distribution to our families, whose response to the students was appreciative and congratulatory. In this case, inquiry was also service, another type of curriculum to be discussed next.

The election in 1972 between George McGovern and Richard Nixon aroused a good bit of interest in our team, and we decided that by creating an inquiry to send to eighth graders across the country we might be able to forecast the outcome. The twenty or so students who chose to participate worked in pairs, studying groups of four of five states to determine population distributions in each state based on the 1970 census. Once we had identified several communities that appeared to be representative of each state, we obtained school names and sent handwritten letters addressed to the Eighth Grade Social Studies Teacher. The letter explained our inquiry and asked the teacher to conduct a show-of-hands poll of which candidate the eighth graders believed would carry their state. We were careful to explain that we sought their opinion of who would win, not who they wanted to win. A self-addressed, stamped postcard was enclosed for the teacher to return the results.

The return rate was amazing—in excess of 70 percent! Excitement about the election mounted as each day's mail brought additional postcards of data. All returns were tabulated on a wall-size map we had drawn by projecting a map transparency onto butcher paper taped to the wall. Our mounting electoral data clearly forecast the landslide win Nixon was going to receive. Given that our own state (Massachusetts) was a hotbed of support for McGovern, my students' individual predictions (a requirement of the project) were torn between the community loyalty they felt toward McGovern and the harder evidence they had gathered that predicted a huge Nixon win. They were torn between thinking and feeling, head and heart.

On election day they brought sleeping bags to school, and late in the afternoon we gathered the makings for a spaghetti supper. We also borrowed a couple of extra television sets, so that we could follow each major network's report of returns. We'd stay up as late as anyone wished, watching and recording the returns together, comparing our data one state at a time with those of the television professionals as the results came in. The party-like atmosphere of our evening faded early as the networks quickly declared Nixon a landslide winner, confirming the predictions of our own data. None of us had much stomach for continuing to watch McGovern's disaster, even though our research had predicted it. The evening was salvaged, however, by music and dance—a certain antidote for such disappointment. (In the Greek tradition, mourners may dance at a funeral to work out their grief.) That project taught the rationality of systematic reasoning in an aura that celebrated the solemnity and intrigue of history in the making, which few if any of those students will ever forget.

This type of inquiry curriculum is unlikely to occur unless it has been initiated and modeled by teachers. I proposed and carried out numerous inquiry projects before my students began to invent their own. Regardless of the subject matter of any curricular study, middle grades teachers are encouraged to maintain consciousness of how or where inquiry might be employed to help personalize the study. Not every topic, of course, lends itself equally to inquiry. However, when the subject can be extended and brought home by involving students in expressing personal opinions and beliefs, inquiry is appropriate and valid as scholarly work.

Service

One of the most remarkable accounts of young adolescents rendering service through education is described in Jonathan Kozol's (1980) report of the Cuban Literacy Campaign. Much of Cuba's poor population was illiterate, living in primitive housing without electricity and proper sanitation and isolated from the world of learning accessible through education. The call went out from Fidel Castro for 100,000 volunteers to leave their homes for a year, going into the countryside to work in the fields with campesinos by day, teaching them reading and writing by lamplight at night. The volunteers came, ranging from as young as nine years old to octogenarians. More than 40,000 of the volunteers were young adolescents, ten to fourteen years old, who left their homes with relatively comfortable lifestyles to serve the national need. Even though the intended beneficiaries were personally unknown to them and the living circumstances were harsher than anything they'd known, most of these young adolescents fulfilled the promise of service to their fellows. The interpersonal values these young tutors acquired through their service is persuasive testimony to their sense of empowerment.

The realization that one's work has helped others is a most powerful reinforcer of learning. Such affirmation is especially compelling to young adolescent students, whose needs to be known as producers, workers, and contributing citizens are so intense and timely. Some of our youngsters have achieved this quality of self-affirming recognition through scouting, but responsive middle level educators see to it that all young adolescents grow from this quality of experience. Service is also an avenue by which schools can take public value positions that are consistent with the mainstream of American life and relatively free of controversy. That students learn about themselves and also learn basic values of democratic citizenship through helping others is recognized as "an essential part of the core academic program" (Carnegie Corporation, 1989). Excellent examples of such service projects based in middle level schools show how students learn skills of organizing, planning, and assessing their contributions (Lipsitz, 1984; Arnold, 1990; Ames & Miller, 1994; Fertman, White & White, 1996). Whether youngsters are helping elderly citizens, working to promote environmental causes, supporting community recycling projects, or supporting each other through a school-based peer tutoring program or buddy system, the underlying principle of learning through service is well established in exemplary middle schools.

Excellent guidelines, suggestions, and resources are available to help prepare educators and parents interested in providing a service dimension in their middle grades curriculum (Conrad & Hedlin, 1987). For the sake of brevity here, the following five criteria developed by the National Commission on Resources for Youth (NCRY) are recommended for conceptualizing service projects (Shine & Harrington, 1982, p. 13):

1. Youth take active roles in activities that meet real needs of other people.

2. Youth carry real responsibility and make decisions affecting others.

3. Youth work collaboratively with adults.

4. Youth work as a group toward a common goal.

5. Youth have an opportunity to reflect critically on their experience through group discussion.

There often appear to be too many interests competing for limited school hours, and other curricular priorities often displace the benefits of learning through service projects. To give an entire year as the Cuban youngsters did is impractical here, so we must look for smaller but comparable legitimate ways for contemporary youth to know the benefits that derive from this work and to acquire social values that serve everyone well. We must also form partnerships with our students' parents and adult organizations that provide community service. This type of curriculum especially benefits from arrangements in which students work with adult community members whom they would not otherwise be likely to know.

Opportunities for service learning abound, and they are available to most schools (see Fertman et al, 1996). Consider these several examples of service opportunities that are responsive to young adolescents' needs and that can be created in most schools and communities:

> Writing stories, illustrating them, and making books to read to primary children, which they can learn to read for themselves
>
> Tutoring younger students
>
> Forming a buddy system in which young adolescents develop friendships with a younger student or a high school student
>
> Designing and decorating a classroom or hallway bulletin board
>
> Landscaping at the school or in the community
>
> Adopting a local street or public building to help maintain it
>
> Participating in an adopt-a-grandparent program or volunteering at a nursing home
>
> Volunteering at the local library and in public service agencies
>
> Working in a soup kitchen or emergency food pantry
>
> Contributing articles/letters to the local newspaper
>
> Sponsoring events such as Arbor Day, Earth Day, community clean-up day, bicycle safety rodeo, CPR seminar, community recycling project

Each of these service examples requires initiative and responsibility—personal qualities that correspond directly to the young adolescent's need to establish a distinctive identity. Regardless of what the service project may be, students will have direct experience that should be processed through reflective discussion. Ideas and insights deriving from this reflection help characterize this real-life experience so that it becomes the focus of writing, whether the copy is for publication or for personal use, such as journal writing. This kind of writing is elevated from the assigned topics that are often contrived. A service curriculum can complement academic and citizenship goals.

Orbital/Expert Studies

There may be no adolescent need greater than the desire for personal expertise and accompanying attention from peers and adults. It is fundamental to every youngster's healthy development that he or she be known as especially accomplished in distinct ways that are at least recognized if not admired by others. Recognition includes, but is not limited to, medals and trophies received for performance in sports, and honor roll designations for academic performance. In recognition of this fact of young adolescents' need for commendation, scouting has for many years provided merit badges for accomplishment in a host of specialized, prescribed topics. Earned merit badges are subsequently worn as part of the scout's uniform, representing the wearer's accomplishments. The middle level curriculum should incorporate equivalents of this effective way to recognize achievement and thereby encourage further meaningful learning by every young adolescent student.

The concept of Orbital Studies as a dimension of the middle level curriculum comes from Charity James's Fourfold Curriculum (1972, 1974). The essence of this idea is that students work autonomously on topics of special personal interest that "orbit" or revolve around other curricula. Unlike the merit badge process in scouting, where acceptable topics have already been designated, however, the topics for these studies may be anything the student wishes to learn more about for the purpose of acquiring expertise. The teacher's role is to help the student plan the study, to locate print and human resources, to be available as needed as a consultant, and to help the youngster evaluate and bring closure to the study by presenting it to classmates.

The most direct way to go about identifying a list of possibilities for Orbitals is to conduct an inquiry that solicits both individual and group interests, building an initial list of interests. That list can be augmented by information about parents' vocations and hobbies taken from another inquiry that solicits their participation as mentors (see Chapter 11). Further possibilities emerge from the ongoing events of a single community or from world events. Looking through the daily newspaper and reviewing the yellow pages of the telephone book may stimulate additional ideas about possibilities that are immediately accessible. The task of selection is more often a matter of too many competing interests than too few.

Consider this assortment of some Orbitals being pursued simultaneously by individuals on a forty-five-student team: Victorian Architecture, the World Wars, Needlepoint Stitches, the 1967 Boston Red Sox, Bicycle Routes Through Boston, Barns, Conchology, Fly-Tying for Trout, World Cup Soccer, Sailor's Knots, Medical Practice in the Civil War, Quilt Making, Horse Care and Riding, Shipwrecks and Treasure, Plant Parasites, HO Railroads, Baking Bread, Flags of the Western Hemisphere, Model Airplanes, Local Artists, Ethnic Restaurants, History of Skates and Skateboarding, Roman Myths, Baseball's Hall of Fame, Rock Climbing, History of the Beatles, Hiking the Long Trail, Telemark Skiing, Country Stores, the Charles River.

Each of these topics was being studied by a single student whose overall purpose was to become as much of an expert on the topic as possible during a three- to six-week period of time. Some of the topics grew out of students' hobbies or the hobbies of people known to them. In every case, however, the initiative came from individual students, who used teachers, classmates, parents, and other community members as they needed them to plan and carry out the study. Teachers served as consultants and coaches, monitoring progress and giving encouragement as needed. Although there is no single universal set of requirements for Orbitals, these students were responsible for accomplishing the following steps:

1. Maintain a log of time spent, resources, and contact people.
2. Write a summary/outline or construct a concept map of what was learned.
3. Assemble a display about the study to be on view for one week.
4. Make a ten- to twenty-minute presentation to at least five teammates.

Written materials were reviewed by a teacher, who wrote a brief response identifying strengths in the study and any remaining deficiencies or needs. The display, which might be a tabletop arrangement, poster, or bulletin board, was photographed. Presentations were made periodically as Orbitals were completed, during times specially designated by the teachers. This final sharing period was especially important, for it was in a student's presentation that what was done and learned became a subject of discussion not just for the moment but in subsequent interactions within the class or team. All writing, drawings, and photographs then become part of the student's personal portfolio for the year.

One team created Personal Improvement Projects (PIP) as a major component of its team curriculum. At the beginning of the school year, each student carried out a self-assessment to identify specific academic areas in which he or she needed to grow stronger. With the teachers' help, they decided on specific work that would help them improve plus a time agenda for doing the work. Periodically they reviewed their PIP with a teacher and assessed their needs again. Since everyone always had needs to improve at something, no one was singled out as deficient or remedial. These projects also constituted ongoing homework that they and their parents understood. By sharing the responsibility for identifying and addressing needs with individual students, these teachers effectively helped their children grow both in academic competence and in personal responsibility.

I know of no other type of curriculum that so effectively brings home to young adolescents such a personally managed level of responsibility for one's own learning. It is a subjective process in that the student must find his or her own level of comprehension of the topic. When students begin sharing their work and consulting with each other, a tone of intellectual and academic purposefulness becomes apparent. Behaviors and attitudes toward work rise a few levels. A new and loftier education becomes palpable as students go about their work.

Students with learning handicaps can become experts because they can function in ways that work best for them. Since there are no external teacher-imposed standards of mastery, every youngster is able to become expert in a field to the extent that he or she is capable of grasping it. Orbitals provide every youngster with an opportunity to not only enjoy the learning fruits of their labor but gain in self-respect as well as the esteem of peers.

Apprenticeships/Internships

In the years before public education occupied the bulk of children's time, it was common for emerging adolescents to learn trades by serving apprenticeships—the quintessence of learning through doing. Two deficiencies of this model of learning eventually led to its demise: employers' exploitation of youth as workers and a lack of communication and coordination with formal schooling. The former problem led to protective child labor legislation during the twentieth century that has virtually eliminated apprenticeships below the age of sixteen. The latter issue remains a promising but largely unfulfilled opportunity for middle level educators and representatives from community businesses and organizations to work together to educate eager young adolescents to the nature of the world they will soon enter as adults. This experiential education assures authentic learning that can only be simulated so long as schoolwork is confined to classrooms.

I know the potential benefits of this arrangement from personal experience. At the age of ten, I began working after school and on weekends for the pharmacist in our small Alabama town. My job was to deliver prescription medicines by bicycle. It was a wonderful job, usually requiring no more than an hour each day. It also paid a hefty two dollars per week—four times what I had earned from the newspaper route that had originally introduced me to the pharmacist, Mr. Maxwell. After I had delivered his newspaper for a few weeks, he offered me the delivery job. With my parents' approval, I happily accepted. Even though forty years have passed since that occasion, I still feel the exhilaration of Mr. Maxwell's telling me, "I like the way you work."

During the next few years I gradually learned just about everything having to do with Maxwell's Pharmacy except how to fill prescriptions. Because Mr. Maxwell's health was not very good, he showed me how to look after many details of the store's operation that he would otherwise have handled himself. By the time I was in eighth grade, I was handling most of our orders to the wholesalers from whom we received everything from patent medicines to candies and cosmetics to greeting cards. I'd telephone the orders long distance to the wholesalers—heady responsibility for a thirteen-year-old in those days.

When the orders arrived, I checked the bills of lading and marked prices on the items, including our wholesale code. My responsibilities were as mundane but necessary as sweeping floors and emptying the trash; they were also as varied and challenging as posting charge accounts and dressing windows.

After four years, Mr. Maxwell's declining health forced him to sell the store to a young pharmacy graduate from a nearby university. By then Mr. Maxwell had dubbed me Assistant Manager, and my salary had risen to twenty-four dollars a week. Since my family was about to move away, I would also shortly be leaving my job. It became part of my responsibility to orient the new owner to the role I had played. I recall feeling proud of how much I knew and could pass along to Mr. Maxwell's successor. But much more important, I had learned I could function successfully in the adult world.

Those responsibilities and work experiences at Maxwell's Pharmacy stand out in my mind as one of the two truly significant dimensions of my education during early adolescence. To this day I recall volumes of trivia from that experience: our wholesale code (DOSTAYMINE), names and faces of customers and salesmen, the floor plan including each of the departments such as cosmetics, patent medicines, stationery, and school supplies. I still smile about some awkward moments when the customer wanting to buy condoms was faced with a young adolescent clerk. But I believe the most important learning I gained from that experience was that I was a capable person, a kid who could learn how to function successfully in an adult context. Those experiences were very influential in the formation of my self-concept and the strengthening of my self-esteem.

The other significant dimension of my education in those years was the legion of books I read, many of which I still recall forty years later, none of which were associated with my formal schoolwork. In fact, formal schooling held little interest for me. I recall that my teachers were generally nice, but their classes were boring. I'm convinced that learning through doing combined with a steady reading habit provided me, nonetheless, with an excellent education augmented from time to time by lessons learned at school. Furthermore, it was outside of school that I learned about the correlations between work and dignity—the bedrock of self-esteem.

There's always a risk in generalizing from personal experience, of course, but after a few years of being a teacher and observing how difficult it was to genuinely engage so many of my young adolescent students in the established curricula, I began to reflect upon some of the unique content of my own education at Maxwell's Pharmacy and that of my friends, most of whom had similar part-time jobs. I consequently negotiated arrangements with business and professional people in our school community to provide youngsters with opportunities to learn through work as an apprentice or intern. Some attributes of those work situations that I believe contributed to the effectiveness of that learning are appropriate for creating effective apprenticeships or internships.

Adultlike Responsibilities. In the adult workplace, youngsters see the part they play in an elaborate, interdependent network of people and functions. At school, responsibilities have to do with isolated chores such as bringing in homework, studying for quizzes, obeying rules that mean little beyond carrying out one's sense of duty. Apprentice functions are important, to be sure, and they provide stature and significant responsibilities comparable to those of the adult world.

Real Consequences. There's also an urgency about doing work well in the adult world, because others depend upon you. A conscientious work ethic is rewarded by others who recognize responsibility. Failure to attend to tasks and details causes real problems. School consequences are contrived to coerce obedience and complicity rather than to demonstrate the importance of one youngster's role to the lives of others.

Meaningful Dialogue with Adults. When there's a job to be done in the workplace, dialogue tends to be candid and direct. Informal conversations, however, might be about anything of interest to either students or adults, such as sports or politics. Because adults are so greatly outnumbered at school and because their task is basically to supervise students, there is little if any opportunity for parity between the generations.

Necessity of Self-Reliance. The busy activity and urgency of the workplace often provide general directions, but there is always individual interpretation, judgment, and expression. It is beneficial for youngsters to have to rely upon their own interpretation and judgment when expectations are unclear. An attitude of minimalism too easily grows out of dependency fostered in school. "How long must the paper be? What do I have to do to pass?"

Teachers and community members are overdue to take advantage of existing opportunities for these qualities of learning. During my years of middle grades teaching in urban schools, where transportation was not a severe problem, numbers of my students apprenticed for short periods with local businesses: a printer, several grocery stores, a veterinarian, architects, a hardware distributor, a bookstore, a pharmacy, a florist and nursery, and an assortment of retail businesses selling items such as stationery, clothing, toys, or automobile tires. These youngsters were charged to "learn how it operates." In addition to providing useful assistance to the proprietors, they learned by asking about such things as budgeting, overhead costs, supply and demand, zoning, taxes, and other legalities that pertain to operating a business. They also drew floor plan maps, classified and inventoried items or services, and learned by interviewing about a typical day of work. These apprenticeships rarely lasted longer than a week, but the stimulation and intellectual connections that accompanied those few days of functioning in the adult world were momentous.

My students were not legal employees as I had been. In fact, part of the agreement we had with our business collaborators was that they were not to be paid for their apprenticeships. The emphasis was upon their learning all that they could learn during this brief period. They reported their experience through presentations to our team, and they wrote a summary paper synthesizing their experience as noted in their daily journals. A copy of the paper was sent to the business collaborator, who was asked for a written response. All were complimentary and supportive. Inasmuch as we were able, we replicated the best of the apprenticeship model of learning with one major change: "school and community organizations . . . shared responsibility for each middle grade student's success" (Carnegie Corporation, 1989, p. 70).

Experiential Education

Every experience precipitates learning, and learning thrives on experience. Experiential education is a curriculum design based on this axiom and created to ensure that formal as well as incidental learnings are identified, shared, and documented. For example, a group of sixth graders in Missouri became involved in the proposal for construction of a dam on a river in their community (Phillips, 1978). Students read and analyzed newspaper articles and editorials, interviewed local citizens and political figures, debated the arguments for and against the proposed dam, and visited the probable dam site for a campout, where they rappelled and explored caves the dam would flood. These students were engaged in an original curriculum project in which they organized and interpreted existing resources while creating others. In so doing they learned that controversy is natural, that people of good will have honest differences, and that effective communication is vital to the democratic process. Another group of seventh graders in Oregon spent a week visiting a small rural community that was going to be wiped out by a new dam. They learned about the concept of eminent domain, and they learned firsthand the complexities and difficulty of defining and deciding the public good. By interviewing people who were going to be displaced, they further appreciated the contrasts between sentimental and market values. In both of these examples, experience that was deliberately planned and ordered was the foremost teacher.

Theory and procedural details pertaining to experiential education are more thoroughly described elsewhere, and readers particularly interested in developing this kind of curriculum are urged to investigate further (Kolb, 1984). For our brief purposes here, however, experiential curriculum is viewed simply as an intentional plan to engage learners with the actual world outside the classroom or school. Teachers envision an opportunity to capitalize upon an issue likely to interest young adolescents, and then formulate a plan to ensure that they participate in activities most likely to generate formal learning in much the same ways as those suggested for apprenticeships and internships. The study may be focused on an event such as the preceding dam proposals, or it may be part of an ongoing curricular commitment such as the following examples.

The Paradise Project is a seventh- and eighth-grade program taught by a two-teacher partner team (Arnold, 1990, p. 7). A significant portion of the program's curricular emphasis is on students planning and then taking trips that carry out an educational theme. The students write daily about their travels—the real events of their lives. During the course of the year, each teacher will be away from the school numerous times with groups of eight to ten students, traveling in a van. Some of the trips are for a single overnight, others may last as long as three weeks. The travelers sleep in the homes of friends and relatives across the country, in churches, and at campgrounds—wherever contacts have been established. The emphasis is upon engaging America directly, sharing observations and impressions, and writing about the experience—all of which occurs within the comfort and security of a group of classmates and a teacher.

Another version of using travel as a basis for experiential curriculum is the Traveling School, a program that takes groups of thirty-two students on a school bus for a seven-week tour of the United States (Arnold, 1990, p. 9). Three curricular principles undergird the learning achieved in this program:

1. Information is gathered in order to analyze and interpret, reflect, form generalizations, and develop further questions.

2. Firsthand experience makes learning more meaningful.

3. Learning includes testing oneself and stretching to new limits.

As a teacher taking groups of ten to fifteen students on trips and also as a guest traveler on a Paradise trip, I attest to the purposefulness and challenges of such experiential learning.

Although actual events occurring in one's community and travel are the most commonly found exemplars of experiential education, studies can be created out of teachers' imagination. Consider the example of The Company, an experience in the free enterprise system at the Kennebunk Middle School in Maine. Eighth graders "hold jobs, own stock, design, produce and sell merchandise, and provide various services" (Arnold, 1990, p. 87). As The Company evolved over its first five years of operation, it diversified to include several new businesses such as a travel bureau, a computer division, and services for both younger children and senior citizens. It is important to understand that this curricular project is the real thing, not a simulation of a business. Students and others who own stock and work in the company learn about free enterprise firsthand, and all of the issues encountered by adult-run businesses, except legalities, are confronted, studied, and resolved.

As part of an ongoing theme study of island cultures, I took a dozen of my seventh and eighth graders from Boston to St. Croix to study the conditions affecting life there. We stayed in the homes of families at the host school, and while our hosts and hostesses attended classes during the day, we visited places that were factors in island life: the remnants of a tropical rain forest; a lagoon formerly protected by a barrier coral reef destroyed by irresponsible industrial dredging; a great house and museum depicting a former sugar plantation; Buck Island, a magnificent healthy coral reef. We read the island's history of slavery and commercial exploitation, and we saw the resulting poverty and damage to ecosystems. Twice each day we stopped somewhere to write and draw, describing and reflecting our experience. This immersion in a culture we could otherwise know only through abstractions of books and visual representations was a profound teacher. And prior to this experiential exploration, several of those travelers had never even been to Boston's Logan Airport.

Anyone who has experience with well-designed and effective experiential learning recognizes the special potential of this kind of curriculum for young adolescents. The interest of youngsters who have become indifferent toward conventional schoolwork becomes resuscitated, responsibilities and types of work can be adapted to individual learners, the uncertainty of new experiences is individually challenging, and stronger interpersonal bonds among students and between generations grow out of such learning. Because students are so developmentally variable yet able to handle experiences that would more likely overwhelm younger students, the middle grades present a unique opportunity for experiential learning.

Simulations

Where circumstances are such that experiential education is impossible or impractical, simulations can be a very engaging, effective way for young adolescents to learn. Often referred to as simulation games, they teach a variety of concepts, especially those involving negotiated problem resolution. Excellent published simulations are available (see Resources at the end of this chapter), and computer simulations are often organized so that students may work individually or in collaboration. In fact, one of the most effective applications of contemporary technology to young adolescent learners is through computer simulations. Teachers are cautioned, however, to review computer simulation programs thoughtfully. Not all of them stimulate the quality of judgment, analysis, reflection, and decision making that teaches, and mere entertainment is not to be equated with learning.

Teachers have also created many original simulations that involve fulfilling a distinct role and participating in lots of individual and group communication activities. This curriculum usually embodies some of the qualities of games such as group activities, a contested issue, rules, and an identifiable outcome. (See Jones, 1985, for guidelines and suggestions about creating original simulations.) Furthermore, these replicas of reality cultivate both cognitive and affective growth, not just as they relate to conventional academic learning but also in terms of the transference of general problem solving skills. Teachers experienced in using simulations with young adolescent learners generally find changes for the better in an assortment of student attitudes (Heitzmann, 1987).

Consider an original, teacher-designed study of colonial American life, especially as it was affected by the tensions between Whigs and Tories in the early 1770s regarding a proposal to seek independence from British rule. The teachers on one middle school team organized their study of this period of history around a simulation whereby each student on the team received a brief sketch of a mock identity he or she was to assume. Some examples of those mock identities follow.

1. *Josiah Jones.* You are an orphan, age seventeen, a cooper's apprentice. You live in a barn belonging to your Tory employer. You suffer from a chronic bronchial condition that requires medications available only from London.

2. *Martha Lloyd Merrystone.* You are a forty-year-old widow and mother of two girls, ages twelve and seventeen. You own and operate a millinery shop in Boston. Your parents, four brothers, and two sisters reside in Wales, and you have saved fourteen pounds of the forty-five pounds needed to pay transportation for you three to rejoin your family there.

3. *Peter Windsor Hartford.* You are a twenty-three-year-old captain in the King's Infantry, son of a wealthy retired general who is an advisor to King George III. You are engaged to marry Harriet Paine, eighteen, daughter of the outspoken writer and organizer of opposition to British rule, Thomas Paine.

Each student further developed his or her character and recorded that development in a journal as incidents affecting them that were part of the simulation occurred from day to day. For example, one day Peter Hartford received a note from Harriet Paine explaining that her father had annulled their engagement. She had fled her home and gone into hiding, waiting to elope with Peter. Meanwhile, Peter received an order from his commanding officer to use whatever force was necessary to suppress a planned colonial demonstration against unfair taxation. The personal conflicts simulated in these incidents aroused empathy for the real priorities people had to weigh in 1775 as they contemplated whether or not to support a revolution. The final stages of this simulation brought all the students together in a convention format. Students dressed in costumes they had created for their characters. Proponents of both sides gave speeches in an attempt to gain support for their position on the issue, and selected students were assigned to lobby votes for and against independence. Each student ultimately had to weigh a host of personal circumstances in coming to a decision about which way his or her character would have voted.

Sometimes this simulation resulted in the majority of students voting to support the move toward independence, but other times the vote was to remain loyal to England. Even though the students knew how their forefathers had actually voted, they had to make their personal decisions in the simulation according to their best judgment about the welfare of their mock characters. The ultimate value of this simulation was that every student had to listen, think, reflect, and then decide which way to vote—much as our colonial ancestors had before coming to their personal decisions.

Many large concepts that are germane to our culture lend themselves to original teacher-made simulations: the stock market, immigration, courtroom trials, the legislative process, a community economy, labor-management negotiations, trade agreements between imaginary nations, issues of discrimination (races, ethnic groups, sexes, ages). Wars and other notable events that have affected the course of our national agenda invite creations of simulations that engage students in learning from direct exchanges of viewpoints, the search for compromise, and personal reflection.

Field Studies

During my first few years as a middle grades teacher, I took whole classes of students on several one-day field trips. I came to know too well the anguish of trying to preserve the educational integrity of a trip while numbers of them were content simply to have a jamboree. There were always those who did their work either because they were genuinely interested or because they were intimidated, but not until I began to take only small groups on outings did I recognize the enormous potential of field studies. I took eight of my seventh grade boys for a long, one-day visit to the battlefields at King's Mountain and Cowpens in South Carolina because they were doing a group project on the history of the Carolinas in the American Revolution. Because a few of the boys had personal histories of indifference to schoolwork, I thought they might become motivated and more involved in a personal exploration of the battlefields. On this long, potentially disastrous day, they surprised me by how much they read, asked questions, speculated, studied maps and made some of their own, drew, measured, photographed, and reenacted the flight of the defeated British troops. They were energized and curious to know more than I could answer or find out immediately. I was simultaneously surprised and delighted by the degree of their interest as well as exhausted from it all.

Since that occasion in 1962, I have led countless other field studies, but since then I have never again taken an entire class on a field trip. I learned pretty much by chance that the key ingredient to a successful field study is in creating a sharply focused curricular plan around some specific purposes that make sense to a small group of students who share a common interest. The group may be as small as only three or four students, or it may be as large as fifteen or so. It is very difficult to have much more than a jamboree with larger numbers, and while there may be a place for jamborees, they should not be confused with authentic field studies.

A later example of this kind of field study was carried out by seventh graders who were members of a sixth to eighth grade interdisciplinary team on which I taught. On the basis of ideas they had expressed in an ongoing theme about island cultures, I proposed a field study of a nearby island community that had permanent residents, Block Island in Narragansett Bay. Fourteen students elected to join this five-week study. Our primary academic goal was to learn about the residents' lives on the island through polling and interviewing so that we could make more informed comparisons between the life we knew in a city and island life. In addition, I identified some two dozen distinct topics from which each student could select one in order to become an expert. These topics included architecture, bird life, flora and fauna, government, and so on. They needed to find out as much as possible about their topics in the month prior to our week on the island where they could learn more specific information.

Books and especially periodicals available through the public library became extremely important to the kids' search for background information about their topics. Using the telephone, they located an assortment of people who knew something about the island. One elderly couple who had lived there many years and still returned for the summers visited us and brought old photograph albums portraying Victorian houses, hotels, and the waterfront area at the turn of the century. A geologist came to explain to us the island's formation as a terminal glacial moraine. A local college student who had attended the island's K–12 school spent parts of several days with us, proving to be especially helpful with our map making. Every day of the study turned up new resources to inform us and orient us for the trip.

Students volunteered for the various tasks associated with planning the study and a week-long field trip to the island. They also worked out an equitable schedule for dealing with chores such as cooking and cleanup once we were there. I functioned as consultant and advisor to the planning process. Where something was being overlooked or misinterpreted, I pointed it out. Otherwise, I responded to their questions rather than telling them how to do their jobs. To live as economically as possible, we took most of our food with us and lived in tents. To raise money, the students decided to make and sell quiche on Fridays to parents who telephoned orders in advance. They also enlisted parents to help us with transportation to and from the ferry dock. Their preparatory studies and planning for the trip went wonderfully well.

The week's visit passed quickly, and it was laden with unplanned, unpredicted events. The constable, a grandfather of twelve-year-old twins who lived on the Island's west coast, took us under his wing, introducing us to people we would not have met otherwise. The scientist at the meteorological station intrigued us all with his explanations of weather changes and the functions of his instruments. A technician at the power station who was an amateur ornithologist took us to his favorite bird-watching sites. An automobile mechanic directed us to a bluff from which we could observe a nuclear submarine in sea trials. Two elderly sisters brought homemade ice cream and cookies to our campsite late in the afternoon of our final evening on the island. The cooperation and acceptance of our project by the people we met could not have been better, and when we returned to our school to publish our study, we unanimously chose to call our sixty-page book *The New Islanders*. In just one week we sold out the hundred copies we printed. Each of us learned a great deal of academic content about the island and island life, but we also learned valuable lessons about being learners and neighbors. And I learned valuable lessons about being a better teacher, as well.

There is no prescribed collection of topics for field studies, yet teachers are surrounded by possibilities. A teacher in California created an original field study, "Night Life in the Mojave," by spending three days on a field study of that desert. Another teacher from a Chicago suburb and his students spent three different weekends in three different Chicago ethnic neighborhoods, conducting field studies of those cultural groups. Another teacher took his students to three consecutive sessions of night court in the Bronx, where they observed, listened, and wrote their thoughts for later sharing with classmates. These examples were created by teachers who were tuned in to their students and whose minds were open to possibilities for curriculum design that would teach and help refine students' academic competencies, stimulate their interest, and influence their values about both scholarship and living a responsible life.

Competitions

The emphasis on competition within and between schools has become a dubious characteristic of our contemporary society. Exaggerated values placed on winning, especially in academics and sports, have created some unhealthy, premature pressures on impressionable young students to outperform classmates, encouraging a beat-your-neighbor mentality. An example of how this point of view has become institutionalized is the often-followed policy of grading on a curve and then honoring only those students with the highest marks. Meanwhile, we know that our students are neither equally gifted nor developed to an equal degree. Reward and recognition policies, originally intended to commend hard work and perseverance, become discriminatory in ways that are inappropriate and undesirable at the middle level, where the dominant emphasis should be on helping every student achieve as many successes as possible according to his or her individual abilities.

A similar dynamic works against the development of a healthy appreciation of sports in schools where degrees of emphasis better suited to older students are placed on winning interscholastic competitions. At a time when the welfare of all students appeals for a variety of intramural activities, we must not be misled into making decisions that are not in the best interest of all of our students. The ring offer of limited rewards to students whose athletic gifts are exceptional creates unfair competition for developing young adolescents, who are psychologically vulnerable to unnecessary losses and failures. People of any age who constantly lose in academic or athletic competitions soon lose their taste for participating at all, and at the middle level the goal should be full participation by all.

In spite of these risks, however, the excitement of participation and the possibility of being successful appeal to young adolescents. As their teachers, we should be concerned not to eliminate competition but to present competitive contexts for learning in a variety of ways that ensure a healthy perspective. Competition can also be a powerful incentive for learning, collaboration, and hard work so long as it constitutes just one type within a curriculum that is balanced among the types described in this chapter. In American education the greatest risk is preoccupation with competition to the exclusion of other approaches to learning.

An example of overemphasis is a game created by a well-intentioned middle school principal. The game was called Quiz Bowl, and it was based on television games in which school teams competed for answers to short-answer questions. Every student in this middle school was assigned membership on a four-person team composed of one student from each of the four grades in the school. Eighth graders were designated as team captains, and they were responsible for organizing their teams' preparation. Study sheets based on the school's curriculum content were distributed for the teams to prepare. The kids' initial enthusiasm for Quiz Bowl was impressive. Many teams worked diligently to win matches and earn points. In a short while, however, the school climate began to deteriorate. While the performance of the most successful teams was impressive, the large majority of the students lost interest, performances dropped off, and squabbles proliferated between teams and among members of individual teams. Within two months, the principal and faculty decided to eliminate Quiz Bowl and try to regain a less conflicted interpersonal climate.

Once again, the key ingredients to the successful employment of competition in middle level curriculum are variety and balance. The Quiz Bowl game wasn't a bad idea. It simply was defined too narrowly, and it became the only game in town, so to speak. Far more teams lost regularly than won, and the worship of winning became its undoing. Other competitions such as spelling bees, geography bees, treasure hunts, hangman, twenty questions, board games like Trivial Pursuit, riddles, and puzzles are also effective ways to enjoy competition that appeal to a variety of talents and interests without becoming so intense that students are intimidated or made unnecessarily self-conscious by the risk of losing. Whatever competitions may be used, teachers need to pay thoughtful attention to the values being taught as well as the content.

In my experience teaching at the middle level, the curriculum that has created the greatest interest and participation from students who don't otherwise tend to become involved in competitive activities is hands-on problem solving. Probably the most publicized of such competitions is the egg drop, wherein the problem is to design a container for an egg that will cushion the shock of impact when the egg is dropped from a height. Students experiment with assorted ways to protect the egg, and the winning entry is the one that can be dropped from the greatest height without breaking the egg. Although this kind of problem solving may be seen by some people as play that is too frivolous to be included as schoolwork, it is curriculum that teaches thinking: theorizing, testing, and evaluating. This basic process is the same as that employed by laboratory scientists. At the most basic level, a youngster thinks theoretically about how to cushion the egg, tests that idea, and evaluates what worked or didn't work. The evidence then spawns new theory, and the cycle continues. Leading engineering schools offer similar competitions to promote this same problem solving process, although those competitions understandably entail more complex theories.

Not only is this experimentation stimulating and satisfying for lots of our students, it nurtures systematic thought in a way that is responsive to how many young adolescents learn how to think. Consider, for example, a contest to construct paper airplanes to achieve (a) the longest flight time, (b) the greatest distance, (c) the most accurate flight to a target, (d) the greatest number of complete circles (turns or loops), (e) the most beautiful airplane. This contest calls for the same process of experimentation as the egg drop but with less potential for waste and mess. The size and weight of paper should be standardized, but students are free to research airplane designs in the library as well as on their own. I always required students to keep a log of their designs and the results as measured by a stopwatch or tape measure. Beauty was always judged by a committee, usually composed of our school secretary, a parent, a teacher, and/or some nonparticipating students. Not only does this kind of competition teach, it also exudes an atmosphere of good fun that offsets the tendency for it to become grim and cutthroat.

Just as there are countless possibilities for field studies often associated with the locale of a school, there are also numerous possibilities for competitions deriving simply from available materials and the teacher's inspiration. For example, when our school became the recipient of over a thousand marbles, one teacher created marble-run problems.

Another created some balance challenges. One team worked to create a marble run that would descend the stairwell of the school. The principal offered the reward of a pizza lunch to any individual or crew of students who could solve a problem. Although not every student in the school was disposed toward working on marble problems, those who were interested pursued their ideas and manifested the value my colleagues and I attempted to teach through competitions. On another occasion when we obtained two large boxes of popsicle sticks, the challenge was to construct a bridge that would span a distance of one meter and support a brick with a sag of 5 cm or less. Again, not everyone opted to address this problem, but those who did learned a great deal of theoretical and practical information about various bridge designs and engineering, not to mention problem solving.

The classic competition that has been an annual event in our school for two decades is the Hopameboatafloata Regatta. The challenge is to construct a sailboat no more than 25 cm in length, 10 cm in beam (width), and 100 square cm in sail area. The boat must sail downwind before a window fan in a pond constructed of 2" × 6" lumber and sheet plastic in a rectangle approximately 4 m long by 1 m wide. Concepts of buoyancy, displacement, balance, and steering are addressed straightforwardly, and it is satisfying to observe the students' maturing applications of the theory–testing–evaluation cycle common to such competitions. The effort, ideas, and willingness with which students offer observations and suggestions to each other for improving the boats further contribute to the values of cooperation and recognition for every individual that we try to develop in our students. In a very real sense, students' interpersonal communications are twelve-year-old equivalents of the collaborative problem solving that is characteristic of engineers or physicians or business people seeking solutions.

One of the most ingenious problems and impressive subsequent efforts from students that I've seen came from four-member seventh grade cooperative groups as they worked to solve a problem their teacher, Tom Keck, had created: to construct a robotic arm that would pick up an egg, move it a distance of one foot, and then deposit it in an egg carton. The physics the students worked with involved friction, leverage, balance, and hydraulics. The robotic actions or "movements" were accomplished by use of hypodermic syringes (without needles) connected by plastic tubing. When one syringe was depressed, the one at the other end was pushed out. Likewise, when the syringe at one end was withdrawn, the corresponding one was drawn in. Initially the teams were preoccupied with solving this complex problem. But as is often the case in such curriculum projects, after a few sessions the work atmosphere evolved into one of mutual consultation and encouragement rather than competitiveness. The problem itself was challenging enough for everyone, and the students behaved toward each other as though they wanted every team to be successful. Whether the challenges are formed around conventional academic material, hands-on problems, or arts projects, the underlying principle of competition in curriculum must be to assure variety and balance that will provide opportunity for success for every student.

CURRICULUM CHOICES AS A CONTINUUM

One very useful way to think about middle level curriculum is reflected in Figure 6.5, "curriculum continuum" (Brazee & Capelluti, 1995, pp. 28–29).

Point 4, Integrative Curriculum, refers to the involvement of students with their teachers in planning curriculum. It is at this Point that educators recognize the unique

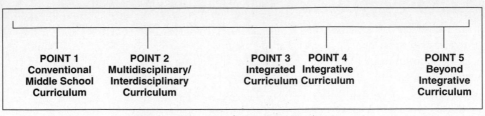

Figure 6.5   The Curriculum Continuum.

perspectives and ideas students have and build upon them in shared exploration. They go on to describe this dimension as where "the focus [is] on finding the answers to authentic questions of young adolescents, not as an add-on to the 'regular' curriculum, but rather as THE curriculum" (p. 34).

This chapter has emphasized the urgency of middle level teachers engaging their students in the responsibility of making decisions about what the curriculum is going to be. The traditional school paradigm relegated that responsibility entirely to an assortment of adults: teachers, department chairs, district administrators, subject matter experts, school board members, and so on. That process was and is completely removed from the interests and ideas of students themselves. Increasingly, middle level educators are recognizing and responding to the importance of engaging students in making decisions and choices about what is to be learned. It is crucial to recognize that the other extreme—children making all of the decisions—is as onerous and inappropriate as not involving them at all. The essential idea of this chapter is that a partnership between adults and children about what constitutes the curriculum for a team or a class ensures optimal opportunities for authentic engagement and learning.

I recognize that for some teachers the thought of sharing the curriculum decision making process with students is uncomfortable if not terrifying. Yet, no one can deny that young adolescents have their own ideas and interests that often do not correspond to the school's externally defined agenda. I also struggled as a young teacher with this challenge. Over thirty years ago I read somewhere that most school curriculums were in urgent need of major overhaul. Since most of my students at that time appeared to be merely going through the motions of learning, I took a lot of interest in the notion of curriculum overhaul. The piece went on to caution that it would be folly to throw out what we have in order to start over. The inevitable result would be chaos. The writer suggested something very reasonable, however: namely that every teacher should decide to make 15 percent of the curriculum an innovation for the purpose of learning more about "what works." This kind of action research made great sense to me, and I thus embarked on semesters and years of innovation that have contributed significantly to my work with young adolescents and college students. I propose that EVERY middle level educator decide to arrive at least 15 percent of what they teach as a partnership with students. Pay close attention to their attitudes, behaviors, and products—in short, their learning. Then use the insights you derive from that action research as you undertake revisions in the remaining 85 percent of what you do. I believe this is the most promising and professionally responsible way for us to better help our students learn as well as to help us better understand our work and possibilities yet to be realized.

Supporting Activities

1. Seven questions are raised at the beginning of this chapter. In light of your personal learning experience as a young adolescent and your reading of this chapter, share your answers to each question.

2. Examine published curriculum guides for the middle level. Look especially at those published by learned societies such as the National Council for the Social Studies (NCSS), National Science Teachers Association (NSTA), and others. How do formal guides reflect an accommodation to young adolescent development?

3. Interview selected middle level teachers to learn the basis on which they make decisions about curriculum. How do their choices reflect an understanding of the students in their immediate charge? What evidence do you find of curriculum based upon students' identified interests? What student outcomes are valued?

4. Using the description and examples of Integrated Interdisciplinary Units (IIU), draft a discipline web, a concept web, and an outline of a unit likely to be interesting to young adolescents. What connections can you make between your design and appropriate pedagogy as described in Chapter 5? Carry out a similar exercise for topics that could be learned through Orbital-Expert Studies. Develop from your community a list of potential apprenticeships or internships appropriate to young adolescents. Create a similar list of topics and sites for field studies.

5. What specific concepts and skills appropriate to young adolescents could be learned through the resources listed in your responses to activity 4 above?

RESOURCES

Association for Experiential Education, CU Box 249, Boulder, CO 80309. Examples and information related to the experiential education curriculum design.
Center for Youth Development and Outreach, University of Minnesota, 386 McNeal Hall, 1985 Buford Ave., St. Paul, MN 55108. Resources from the National Commission on Resources for Youth.
Foxfire, Rabun Gap, GA 30568. Write for a list of publications.
INTERACT, P.O. Box 997–S90, Lakeside, CA 92940, Catalogs of published simulation programs appropriate to young adolescent learners.
Listen to Us (New York: Workman, 1978), edited by Dorothy Kavanaugh. A good source for examples of young adolescents' writing about local and world events.
Middle Level Curriculum: A Work in Progress (Columbus, OH: National Middle School Association). A position paper about curriculum available on request.

REFERENCES

Alexander, W. M., & George, P. S. (1981). *The exemplary middle school.* New York: Holt, Rinehart, & Winston.
Ames, N., & Miller, E. (1994). *Changing middle schools: How to make schools work for young adolescents.* San Francisco: Jossey-Bass.
Armbruster, B. B. (1984). The problem of "incomplete" text. In G. G. Duffy, L. R. Roehler, & J. Mason (Eds.), *Comprehension instruction: Perspectives and suggestions.* New York: Longman.
Arnold, J. (1990). *Visions of teaching and learning: 80 exemplary middle level projects.* Columbus, OH: National Middle School Association.
Arnold, J. (1993, Fall). A curriculum to empower young adolescents. *Midpoints: Occasional Papers 4*(1), Columbus, OH: National Middle School Association.

Atwell, N. (1987). *In the middle: Writing, reading, and learning with adolescents.* Upper Montclair, NJ: Boynton/Cook.

Atwell, N. (1990). *Coming to know: Writing to learn in the intermediate grades.* Portsmouth, NH: Heinemann.

Beane, J. A. (1990). *A middle school curriculum: From rhetoric to reality.* Columbus, OH: National Middle School Association.

Brazee, E., & Capelluti, J. (1995). *Dissolving boundaries: Toward an integrative curriculum.* Columbus, OH: National Middle School Association.

Brodsky, M. A. (1987). The roaring twenties—An interdisciplinary unit—or how to make use of that old raccoon coat in the attic. *Middle School Journal 18*(4), 7–9.

Burkhardt, R. (1995). The inquiry process: Student centered learning. Columbus, OH: National Middle School Association.

Burns, J., Shinas, K., Jeffryes, L. (1994, Spring). Katelyn's inquiry: What we learned. *New Mexico Middle School Journal, 4*(1).

Calkins, L. M. (1986). *The art of teaching writing.* Portsmouth, NJ: Heinemann.

Carnegie Corporation. (1989). *Turning points: Preparing American youth for the 21st century.* Washington, DC: Author.

Combs, A. (1987). Keynote address, annual conference of the National Middle School Association, St. Louis, MO.

Conrad, D., & Hedlin, D. (1987). *Youth service: A guidebook for developing and operating effective programs.* Independent Sector, 1828 L Street NW, Washington, DC 20036.

Dewey, J. (1938). *Education and experience.* New York: McMillan.

Educational Products Information Exchange. (1977). *Report on national study on the nature and the quality of the instructional materials most used by teachers and learners.* (EPIE Report No. 17). Stonybrook, NY: EPIE Institute.

Epstein, H. T. (1978). Growth spurts during brain development: Implications for educational policy and practice. In J. S. Chall & A. F. Mirsky (Eds.), *Education and the brain.* Chicago: Society for the Study of Education.

Fertman, C., White, G., & White, L. (1996). *Service learning in the middle school.* Columbus, OH: National Middle School Association.

Flood, D. (1989). Keynote address, annual conference of the National Middle School Association, Toronto: Ontario.

Fulwiler, T. (Ed.). (1987). *The journal book.* Portsmouth, NH: Heinemann.

Glatthorn, A. A. (1990). *Curriculum development.* (Instructional Leadership Series). Reston, VA: National Association of Secondary School Principals.

Goodlad, J. I. (1984). *A place called school.* New York: McGraw-Hill.

Goodlad, J. I., & Associates. (1979). *Curriculum inquiry: The study of curriculum practice.* New York: McGraw-Hill.

Heitzmann, W. R. (1987). *Educational games and simulations* (rev. ed.). Washington, DC: National Education Association.

Irvin, J. L. (1990). *Reading and the middle school student.* Boston: Allyn & Bacon.

Irvin, J. L. & Connors, N. A. (1989). Reading instruction in middle level schools: Results from a U.S. survey. *Journal of Reading, 32,* 306–311.

Jacobs, L. B. (1989). What is whole language? *Teaching PreK–8, 19*(8), 34–36.

James, C. (1972). *Young lives at stake.* New York: Agathon.

James, C. (1974). *Beyond customs: An educator's journey.* New York: Agathon.

Jones, K. (1985). *Designing your own simulations.* New York: Methuen.

Kavanaugh, D. (Ed.). (1978). *Listen to us.* New York: Workman.

Keizer, G. (1989). *No place but here.* New York: Penguin.

Kolb, D. (1984). *Experiential education.* Englewood Cliffs, NJ: Prentice-Hall.

Kozol, J. (1980). *Children of the revolution.* New York: Dell.

Lipsitz, J. (1984). *Successful schools for young adolescents.* New Brunswick, NJ: Transaction.

Lounsbury, J. H. (1990). Interdisciplinary teaming—Destination or way station? *Middle School Journal, 21*(4), 41.

Lounsbury, J. H., & Vars, G. E. (1978). *A curriculum for the middle school years.* New York: Harper & Row.

Marshall, S. (1968). *An adventure in creative education.* London: Pergamon.

Mathematical Sciences Education Board. (1990). *Reshaping school mathematics: A philosophy and framework for curriculum.* Washington, DC: National Academy Press.

Melton, G. (1990). I dare you! Keynote speech. New England League of Middle Schools Ninth Annual Conference, Hyannis, MA, March 26, 1990.

National Council of Teachers of Mathematics. (1989). *Curriculum and evaluation standards for school mathematics.* Reston, VA: Author.

Phillips, J. (1978). A cave, a dam, a river. *Phi Delta Kappan, 59,* 703–704.

Rogers, V., & Stevenson, C. (1988). How do we know what kids are learning at school? *Educational Leadership, 45*(5), 68–75.

Sayre, S., & Hall, D. W. (1975). Piagetian cognitive development and achievement in science. *Journal of Research in Science Teaching, 12,* 165–174.

Shayer, M., & Arlin, P. (1982). The transescent mind: Teachers can begin to make a difference. *Transescence, 10,* 27–34.

Shine, J. G., & Harrington, D. (1982). *Youth participation for early adolescents. Learning and serving in the community.* (Fastback 274) Bloomington, IN: Phi Delta Kappa Educational Foundation.

Smith, F. (1986). *Insult to intelligence.* New York: Arbor.

Stevenson, C. (1986). *Teachers as inquirers: Strategies for learning with and about early adolescents.* Columbus, OH: National Middle School Association.

Stevenson, C., & Carr, J. F. (1992). *Dancing through walls: Integrated studies in the middle grades.* New York: Teachers College Press.

Vars, G. F. (1987). *Interdisciplinary teaching in the middle grades.* Columbus, OH: National Middle School Association.

Weaver, C. (1990). Weighing claims of "phonics first" advocates. *Education Week, 9*(27), 23.

Wheelock, A. & Dorman, G. (1988). *Before it's too late: Dropout prevention in the middle grades.* Report by the Massachusetts Advocacy Center (76 Summer Street, Boston, MA 02110) and the Center for Early Adolescence (Suite 223, Carr Mill Mall, Carrboro, NC 27510).

Wigginton, E. (1985). *Sometimes a shining moment: The Foxfire experience.* New York: Anchor (Doubleday).

Wiles, J., & Bondi, J. (1981). *The essential middle school.* Columbus, OH: Merrill.

Chapter 7

Organizing for Responsibility and Harmony

○ *Will the kids listen to me? Obey me? Like me?*

○ *How do I get them to do their work?*

○ *How can I get them to behave?*

○ *Will they work together?*

○ *What do I do first?*

○ *Then what?*

It is absurd to suppose that a child gets more intellectual or mental discipline when he goes at a matter unwillingly than when he goes at it out of the fullness of his heart.

John Dewey, *Interest and Effort in Education*

The essence of any institution that thrives is that its people enjoy the "fullness of heart" of which Dewey writes. Our most civilized schools and classrooms are places where all the occupants believe that they belong, where they are living and learning successfully, in a climate much like that of a nurturing extended family. The adversities that emerge from social and academic competition can become savage and merciless among emerging adolescents who perceive themselves to be pitted against each other. There is perhaps no greater casualty of a traditional bifocal conceptualization of schooling into elementary and secondary configurations than the profession's failure to recognize the early adolescent school years as an opportunity to empower students to learn how to govern themselves responsibly and harmoniously.

Understandably, the preoccupying concern of most beginning teachers is their own survival. Questions such as those listed above are very much on their minds—uncertainties that can and will be answered only through their own work with students. As in the sailing metaphor that introduces this book, teaching is learned through the action of teaching accompanied by reflection, study, and modification. In the spirit of that adventure, this chapter pursues the goal of constructing an atmosphere in which responsibility for the interpersonal relationships, academic initiative and responsibility, and work ethic about learning are shared by teachers and students in recognition of the benefits they bring to all. This chapter is about a merging of teachers' and students' volition around conditions that will help cultivate a "fullness of heart" for all.

The case has been made in previous chapters about ways in which students change during the years of early adolescence. Their readiness for schooling complements their emerging abilities to understand and settle all kinds of needs and problems in new ways. This chapter deals with some of the ideas and strategies conventionally referred to as discipline and classroom management. The dominant theme in this particular treatment, however, is to cultivate individual and collective responsibilities for learning in an atmosphere characterized by recognition of differences and commitment to harmony. The strategy is to approach the organizational issues of teaching with the same educational values and priorities that have been applied throughout this text: responsive designs and partnerships.

To begin, we need to conceptualize what takes place when young adolescents are engaged in learning. We need to remember that, as Chapters 4 and 5 described, they vary substantially from one another in a host of ways: sophistication of reasoning, special talents or abilities, attention span, preferred modes of learning, personal interests, facility with oral and written language, and so on. We have students who have exceptional intellectual and aesthetic abilities, and we work with students who sometimes struggle to achieve a functional degree of facility. Any attempt to describe or define what is "normal" among young adolescents working at their best must begin by emphasizing their interpersonal variability. While a significant portion of learning activity will be the same for every student, much of the individual and small group work they do will reflect their inherently varying approaches to learning. The prudent teacher will seek a balance between work that is directed and focused around the teacher's presentation and work that is student centered, accommodating students' varying approaches.

The stereotype of a classroom of young adolescent students sitting attentively in rows, oriented toward the teacher's lecture or demonstration and speaking only when called upon, is a misleading depiction of the kind of schooling that is both possible and desirable for these youngsters. Yet, this classic image of teaching is common among those of us who have fallen victim to the occupational hazard of preoccupation with ourselves and our presentations. Although direct instruction is the most effective way for students to learn many things, they must also work in a wide variety of learning activities in which the teacher's role is to respond where help is needed according to the calling of individual learners. Correspondingly, students move about deliberately and purposefully according to the nature of their tasks, much as travelers move about an airline terminal.

I often hear conflicting opinions and sometimes anxious arguments among experienced teachers who advocate "treating kids like grownups" over "treating them like babies." Teachers who were originally prepared to be secondary teachers or who see themselves as secondary teachers seem to most often express their passion over this false dichotomy. When young adolescents don't measure up to these teachers' expectations, the students are admonished to "act your age." That is, in fact, precisely what they are doing. I submit that tensions between choosing to organize schooling as either teacher-and-curriculum-centered or student-centered divert attention away from the real issue, namely, that we must do whatever best serves the overarching goal of "qualities . . . we envision in the 15-year-old who has been well-served in the middle years of schooling" (Carnegie Corporation, 1989). These qualities are "embodied in five characteristics associated with being an effective human being" (p. 15):

An intellectually reflective person
A person en route to a lifetime of meaningful work
A good citizen
A caring and ethical individual
A healthy person

In my judgment, nurturing these qualities in our students must always be our predominant goal. When we lose sight of them, we risk losing everything. Furthermore, we who work in the middle grades have the very best opportunity in all of public education to cultivate youngsters' potential for becoming responsible human beings who understand and know how to live according to ethical, democratic processes.

SOME SHARED CONCERNS

It is fair to assert that the public expectation of public education is that it is the vehicle through which students will learn how to become self-sufficient, responsible citizens who will make the United States and the world better places for everyone. Let's consider three fundamental values associated with that general expectation. Of course, our society has many expectations of our schools, but the three I choose to emphasize here are repeatedly at or near the top of polls that assess public attitudes toward public schools. (A Gallup/Phi Delta Kappa poll of public opinion about public schools has been published in the *Phi Delta Kappan* annually since 1968. Tabulated annual results of that scientific polling usually appear in the September issue.)

1. A primary purpose of public education in American society is to ensure democratic socialization. The essence of our heritage is its melting pot composition, and public schools constitute the primary setting for uniting people of diverse backgrounds around a core of basic human and institutional values. It is through public education that our history, social and political ideals, and understanding of the American way of life are transmitted to every new generation.

2. An abiding contemporary public concern about our schools has been an apparent lack of discipline. Segments of our contemporary youth culture appear to be out of control, raising the specter of an imminent collapse of traditional American values. Many of our schools are places of violence, intellectual indolence, personal health abuses, and social and racial discrimination. These deficiencies are often attributed to a breakdown of discipline in homes and schools.

3. The American dream is that through diligent work in honest labor, every individual can become successful. The American work ethic appears to have fallen into jeopardy as the reputation of our industrial workers languishes. Stories of easily acquired and often ill-gotten fortunes dominate the media and become the fantasy-priorities of youth. Meanwhile, other industrialized nations are taking over economic leadership in the world, and public education is blamed.

These concerns about the purpose and functions of public schools are and should be fundamental to the deliberations of policy makers and classroom teachers alike. They are especially auspicious for middle level educators, however, because the concerns of the general public have direct parallels in the school-related priorities of emerging adolescents. Their perennial desire is that other students will like them and become their friends. Beyond that primary goal, however, they have specific aspirations that parallel the aforementioned public concerns.

1. Young adolescents need to believe that their school is a place where they will receive fair treatment, where justice prevails, and where individuals have a right to speak their minds freely without fear of retribution—elements of our democratic American heritage that have already become part of their daily lives and expectations. They assume they will be governed by rules, and they expect the rules to be equitably derived, clearly articulated, and fairly enforced. Even the occasional student who rejects democratically derived rules and procedures understands and respects kids' efforts to achieve equitable governance.

2. High in their priorities is the need to believe that they will be safe at school, that order will prevail, and that they will not be victimized either physically or emotionally. These youngsters also recognize that neither adults nor kids working without each other can accomplish the order they both value. The mutual support a legitimate partnership entails is both understandable and desirable.

3. Youngsters desperately need to believe that they will be successful at school, and they recognize that applying themselves through work is usually necessary to achieve success. Thus, they come expecting to work but needing that work to be understandable in terms of their capability and reasonable in terms of volume. When work is thus doable, willingness to work follows.

These two sets of goals are self-evidently compatible and complementary. Surprisingly adults in authority often overlook the truth that many if not all of the basic values children seek are quite consistent with their own. How authority and order are achieved is the organizational crux of learning environments that are responsive to young adolescents.

ORGANIZING STUDENTS AND TEACHERS

The traditional bifurcation of American education into elementary and secondary schools has over the years left a good bit of ambiguity about how middle level schools and middle level programs within elementary and secondary schools should be organized. Elementary schools are usually configured as self-contained classrooms in which one teacher is responsible for all or most of the instruction of twenty-five or so students. The decision to assign a single teacher is a function of the belief that younger children need continuous contact with one adult in order to build interpersonal familiarity. Secondary schools are organized by academic departments. Teachers usually have a daily load of five or six classes, and they typically see as many as 125 to 150 students per day. This arrangement derives primarily from beliefs about older students' needs for teachers who have academic specialization in a single field. While there are advantages to both of these configurations, neither plan is nearly as well suited for responding to early adolescent needs as is interdisciplinary teaming—"an acknowledged goal for hundreds and hundreds of middle level schools" (Lounsbury, 1990, p. 41).

We educators tend to use the terms *classroom management* and *discipline* as synonyms. I propose that we recognize them as similar but distinctly separate concepts. In fact, discipline is but one dimension of a comprehensive classroom management plan—a design that encompasses multiple dimensions of the educational program being employed: vision and philosophy, academic and citizenship goals, a governance process, and so on. The thoughtful observer visiting an effective primary classroom can usually infer very accurately what the management plan is and how it is being implemented. It is usually quite evident how the plan addresses students' behavioral expectations, standards, and consequences for their misbehaviors. So it is in the most successful middle level classrooms. The greatest single difference between primary and middle level organization is the number of students and teachers involved and how they are organized. Middle level teams embody an enormous potential for developing even greater management efficiency through greater initiative and participation by students. First we will briefly examine selected principles and practices associated with successful management through teaming; then we will consider varying perspectives on discipline.

Interdisciplinary Team Organization (ITO)

This distinctly middle school teaming plan has already been described as a configuration of students and teachers that promotes constructive social interactions. However, teaming also enables teachers to achieve a great many more academic and organizational goals. ITOs are usually a student-teacher subset of the whole school, except in a small school where the entire middle level student population may be appropriately sized for a single team. More detailed treatment of team organization is found in Chapter 9.

Teams may consist of as few as two teachers and forty to fifty students, or they may be as large as four to six teachers and upwards of a hundred students. One of the primary purposes of ITO is to promote a closeness between adults and children and among children that is comparable to that achievable in the self-contained classroom. Therefore, teams of two to four teachers and fewer than a hundred students are generally most desirable. Students are most often drawn from a single grade, but there are also multigrade or multiage teams that make it possible to sustain student-teacher relationships over as much as two or three years (George, Spreul, & Moorefield, 1986; Lynch, 1990).

Young adolescents and their teachers enjoy numerous advantages over self-contained or departmental programs when they are part of a team that functions well. The benefits to students are too numerous to fully describe here, but four of the most notable advantages from students' point of view must be mentioned.

1. *Belonging.* The identity needs of young adolescents have already been described in Chapter 4. Teams are responsive to this need to belong, just as a healthy family dynamic means identity and status for every child. Being on a team provides a certain membership, complete with rights to ownership of everything the team stands for, all team activities, and the assurance of connectedness with teachers.

2. *Familiarity.* Students on teams know all of their teammates, because a function of ITO is to promote comfortable interpersonal relationships. During this developmental period often dominated by youngsters' uncertainty about their social status, responsive teaming assures that everyone, students and adults, gets to know everyone else through instructional groupings as well as other team activities.

3. *Recognition.* I have already written at length in earlier chapters about the importance of young adolescents being successful and feeling that they are a success. Within a team, students can be recognized frequently because they and their teachers are better able to know what is being done. Team awards as well as incidental comments by teachers who know what all their students are doing are extremely valuable to kids.

4. *Coherence.* The simple fact that all the teachers on the team are working toward the same general purpose and specific goals gives credibility to a team's educational program in the perceptions of their students. Students recognize unity as well as differences between teachers in terms of their expectations and standards. When teachers are consistent with each other, their programs make sense.

There are also numerous advantages in ITO for teachers. Again, the evidence from research is too extensive to review adequately here, but at least four advantages to teachers on interdisciplinary teams are worthy of brief mention.

1. *Collegiality.* Feelings of isolation can be a serious problem for teachers working alone all day with the same group of children, and the situation is not much better in a departmentally organized school. ITO necessitates a daily schedule built around a common planning time for the teachers on the team. The success of the team rests heavily on their easy access to each other and on constant communication.

2. *Authority.* In order to create and administer a coherent program, ITO teachers must be authorized to make many program decisions such as team procedures, daily scheduling, curricular organization, and student evaluation. This opportunity enables them to become more fully responsible for the education of their students, since they are able to innovate and work out problems to improve their programs.

3. *Problem solving.* No school organization functions without glitches, but since ITO teachers work collaboratively, meeting at least daily, they are able to respond to program or student problems swiftly and with the benefit of collective thought and the unity that derives from collective problem solving. Excellent teams are also conscientious about supporting off-team colleagues and the administration.

4. *Efficacy.* In the simplest terms, ITO makes teaching possible. With the collective effort of similarly committed teachers, it is possible to create education that goes well beyond any other known arrangement for middle level schooling. Teachers who have been members of successful teams frequently comment that they'd leave the profession if they had to give up teaming. Professional efficacy becomes a central, essential goal.

These advantages of ITO at the middle level may vary from one setting to another according to how specific teams have organized themselves and how well they function. The very best teams provide exceptionally comprehensive programs, and they represent education that is truly responsive to the developmental needs of their emerging adolescent students (George & Stevenson, 1989). Those highly accomplished teams have evolved successfully through middle phases of team development over more than a single year (George, 1982). In my experience, excellent schools at any level of schooling are populated by teachers who express a great deal of personal belief in their work and who are enthusiastic about their students and know they are making a difference in their lives. Every middle level school should aspire to conditions whereby "teachers . . . report greater satisfaction with the conditions of teaching when they are organized into interdisciplinary teams" (Erb, 1987, p. 4).

Essentials of ITO

Successful teaming is a somewhat complicated matter, however, and is not accomplished without a considerable investment of time, energy, and especially compromise by the teachers involved. The program details that are important to a single team's success may be situationally idiosyncratic, but underneath the concept of ITO are some foundation elements that are absolutely essential.

1. *Commitment.* Unless participating teachers are individually committed to the ITO concept and to their own team, the chances that they will become a successful team are nil. The interpersonal differences that are always present in any group become magnified, and self-interest rises above team-interest, whether the team is composed of teachers, athletes, or business people (Larson & LaFasto, 1989).

2. *Communication.* In order to collaborate successfully, team members have to understand each other. Understanding derives from dialogue that is goal directed and candid but always mutually respectful. Trust evolves from cumulative experience with such a quality of communication, augmented by shared accomplishments that derive from successful communications and collaborations.

3. *Time.* Time is a precious commodity in schools, but to have a successful team teachers must meet daily for as much as an hour in order to plan programs, address problems, discuss students, and coordinate the myriad of details that are part of the operation of a successful team. These daily sessions must also use time efficiently, following an agenda and effecting rapid turnaround on the host of details requiring attention.

As I mentioned at the outset, ITO is fundamentally different from self-contained and departmentalized school organizations. There are certainly excellent teachers whose outstanding work transcends whatever organizational scheme may be employed in their particular schools. However, those exceptional teachers notwithstanding, ITO is clearly the format by which most teachers can also grow personally, become better teachers than they might otherwise be, and derive greater personal satisfactions from working with other teachers. Excellent resources to enable further exploration of this distinctly middle level, organizational configuration can be found at the end of this chapter.

AUTHORITY

> Educators [must] have a collaborative relationship with students. This doesn't mean students run the class; teachers have a clear idea of . . . goals and most of the strategies to be used. But they encourage students to produce solutions to problems.
>
> *(Nathan, 1990)*

A contradiction that relates to authority is at work in the lives of young adolescents, and the issue begs for teachers' reflective thought and responsive practice in middle level schools. A notable dimension of these youngsters' personal development encompasses their maturing abilities to reason and achieve considered decisions about the most prudent way to respond to personal as well as situational dilemmas involving others. At the same time, these youngsters also want to assert themselves as independent decision makers. This combination of ability and desire is clearly evident to adults who observe and listen to them. We can see this mixture in their argumentativeness and in their readiness to give advice to each other. Sometimes the complexity of their reasoning can be astounding, especially when it concerns the interpersonal dynamics of their social groups.

This authority discrepancy often contributes to counterproductive tensions between generations—tensions that add significantly to the degrading stereotype of young adolescent rebelliousness and irresponsibility. Parents and teachers can become especially frustrated as children change from being relatively obedient and submissive at younger ages to becoming more assertive and even contentious in early adolescence. The new educational potential of this time can be easily lost through diversions brought about by confrontations and arguments, unless the adults involved recognize these signs for what they are: youngsters' attempts to assert their individual identities as independent thinkers and decision makers.

Let's turn for a moment to consideration of the host of people who exercise authority over young adolescents. Parents are their most dominant superiors at home, of course, but older siblings or grandparents or other family members living in the home may also have command over them. At school every adult is a superior, and there are often detailed rules specifying what students may and may not do. Rules are usually the collective authority of other people, not of the students' choosing. Most extracurricular group activities such as scouting and sports teams carry on the tradition that adults are in charge of children and therefore have authority over them. Even in the community, neighbors and business people have informal authority by virtue of their having attained the legal age for adulthood. In all of these contexts, young adolescents must function according to external expectations, controls, and consequences. Living under various authorities is the nature of things in our society, and it is not bad unless it is total and those subjugated have no say in their own lives.

Let's also think about the ways in which ten- to fourteen-year-olds are able to be independent decision makers and have authority over themselves. The extent to which contemporary family life allows choices for young adolescents is unclear; family lifestyles are as variable as individual personalities. Some parents allow choices only about such routine matters as chores and bedtime; other parents have largely abandoned parental responsibilities and leave their children to fend for themselves. Given how nebulous this important dimension of our students' lives may be, exploring the parameters within which students have say in their personal lifestyles is an excellent issue for teacher inquiry (see Chapter 3). Not only will the results help teachers to know their constituents better, but the data will likely provide useful information to parents.

The authority issue tends to be much clearer and more predictable in schools than in homes. The traditional message at school is simple "Obey!" Whatever the rule may be, whoever is giving orders, this dictum remains. Youngsters are left with the choice only to obey or not to obey, to pay attention and learn or to pretend. What is even more disturbing is a syndrome in which apparently mindless submission to obedience on the surface is often countered with devious actions of the child's own choosing. There is something

about totalitarian rule that provokes rebellious or deceitful behaviors among people needing to assert their individuality, whether it is a pretense of doing one's work or petty larceny or the more malevolent drug and alcohol abuse. Middle level educators must be
awake to the actuality that early adolescent youth, given opportunity and examples, are
capable of creditable reasoning and responsible decision making.

The most obvious place to share authority with young adolescents is in creating,
amending, or replacing the rules that guide how their school lives are lived. Once again,
interdisciplinary team organization provides a perfect context for engaging students in exercising their developing capacities for reasoning. To function efficiently and coherently,
teams must have policies and guidelines or rules. What better opportunity could educators desire than to collaborate with students in setting up, maintaining, and refining as
needed the team's routines? Since the youngsters will be working to create a context that
suits their needs and circumstances, their deliberations and decisions will certainly be
meaningful to them.

Consider the following areas in which students and teachers conscientiously communicating can share authority:

Developing team, classroom or project-related rules and consequences for such is-
   sues as behavioral expectations, acceptable language, interpersonal courtesies
Selecting and planning special occasions such as team events, birthday celebrations,
   holiday commemorations, and team/class parties
Choosing curricular studies such as orbitals and service projects
Negotiating dates for tests and due dates for projects, and designing a homework
   schedule
Creating an equitable system for decorating and maintaining the team space or class-
   rooms and the outdoors
Explaining educational goals and programs to parents
Leading team/class meetings and discussions

One knee-jerk reaction to the idea of shared authority is that young adolescents will
seize the opportunity to legislate themselves out of all responsibility and accountability.
My experience and that of others shows that the overwhelming majority of young adolescents are both conservative and cautious as novice decision makers. Often there will be a
minority viewpoint, but so it is in democratic decision making. The majority still rules,
and as teachers we must go beyond a verbalized advocacy of democratic rule to a demonstrated one.

Elementary kids behave according to blind faith.
High school students live according to rules faith.
Middle level kids trust proven faith.

(Arth, 1987)

Finally, the spirit in which decisions are shared affects students' perceptions of the authenticity of teachers' motives. Authority that is shared grudgingly will likely leave an adversarial tone, and while the letter of the democratic process may be observed, the spirit of
democracy will be missing. Where people of good will representing different generations
talk and listen to each other earnestly and in good humor, the spirit of democracy thrives.

DISCIPLINE

No other word seems to catch the attention of beginning teachers more quickly. Discipline portends conflict, a struggle for control over students, a contest for power, and the sinking fear that "they won't behave for me." That all teachers, especially novices, will be challenged by some students is a virtual certainty, and experienced teachers understand that how well they handle these first challenges establishes their credibility with even the most complaisant students. This familiar anguish over an untried teacher's clout in relationship to students is characterized in the reflections of Brian Aspinwall, a fictional first-year teacher and boarding school dormitory proctor, as he writes in his journal,

> There were terrible squeals after lights tonight, and I was in a wretched quandary. How does one cope with forty fifteen-year-olds in the dark? . . . How can I afford to admit that [they] are out of control? I can only pull out this journal and foolishly wish that I could climb inside of it and pull its covers over my shamed and ridiculous head. Oh, Journal, if you could only hide me, if I could only turn myself into ink! . . . Please, dear Lord, keep [them] quiet tonight.

> *(Auchincloss, 1964, pp. 7–8)*

There are probably no more urgent and agonizing worries for the majority of beginning teachers than the questions that introduce this chapter. Whether the teams used are discipline or classroom management or control, the priorities at risk are that students will behave themselves, treat each other and the teacher with civil consideration, and do their work. And underlying these outcomes is the larger concern that students are growing in terms of understanding themselves and others, developing self-control and denial, learning to be understanding and tolerant of others, and accepting the consequences for their failings. Given the intense changes young adolescents are undergoing, this can be a large order.

Few areas of teaching methodology have been researched as thoroughly as discipline or classroom management. Specific programs and organizational systems reflecting diverse philosophies have been applied with success in all sorts and conditions of schools. The four selected approaches abstracted below reveal interesting philosophical differences but generally compatible values. Readers are encouraged to investigate these programs in greater detail by reading the original works of the associated theorists.

Behavior Modification

Positive reinforcement, also referred to as reward, is the critical technique to be employed in using behavior modification. When a student is functioning in ways that are consistent with the teacher's desire, the student's behavior is reinforced through the teacher's compliments and encouragement. Tangible rewards such as stars or bonus grades or credit are also sometimes given according to the age of children. In effect, the desired behavior and the student are affirmed. When a student's behavior does not conform to the teacher's expectations, the student is either ignored or punished by removal of privileges. The underlying assumption is that all behavior is learned, and it is the consequences of their behaviors that affect students' learning and future patterns. While there may be assorted permutations to this basic approach, the underlying theoretical basis comes primarily from the work of B. F. Skinner (1971).

Assertive Discipline

This approach posits that students need the psychological security that derives from order if they are to learn. Therefore, schools and classrooms must be orderly if they are to effectively serve student needs and promote learning. A key to such order is consistency among teachers who are assertive in communicating clear expectations, behavioral limits, and consequences. In order to become effectively assertive, teachers should learn assertive response styles through practice. A critical dimension of assertiveness is learning how to establish and follow through on limitations to student behavior. These conditions are essential to establish a platform upon which more affirmative teacher–student interactions may occur, such as recognition for students' accomplishments and a variety of rewards. The dominant theme of this approach is that the adults are in charge, and they have agreed upon a common approach to discipline. They are asserting their authority and doing what they say in terms of consequences (Canter, 1976).

Logical Consequences

The heart of this approach is democratic. Students participate by discussing behavioral standards and expectations, setting rules, and working out consequences. Furthermore, teachers teach responsibility by helping students acknowledge their motivation for behaviors, most of which are related to a desire to belong. By raising students' consciousness about the four basic goals of misbehavior, they become more capable of recognizing their own motivations and making subsequent self-corrections if necessary. Those goals are (1) attention getting, (2) power seeking, (3) revenge, and (4) displaying one's inadequacy. Teachers must also be attentive to students' behavior patterns and able to assist students in their personal reflections. This system works best with teachers who are disposed to work patiently and consistently with students having difficulty working out behavioral issues. The theoretical basis of this approach and excellent guidelines are found in the writings of Rudolf Dreikurs (Dreikurs, Grunwald, & Pepper, 1971).

Control Theory

This conceptualization of student needs and school discipline reflects a twenty-year evolution in the work of psychiatrist William Glasser (1969, 1985). The theory acknowledges that students have four inherent, fundamental needs: (1) to belong, (2) to have power, (3) to be free, and (4) to have fun. Behavioral problems arise when these needs are unmet, and students act out on their frustrations with their circumstances. Teams and classes organized into small cooperative units that encourage helping and emphasize connectedness among everyone are much less likely to thwart these needs. Teachers shift their management focus from a me–them to a we–us orientation, and team or class meetings become a major vehicle for promoting communication and trust. The overriding goal is to see that students achieve satisfaction for their need quest in ways that enhance the quality of life for the total student community. Glasser claims that "any school that operates without taking [these] needs of students into account will fail badly in its purposes" (Chance & Bibens, 1990, p. 4).

DISCIPLINE AND EARLY ADOLESCENCE

Gumption and initiative are valued human qualities that surface readily as young children grow into and through adolescence. Unrestrained spirit, however, no matter how natural it may be, can be an obstacle to teachers' efforts to create a climate for learning that is safe and comfortable but also purposeful and productive. And perhaps more than any other aspect of being a teacher, unresolved discipline issues drain energy and spirit. Each of the preceding models offers insights about ways to go about helping young adolescents develop whatever personal restraints or initiatives they need to function as complements to their team or class. Drawing from those models and personal experience, I recommend four general but essential provisos for team or classroom plans that will not only accomplish the order necessary for learning but also enable students to draw upon their energies and developmentally natural need for independent authority. After all, the choices youngsters make about how to behave constitute the quintessence of personal authority.

1. *Interpersonal Climate.* A school climate that is responsive to youngsters' needs is aptly described as sunny and warm. If youngsters are expected to appreciate the efforts of their educators, to cooperate, and to show good humor, they must likewise be respected and enjoy good-natured relationships with adults. Partnerships become feasible when adults and children treat each other amiably and respectfully. And teachers are themselves most approachable when they are in turn approaching their students.

2. *Worth and Dignity Assured.* There should be no doubt that every youngster needs to learn to believe in himself or herself, especially when so many of them are going through troubling changes and feel so vulnerable. Self-esteem is a constant need, and for many youngsters it is especially fragile and elusive. Simply feeling good about oneself and optimistic about possibilities is especially hard to come by when others—teachers or students—belittle or degrade. Hurtful teasing isn't acceptable. Embarrassment and humiliation, whether perpetrated by adults or children, have no place in responsive middle level education.

3. *Approximating Democracy.* It should be obvious that young adolescents cannot legally participate as fully as adults in the democratic process. Until students reach the age of legal majority, it is prudent to approximate democracy as much as is possible within school system policies. Not only will firsthand schooling in democratic processes contribute to enlightened citizenship in adulthood, it will also enable teachers to accommodate students' needs for self-determination. Team meetings become a forum for discussion and decision making about the procedures and rules the team will live by, and every member is assured of an equal say in defining how the community will function. The key to clear understanding and subsequent collaboration is dialogue, and the team meeting assures democratic participation.

4. *Redemption Is Always Close, Not Closed.* This is a time when many youngsters are struggling with the question "Who am I?" and in their quest for this identity they will make mistakes. A few youngsters may make many mistakes. In order for them to learn to trust the system and the adults, however, they must understand that their commitment assures them a fresh start. I am not suggesting that teachers should overlook offensive behaviors. However, teachers must maintain their mature poise in

order to separate the behavior in question from the identity of the perpetrator. Forgiveness for past transgressions and the opportunity for a fresh beginning must always be available. It is essential for us as teachers to remember that human development and growth occur irregularly; we must not close any options for our rapidly changing young adolescents.

For several years I was a teacher on a sixth to eighth grade team in a major Eastern city. Some of our students could be described as "street kids," because in moving about their urban setting they had developed the toughness and resilience that survival on the streets demanded. The language of that street culture was rife with swearing, and those profanities came to school with them. Although most of the students on our team seemed generally indifferent to it, the swearing was objectionable to my teammates and me. Thus, appropriate school language was periodically a matter of debate in our team meetings. The kids and we were never completely successful in enforcing a rule about swearing that we had discussed and adopted. The difficulty of judging the circumstances of individual situations left doubts and concerns about equity. Yet, for a few days after every team meeting where we discussed the issue, swearing diminished or disappeared completely. Even those street kids for whom cursing was as normal as any other language were making a deliberate effort to accommodate their teachers. In time they slipped back into lesser consciousness, and after a while the cycle would repeat itself. My colleagues and I came to appreciate how essential it is for people of contrasting ages and cultural dispositions to maintain rational dialogue if they are to come to understand and respect each other. That dialogue was the essence of our ability to share authority and live effectively as an interdependent learning community.

CONFLICT RESOLUTION AND STUDENT MEDIATION

Functions . . . that call forth effort . . . make an individual more conscious of the end and purpose of his actions . . . to turn his energy from blind, or thoughtless, struggle into reflective judgment.

(Dewey, 1913, p. 53)

Interpersonal conflict among young adolescents and between some of them and teachers is inevitable. In any social context where people are working hard to define and establish themselves and their priorities, there is virtual certainty that disagreements and disputes will occur, some of which may intensify into vocal clashes and even physical altercations. School mediation programs are especially appropriate ways for teachers to work with young adolescents to help them learn ways to use these conflicts to learn more about themselves and ways of living equitably and amicably with others. The prospect of a better way to resolve disputes than many of the responses of previous generations also appeals to their natural idealism for a better life for all.

Conflict resolution through school-based mediation programs began in the 1980s and has in a brief time become established as "part of a significant societal trend toward alternative means of resolving disputes" (Koch, 1986). According to an analysis of student mediation programs reported in the Harvard Education Letter, "young people are much more likely to resolve their differences when they—with the help of trained peers—sit down together, name what has been going on without focusing on blame, and work out a solution" (Steinberg, 1989, p. 5). Middle level educators have a unique opportunity to help developing young adolescent students learn how to listen to each other and learn what they can do to work out differences through reflection and deliberate actions. Mediation stands as a hopeful strategy for addressing issues that can otherwise be disheartening.

Young adolescents are becoming increasingly able to look beyond just a personally defensive or egocentric viewpoint in order to grasp how differently but legitimately another individual's perceptions of a common experience or event may be. Their ability to recognize and respect the legitimacy of contrary points of view, especially when one of the opinions is personally held, is a mark of growing maturity. Youngsters' potential for stepping outside their own point of view in order to swap roles or arguments with an adversary in order to understand and empathize is ripe for development through skillfully guided experience. Becoming able to see oneself as a person who said or did a particular thing is a trustworthy indicator of the advancing intellectual development referred to in Piaget's formulation as formal operational thought. When youngsters choose mediation, they also have personal stakes in the results and tend to be intensely interested in how the process works.

In order to teach students the processes of mediation, teachers must first learn and use the method themselves. The techniques are not acquired merely by reading, but like all effective interpersonal transactions, they must be learned through guided use. In a school, classroom, or team where mediation is available, all students are oriented to the process and the kinds of difficulties that are suitable for its application. Potential student mediators may be selected for training by random selection, by nomination from the class or team, or by individual application. At least one teacher who has been prepared in the philosophy and techniques of mediation teaches the student mediators and continues to work with them, meeting regularly to help them process their experiences.

Student mediators first learn how to listen carefully and impartially to the accounts related by the antagonists in order to be able to retell the contrasting points of view and guide the antagonists through the resolution process. They must continuously remain neutral, never giving personal opinions or advice. Personalities must never be allowed to become an issue if the integrity of the process is to be observed. Therefore, litigants have to agree that name-calling, put-downs, and interrupting each other's explanations will be ruled out. In learning mediation, students learn how to ask clarifying questions and how to reflect each person's perception of the conflict. They may also have to reassert the mediation process, policing the antagonists when they sometimes revert to name-calling. Their function is always to guide the antagonists toward a solution that preserves each individual's need for personal dignity and that each of them can support.

Mediation is an organized process that student mediators learn through a thorough orientation and practice before they take on real issues. While on the surface it may appear deceptively easy to simply follow the steps, it is important to remember that patience, calm, and tenacious adherence to the steps in the process are always necessary to achieve progress when strong feelings are involved. The focus must be kept on the particular problem that has aroused a conflict. Antagonists must agree to address the problem candidly and honestly in order to achieve the purpose of the session, namely, reaching agreement about solving the problem.

Although the specific steps of any mediation process may vary somewhat from one setting to another, six elements are usually present:

1. Two trained student mediators convene the session, explaining the ground rules and how mediation works. If the antagonists agree to comply with these conditions, the

process continues; if either or both do not agree, the issue is removed from mediation and turned over to the responsible adult.

2. Each of the antagonists tells his or her version of the conflict.

3. The mediators look for areas of agreement in the two versions and then retell the incident, pointing out where there is agreement and disagreement. They also make distinctions between fact and feelings, and as they restate the incident and the antagonists' feelings, they look to each individual for concurrence or challenge.

4. The adversaries are then asked to brainstorm possibilities for how their problem might be solved while the mediators list and subsequently reflect the proposed solutions in an attempt to identify one or more mutually acceptable possibilities.

5. The possibilities are discussed by the antagonists and moderated by the mediators until a mutually agreeable solution is established. The mediators then summarize the incident, pointing out how the process has identified a positive solution.

6. The mediators write a brief report, sometimes using a special form that includes a brief outline of the incident and an explicit statement of the agreement. Each participant signs the report and receives a copy. One copy of the report also goes to the teacher to be kept in a mediation file.

Usually one of the mediators has a brief follow-up interview a few days later to find out how the solution is working and how the antagonists are feeling about the mediation process. Sometimes students who have agreed to a solution fail to observe their agreement, but my experience has been that these relapses occur rarely. Because some educators are accustomed only to schooling in which adults enforce rules and consequences, mediation may best be offered at first as an alternative to the more conventional disciplinary consequences. Furthermore, specific program procedures and applications may vary from one school to another as students and teachers both grow in knowledge of this excellent way for students to become more responsible for themselves and each other. Student mediation is also not intended for issues in which there are clear violations of the law or of clearly stated school policies such as alcohol or drug use, larceny, or vandalism.

Some excellent resources are listed at the end of this chapter to guide educators desiring to explore student mediation. It is important to understand that developing an effective mediation program takes time and careful teaching. Although mediation will not solve all conflicts in a school, it will have significant impact on the interpersonal climate. At its very best, student mediation is even used to resolve disagreements between teachers and students, showing the extent to which the institution is truly committed to a just, democratic community.

GROUPING STUDENTS FOR LEARNING

Psychologists tell us that the roots of much of human motivation are couched in interpersonal relationships. We middle level educators need to exploit that prospect. No decisions about classroom organization are more consequential than the ones teachers make about grouping students. We know how sensitive young adolescents are about other's perceptions of them. We also know that they are inclined to take on the identity of the groups to which they belong. How fully students achieve the school's or program's goals and objectives, how well they accomplish the academic curriculum, and how successfully they learn to function as contributing members of a school community derive directly from their group experiences. Helping students learn how to function effectively in variously configured groups becomes a central goal of classroom and team organization.

Grouping students by assumed measures of academic ability is an ignoble practice that is gradually being abandoned at the middle level. The terms that refer to this custom are *tracking* or *streaming* or *leveling*. This practice has been controversial because it reflects and helps perpetuate the class and racial inequalities of American society (Oakes, 1985; Wheelock, 1992). For a long time, educators have rationalized it on the grounds that grouping students of like abilities together helps everyone move at his or her own most appropriate pace. The practice and this argument have been particularly objectionable at the middle level for several reasons:

1. Early adolescence is a time of conspicuous change in the rate and dimensions of intellectual development.

2. Group-administered paper-and-pencil measures of "ability" are notoriously deficient.

3. The identity-formation needs of youngsters are especially vulnerable to grouping designations decreed by school officials.

4. Emerging adolescents are naturally inclined toward learning from peers who have various individual abilities and talents.

To the lay person it may appear logical that if the quickest and brightest students are grouped together in one class and the slowest students are grouped separately in another class, both groups will learn better. Despite this logic, however, there are substantial research data to challenge the rationale for tracking (Kulik & Kulik, 1984; Sorenson & Hallinan, 1986; Slavin, 1987). Furthermore, tracking students is conceived as a strategy to accomplish only academic goals, not those related to personal development. Imbalance in the mission of the middle level school results, and what becomes most highly valued is driven by the traditional departmental orientation toward covering curricular content.

Middle level educators must preserve healthy personal development as the uppermost goal. Many excellent schools have shown that students placed on heterogeneous grouped interdisciplinary teams do well in both academics and social terms (George, 1988). In summarizing his excellent review of the implications of research on tracking for middle level education, George wrote:

> Middle level schools of all kinds must immediately move to a school organization based on the interdisciplinary team format, where students are placed on teams heterogeneously [that] must operate in ways which encourage all students to see themselves as important parts of positive and varied groups . . . without damaging the opportunities for increased self-esteem, higher academic achievement, and more positive group involvement.

> *(George, 1988, p. 27)*

Given that tracking is discriminatory and its positive effects on learning are dubious at best, responsible middle level educators are heeding this excellent advice and looking to other ways of grouping that are more responsive to both students' needs and academic goals. These are often referred to as "within class groupings," but they may also be applied as "within team groups." Before examining some of these strategies, however, we should consider some observations about young adolescents' varied preferences for relationship structures.

Although a few youngsters may consistently prefer to work alone, the large majority of young adolescents are generally interested in working in amenable groups, especially those composed of just a few classmates. Remember that being successful is each youngster's first priority, and that includes being with and working with other students as much as it refers to academic or athletic accomplishments. But they can also be quite fussy about whom they will work with and the conditions that pertain to the group process and task. They are also likely to be perceptive and sensitive about teachers' rationales for forming a particular group and its identity, so teachers should not be naive about the accuracy of their students' perceptions.

Although teachers may not like it, they must recognize that some of their students are "groupies" of sorts—their sole reason for wanting to be in a particular group is simply to belong with a group or other students who are also in that group. Even though the motivation may be banal, it is important to accept it as a starting place from which these groupies can learn about being responsible and useful to achieving group goals—not only as membership for social or identity purposes. I have worked with students who were so much in awe of a particular classmate that they wanted to be in the admired peer's group in order to do whatever would help that person be successful. Such a motivation simply to serve someone else may work well in a format based on a superordinate-subordinate dynamic so long as the "servant" also learns how to lead such a group. After all, aside from helping students become more personally involved in their studies, the goal of all grouping strategies must be to help students learn how to be a group member and how to function in a variety of group roles.

Whole Group Direct Instruction and Activities

Some of the time, all students benefit from well-presented direct instruction to the total class or group. In spite of numerous effective strategies for promoting learning and responsibility for learning with students, this classic approach to instruction is still necessary. When a team or class is being oriented to a large group activity such as a geography bee or a library project or an interdisciplinary unit, it is appropriate and far more efficient to instruct everyone at the same time. As is probably self-evident, these whole group sessions should be well organized around direct teaching segments of no more than ten minutes followed by an activity in which individuals or small groups carry out some kind of follow-up. For example, if a class of thirty students is beginning a study of the Industrial Revolution, the pertinent background material might be described by a five-minute lecture followed by three-member group work to brainstorm lists of consumer products in their homes that appear to have been manufactured by use of assembly-line techniques. Each small group might later contribute their ideas to a bulletin board matrix depicting the ideas of the whole class, thus bringing the activity around to another whole group lesson. This arrangement enables personal learning to be based on intermittent sessions in common with the rest of the class.

Small Group Direct Instruction and Activities

Where curriculum content is sequenced into interdependent concepts or operations, small group direct instruction is often necessary. There is no restriction on the size of a small group other than having few enough people to give everyone an opportunity to respond and ask questions. The classic source of examples of this kind of grouping for instruction is mathematics, the most naturally sequential material in the middle level curriculum. Although many of the books and materials from other subject areas are organized in highly serial ways, no other core subject at the middle level has the degree of natural sequence that mathematics has. If, for example, one small group studies bisecting angles while another group is measuring angles, direct instruction using both compass and protractor is appropriate for the former group, while instruction about how to use the protractor is provided for the latter group.

Interest Groups

One of the simplest ways in which young adolescents can exercise some authority about what they learn is through interest groups. Let's return to the earlier example of the unit about the Industrial Revolution. The teacher might identify a list of groups needed to accomplish a class presentation to the rest of the school about their study. One list might include groups about capitalism, child labor, communications, cottage industries, division of labor, guilds and labor unions, iron making, railroads, raw materials, spinning and textiles, and the steam engine. Another list might include invitations, publicity, play writing, refreshments, costumes, decorations, and cleanup. Each student would choose to join one interest group from each list. That choice would enable him or her to act on a personal interest, whether it had to do with particular subject matter or the opportunity to work with particular classmates (or both). The point to be emphasized here is that in every unit of study, regardless of the topic or subject matter, students ought to have an opportunity to express personal interests through such group membership choices.

Interest groups selected primarily because a pair of students or a circle of friends want to work together can be very successful. Their motivation may have little to do with the topic—they simply want to be together. Such natural affinities can become the context for highly productive work, and teachers are well advised to cultivate these preferences along some prudent guidelines.

1. Group members must form a plan that designates a timetable and spells out which members are responsible for which tasks.

2. The group must agree to be self-policing, abiding by a work ethic that will enable them to accomplish their timetable.

3. No one who is not a member of the friendship group can be excluded so long as they observe the two preceding conditions.

When interest groups are being formed, it is also fitting to set up additional structured groups for students whose interests are based on the topics rather than motivated by social choices. There are several other ways to configure those groups as well as interest groups.

Book Groups

During my sixteen years as a middle level teacher, I became convinced that nothing I could teach was as important as the intellectual engagement that students experience when they are truly immersed in reading and exchanging ideas about the text. As a young teacher believing in reading's preeminence from the outset, I worked hard at teaching reading skills by using direct methods, well-conceived packaged materials, and the technologies of the time. As I gained in experience I came to realize that students' choices were the key to reading, not me or the materials I chose for them. From then on, I shifted the emphasis to students reading materials they chose together while I worked primarily as their guide and coach—a technical troubleshooter. I also freely shared my own literary passions and insights, modeling precisely what I hoped they would become. But my enlightened emphasis remained a focus on the individual student's choices and growth as a literary person.

From this personal origin, book groups became a central component of our team organization when our block schedule allowed a varied assortment of groups and instructional activities. These groups were freely formed in that students chose books from our extensive paperback collection. The only requirement was that every student always had to be in a book group. "Not choosing" was unacceptable. The size of a group could be as small as two or limited only by the number of interested students and our collection of eight to ten copies of established favorites. Each group would pick a student coordinator and meet two or three times a week as its members completed previously agreed-upon numbers of pages or chapters. Meetings were used to swap personal reactions, discuss the author's message or lesson, exchange new words for their word books, and negotiate the subsequent pages or chapters to read. One of the teachers would join at least one meeting per week to serve as a consultant to each group. If one of us had not previously read the book, that teacher would be a full member of the group, meeting each time the group met and carrying out the same work as the students, but not serving as coordinator, since we wanted our students to learn from that experience. As books were completed, each participant drafted a minimum one-page review for a teacher's critique prior to writing it formally in his or her portfolio, also described in the next chapter.

Our students often requested particular titles outside our existing collection, and after one of my teammates or I reviewed a proposed book as a candidate for our students' general reading, we'd almost always purchase the requisite copies. Since we were not required to purchase basal readers for every student, the book budget always allowed us to acquire as many new paperbacks as we needed. We also managed to maintain an up-to-date collection of periodicals. While we had classroom subscriptions to several magazines, we augmented that collection by asking families to share their subscriptions as soon as they'd finished reading them. Consequently, we usually received weekly sports and news magazines such as *Time* and *Sports Illustrated* within a week or so of their publication, and we often received several copies of monthlies such as *National Geographic* and *Smithsonian*. Occasionally a parent would subscribe to a periodical as a gift to the class. *New Yorker* came to us that way, and its cartoons as well as some of its short stories were an immediate attraction. A popular writer with our team, E. B. White, had a long-standing affiliation with that magazine, enhancing its credibility with our emerging young literati. Exercising their literary opinions and preferences appeared to fuel their eagerness to read.

Our vision of a team climate defined by high literacy expectations was also realized by the extent to which we shared our passions for our own reading. Although it may be difficult for teachers to read at home on their own during the school year, doing so and sharing the experience is essential if the reading program is to have any credibility. My teammate, Willy Claflin, enjoyed science fiction. His steady commentary of reactions and excerpts from those pieces ignited our students' interest. I recall reading Peter Benchley's

Jaws over a weekend, becoming so excited by the story that I couldn't wait to share it with my students on Monday. They begged for us to buy copies, but since it was available only in expensive hard cover, I agreed instead to do a book group in which I'd read excerpts to them, covering one chapter at a time. They weren't reading it, of course, but in reading to them I found them extremely responsive, so much so that I wound up doing three consecutive groups.

I also shared poetry I favored, occasionally reading pieces aloud alone or with a teammate when there was more than one voice, such as Robert Frost's "Telephone" and "Death of a Hired Man," two of the students' favorites. When I took a community center course in Japanese bonsai, I shared the reading materials and my projects as if my students were my peers. Throughout all of this intergenerational sharing, however, the foundation component was the book group. Students read many things, of course, but the tone was established and sustained by these choice groups in which individual pleasures in reading were augmented by degrees of analysis and interpretation that were understandable for the diverse composition of our team.

Cooperative Learning Groups

No grouping designs are better suited to the social and intellectual needs of young adolescents than the assorted strategies generally referred to collectively as cooperative groups (Slavin, 1987; Johnson & Johnson, 1988). Their common purpose is to promote interdependent learning by establishing conditions that require small groups of students to work productively and positively together, face to face, sharing individual responsibility for a group product. Where students work this way in small groups or pairs and share rewards, not only do they appear to learn the assigned material better but "the shared responsibility and interaction produce more positive feelings toward tasks and others, generate better intergroup relations, and result in better self-images for students with histories of poor achievement" (Joyce & Weil, 1986, p. 216).

Since the resurgence of interest in cooperative methods in the decade of the 1980s, specific strategies have been developed and extensively researched. Some of the most noteworthy of those approaches are briefly described in the following pages. To summarize the research findings, there is general improvement in academic achievement and grades among students working in successful cooperative groups. There are likewise beneficial social outcomes in measures of self-esteem by virtue of the recognition obtained from successful individual accomplishment as well as contributions to team successes. What is less clear is the extent to which the patterns of functioning learned in cooperative groups are transferred to other learning activities. It is also appropriate to examine the necessity of the various scoring systems used to distinguish "super teams" from "great teams" from "good teams" and so on. While competition may motivate students in many settings, the necessity of team competition as emphasized especially in the Student Team Learning methods is questionable.

In order for a group to function successfully, the members must learn how to organize themselves around a common goal in ways that teach listening and processing skills. Individual accomplishment is tied to the group's accomplishment. Group successes reflect the individual efforts and talents of members plus their effectiveness in collaboration. In my experience, the optimal group size is three students, although the cooperative methods currently being employed allow for organization primarily into four- to six-member teams that follow fairly explicit directions. I've found that larger groups sometimes tend to become reformed into subgroups, and achieving the oneness of a single group effort becomes more problematic. As the number of people in a group increases, the likelihood that individual members will slip into the background is also increased.

The teacher's role in cooperative grouping shifts from being the control center of learning to functioning more like a coach, moving among the groups, giving individual help as needed, helping to clarify issues and answer questions, and offering encouragement and compliments. When a group is struggling, the teacher is able to more easily give assistance directly where it is needed, whereas in a teacher-centered class, everyone else has to wait until one group's problems have been resolved. Students who need particular help have a better chance of getting it, because they can draw on their fellow group members as well as the teacher. Because all group members have responsibility for carrying out collateral work, their intensity in learning is enhanced. Helping each other becomes the established expectation, not something that the teacher regards as objectionable.

Teachers wishing to employ cooperative learning strategies should not rely solely on the characterizations that follow as adequate for classroom implementation. Cooperative group skills are acquired through directed experiences over time, whether the learners are teachers or young adolescent students. Successful implementation is very dependent on thorough preparation, and teachers must learn for themselves the dynamics of these strategies if they are to be adequately prepared for teaching them to their students. The reorientation from a setting that is primarily individually and competitively oriented to one that emphasizes collective successes requires time and experience. Workshops or seminars in which teachers function according to different types of cooperative groups are probably the best way to learn these techniques. Several effective and thoroughly researched protocols for cooperative groups will be described briefly.

Learning Together

The Johnson brothers, David and Roger, have been pioneers in the development of cooperative group work among students (1988). Their Learning Together model engages small groups of students in cooperating to complete a single assignment. Rewards are tied to how well the students functioned as a group as well as the quality of their group's product. Groups are usually made up of four or five students, and they are not deliberately formed according to measures of ability, popularity, or any other criteria. An example of implementing the Learning Together model is an assignment to a group of four students to list and illustrate the chronology of steps occurring in the evolution of an acorn into an oak tree. A single product reflecting their collective work is submitted and evaluated. Their individual grades for the project is the project grade plus whatever grade is derived from the effectiveness of their collaborative process as judged by the teacher. Group members might also participate in evaluating their group. Individual grades might be further augmented by performance on a test about the study.

Group Investigation

This model emphasizes the role of students as decision makers as well as workers and learners. They exercise choices about the composition of their two- to six-member groups, what they will study, the steps they need to follow in accomplishing their project, and how the work will be divided (Sharan & Sharan, 1976). Six successive stages may be spread over one or more weeks; teachers of young adolescents are reminded to try to complete a Group Investigation within three weeks or less. The stages are listed below and described in detail elsewhere (Sharan & Sharan, 1989/1990).

1. Identifying the topic to be investigated and organizing students into research groups
2. Planning the investigation in groups
3. Carrying out the investigation
4. Preparing a final report
5. Presenting the final report
6. Evaluation

Consider this example of Group Investigation as it was applied to an interdisciplinary unit, "Transportation." From the opening stage of the unit, the four students especially interested in sea travel organized themselves as the Sea Group, with one student serving as the coordinator and another as the recorder. Then they brainstormed questions they wanted to investigate about the topic and solicited questions and ideas from classmates who were not part of their group. These possibilities were then condensed into an outline of four topics, complementing the number of students in the group: sailing ships, ocean liners, submarines, nuclear ships. The coordinator's task was to keep discussion focused on the investigation, and the recorder documented the group's decisions and plans. Their final task was to list the questions to be addressed by each member and to write out a worksheet and timetable for each other and the teacher. In the third stage they met briefly each day to update each other about what they learned and to identify where they might need to help each other or get outside help. Then in the fourth stage they prepared their project according to their plan: a time line and a three-page written history of sea travel linked to a classroom display of drawings of ships on poster board. Presentation of their study, the fifth stage, was accomplished via a tape-recorded radio show dramatizing fictional students traveling on the sea at different times in history. Closure was brought to the project by two forms of evaluation. First, students completed an individual form that solicited an evaluation of the quality of their project and assessed their group-mates' contributions. Second, they took a test they devised themselves based on their project. Every participant had an almost unavoidable opportunity to succeed in such a Group Investigation.

Student Team Learning

The most comprehensively researched forms of cooperative grouping are those included under this category of strategies developed primarily by Robert Slavin and his colleagues. More detailed descriptions of their designs for team learning may be found elsewhere (1980); general descriptions of these organizational and instructional strategies are described below.

Student Teams Achievement Division (STAD). Teams of four to five students are formed by the teacher to reflect both the academic and the social-cultural composition of the class. A direct presentation of subject matter by the teacher is followed by distribution of worksheets to all students. The emphasis is on team members working together to teach each other and quiz each other until the subject matter has been mastered by every team member. Each student then takes a quiz on the material, and individual scores are compiled to generate a team score. The incentive for doing well comes from the need to uphold the team plus the reward of an inventive scoring system that rewards individual members for improving on past quizzes or sustaining a high level of performance. The scoring system establishes a base score for each member that is five points less than the average of quizzes in the past. For each point above one's individual base score, students earn up to ten additional points. This scoring system assures that every student, regardless of his or her past performance, can contribute positively to the team performance. This method enables every student to be successful and to contribute to the success of peers.

Teams Games Tournaments (TGT). The tournament pits students of comparable past quiz performances from each STAD team against each other in a novel question-answer competition that shifts the focus from quizzes to games. Consider this example: team representatives whose averages are approximately 80 are gathered around a table where numbered question cards are stacked face down. Those students compete for points for their STAD teams according to the following game rules (Slavin, 1980, p. 28).

Reader

1. Picks a numbered card and finds the corresponding question on the game sheet.
2. Reads the question aloud.
3. Tries to answer.

First Challenger

Challenges if he or she wants to (and gives a different answer), or passes.

Second Challenger

Challenges if first challenger passes, if he or she wants to. When all have challenged or passed, second challenger checks the answer sheet. Whoever was right keeps the card. If the reader was wrong, there is no penalty, but if either challenger was wrong, he or she must put a previously won card, if any, back in the deck.

Scoring is based on the number of cards each player wins, and their points then figure for their STAD team in the tournament scoring. To keep students rotating among the tables, the highest scorer at one table is moved to another table composed of members whose past averages are higher than 80 while the lowest performer moves down a notch. This maneuver helps maintain equity in the competition and also ensures that every student is able to earn points for his or her STAD team.

Jigsaw I and II. Jigsaw II teams are also configured into four- to five-member heterogeneously mixed teams, but the cooperative group process is different from STAD and TGT. The emphasis is on students' dividing and sharing an assignment in order to learn one section well enough to teach it to the other team members. All team members initially cover the same material together before the individual members take responsibility for sections as designated by the teacher. Each team member then works with students from each of the other Jigsaw teams who are responsible for the same sections. They cover their sections thoroughly, becoming experts about them, before returning to their teams to teach their teammates. Then each Jigsaw team studies the total assignment together, teaching and quizzing each other within the team. Upon completion of this studying phase, they take individual quizzes that are again weighted in terms of improvement and subsequently expressed as team scores similar to STAD and TGT. Jigsaw II was developed from a previous Jigsaw group learning process that did not utilize cooperative learning incentives as fully as the preceding Student Team Learning methods (Aronson, 1978).

Team Assisted Individualization—Mathematics (TAI). TAI combines cooperative learning incentives and programmed or individualized instruction in mathematics where a comprehensively sequenced course of study that accommodates individualized instruction already exists. In order to designate TAI team composition, all students are first pretested to establish a class profile of their levels of skill in math operations. Then, heterogeneous teams of four to five students are formed, ensuring that each team is also mixed in social-cultural terms. The daily routine includes the teacher working with groups of students who have similar needs from the several TAI teams while the remaining students work within their teams on self-paced materials that constitute the course of study. These materials are organized into compact booklets that describe the concept being studied and integrate it with step-by-step explanations of the skills being learned, practice problems, formative tests, a unit test, and answer sheets. Students do most of the checking in the team and judge when further work on a skill is needed. The careful ordering of the math content in these booklets enables every student to work at a level appropriate to his or her existing competence and then move ahead at a complementary pace.

The cooperative feature of TAI begins with the help-giving interactions within a single team. Students turn to each other to clarify explanations, and they check each other's work. In fact, students are urged to try to resolve needs within their teams before seeking the teacher's help. When a team member has demonstrated proficiency on self-administered formative tests, the student goes to another team where another student is designated as monitor. That monitor then administers and checks the unit test. The unit test scores are recorded by the teacher, who periodically calculates team scores in a manner generally similar to that of TGT. This approach to teaching mathematics is particularly appealing in contrast to traditional formats because it accommodates in a single class a great heterogeneity in terms of student competence, all the while promoting belonging and cooperation—learning incentives that rank high in the priorities of young adolescents.

Cooperative Integrated Reading and Composition (CIRC). This design was developed as a complement to TAI to address language arts learning among elementary students by using cooperative methods (Madden, Slavin, & Stevens, 1986). Students are grouped into pairs or triads based on the teacher's designation of three or four reading levels within a class. Teams are formed to include pairs or triads from two different reading levels. Most of the team activities are carried out by students working in pairs as well as a whole team, usually independent of the teacher. Three types of pedagogy are employed: basal-related activities; direct instruction in reading comprehension; integrated language arts and writing. The emphasis is on exchanging understandings, ideas, interpretations, and questions from reading in pairs or triads or as a whole team. Brief conferences are used to maintain student–teacher communication as well as to build an atmosphere of interdependence among the students. In ways similar to the preceding STL methods, students critique each other's work and quiz each other to enhance their performance and grades on tests, compositions, and book reports that contribute to their team score. There are numerous essential particulars in the CIRC process that should be studied and tried out on a small scale before full implementation is attempted.

Mainstreaming

The philosophy of mainstreaming is quite compatible with middle level education's emphasis on young adolescent growth and development as the quintessential purpose of schooling. For the better part of three decades, beginning in the early 1950s, students with learning difficulties or disabilities were removed from regular classrooms for special education. The rationale was that they would only be frustrated and defeated by having to constantly try to keep up with and compete with age-mates who learned more easily. With the growing realization of the variability among all young adolescent learners and their concomitant irregular rates and patterns of development, middle level educators began to recognize that their most appropriate emphasis should be upon the improvement of individual students, regardless of their particular intellectual gifts or deficiencies. The emergence of the middle school's emphasis upon the development of multiple grouping configurations further argues for returning these special education students, especially those with relatively mild handicaps, to the "mainstream" of the school as much as possible.

Young adolescent students who have remarkable intellectual and aesthetic abilities also need the benefit of being able to work on their special interests and with classmates who share their priorities. One of the risks inherent in designating gifted students, however, is the tendency to segregate them from the rest of their classmates. Such arrangements often exacerbate the tensions among students and sometimes among teachers as well. Multiple grouping options assure every student of opportunities to work in contexts that more nearly match their interests, readiness, and work habits without fostering the kind of resentment and rivalry that can easily become destructive to interpersonal relationships and the school climate.

With cooperative learning's emphasis on heterogeneously blended student teams and groups, many students who were previously segregated can be included in class work with their age-mates. Even though some of them may have particular struggles, especially with basic reading, writing, and mathematical skills, they especially benefit in terms of social recognition from working with classmates under these controlled group dynamics. The data are less clear about the degree to which mainstreamed students achieve greater academic benefits from participating in cooperative groups rather than in other settings. However, it is apparent that they do at least as well in cooperative group settings. Furthermore, less handicapped students do not show any losses as a consequence of working with classmates formerly relegated to pull-out programs and segregated classes. We do not yet know just how far all students, but especially handicapped learners, can progress in a setting where cooperation is the constant goal and celebrations of individual accomplishments are the norm.

Cooperation or Competition?

At a recent gathering of middle school teams participating in a statewide Odyssey of the Mind competition, I noted the healthy balance that seemed to exist among young adolescent youngsters striving to support their teammates in their own presentations while also enthusiastically cheering the performances of competing teams from other schools. Unlike most athletic competitions I've participated in or observed, this event appeared to be more of a celebration than a competition. Even though there was a payoff for winning teams through trophies and travel to further events, the detectable atmosphere in the gymnasium was clearly one of revelry instead of the more cutthroat competition of the activities that took place on other occasions in that same space. The fierce rivalries and sometimes behaviors by derisive fans that often accompany athletic contests were absent. Emphasis on teamwork, ownership, and participation was the overriding value that established the natural celebratory atmosphere.

The traditional American value that favors survival-of-the-fittest competition must be kept in a cautious perspective during the middle years. While the exultation of winning can be self-affirming, it can also become intoxicating, bringing about competitive values that are unhealthy for individuals and destructive to a harmonious team or classroom climate. With the critical identity formation processes of these transitional years in mind, middle level teachers must be especially sensitive to how their students are handling competitive activities, whether they win or lose. Learning to be equally adept at handling winning and losing are notable developmental tasks.

I don't know any formula for calculating exact proportions of these activities. Every class and team is a unique blend of personalities that have been influenced by a unique combination of societal values. It is true that our students live in a competitive society, but what is often overlooked are the far more numerous examples of cooperation that are necessary to our society. Choosing organizational schemes for learning will always be left to the judgments of teachers who study their students and assess their attitudes. As a teacher I recognized differences in what I'll call "neediness" for being on a winning team or being the team champion of spelling or geography. I always had students whose approaches to competition were much more intense than others. Some would approach these activities with a scoreboard mentality wherein their only concern was to come out on top. Learning was incidental to winning. Manipulating team memberships and activities to feed those needs was always a judgment call I tried to make in light of what I reasoned to be the best interest of individuals and of our whole team. My abiding concern was that every student who responded to team competitions had the experience of winning. I took for granted that every student who cared at all needed to experience the joy of winning.

The overriding message of these activities is, however, that cooperation is good for its own sake. Two people can always accomplish more than one, and a smoothly functioning synergic team can accomplish more than the sum of its individual members. Furthermore, cooperation skills have seemed to me to be easily transferred to other activities. I have found that students who know how to organize and carry out academic tasks cooperatively are more inclined to demonstrate their facility in small group work outside academics, such as planning a social event or performing a community service. They are motivated by the satisfactions of working in successful collaboration rather than by the contrived diversions of score keeping. Shared successes and accomplishments stand on their own as educative and worthwhile.

THE PHYSICAL ENVIRONMENT

An inquiry I've used many, many times with young adolescents as well as with university students is simply the charge to "draw and label the space where you most like to work (or study/learn/read/be)." Their drawings suggest a great deal about what they value, the things they like to have close by, and the elements present in their preferred work contexts. Even those who initially respond with "but I can't draw" tend to become serious and deliberate as they develop their pictures. When we subsequently share our drawings (or verbal explanations of what they include for those who are uncomfortable with showing their pictures), it becomes evident that the physical context for work matters a great deal to us. The drawings also show that people share lots of values related to their preferred workspaces: access to the outdoors evident in positioning the desk or table or other work surface next to a window; the presence of living things, especially pets, plants, and other people; valued personal artifacts, especially those associated with friends or family; posters and other artwork; easy access to music. Through this simple inquiry we learn specific things about each other and some of our shared values, and these elements are testimony to the value we give to our physical contexts.

One important but sometimes overlooked dimension of the identity formation process occurring in early adolescence is the need and desire of many youngsters to define themselves not just through dress and hairstyle but also through the things they call "mine." Consider how youngsters decorate the insides of their lockers. Even these tiny cubbies are often carefully dressed up with pictures, favorite sayings, and artifacts. Other students may decorate book covers. Others, on the other hand, may seem to be completely indifferent to any of these modes of self-definition.

My teammates and I would usually begin working to set up our team rooms and other spaces a couple of weeks prior to the opening of school. We'd always invite students to join us in this process, and invariably some of them would come. Some of the most authentic interpersonal bonding I ever experienced with my young adolescent students occurred through our shared work to prepare or renovate our physical spaces. By the time the first day arrived, our rooms would reflect our thoughtful collaboration. As I have visited team spaces and classrooms in numerous other schools, I have become accustomed to recognizing where other teachers have also capitalized on their students' interest in being involved with defining their work context. Spaces that have been prepared by kids are quickly evident.

One team room in a nearby middle school includes small, carefully detailed frescoes (wall murals) rendered by past and present students that depict what they have designated as "Great Moments in the History of Science." Another room has a collection of teddy bears, the team mascot. Another has a "Wall of Fame" showing photographs of adults who have befriended the team. Another particularly expansive team space with folding interior walls is decorated with papier-mâché circus figures created for a unit of study two years previously as well as backdrops from a play the team had presented a few weeks earlier. Students there are surrounded by reminders of their accomplishments. More poignantly, another room has a dusty, aging, almost finished model of an English castle that sits on a shelf behind a protective Plexiglas window. Several years previously the student who was building the model died tragically one afternoon after school when an automobile struck him on his bicycle. The model is exactly as he left it, representing the sentiments the teachers feel for the student they lost and serving as a statement of their ongoing regard for their current students. In each of these examples, the ways the spaces are outfitted and decorated portray humanity and collaboration between adults and young adolescents.

Some of the planned physical characteristics frequently evident in middle level classrooms and team spaces are

Rooms painted to highlight the team's colors

The team logo and motto evident on walls and/or on student's shirts, buttons, pencils, and book covers

Bulletin boards and displays produced by students

Team or classroom announcements, membership list, calendar, schedules, rules, newspaper clippings, letters about the team or school, and so forth posted in central traffic areas

Artifacts from team events and history, mounted photographs of students doing projects, and samples of exemplary work

Materials and equipment organized and labeled for easy access

Storage arrangements that accommodate team members' records and work in progress

Readily accessible periodical reading materials, especially daily newspapers and magazines

Just as homes and private rooms reflect personal tastes and preferences, physical spaces in middle level schools should reflect the collective values of the adults and young adolescents who inhabit them. Sometimes individual tastes clash, and those occasions become opportunities for negotiation that give students a legitimate voice in making decisions that matter to them and reflect their deliberations.

Resources for Learning

Classroom resources necessarily reflect the particular subject matter that is taught in those spaces. For example, maps are usually in a social studies classroom, lab equipment is in the science room, and so on. There are selected tools, materials, and resources for learning that overlap subject matter areas and can expand ways of learning. Although the suggested items that follow might in some cases appear extravagant, the kind of work young adolescents can do stipulates particular resources that are not unreasonable in view of the costs of a set of textbooks.

Telephone

At first thought, some people would see a classroom telephone as an invitation to abuse. However, in the several team rooms I've visited that include outside telephone lines, teachers report that their students protect this special resource, recognizing that they must monitor its use. Consequently, abuses have been rare. During the last five years I taught young adolescents, our team space had two outside lines. The set had locks on the dials, so we didn't even have to put them away and then take them out to use them. I don't recall a single incident of students abusing our telephones, yet they used them frequently in the course of their daily work. All of our students' parents, especially families in which both parents worked during the day, also appreciated knowing there was a direct telephone link with their children.

Resource Filing System

The roll-file (Rolodex) of human resources my teammates, my students, and I developed over several years grew to 126 categories and over 650 entries in a five-year period. Beginning with categories such as Air, Animals, and Architecture and ending with Weaving, Whales, and Zodiac, this file was our own continuing collection of names of local people who knew something about the topic as well as print and site resources available to us. As students pursued both group studies and Orbitals as described in the previous chapter, they regularly found new resources that were added to this file. From the information sheets we solicited from parents each year, we also identified resources for the file. Although our records were maintained on cards in a roll file, the quality of information storage and retrieval that is now possible through computers is infinitely superior, leading to the next suggested resource.

Microcomputer(s)

Aside from the abundance of instructional programming now available, the microcomputer is by far the most comprehensive way for teachers and students to maintain records of student work. The years in which I taught young adolescents predated microcomputer technology, so we kept samples of our students' work and day-to-day records of how they used their time in folders stacked in recycled banana boxes (see Chapter 8). It is still essential to document students' work with hard copy samples, but the capacity of classroom microcomputers makes it more possible than ever for students to efficiently log their academic activities. By keeping more detailed records of their work, they become more responsible for how they use their time and can become more fully accountable for their own academic development. An additional benefit of using this technology is the greater ease in producing team or class publications. Team newsletters published at regular intervals are essential to keeping everyone else informed about team activities. These publications should be written, edited, and produced by students with coaching by the teacher. The many word processing programs that are easily learned by young adolescents simplify production of these vital communication links to parents and other teams.

Electric Typewriters

Although writing by hand remains an important academic skill, pieces produced for newsletters or other publications usually must be rendered in print. While the microcomputer is easily the preferred way to make this conversion, many classrooms are unable to include an adequate number of workstations. Electric typewriters are less expensive, easily portable supplements. They are also very useful to make labels for drawings and charts that may not be so easily accomplished on the computer, depending on the word processing program being used and the extent of students' experience. Double-spaced, typewritten drafts are also helpful for editing by peers among young adolescents as well as with university students.

Printing Equipment

One of the most valuable pieces of equipment in our team room was a second-hand spirit duplicator one of my teammates picked up at a garage sale for twenty-five dollars. As I recall, it required a couple of minor repairs he was able to make, so for very little money that machine suddenly made it possible for our students to produce several publications we subsequently marketed to parents, visitors, and others interested in their writing. Three times a year we published *Facets,* a magazine made up of our favorite original writings, and each Integrated Interdisciplinary Unit (IIU) culminated in a book about the study.

Some of those books had as many as twenty authors and were as long as seventy-five pages. Microcomputer and photocopy technology currently available make it possible for students to publish their work more quickly, attractively, and with much less hassle and mess than is possible with the purple stencils and duplicating fluid. The essential need is to have some sort of effective printing equipment readily available for kids' use.

Graphic Arts Materials

The materials students need to represent their understandings and ideas are as necessary as woodworking tools to a carpenter. Consequently, every classroom—not just the art room—needs an assortment of types of paper, cards, pens and markers, fasteners, clipboards, and so on. My teammates and I found treasures of these kinds of supplies at little or no cost by soliciting recyclable materials from industries, especially print shops and bookbinders. We also oriented our parents to be on the lookout for material possibilities for our general arts supply, and they came up with some of the most interesting: discarded X-rays from a local hospital, assorted tapes from the ends of industrial rolls, ends of lots of brilliant high-intensity dyes, architects' blueprints, large paper tubes left over from rolls of newsprint, and an unending supply of bunting and other fabrics from a flag maker and a couple of textile plants. As long as the physical space lends itself to short-term storage, having such materials available stimulates imagination and enthusiasm for students to create representations of their knowledge.

Camera(s) and Film Processing Capability

I can't overstate the potential benefits of having students use 35-mm black-and-white photography to document their work. Regardless of the kind of exploratory studies students are carrying out, photographs enrich and document their experience as readily as they enhance newspaper copy and magazine stories. I have been amazed and enlightened by my students' often inventive use of photographs to convey both content and meaning. The basics of film processing, printing, and enlarging are also easily acquired by many young adolescents. Costs can be kept to a minimum when film is purchased in bulk and the students load it in cartridges and then share responsibility for the necessary lab work. For a time our team darkroom was a closet. Later we acquired two small basement rooms where three or four students at a time could do this work. Eventually we learned how to make photographic silk screens, and we constructed most of the equipment required to expand our work to include publishing calendars and printing on T-shirts. Every piece of this equipment that our team owned was acquired through either donation or second-hand purchase, enabling us to maintain this valuable resource for only the price of supplies.

Television and Radio

The aural and visual media are a primary source of information and values for our students. Some of our youngsters take television programming more seriously than their schoolwork, and many of them spend considerably more time with these media at home than on reading and other more challenging intellectual pursuits. Who is teaching them how to be thoughtful, discriminating, wise consumers of these media? It is naive to assume that very many parents are providing much consistent, penetrating analysis. It becomes yet another crucial task of schooling to help youngsters understand this central

American industry and how it affects our values, habits, expectations, and economic be-haviors. Many of the fundamental values of contemporary society can be identified; what content could be more basic to what we refer to in the curriculum as social studies? Every year that I taught an IIU about television, we studied programs together in order to ana-lyze their market appeal and formula. With today's video recording devices, that kind of study can be made even richer by recording programs broadcast after school hours for later dissection in class.

Audio and Video Recording/Editing/Playback Equipment

One teacher created a project he called "What Kids Want to Know." Sixth through eighth graders identified topics they'd like to know more about that could be reported in a news documentary format. With contemporary programs such as *60 Minutes* and *20/20* in mind as examples, they created ten- to fifteen-minute segments that were then aired weekly on the community's public access television channel. Each thirty-minute program was a com-bination of two or three student-directed and photographed segments about topics such as the work and adventures of the police chief, an interview with a pilot (also a student's father) from the cockpit of the airplane he flew, a practice session of the local university's ice hockey team and interviews with players, the World War II experiences of a local war hero, a visit to the shop and an interview with the proprietor of a baseball card business; a tour of the tunnel roadways where delivery trucks service stores in a large shopping mall, the jelly-making process of two grandmothers of students in the class. In creating and pro-ducing each segment, students made story boards and wrote interview questions accord-ing to essentially the same format as that used by professionals. As this project gained pop-ularity and notoriety in the community, moneys for additional equipment came more easily from the local school board. A few small grants were also awarded by outside agen-cies to support the project.

References

The school library is the traditional home of reference books, but teams should augment the library by building and housing their own selection of reference materials. At the very least, the collection should include one recent encyclopedia, several dictionaries, and a thesaurus. Beyond this minimum that should be provided from school resources, the col-lection grows and expands according to the teachers' successes in soliciting references from parents or shopping perceptively at garage sales. Among the most heavily used of these kinds of references in our team were encyclopedias of classical music, rock and roll, and the opera; two biographical dictionaries; several different literary anthologies; a dozen or so art books that included full-color reproductions (Renoir and Peter Max were the fa-vorites!); a medical dictionary; a book about how musical instruments work that began with "accordion" and ended with "zither." Each of these acquisitions had its own story. Some were gifts from parents and friends, some were brought in by students, but most of them were acquired by the teachers. I don't recall that we ever bought one of those vol-umes new. We picked them up as we found them, paying as little "for my classroom" as the seller would accept. Nonetheless, through this admittedly serendipitous acquisition process, we created a functional team reference library. We also taught students to value books and to go to them and find out what was needed. And, after all, that was one of our primary goals—modeling the natural behaviors of learners.

Tools

I've never been able to get along very well without some screwdrivers, pliers, and a hammer. There is always something that needs fixing or improving. Whether or not I've made similar repairs in the past, I'm inclined to tackle mechanical breakdowns. At some point early in my teaching career I realized that in a limited but vital way, tools are teachers. Using them successfully as they were designed to be used is inherently satisfying, and finding new applications and uses is a bonus. Since that realization I've maintained a continually growing collection of tools, and those that suited my students' use stayed at school most of the time. While I've never compiled a particular list of essential tools for middle level learning and teaching, the process of collecting, using, and filing tools models to a considerable extent the process of learning, whether the students are writing an essay, creating a project, or mastering an algorithm in mathematics. This tool mentality has been useful to me both practically and metaphorically.

Supporting Activities

1. Visit a local school that serves young adolescents to observe and interview students, teachers, and administrators. Inquire about the following:

   How are students and teachers organized?

   What are the citizenship expectations for students at school?

   How are violations of those expectations handled?

   How are students' interpersonal conflicts addressed?

   How are cooperation and teamwork taught?

   Compare your findings with the pertinent discussions in this chapter.

2. Arrange a book group with a small group of young adolescents. Use your experience in the group to learn how and what the students think about the problems of being together in any setting. What are their ideas? What might you do to teach them how to work together cooperatively?

3. Study the physical environment and resources of a school serving young adolescents. Describe its aesthetic qualities. Inventory the resources you observe being used by students. How are these features appropriate to the students? What have students contributed to make the place their own?

RESOURCES

Student Mediation

Kreidler, W. J. (1984). *Creative conflict resolution*. Glenview, IL: Scott, Foresman (Goodyear Books).

The National Association for Mediation in Education (NAME, 425 Amity Street, Amherst, MA 01002) publishes a comprehensive array of materials pertinent to student mediation. Especially useful are:

Cheatham, A. (1989). *Annotated bibliography for teaching conflict resolution in schools* (2nd ed.). (Order # SUP1, $6.00).

Cheatham, A. (1988). *Directory of school mediation and conflict resolution programs.* (Order # SUP2, $12.50).

Richard Cohen, Director; School Mediation Associates, 702 Green Street, #8; Cambridge, MA 02139.

REFERENCES

Aronson, E. (1978). *The jigsaw classroom.* Beverly Hills, CA: Sage.

Arth, A. A. (1987, April). Keynote address at a middle level conference sponsored by the Maine Association of Secondary School Principals, Augusta, ME.

Auchincloss, L. (1964). *The rector of Justin.* Boston: Houghton Mifflin (Riverside Press).

Canter, L. (1976). *Assertive discipline: A take-charge approach for today's educator.* Seal Beach, CA: Canter and Associates.

Carnegie Corporation. (1989). *Turning points: Preparing American youth for the 21st century.* Washington, DC: Carnegie Council on Adolescent Development.

Chance, E. W., and Bibens, R. F. (1990). Developing quality middle schools—an interview with Dr. William Glasser. *Middle School Journal, 21,* 1–4.

Dewey, J. (1913). *Interest and effort in education.* Boston: Houghton Mifflin (Riverside Press).

Dewey, J. (1916). *Democracy and education.* New York: Macmillan.

Dreikurs, R., Grunwald, B., & Pepper, F. (1971). *Maintaining sanity in the classroom.* New York: Harper & Row.

Erb, T. O. (1987). What team organization can do for teachers. *Middle School Journal, 18*(4), 3–6.

George, P. S. (1982). Interdisciplinary team organization: Four operational phases. *Middle School Journal, 13*(3), 10–13.

George, P. S. (1988). Tracking and ability grouping: Which way for the middle school? *Middle School Journal, 20,* 21–28.

George, P. S., Spreul, M., & Moorefield, J. (1986). *Long-term teacher-student relationships: A middle school case study.* Columbus, OH: National Middle School Association.

George, P. S., & Stevenson, C. (1989). The "very best teams" in "the very best schools" as described by middle school principals. *TEAM, 3*(5), 6–14.

Glasser, W. (1969). *Schools without failure.* New York: Harper & Row.

Glasser, W. (1985). *Control theory in the classroom.* New York: Perennial Library.

Johnson, D., & Johnson, R. (1988). *Cooperation in the classroom.* Minneapolis, MN: Interaction Books.

Joyce, B., & Weil, M. (1986). *Models of teaching.* Englewood Cliffs, NJ: Prentice-Hall.

Koch, M. S. (1986). Schools can replace gladiators with mediators. *Education Week, 5,* 28.

Kulik, J. A. & Kulik, C. L. (1984). Effects of ability grouping on secondary school students: A meta-analysis of evaluation findings. *American Educational Research Journal, 19,* 415–428.

Larson, C. E., & LaFasto, F. M. J. (1989). *Team work: What must go right/what can go wrong.* Newbury Park, CA: Sage.

Lounsbury, J. H. (1990). Interdisciplinary teaming—destination or way station? *Middle School Journal, 21*(4), 41.

Lynch, J. (1990, March 27). *Multi-year, multi-graded teaming: The third year results!* New England League of Middle Schools Annual Conference, Hyannis, MA.

Madden, N. A., Slavin, R. E., & Stevens, R. J. (1986). *Cooperative integrated reading and composition: Teacher's manual.* Baltimore, MD: Center for Research on Elementary and Middle Schools, Johns Hopkins University.

Nathan, J. (1990). Toward a vision of students as "citizens." *Education Week, 9* (31), 32.

Oakes, J. (1985). *Keeping track: How schools structure inequality.* New Haven, CT: Yale University Press.

Sharan, S., & Sharan, Y. (1976). *Small group teaching.* Englewood Cliffs, NJ: Educational Technology Publications.

Sharan, Y., & Sharan, S. (1989/1990). Group investigation expands cooperative learning. *Educational Leadership, 47,* 17–21.

Skinner, B. F. (1971). *Beyond freedom and dignity.* New York: Knopf.

Slavin, R. E. (1980). *Using student team learning.* Baltimore, MD: Center for Research on Elementary and Middle Schools, Johns Hopkins University.

Slavin, R. E. (1987). Ability grouping and student achievement in elementary schools: A best evidence synthesis. *Review of Educational Research, 57,* 293–336.

Sorenson, A. B., & Hallinan, M. T. (1986). Effects of ability grouping on growth in academic achievement. *American Educational Research Journal, 23,* 519–542.

Steinberg, A. (Ed.). (1989). Talking it out: Students mediate disputes. *Harvard Education Letter, 5,* 4.

Wheelock, Anne. (1992). *Crossing the tracks: How "untracking" can save America's schools.* Massachusetts Advocacy Center. New York: The New Press.

Chapter 8

Evaluation and Assessment: Understanding What's Happening

___

○ *How do we know what our students are really learning?*

○ *What does a ten- to fourteen-year-old student's knowledge look like?*

○ *How can students become more responsible and accountable for their learning?*

ITEM

Travis is an eighth grade boy from a large farm family. His schoolwork has been marginal and he has been indifferent toward it for as long as any of his teachers can remember. He is also routinely in trouble with a teacher or the principal. In one two-week period, for example, he was reported for smoking in the rest room, roughhousing in the hallways, and two incidents of acting insolent toward teachers. Four years earlier, his fourth grade teacher had believed that he might be mildly retarded, and some diagnostic tests were conducted. The results were inconclusive, but the evaluation did indicate that his intelligence was at least average. He likes to boast that he'll leave school as soon as he's fifteen to get a job and buy a motorcycle. He likes to tell whoever will listen that he'll ride past the school every morning and wave.

The two teachers responsible for eighth grade social studies and English decided to plan a community study in observance of the one hundredth birthday of their Vermont town. Students were given the option of doing a project about any feature of the community that related to its history. Every student except Travis picked from a list of suggestions that included oral history interviews with elderly lifelong residents, drawing pictures of town buildings, writing reports about townspeople, and making historical costumes. True to his fashion, Travis didn't indicate that he was doing a project.

The town's official birthday celebration was to take place all day long on a Saturday. Travis didn't meet the school bus on the Friday morning when students would be busy decorating the school and setting up their finished projects in the hallways. At noon he arrived in a pickup truck with his older brother, who helped him unload a scale model of a sugarhouse on a four-foot square piece of plywood. The model displayed a network of taps and tubes to carry sap to the separator. There was also a cross section of a sugar maple tree with a tap attached. The tree's life rings and two scars from past tappings were labeled with small tags attached to finishing nails. The third piece of the project was a carefully illustrated and lettered poster made from one side of a cardboard refrigerator box. The poster explained the sugaring process, and mounted on it were two aged black-and-white photographs of his grandfather at work in his sugarhouse. Although the lettering was irregular and there were several misspellings, Travis's work reflected a solid grasp of sugaring—a constant in the economic present and history of his community.

ITEM

Two university teacher education students and I visited a junior high school eighth grade science classroom that contained an impressive array of displays the teacher had prepared to explain the current lesson on animalia phyla. The classroom atmosphere was busy, and the students' work ethic seemed purposeful. They were working dutifully to complete worksheets on which they were to list plants and animals according to the framework they had been studying, which was posted on one of the bulletin boards. Their primary source was a textbook, but the cheerful young teacher freely supplied guidance and even occasional answers as she moved among the students' desks. She seemed a perfect model for my students, for she smiled a lot, giving encouragement and frequent pats on the back. Any casual visitor would certainly have been favorably impressed by this example of schooling.

When the science period ended, each of us who was a visitor was escorted to lunch by one or two students who had been designated hosts and hostesses as a consequence of their being good students. Amy and Susan, my escorts, were very polite and seemed eager for me to enjoy my visit. After we collected our lunches and found a table, they offered to answer any questions I had about their school. Their courtesies seemed genuine, and their affection for their teacher and enthusiasm for their school were palpable.

After a quarter hour or so of lunch and chitchat, mostly about other kids and sports, I mentioned that I was very impressed by what I had seen in their science class. Then I suggested, "Tell me about animalia phyla." Both girls seemed startled, and they glanced uneasily at each other. For the first time since we had met, they were uncomfortable. Amy responded with "What do you want us to tell you?" I asked that they simply tell me about what they were learning. For the next minute or two they offered some awkward generalizations, finally commenting how they weren't exactly sure what they were doing but assuring me that "Mrs. Potter is a great teacher."

ITEM

Ben is an eighth grader who is very interested in everything. An avid collector, he has kept what he refers to as "my museum" at home since he was a third grader. His collections include rocks, shells, arrowheads, coins from other countries, automobile models, computer games, and Agatha Christie mysteries. In addition to the collections, his museum includes what he refers to as "interesting artifacts" such as a shark's jaw and some Roman nails. Ben is also an avid reader of medieval fiction in addition to the mysteries he collects.

While being interviewed about his interests, Ben asked if there was anything he would like to be able to do better. His answer was immediate: "I'm not a good test-taker." When asked to explain, he went on to say, "I study a lot, but I guess I just don't study enough." Upon being pressed for an example, he went on to say, "Well, right now we're reading *Call of the Wild* in English class, and we have a quiz at the end of every chapter. The quiz yesterday was true-false. There were ten questions and I missed three. And they were all details like 'The dogs ate caribou meat' when it was horse meat. I got that wrong. I like to go smoothly through the book. I don't like it when it's all chopped up. It's sort of a pity when I have to read a wonderful book this way. The quizzes make me not want to read the book."

These anecdotes remind us that the conventional evidence upon which we make assumptions that learning has occurred (for example, classwork, homework, tests) doesn't necessarily coincide with any individual student's actual understanding. Amy and Susan did what they were expected to do—they carried out their deskwork, they scored well on daily quizzes, and they participated fully in group activities. Beyond those behaviors, however, they apparently had very little grasp of the subject matter, at least insofar as they were able to explain what they had done. Travis, on the other hand, did just about all of his routine schoolwork incorrectly, incompletely, or not at all. Yet, in a context suited to him, his work showed both substantial knowledge and pride. Ben, very knowledgeable and interested in an abundance of topics, struggled with often ambiguous short-answer questions. His actual understanding and appreciation of the subject matter was of a much higher quality than his test performances indicated. And even more disturbing is that he thought less of himself because he didn't handle such items as effectively as he desired. In each of these cases, traditional paper-and-pencil modes of evaluating how much individuals understood about subject matter failed to reflect how much they actually knew.

This chapter describes assessment and evaluation strategies that include some traditional practices but also go well beyond them in order to help teachers develop a context that will generate a more comprehensive and realistic understanding of their students' learning. Before turning to strategies, however, let's examine some issues raised by the questions that introduce this chapter. First, on what evidence do we assume that students have learned?

In general, teachers feel most confident that learning has occurred when students perform well according to familiar measures—usually homework, classwork, and tests. There is considerable pressure on teachers to cover material as efficiently as possible, test students to establish how much has apparently been learned, assign grades according to test performance, and then move on to the subsequent unit of study. Furthermore, there are always some students present whose inherent dispositions are suited to these modes—children whose retention of facts and details comes naturally and who enjoy demonstrating their abilities to reflect their learning in these ways. Whether the stage is set for making classroom recitations or for memory games such as Trivial Pursuit or Facts-in-Five, they enjoy performing in accord with teachers' expectations. It is natural for teachers to perceive students who do not perform well on these measures as deficient. Such youngsters are often regarded as either intellectually inferior or failing to work up to their natural ability. Sometimes they are even tracked in slower classes and given remedial work in which the very same modes that have already been demonstrated as ineffective are continued with a smaller student–teacher ratio. Travis is an example.

I often urge teachers, especially those who are committed to traditional paper-and-pencil learning measures, to examine the effectiveness of their practices by inquiring into the validity of such techniques. I suggest that they select a test or some other written assignment that students had undertaken several weeks before and for which the teacher has kept the original work. Then, promising students that their performance on a second testing will not count against them, have them do the test or assignment again. What is evident from their overall performance? Which items were most frequently incorrect in the original work? the current work? Which items were handled correctly on both occasions? This inquiry never fails to generate ideas about the activity and patterns of learning within the class. It may also help teachers understand better how individual students function. My own uses of this inquiry revealed that middle grades students handled concrete material most successfully, and their grasp of much of the content I taught was poor (Rogers & Stevenson, 1988).

Because students are at developmental extremes during the early adolescent years, their classroom performances will be likewise variable. In the midst of teachers' efforts to keep students productively involved and socialized, it is not surprising that student achievement becomes equated with what they appear to know or don't know according to conventional measures. Many teachers slip into the delusion that recitations on tests and through homework are the only efficient and valid measures of knowledge, so they become the custom for all students. What actually results, however, is essentially a sorting process. Youngsters who do well become identified as "the A students" and the others are likewise labeled according to the grades they receive. In the opening anecdotes, Amy and Susan were described as "A students," Travis was a "D or F student," and Ben was regarded as a "B and C student." In truth, however, the understanding and accomplishments of each of these students is infinitely more diverse, complex, and idiosyncratic than conventional letter grades based on classwork, homework, and tests can possibly reveal.

What does a ten- to fourteen-year-old's knowledge look like? Many knowledge paradigms can be useful in thinking about how knowledge may be organized (Bloom, 1956; Ausubel, 1963; Gagne, 1965). How teachers conceptualize knowledge structures certainly affects how they plan instruction. Our purpose here, however, is to learn to recognize the various evidences of a young adolescent's intellectual engagement and learning. Chapter 4 provides an overview of the array of the developmental changes characteristic of early adolescence. Those changes may precipitate differences in terms of personal learning styles and approaches to intellectual or academic work. And although there may be fairly extensive commonality of values and social interests, their individuality is still recognizable through their work and representations of knowledge. Knowledge structures are often idiosyncratic, and during this time of personal change, understandings are especially in flux. Compared with teachers' conceptualization and organization of subject matter, young adolescents' knowledge often appears incomplete, flawed, and uneven. There may be little relationship between lessons taught and subject matter learned. It is essential for us to anticipate this natural diversity in our students' learning and knowledge.

SHARED RESPONSIBILITY

Teachers are traditionally expected to give students academic assignments and tests, record grades, and produce an overall grade average for each class every six to nine weeks for report cards. Virtually everyone knows firsthand the motivational effects and consequences of this system. It is generally assumed that this method indicates how students are doing in terms of academic growth relative to their classmates. Perhaps. While this system is familiar and most comfortable for those who thrive, it fails to identify or report insights about an individual's growth. It also overlooks the most important elements of education: the specific areas of growth the student has accomplished. It is only when students participate in planning their educational goals, log their investment of time and energies, and critique the results of their labors against understood criteria of excellence that enduring educational growth is being achieved. Just as the case was made earlier for partnerships between teachers and students with regard to curriculum, so should a state of partnership characterize the related but distinct processes of assessment and evaluation.

ASSESSMENT AND EVALUATION

As teachers create learning conditions designed to complement young adolescents' developmental conditions such as those described in the three preceding chapters, they must also devise arrangements by which their students can keep them informed about how they're doing. Students need an effective system they can use to let teachers know what they understand and what is unclear. Teachers need to know much more about how students are doing than can be judged from a homework or test paper. Teachers' expectations and scholarship standards need to be communicated explicitly through the students' responses to individual work, but teachers also need to understand how students perceive those same criteria. Thus, for our purposes here, distinctions will be made between the purposes and functions of assessment and evaluation. While one single comprehensive documentation strategy can be used to keep up with students' school experiences, virtually all types of evidence may be used for assessment, whereas only selected types of data are appropriate for evaluation. Consider the following operational definitions.

> *Assessment:* the process of collecting information that helps students and teachers understand how students are doing. Student journals that are shared with teachers are a commonly used assessment device. Written anecdotes enable the student to both clarify an issue or idea for himself or herself through writing and at the same time convey it to a teacher.

> *Evaluation:* the process of employing selected, specific criteria for the purpose of judging and critiquing the quality of a performance, production, or other evidence of learning. A familiar example of evaluation is a spelling test composed of words drawn from classwork. This device evaluates students' knowledge of the correct spelling of selected words.

Often an event provides both assessment and evaluation information. A teacher I know regularly steps outside her classroom when students are taking a test, because she is curious to understand how her students react to being left alone during a formal evaluation. Teachers on a two-person seventh–eighth grade team where each student's responsibility to the team is heavily emphasized periodically write on a chalkboard first thing in the morning, "Today is a teachers' in-school day off." Students understand that although their teachers will be in the classroom, they will not teach or respond to questions except in an emergency. They further understand that this is an occasion for them to demonstrate their responsibility for themselves. Generally it is the eighth graders who have had at least a year's experience with this ritual who lead the classes, mediate disagreements, and so on. Another teacher gives her students copies of the final test they will take on the very first day of the unit. She then observes how students use the test as a learning tool in order that she can better understand them, their motivation, and standards. Arthur Costa urges us to "constantly remind ourselves that an ultimate purpose of evaluation is to enable students to evaluate themselves" (1989, p. 2).

Although assessment and evaluation are words sometimes used synonymously, they will be employed as separate concepts in this chapter. Assessment enables teachers to better understand how schooling is being experienced from the students' point of view, and evaluation helps students better understand standards and quality in terms of their production. The subsequent pages of this chapter describe assorted strategies for documenting each student's school experience so that both assessment and evaluation needs are served.

DOCUMENTATION THROUGH PORTFOLIOS

Documentation is simply a purposeful, orderly process of maintaining documents about a series of events. The documents of concern to middle level teachers are those that pertain to their students' learning, their activities, and their ideas and reflections. Documentation requires setting up individual portfolios to which students regularly contribute samples of their schoolwork and other anecdotal records of their experience. Teachers also contribute comments, suggestions, and formal evaluative reports at periodic intervals. While teachers set up the files and establish guidelines for their maintenance, it is the students' responsibility to maintain them. Files are in turn monitored by teachers for assessment and evaluation purposes. When these documentary files—also known as portfolios—are kept systematically and thoroughly, they more nearly reflect students' actual learning and development than the teacher's traditional grade book and permanent record folders usually kept in the school office.

One of our primary goals in the schooling of adolescents must be to see that they become accountable for themselves as learners and as citizens. Our youngsters are developmentally advanced to the degree that their present and future academic progress is commensurate with their willingness to invest themselves in their own development. While primary grade teachers may have been able to get away with exercising dictatorial authority about what happens during the school day, a large part of becoming adolescent is the child's growing need to assert his or her independence of thought and action. Consequently, middle level teachers are well advised to acknowledge this transition and to work with their students as partners in their subsequent learning and development. One dimension of the partnership is sharing accountability. If our youngsters are to be truly educated, they must learn to make responsible choices and decisions thoughtfully and wisely. They must gain insights about themselves as learners, and they must personally experience the dignity that accompanies being increasingly responsible for oneself and one's education. Furthermore, they need to recognize that their improvements as learners and personal growth are real accomplishments, whether or not they are accompanied by grades or other forms of reward.

Often in large junior high schools teachers may see a hundred or more different students each day. Staying frequently and continually in touch with every student's work in such circumstances is extremely difficult, if it is even possible. In addition to the impersonality forced by such numbers, it is difficult to simply find adequate space that provides easy access to each folder. And although students are primarily responsible for keeping their portfolios current, it is essential for teachers to review them regularly, offering feedback and suggestions and raising questions as needed. As a member of a two-teacher team working with forty-five to fifty-five students each year, I could easily review each student's folder a minimum of at least once a week. There were also a few students whose work I'd review daily, often having the student guide me through it. I learned that if young adolescents were to become truly responsible for their own learning, I needed to be patient but persistent and consistent in having them demonstrate that they were being accountable for keeping my teammate and me informed about their school experience. This relationship also helped them participate more effectively in the three-way parent conferences that were part of our design for helping parents understand their children's educational experience.

USING PORTFOLIOS

Three fundamental communication goals can be served by maintaining portfolios that document students' work and experience:

1. The teachers' need to understand what each student is doing and learning
2. The students' need for understanding about themselves as learners
3. The school's need for formative information about programs

The primary emphasis is, of course, on communication between students and teachers. Remembering that communication denotes a two-way process, the credibility of that communication has a great deal to do with how seriously and responsibly youngsters go about their school lives. Students who are convinced that their teachers are their advocates will reciprocate with trust, even when they have doubts. Communication and trust are a lot like dancing in that all three require partners who work in rhythm, taking turns as leaders and always facing each other directly.

Although drawings and photographs are excellent ways to document students' work in portfolios, the dominant content is written work. Writing is a discrete representation of thinking; therefore every teacher should consider himself or herself to be a writing teacher.

> Language is the medium of the mind. It forces us to find the words that most persuasively express our point of view and, in the process, forces us to clarify our point of view. Writing, in particular, exercises the intellect. The habit of good writing—the organizing of ideas, the marshaling of evidence, and the choosing of the most appropriate words to express an idea—is virtually indistinguishable from clear thinking. (Honig, 1987, p. v)

One of the most satisfying benefits of reviewing my students' portfolios was how effectively the process helped me shift my frame of reference about what was going on. Since I easily tend to become preoccupied with my own agenda for teaching, the process of reviewing portfolios helped me gain understanding about how students were perceiving both their studies and events that occurred within our team. It was common for me to have questions as I looked through a youngsters' collection of materials, so I'd often raise those questions on a note attached to the folder. Students always knew when their folder had been reviewed by the note attached with a paper clip. Some of my questions required a direct response; others were rhetorical questions intended to provoke a thought about the student's work.

TEACHER'S LOG

Some teachers are amazing in their ability to remember important incidents that occur with their students. Most of us, however, are so busy keeping up with the multitude of activities that insights of a given moment are unwittingly lost all too quickly. One strategy for recording these observations is to maintain a teacher's log. Entries can be made daily if the purpose is to maintain a chronological record of teaching. If the purpose is to log observations of students, the log can be alphabetized by students' names. As noteworthy events, ideas, or insights occur, they can be entered and subsequently used for the teacher's own reflections.

One teacher who had a long daily commute arranged a schedule whereby her students would tape-record a weekly progress report to her. She would listen to the tapes while driving back and forth and then record her suggestions and other reactions for her students to listen to. The tapes became a communication log between that teacher and her students, who would receive them at the end of the year as a personally documented record of a year in their lives.

I maintained a three-ring binder with sheets for every student on our team and additional sheets on which I could make notes pertaining to curriculum. The student notes were extremely valuable for sharing in conferences. Students were always quite interested in the things I had written about them over the course of a few weeks, and since I kept a sharp eye for positive things to note, I usually had several compliments to give them in conferences.

It also served me well to keep three- by five-inch index cards in a shirt pocket; on them I could make a variety of other notations about the events occurring over the course of a school day. Those cards gave me security, because I don't have good natural recall for many details. Although my teaching role today in a university setting is qualitatively quite different from the daily intensity of being on a team, I continue to rely on index cards.

Through these devices it is both possible and appropriate for teachers to model documentation processes for their students through the ways they keep their own records.

CONFERENCING WITH STUDENTS

One of the benefits of teaching young adolescents is that they are becoming increasingly able to take on some of the responsibility for conferences. Conferencing is another dimension of accountability. In schools that provide teacher advisories (see Chapter 10), students make periodic reports of their progress to their advisors, using their portfolios as evidence of their work and activities. It is increasingly common in middle schools that private teacher–student advisory conferences are held monthly to make sure that the communication vital to the student's welfare is occurring.

A neighbor shared his complaint that a conference with his seventh grade son's homeroom teacher revealed that the teacher was largely ignorant about his son. She was well prepared for the conference in terms of having grade averages from Bobby's various teachers, but there was almost no information beyond number grades and vague platitudes such as "He's doing just fine." My neighbor decided to quiz his son about his schoolwork, but Bobby offered little more insight. Although this youngster was indeed "doing just fine" as far as academic and deportment grades were concerned, they constitute merely a snapshot when information approximating a portrait is possible. Since I occasionally employ Bobby to help me with yard chores, I've had lots of opportunities to learn about his interests and ideas. Our several conversations while stacking firewood and painting the fence have revealed Bobby's ample capacity for being responsible for documenting his work and other school activities as well as participating meaningfully in conferences with his teachers and parents. Here is an opportunity being overlooked.

Since most students stayed for three years on the team on which I taught, I was able to observe them growing and developing in terms of both their initiative and their skill in sharing conferences about their progress. In fact, by eighth grade our conferences tended to become well focused and efficient, because students had learned through experience how to prepare and present themselves. As will be described later in this chapter, most of our parent conferences brought teachers, parents, and student together. By the time students were in their third year on our team, we expected them to lead those conferences, drawing on their portfolios to support generalizations about their accomplishments and progress. Occasionally a private adult conference that excluded the student were necessary, but they occurred infrequently.

ESTABLISHING AN ACCESSIBLE STORAGE SYSTEM

In order for a documentation-portfolio system to function successfully, the system for maintaining student files must be well planned so that students can maintain a thorough representation of their work and can have easy access to their files. Standing vertical file cabinets are often available, but because only one student at a time can access a file in a drawer, they are inconvenient. Besides, portfolios don't usually contain the kind of confidential information that requires security. Personal, private materials are maintained in a secure system, usually in the school office. In fact, I have not ever been aware of a student being so interested in another student's portfolio that privacy was violated. It was common for students to share their files with friends, and more experienced students sometimes helped novices with suggestions about keeping their files.

Hanging files are more efficient than drawer files. When they are placed on a shelf or table, students can locate their files quickly, make additions or changes, and remove them easily if necessary. Sometimes large plastic or metal milk crates have been used effectively. My personal preference after years of using this system was banana boxes. These heavy-duty boxes are heavily constructed of cardboard to protect their cargo from bruising, and they are just the proper width for large file folders. They are also long enough to hold a large number of files. Finally, they are lightweight and have handle cutouts on the ends for easy movement. The banana boxes I used for my students' folders were heavily used, but each one survived several years' use, including countless occasions when I took boxes of files home on weekends to review my students' folders.

Microcomputer technology can be applied very effectively for keeping particular types of student records. For example, where student progress according to an extensively defined collection of academic competencies was mandated in eighth grade, a teacher wrote a computer program that accounted for many competencies. Students could demonstrate their progress through records they kept on a microcomputer. Each student was required to show mastery of selected competencies on an individual disk that contained only his or her data. For example, one of the language competencies was the ability to write single and plural nouns as possessives. An exercise requiring the students to show mastery of that competency was incorporated in the program.

Even though many competencies did not lend themselves to computers, a record of each student's accomplishments of those competencies was also added to his or her disk by the teacher. This single data source served that particular accountability need particularly well. Furthermore, each student on that team had constant access to information about where he or she stood in relation to the school's academic expectations. Another middle grades teacher who used a similar system for recording attendance, grades, and competencies took classroom use of the technology a step further and corresponded with his students on their disks. He modeled much of what he expected his twelve-year-olds to learn.

DECIDING WHAT TO SAVE

There's no single recipe for what should be included in documentary portfolios so long as the agglomeration accurately represents the variety and quality of work being done plus the communications between teachers and the student regarding his or her school experience. Among the types of materials most commonly included are the following:

1. Cumulative reading log since the beginning of the school year
2. Writing samples, especially those that show progression from an initial draft to a finished product
3. Papers written as long-term assignments as well as daily homework
4. Test papers, especially those representing evaluation of a unit of study
5. Written or tape-recorded messages between the student and teachers
6. Activity log, records of time use
7. Photo or drawings of projects or constructions too large for the folder
8. Agenda/goals and work plan for independent or Orbital studies
9. Peer evaluation reports from group projects
10. Records of progress in self-paced instructional materials or kits
11. Communications with the student's parents
12. Interim school reports such as citizenship comments
13. Academic competency log (if applicable)
14. Teacher's notes about the student's presentation, debate, and so on
15. Records of extracurricular activity: sports, clubs, service projects
16. Periodic self-evaluations based on previously stated goals

Even though the portfolio is intended to be a warehouse of samples, students who are doing well tend to be especially eager to keep their files filled. Students also tend to save only those papers that reflect most favorably on them and their work, invoking the issue of candor in self-examinations. This outcome presents a relevant opportunity for encouraging youngsters to work for successes in order to be able to fill their folders with their best work. This rationale also appeals to students who enjoy looking through their folders and reliving their accomplishments.

A newcomer to documenting students' schoolwork and other experiences may be surprised at how quickly many students' folders will grow. As the folder swells, a new issue is presented: the need to create a written summary of the work to date. While the student has the primary responsibility for writing this recapitulation of his or her productivity, the teacher or advisor helps organize and outline it. I expected my students to conduct four to eight of these interim self-evaluations during the course of a year. Some suggestions for guiding the self-evaluation process are found later in this chapter.

Documentation Examples for Portfolios

Rather than recommend a single formula, I alphabetically list examples of specific items students might include in their portfolios. According to their own priorities, teachers may wish to require that selected items always be included. The basic guideline to teachers is to see that whatever will help them and their students understand what is taking place in the students' school lives should be included. It is furthermore very important to date everything that is filed, whether or not it is material that is likely to remain for a long time. Having dated material becomes self-evidently valuable after only a few weeks when students analyze their work and organize it chronologically.

Anecdotal Notes and Notations

When a teacher writes a student a note or adds thoughtful annotation to a student's paper, that particular communication should be saved. Teachers' notes offering critical suggestions as well as encouragement or approval should be documented, and students' notes to teachers should be returned for the portfolio, especially when the note has been answered. Similarly, communications such as a classmate's critique of a draft of writing or communications between students about a shared project should be preserved in one student's portfolio.

Awards

Whether the student is recognized in a team meeting or by the principal in a schoolwide recognition, written records of the accomplishment should be kept.

Brainstorming

Students in middle level classes often work together exchanging ideas about a project or developing responses to questions in a cooperative group. A written record of their process should be kept by each student.

Bulletin Board

When one student or a group of them creates a bulletin board design, each of them should save a sketch or photo of the product.

Chart or Poster

Large portrayals of a concept such as the water cycle or a chart of data done by students are too large for their portfolios. Yet, they represent a student's work and learning. A sketch or photo belongs in the creator's folder.

Classes Taught

When students take responsibility for formally teaching classmates or younger students planned lessons, a record of that service belongs in the portfolio. The record may be written by the student, the teacher, or those who benefited from the service.

Concept Map

A map created by a student as a tool for organizing new knowledge, as well as one done for the teacher as evaluation, documents understanding.

Construction

Whether a student has constructed a building model or baked a casserole, a written, drawn, or photographic record of the construction needs to be kept.

Contract

A learning contract between a student and a teacher spells out precisely what the student will do, the record of how the teacher has monitored the work, and the payoff for the student. Contracts should be kept in the portfolio at all times for easy reference and as documentation.

Debates

Although recording an entire debate may be impractical, a record of the student's participation in the form of notes or a summary and feedback from the teacher or classmates belongs in the portfolio.

Demonstration or Presentation

There's no better evidence of a student's understanding of a topic than his or her demonstration of that knowledge to others. The teacher and/or several students who receive the demonstration should provide brief feedback to be attached to notes prepared by the presenter.

Display

Whenever students create displays—whether a personal hobby such as a stamp collection or a portrayal of materials describing another country—a written, drawn, or photographic record of that creation should be kept in the portfolio.

Drama and Role Playing

Whether a performance is formal, as a role in a play given before an audience, or instructional, as in role playing for a classroom simulation, some kind of memorandum documenting the student's activity is appropriate for the performer's folder.

Drawings and Illustrations

Whenever a student creates a thoughtful expression of a concept, a copy of that work documents that understanding and contribution.

Enterprise and Leadership

Initiative in leading or helping others accomplish a group task is a quality worthy of every student. Leadership, whether spontaneous or designated through the selection of others, should be documented, recorded, and saved as an example of significant personal growth.

Homework

Routine homework such as mathematics calculations or notes from reading tend to clutter the folder without adding useful information unless, in the judgment of the student or the teacher, they represent a significant change.

Inquiry

Student-conducted inquiries represent both curiosity and new understanding, so they should always be saved.

Interview

Students often formally interview a classmate, a parent, or a person in the community. Whatever constitutes the final version of the interview or its summary belongs in the portfolio.

Inventory

Some students are natural list makers. They enjoy keeping up with their tasks and accomplishments by making lists and checking items off when they've been handled. Such inventories are precise records of goal accomplishment, and they should be added to the student's folder as they are completed.

Journal

Student-maintained journals document thoughts as well as activity. I always maintained students' journals separate from their folders because their writing was sometimes more personal than the contents of their folders. Therefore, students' preferences should dictate how these documents are stored.

Letters

Correspondence associated with curriculum projects forms communication records that document a student's scholarly work.

Mediation Record

When students have participated in peer mediation sessions they usually write some kind of summary as part of that experience. Such experience should be documented and utilized as a benchmark in assessing the student's progress in citizenship.

Microcomputer Work

Since data disks are a documentary record in themselves, printing everything one has done is not necessary. However, a periodic printed summary of programs completed or competencies achieved should be added to the portfolio, since that folder is the central repository for a student's schoolwork. Such records also simplify conferencing because everything is in one place.

Mnemonics

Whether the device is created by the student to recall information in a particular order or whether it is offered by the teacher, the folder is an excellent place to store a record of memory strategies used by individual students.

Parent Communications

Notes from parents, and teachers' responses that have to do with the student's school-work, belong in the student's folder. Sometimes the message is private between the adults and inappropriate for inclusion in the folder, but whenever possible the student should be an active part of such communications and thus the keeper of any records of communications about him or her. When the student and the parents work together on a project, the student should be accountable for keeping a record of that work.

Partner Learning

When students work together in pairs, they should maintain at least a summary record of time spent and work accomplished. I found it helpful to have each member of the partnership summarize what the other partner did, swapping these accounts for their folders. The products of partner learning work, regardless of what it is, should be noted in each student's folder.

Peer Evaluation

Forms such as the example included in Figure 8.6 should be part of the teacher's record. It is then appropriate for the teacher to convey periodically to each student a general summary of how that student's contributions are being reviewed by classmates. In order for students to be authentic in responding to peer evaluations, they must be assured that their communications with the teacher are confidential.

Peer Tutoring

Whether the individual gives or receives a tutorial, a record of that service should be filed. Any evaluation should also be saved.

Reading Record

A single booklet such as those often used as exam books in university courses is adequate for the student to record each book read and a thumbnail sketch. More formal writing about the book is a separate item for inclusion because it is more than just a record of material read.

Recitation

The teacher must judge the propriety of documenting a recitation for inclusion in the student's folder. For example, a student who has memorized a poem when such a task is especially difficult needs to receive recognition for that particular accomplishment. A congratulatory note will do the job.

Service

Information that documents a student's service work should be kept and filed. Often the experiences in a service activity become a topic for writing in an English or social studies class. Whether or not the student writes about the experience, however, at the very least a record of activity should be maintained by the student.

Student Team Learning

The STL groups described in the previous chapter produce sometimes detailed records of both group and individual accomplishments that are appropriate to save in documenting each student's experience.

Suggestion Box

Although the suggestion box described in Chapter 3 is designed to help teachers understand their students, students may also be asked to write their personal reactions to suggestions shared publicly in class.

Tests

Much careful thought must be exercised in the design and use of tests with young adolescent students. They are especially sensitive about their test performance as it relates to personal identity. Teachers face the double task of using tests responsibly to evaluate learning while at the same time teaching students how to do well on them, enhancing their views of themselves as successful learners and students. The tacit notions of using tests "to separate the sheep from the goats" has no place in a program where student advocacy and promoting successes are emphasized. Learning how to perform successfully on the various forms of testing briefly described below should also be a vital instructional goal, not just an evaluation process.

Criterion-Referenced Tests. These tests are composed only of items that have been directly taught. They have traditionally been used to determine students' mastery of one unit of material prior to moving on to a subsequent, more complex level or application. They have also been used to gauge where a student's deficiencies may lie within a unit of subject matter. These tests are especially useful in evaluating a student's learning within subject matter that is highly sequential, where continued skill development is dependent upon success at the prior level. This form of evaluation is especially used in mastery learning programs where the curriculum material has been carefully sequenced. Criterion-referenced tests are also especially useful for informing the teacher about how well students are accomplishing the specific learning objectives of the unit or lesson. It is appropriate to save selected representative criterion-referenced tests in student portfolios.

Norm-Referenced Tests. These published, standardized tests purport to show evidence of a student's learning relative to that of other students of the same age and grade across the country. They are almost always made up of so-called objective items, the answers to which are marked on a separate answer sheet using No. 2 lead pencils. For virtually all of the items, the student must choose one answer from several that are offered. Student results are usually reported in terms of percentile rank, and many test makers also express percentiles in terms of "grade level scores." The public often judges the merit of a school or system on the basis of students' performance on norm-referenced tests. Furthermore, educators sometimes misuse such test information in making superficial judgments about their students' abilities. The apprehension associated with norm-referenced tests often intimidates educational innovation. Materials pertaining to these tests are generally kept in students' permanent records in the school office. However, I have found it both useful and popular with many students to dissect a test booklet during a unit, "The Craft of Test-Taking," analyzing how items are written and cultivating skill in thinking like a test maker. I believe that as students learn how they missed particular items on a test, they become more savvy about handling similar items they encounter in future testings.

Diagnostic Tests. Countless testing instruments have been devised to produce helpful information about the intellectual and academic issues of individual students. These tests are generally used by a specially trained professional, such as a reading specialist. While such materials don't belong in the portfolio, a copy of suggestions or recommendations from the specialist to the student is appropriate to include. Such expert insights should be included in whatever planning the student may be doing.

Collaboratively Designed Tests. Students have demonstrated excellent ideas to me about which items are important to include on tests, how to clarify questions in ways that help them understand what is being asked, and their preferred ways to reflect particular types of learning. Their viewpoints have helped me understand far more about what they think and believe is worthwhile than a test I may have constructed in isolation from their input. Tests that are designed collaboratively provide useful data for both assessment and evaluation purposes. Furthermore, the sudents are often more exacting in judging what we agree to refer to as "essential knowledge" than I am inclined to be. Most of them take seriously the invitation to identify important material, create questions, and design ways to access knowledge through paper-and-pencil items. I do not always agree with their priorities, of course, but by including the items they select, I convey my regard for their ideas about scholarship. I also show that my purpose is to confirm their learning, not to trip them up. These jointly constructed evaluations are particularly appropriate for inclusion in portfolios, because they reflect not just a single student's performance but also the collective thought of the class about what is important in a unit of study.

Types of Items and Questions. I've been especially interested in learning which ways of asking questions appeal to individual students. Some students prefer short-answer items; others prefer short essay questions. Matching items from two columns appeals to one youngster, while sentence completion is another's favorite. In my experience, the least favorite format is multiple-choice, especially when the choices appear ambiguous. I treat this kind of information as extremely important assessment information, because it enables me to ask questions in the mode my students prefer while also offering a workshop around strategies for improving one's performance on items that the student feels inadequate to do well on, for whatever reasons. Since norm-referenced tests rely heavily on the multiple-choice format and analogies, helping students become more comfortable with those layouts is especially crucial as they approach a period of life when their options will be increasingly affected by how well they perform on standardized tests.

Time Use Records

There may be no more urgent conservation need in youngsters' lives than time. School hours are frequently chopped into small units of twenty to forty minutes in order to let everyone "cover the curriculum/book/course." Many kids' lives outside school are similarly segmented by lessons, sports, activities, and even daily television schedules. Their daily schedules are often organized, in fact, like a page from *TV Guide*. A pitfall of contemporary adolescent life is that students fall into a mindless flow from one event to another without stepping back, looking at the options, and making a deliberate plan for how they will use their time.

To raise students' consciousness about this increasingly pressing issue in their lives as well as to help them learn how to make responsible choices, it is useful to have them maintain a record of how they use their time. The information collected will help them gain perspective about their lives, and it is also extremely helpful assessment information for the teacher. No single format is required for keeping time records, but Figure 8.1 shows a format that can be used or adapted according to the teacher's interest. Time use records constitute very useful data when they are kept in student portfolios for use in periodic assessments/evaluations.

There are team settings where students are expected to formulate a plan for using a block of school time such as that illustrated in Figure 8.1. Each student plans his or her work for the time block and files that plan with one of the teachers. At the end of the day that record goes into the student's portfolio. Periodically the student reviews these daily records and assesses the uses he or she has made of this personal planning opportunity. Each student shares that assessment in a conference with the teacher, when the compiled data help with both guidance and future planning. This kind of information is also valuable in helping parents understand issues related to their child's use of time at school. I should add that I have worked with many students who make responsible choices about time and seem to naturally apply their time productively. Although some of them have been interested in keeping personal time use records, the practice has been superfluous for others. However, most young adolescents can benefit from examining their time use patterns.

Student _____ TA _____ Day _____ Date _____

TA Summary

8:00

Learning Activities	Time Spent	Accomplishment
8:20 11:45		

— Team Lunch —

| 12:15

 2:50 | | |

Self-Assessment (Circle)   1 (low)   2   3   4   5 (high)

Comment:

_____
Signature

Figure 8.1   Daily Student Plan.

Unit Feedback Records

In order for teachers to understand how students are reacting to a unit of study, it's important to solicit formal feedback at regular intervals. Sometimes it is appropriate to have students respond anonymously, in which case the feedback sheets can't be returned for portfolio storage. However, Figure 8.2 shows an example of such an assessment that is

Unit Feedback

Topic or Unit _____   Teacher (s) _____

Most interesting things about the study:

Activities which helped me learn:

Suggestions for improving the unit:

Advice for next year's students about this unit:

Signed _____   Date _____

Figure 8.2   Unit Feedback.

signed by the student and should be returned for inclusion in the portfolio after the teacher has examined the student's reviews.

Writing

The part played by students' writing as access to their thought has already been discussed. It is notable to emphasize again, however, that their reflections about what they are learning and doing as revealed through regular writing is vital to their becoming increasingly accountable for themselves. Whether they are writing about math class, about a sports activity, or about working with classmates, their written records document the youngsters' school-related perceptions. And insights expressed in writing are valuable not just to the student but also to teachers and parents as they attempt to understand the youngster's perspective.

STUDENTS' ACCOUNTABILITY FOR SCHOOLWORK

If one of our goals is for students to learn to take more responsibility for their education and to become more personally accountable, we must show them how to do so. There are specific things they can do to demonstrate increasing self-reliance. The changes they're undergoing in early adolescence present a perfect opportunity for them to achieve progress toward greater self-sufficiency. At a time when they are trying to define themselves, establish relatively greater independence, and assert their individuality, we can support them by beginning to share some of the evaluation work that heretofore had been strictly a teacher's function. We can further develop partnership with students by showing them how to set reasonable personal goals, work purposefully toward accomplishing them, and at appropriate times monitor their progress.

Josh, a seventh grader, set several personal goals to accomplish over a four-week period. His plan was reviewed by Mrs. Pitt, his advisor on the Explorer team, and she signed her approval as shown in Figure 8.3. Figure 8.4 shows the ratings and explanations Josh gave himself four weeks later. It was his duty to show Mrs. Pitt again what he had originally set out to do, the materials from his portfolio that he had completed in the interim, and his self-evaluation rating and written comments. Mrs. Pitt would add her own written comments.

Once this follow-up discussion was completed, the papers would be stapled together and returned to Josh's portfolio. He would then select new goals, repeating this cycle. In the event that Josh failed to follow through on one of his goals, Mrs. Pitt would need to decide whether or not to require him to retain it for another period of goal setting. That judgment would be made on the basis of her knowledge of the exigencies of Josh's circumstances. ("MyGET" is the acronym for "*My Goals—Explorer Team*.")

Josh's goal statements show his assessment of his academic needs, and in electing to work on them he has chosen a responsible action. His portfolio documents the work he did over approximately four weeks in mastering the calculation problems, and he also wrote multiple drafts of two stories—no small accomplishment in light of the fact that he was also responsible for academic work in his ongoing classes. As his advisor on the Explorer team, Mrs. Pitt stayed in regular contact with Josh to offer help and encouragement.

MyGET Plan

Name __Josh B._____ Dates: From ___Oct. 14___ Until ___Nov. 5___

Improvements I need to make:

1. fractions
   multiplying + division

2. reading one hour everyday

3. alot of writting

Things I want to learn more about:

1. how a motorcycle works

2. New York giants + Lawrence Taylor

3.

Student _____Josh B._____ Teacher __M. Pitt_____ Date __10/15/90___

Figure 8.3

She also kept Josh's other teachers on the Explorer team informed about his goals, so they too were able to help him become successful. When youngsters pinpoint things they know they need to learn, then design and carry out a plan to resolve those needs in a supportive atmosphere, they justifiably feel and act more maturely. They are learning about growing up in ways that adults already know is vital to their future success.

The MyGET system serves the aspirations of the four teachers on the Explorer team, who agreed that they needed to find a way to teach students how to become more responsible. It helps them pursue their educational goal of teaching students a way they can become more goal oriented and aware of their actual progress. However, this is but one design for formalizing partnerships with students around issues of personal accountability.

Given youngsters' need to know how they stand in relation to long-term goals and expectations, it is helpful to spell out some achievable targets that guarantee recognition.

MyGET Plan

Rate yourself according to how you think you did on each goal. Give
yourself a 5 if you were completely successful, 4 if you were
mostly successful, 3 if your success was average, 2 if you had
less success than usual, and 1 if you didn't make much progress
at all. Then list reasons why you gave yourself that rating.

Improvements:

1. Rating: _4_   I get them right most of the time.

2. Rating: _5_   I read Hatchet and Savage Sam.

3. Rating: _5_   I rote a letter to Lawrence Taylor,
a report about the history of motorcycles.

Interests:

1. Rating: _5_   I read alot about them and I went
to the Honda and Kawasaki dealer.
I got a A- on my report.

2. Rating: ___   I watched 3 games on T.V. and I
counted how may L.T. tackled. He got
a fumble once and a interseption. I
rote him a letter.

3. Rating: ___

Student ___Josh B.___   Teacher ___M. Pitt___   Date ___11/6/90___

Figure 8.4

Scouting has provided such structures for many years, suggesting possible goals (merit badges), supporting individual choices, and promoting personal accountability by their young adolescent constituents. Paradise Project, a seventh–eighth grade two-teacher team, promotes responsibility and personal accountability through what they refer to as the Paradise Achievement Program (Figure 8.5). Entering seventh graders are shown that they have a great deal of control over their own destiny during the two years they will be on the

Paradise team. Every student is responsible for maintaining a record of his or her accomplishments, and by showing portfolio documents to classmates and a teacher who constitute the achievement committee, they can move upward step by step through the six levels. Usually half of the team completes the top level, and students display genuine pride and confidence when they describe their individual positions in terms of the achievement program.

STUDENTS' ACCOUNTABILITY FOR CITIZENSHIP

Broadly defined, I use *citizenship* in reference to the social responsibility students demonstrate. Whatever the setting—a formal class, a team meeting, a small project group, a field trip into the community—young adolescents must be accountable for the choices they make about how they behave. Those who are constitutionally unable to restrain their impulses are rare. It is appropriate for teachers to expect young adolescents to conduct themselves in ways that show consideration toward community standards and toward other people. Sometimes younger children lack adequate understanding of the circumstances and consequences of their conduct, so teachers police them. By the early adolescent years, however, youngsters are able to comprehend expectations, limits, and responsibilities toward others. In fact, many kids are preoccupied with concerns about how they think other people are perceiving them. At this time in their lives they are developmentally advanced enough to take full responsibility for their actions.

Again, teachers can help students look at themselves and their growth toward increasingly responsible citizenship more dispassionately and analytically than was possible in their younger years. Although Josh's goals in the previously described MyGET format concerned only academics, he might also have chosen citizenship goals. Young adolescent society tends to be dynamic and sometimes tense. The school, especially within teams, is also an appropriate context for students to set social goals such as getting to know another student better, resolving to work out a troubled relationship with a classmate, taking initiative on cleanup chores, and so on.

Small groups are excellent settings for such self-evaluation and peer evaluation because they are microcosms of the larger student community. When students work in a project group for several days, they will form certain judgments about their group-mates' participation as well as their own. Such fresh information constitutes excellent data for assessing citizenship. Consider the student group evaluation depicted in Figure 8.6.

In the spirit of inquiry described in detail in Chapter 3, it is appropriate to ask students to respond to additional questions that raise their consciousness about their progress as a contributing member of a team, class, or small group. For the questions listed below that students might be asked to respond to in writing, insert "group, advisory, class, team" according to the setting.

> What have you learned about how to be a successful member of your _____?
> What are the things you do that help the _____ be successful?
> What steps do you need to take to become a more effective _____ member?
> What are the (advantages/most difficult things) about being in a _____?
> What changes do you suggest to make the ——— function better?

The Paradise Project Achievement Program

As an ongoing, changing, and evolving program, the Achievement Program should provide approximately thirty to forty skills from which a student might choose when advancing. Some skills have two levels of achievement, Intern and Master, and are considered separate skills. Skills and advancement will be awarded only for work done after completion of the sixth grade.

Although there will be a wide variety of skills from which to choose, we feel that some skills are basic to growth within the Project and should be achieved by all. Therefore, some specific skills are required for advancement to the next level of achievement. A total of twenty-five skills must be achieved by Level Six, twelve of them specific required skills in the areas listed below:

Community & School Service	Academic Achievement	Fundraising
Trip Planning	Public Speaking	Teaching
Interviewing	Emergencies	Contributor to Publications

To move from one level to the next a student must be demonstrating a positive attitude toward self and others, earning a passing grade in all subject areas, participating actively in the Paradise Project, performing service for family or community, and earning a specific number of skills. At each level a student must also choose a goal for personal growth.

LEVEL ONE

_____ Demonstrate a positive attitude toward the Paradise Project.
_____ Be earning a passing grade in all subjects at the time of advancement to next level.
_____ Earn one skill award.
_____ Participate positively in classroom or Project activities.
_____ Perform a service for your family:
_____

_____ Choose a personal growth goal for Level Two.
_____ Review by a Project Director   _____ Date

LEVEL TWO

_____ Demonstrate a positive attitude.
_____ Be earning a passing grade in all subjects at the time of advancement to next level.
_____ Earn "Trip Planning" skill and one other skill award.   (Total of 3 skills.)
_____ Participate in at least one Paradise Project day activity.
_____ Perform a total of six hours of family, school and/or community service. List services
          and hours below:
_____
_____
_____

_____ Participate in a school fund raising activity:
_____

_____ Complete the personal growth goal described below:
_____

_____ Choose a personal growth goal for Level Three.
_____ Review by a Project Director   _____ Date

LEVEL THREE

_____ Demonstrate a positive attitude.
_____ Be earning a passing grade in all subjects at the time of advancement to next level.
_____ Earn Emergencies skill, School Service Intern <u>or</u> Community Service Intern skill,
          and earn two additional skills of your choice.   (Total of 7 skills.)
_____ Participate in at least one Paradise Project overnight activity.
_____ Perform a service for your family or neighborhood:
_____

_____ Complete the personal growth goal described below:

_____ Choose a personal growth goal for Level Four.
_____ Review by both Project Directors _____ Date _____ / _____ Date _____

LEVEL FOUR

_____ Demonstrate a positive attitude.
_____ Be earning a passing grade in all subjects at the time of advancement to next level.
_____ Earn Contributor to Publications Intern skill, two other skills from the Level
         Six list, and any two additional skills of your choice.   (Total of 13 skills.)
_____ Participate in a Paradise Project trip of three or more days.
_____ Perform a service for your family or neighborhood:

_____ Organize, lead, and successfully complete a service or fund raising activity:

_____ Complete the personal growth goal described below:

_____ Choose a personal growth goal for Level Five.
_____ Review by both Project Directors _____ Date _____ / _____ Date _____

LEVEL FIVE

_____ Demonstrate a positive attitude.
_____ Be earning a passing grade in all subjects at the time of advancement to next level.
_____ Earn Academics skill, School Service Master, or Community Service Master skill,
         and any four additional skills of your choice.   (Total of 20 skills.)
_____ Become certified to serve as an Instructor in a skill:

_____ Perform a service for your family or neighborhood:

_____ Serve as leader for a trip of three or more days or lead a Trip Journal:

_____ Complete the personal growth goal described below:

_____ Choose a personal growth goal for Level Six.
_____ Review by both Project Directors _____ Date _____ / _____ Date _____

LEVEL SIX

_____ Demonstrate a positive attitude.
_____ Be earning a passing grade in all subjects at the time of advancement to next level.
_____ Earn five more skill awards, including the remaining skills from the Level Six
         required list.   (Total of 25 skills.)
_____ Serve as a Certified Instructor in two more skills:

_____ Perform a service for your family or neighborhood:

_____ Serve in a leadership position for at least three months or lead a major trip of at
         least five school days:

_____ Develop, organize, and lead a major community service project (preapproved):

_____ Complete the personal growth goal described below:

_____ Review by both Project Directors _____ Date _____ / _____ Date _____

Figure 8.5   The Paradise Project Achievement Program.

Student Group Evaluation

Group Members: _____

Place group members' initials in the box that matches your
evaluation for each statement. Be sure to include yourself.

	Always	Frequently	Sometimes	Never
Did a fair share of the work				
Contributed ideas				
Was cooperative				
Used group time well				
Took the project seriously				
Was fun to work with				

Title of Project: _____

Your Name _____   Date _____

Figure 8.6   Student Group Evaluation.

GRADING

This chapter is concerned with strategies teachers can use in order to better understand both what students are actually learning and what they believe about their school experiences. These dual processes have already been explained as evaluation and assessment. The intended theme is understanding—being aware of students' learning and development.

The traditional way in which teachers have reported their evaluation to students and parents is through grading or marking systems, most often represented by the familiar A, B, C, D, and F that are sometimes further refined by pluses (+) and minuses (-). Since virtually every adult has attended schools, most people accept this system, whether or not they agree exactly about how it is constituted and what the grades actually represent.

Therefore, the grading issue becomes extremely important for teachers to communicate explicitly to students and parents.

I recall being a mediocre student in seventh and eighth grades in the small-town junior high school I attended in Alabama in 1950. My dominant recollections have to do with struggles to catch on to things some of my classmates seemed to grasp effortlessly. While I think I was generally obedient about doing homework, I can't recall a single school project or study from those years. I was an avid reader, however, and I can still name books, characters, authors, and many, many important learnings from my life outside of school. I recall myself as being essentially average, a "C student" if not a "C person" as far as my school status was concerned.

On my fiftieth birthday, my mother sent my report cards from those two years. I had no idea they still existed, and had they not borne my father's distinctive signature signifying that I had dutifully delivered the card every six weeks, I would have doubted their authenticity. During those two years my actual grades were almost entirely As. In fact, the only B grades shown were in Conduct. I wonder how it could be that those grades had absolutely no correlation with my sense of myself as a learner or as a person. What did I learn that merited those A grades? And what did those grades have to do with what I was really thinking about and learning at the time?

My young adolescent intellectual life was certainly as rich as could be expected under the circumstances. I read a good bit, I obsessively followed all sports through the newspaper and radio, and my job at Maxwell's Pharmacy stretched me in lots of educative ways. I'm especially curious now to know what I did that resulted in Bs for conduct. I recall being what my parents called "a good boy." I clearly recall Mr. Maxwell treating me as an adult and praising my work. I continue to ponder the substantial differences between my perception of myself as a student and what these school records suggest. There was an obvious gap between how my teachers evaluated my performance and what I thought.

When I have the opportunity to chat with students on my frequent visits to middle level schools, I enjoy asking them to "tell me what you've learned" or "describe yourself as a learner." The first question usually (but not always) seems to be somewhat startling. And the eventual answers almost always have to do with something the student is doing in a particular class at the moment, such as "We're studying Africa." The second question is almost always countered with "What do you mean?" This apparent neutrality and detachment of youngsters' intellectual lives not only is unnecessary, it exacerbates their natural apprehensions about how they're doing. High marks or grades seem to have little to do with the kind of self-knowledge they seek and evidence they crave.

Teachers face a common dilemma over determining academic grades. There's tension between the desire for students to be successful on one hand, and society's expectations that teachers maintain high academic standards on the other. This tension is especially troubling for middle grades teachers, because they in particular understand how very important it is to a young adolescent's identity formation process to have lots of successes and to receive recognition and respect from peers and adults for their accomplishments. Not only do we have to create a new context for evaluation and accountability, such as the portfolio documentation already described; we must also help parents understand this more authentic way of examining youngsters' work and learning.

During my years as a teacher I was usually somewhat concerned when students referred to "making all As" or "making the honor roll" as a goal detached from learning. Sometimes such a goal was tied to external rewards offered by a parent. But on the whole I understood, of course, that students were setting their sights on a target that virtually everyone recognizes as worthwhile. I understand youngsters' need for accomplishment and recognition, and I have no quarrel at all with their setting such goals. However, my concern was and is that such motivation is too often expressed irrespective of authentic learning. And I know from countless interactions as a teacher with young adolescents that they are quite capable of setting appropriate learning goals for themselves without regard to external recognition. Young adolescents are remarkably savvy about the differences between work as an expression of personal need and work aimed at an external goal. While I advocate celebrating accomplishment at every opportunity, I also warn that we must be mindful not to underestimate our students' awareness of their needs and capacity for real accountability.

Subjectivity versus Objectivity

All grading is subjective. Regardless of the claims of "objectivity" some might make, the very fact that human judgment has been involved in decisions about what is to be evaluated and how performance or knowledge will be equated with number or letter grades renders the process and the outcome subjective. It becomes extremely important, therefore, that we clarify relationships involving our educational goals, learning objectives, instructional activities, and strategies for evaluation and assessment. These relationships not only must be thought out carefully in advance by teachers, they also must be conveyed clearly to students and parents. One way to achieve such clarity is through explicit definitions of evaluative criteria for each letter or number grade.

Grades Earned versus Grades Given

The ordinary language used by students and sometimes by teachers fails to make a distinction between two central concepts: "earning" versus "giving." Although there may be times when a teacher opts to give a student a grade as a bonus or incentive, the vast majority of grades should reflect the fact that a student has earned recognition through the accomplishment of explicit criteria. When criteria are unclear, confusion is a certain result, and distrust is likely. When tests include items that were not taught or questions designed to mislead students into errors in ways that are incompatible with the unit objectives, alienation is a virtual certainty. Anything the teacher can do to help students clearly understand the relationships between what they do and how grades are determined for that work will clear the air. Such clarity also enhances a trusting climate.

Learning Contracts

One example of clarity in spelling out the relationships between schoolwork and grades is represented by a learning contract such as that in Figure 8.7.

While such a contract system is very helpful for many students, some disadvantages should also be pointed out. First, the contract will be superfluous for some students who

Learning Contract

Unit: <u>The American Revolution</u>　　　　　　Dates:　Oct. 14–Nov. 17

Work Required for a "C"	**Due Date**	**Check Off**
1. Make a political map of the colonies (*)	_____	_____
2. Make one biograpy presentation (*)	_____	_____
3. Read & study assigned chapters, handouts (*)	_____	_____
4. Read and discuss *Johnny Tremaine* (*)	_____	_____
5. Keep a sketchbook (e.g., fashion, tools, etc.)	_____	_____
6. Score a minimum of 80% on 11/2 vocabulary test	_____	_____
7. Score a minimum of 70% on 11/12 unit test	_____	_____

Work Required for a "B"		
8. Make diorama portraying a historical event (*)	_____	_____
9. Daily journal entries for your character	_____	_____
10. Letter about America to your old-country family	_____	_____
11. Score a minimum of 90% on vocabulary test	_____	_____
12. Score a minimum of 80% on unit test	_____	_____

Work Required for an "A"		
13. Inquiry involving at least 10 adults (*)	_____	_____
14. Recite Constitution Preamble	_____	_____
15. Score a minimum of 90% on unit test	_____	_____

Memorandum of Understanding

I _____ contract for a grade of _____ for the American Revolution unit. I will do my best work and complete everything by the due dates. Mr. Simpson has the right not to accept any of my work that he finds unsatisfactory. I understand that I may work with classmates on the items marked (*), and if I need to take quizzes or tests more than once, only the average grade will count toward my contract. If I decide later that I want to renegotiate my contract for a higher grade, I may do so after Nov. 12.

Signature _____ Teacher _____ Date _____
　　　　　　　　　　　　　　　　　　(R.J. Simpson)

Figure 8.7

are naturally motivated and who object to such a detailed agreement. Therefore, teachers should use contracts judiciously, according to students' disposition and work habits. Second, the contract shown in Figure 8.7 doesn't allow students many significant choices. Mr. Simpson would be well advised to invite students to add their own interests and ideas about studying the topic, perhaps in lieu of some of his items. Third, such a contract suggests that learning has a production-line orientation. The process of forming understandings is not as chronological and impersonal as the contract implies. Fourth, although the teacher is the judge of whether or not the student's work is satisfactory, no distinctions are made between marginal and exceptional work. Nor does the contract allow for unanticipated developments that might impinge on the student's ability to deliver the agreed-upon work by an agreed-upon time. In spite of these limitations, however, contracts can be extremely helpful in clarifying everyone's understanding about expectations and how standards will be interpreted.

PARENT CONFERENCES

The most effective way to accomplish communication is talk—not report cards, memorandums, or notes delivered back and forth by children in lieu of direct conversations. That face-to-face dialogue ought to be focused on the actual materials that a well-kept portfolio contains. Samples of the youngster's work illustrate the child's personal abilities, talents, interests, and areas of progress as well as specific deficiencies. In a conference over a portfolio, teachers can point out specific characteristics of work that show the student not just what he or she is learning but patterns of ongoing needs, both in terms of academic gains and in terms of the student's developing responsibility. A thoughtful demonstration of what the student has accomplished and suggestions based on a context of actual materials also make much more sense to the student than the abstract representation of a letter grade or check marks. A periodic teacher–student conference based on the student's portfolio must become the teacher's central communication strategy.

The teacher's advice makes a great deal more sense when it is offered as part of a context established through firsthand examinations of the student's work. Discussions are focused on the work itself, enabling everyone to avoid awkward clichés such as "Susie just needs to work harder" and "Johnny has to study more." In addition to making the student's actual work and self-evaluations visible, portfolio materials also provide clues about the student's conceptual development. Realizations about how one's child thinks can help a parent gain a more appropriate perspective on the youngster's intellectual and social maturity. Expectations can then become more realistic and consistent with the child's development. The very best way to make certain that issues are understood is to participate in dialogue about actual work.

Synergy with parents is likewise enhanced by periodic telephone conversations initiated by teachers at periodic times following conferences where the portfolio has been reviewed. As a student makes progress on a particular need or deficiency previously identified, the prudent teacher telephones the parents to let them know about their child's improvement. In addition to feeling greater confidence in the teacher as an advocate for their child, parents will likewise become more generally supportive of the teacher, the school, and the educational agenda for their child. The power of concurrence between home and school is also considerable, especially when it is clear to a youngster that these two important influences in his or her life have common values and are advocates for the student.

THREE-WAY CONFERENCES

By the time youngsters reach early adolescence, it is crucial that they accept the bulk of the responsibility for their actions. Learning how to account for one's use of school time and performance requires, first of all, an adult's sensitive, informed guidance. In order for students to be able to talk responsibly about their progress, they need to be able to review their actual materials in the portfolio. As a starting point to organize thought, general questions included in the earlier discussions of student accountability and citizenship can be adapted to the following: What are the things I've learned and done well? Where do I still need to improve? How do I contribute and benefit as a member of this (team/ class/school)?

Very few children cannot at the very least make a list of responses to these three questions. According to their seriousness and intellectual maturity, they can move from a basic list to an outline. Ultimately, they should be able to begin to look at themselves and their work in a somewhat detached way, finding ways to categorize their reflections on their work. I required my students to make such self-assessments periodically, usually at intervals of four to five weeks. Their higher-order thought involved improved with practice.

The Alpha team teachers have long been committed to teaching their students how to set personal learning goals within what they have established as Alpha's Five Essential Learnings (Kenny, et al., 1995). These learning areas are communication, personal development, reasoning and problem solving, functioning independently, and social responsibility. Students set personal goals every trimester, and they document their work and progress weekly, collecting and sorting related work samples. On the basis of these working portfolios, students prepare an outline for a parent conference focusing on their schoolwork and their progress. The teachers have evolved a balanced delineation of responsibilities that stipulates responsibilities and tasks for teachers, students, and parents.

Teachers will

- inform parents about the rationale and procedures of this assessment and evaluation scheme
- establish and administer an organizational framework
- teach the steps and process of leading conferences
- schedule time for portfolio and conference preparation
- meet and greet parents at the beginning of the conferences
- answer students' and parents' questions at the end of the conference
- clarify team and/or school policies and procedures as needed
- call attention to and celebrate the student's effort and growth

Students will

- maintain a working portfolio throughout the trimester
- assess each piece of work for strengths, needed improvement, and connections to their goals
- anticipate parents' questions and concerns, and plan responses to them

- organize work samples in the portfolio
- rehearse the conference with a classmate
- rehearse the conference with a teacher
- show parents the portfolio prior to the conference
- conduct the conference
- set new goals for the next trimester

Parents will

- review the portfolio contents prior to the conference
- attend and participate at the scheduled conference time
- trust the student to assume responsibility for reporting his/her progress
- ask thoughtful questions and listen to the answers
- help the child conceptualize and determine appropriate goals for the next trimester
- evaluate the conference process
- write a positive, supportive letter to the child about his/her growth

Students need some successful experience in assessing their work and participating in conferences with parents before it is reasonable to expect them to take this much leadership, but teachers should begin, as these teachers do, with the assumption that their young adolescents are capable of being accountable for themselves and their learning. An advantage of teaching on a multiage team such as Alpha is that the teachers have the opportunity to nurture their students' skills to the point where after a year of learning about leading by observing their teachers lead, students are sufficiently experienced to lead their own conferences. With their portfolios as the resource, youngsters can and should learn how to participate and subsequently lead conferences involving their parents and teacher or teacher advisor. Failure to involve them in this kind of accountability prolongs dependence and in many cases irresponsibility, which are counterproductive. When the teacher and parents are certain advocates for the student, the child can grow rapidly in being accountable for his or her own education.

CELEBRATING ACHIEVEMENT

It is fairly common in the first weeks of a new school year for middle level schools to conduct some kind of evening presentation for students' parents. These are sessions during which parents and teachers are introduced, and parents often go through an abbreviated version of their child's daily schedule. These evenings are especially useful in helping parents gain a sense of the school context, but there usually isn't sufficient time to show students' collective work adequately.

Completion of a unit of study creates both a need and an opportunity for students to share their accomplishments with parents. In fact, it is fitting for them to teach their parents what they have done and learned as a group. When a team has conducted an IIU, for example, the unit should culminate with a group presentation. One team studied businesses in their small town. On the evening of the study's final day, they set up their classrooms as a series of individual booths, one for each business, so that parents and invited community members could examine the booklets, drawings, photographs, artifacts, and so on that were derived from the study. Visitors to each booth received a brief lesson on that business from the student who had done the study. Another team had studied landfill problems in the community, and they finished their study with a student debate followed by a roundtable discussion in which parents and other guests participated.

On these occasions, parents and community members gain a much clearer understanding of how their young adolescents think, the intellectual and academic context of which their child is a member, and what is actually being learned. The rationale for these particular events is twofold. First, it is an occasion for adults to learn about and celebrate what students are doing and learning. Every achievement celebration I have ever attended impressed guests with the quality of kids' learning and generated lots of compliments and congratulations. Second, it is another dimension of the communication between school and home that is essential if the adults involved are to support each other's efforts to raise children well. One of the most exciting outcomes of these evenings is to observe parents and kids discussing issues in ways that provide mutual enlightenment.

PRESERVING PERSPECTIVE

Earnest teachers I've known have spoken candidly about the pressure they feel to cover given amounts of subject matter in the time allowed, pacing classes so that more advanced students don't become bored and slower students don't get lost. Where that historical instructional model prevails, conventional approaches to evaluation and grading are usually equally well entrenched. Practices such as tracking by ability, calculating students' class rank, and grading on the curve are also often found. Those consequences of an exaggerated emphasis on subject matter to the sacrifice of the child-centered values described here constitute a central dilemma for teachers whose primary commitment is to the welfare of all students, irrespective of differences in their talents for competitive academic performance.

Middle level teachers who choose healthy adolescent growth and learning over the profession's unnecessarily competitive tradition will do well to keep three points in mind.

1. Every student needs to be successful as much as possible, and a well-maintained portfolio system documents progress and successes.

2. Achievement ultimately requires initiative and responsibility; the portfolio is an accurate, up-to-date reflection of the extent to which a student manifests these qualities.

3. Young adolescents preoccupied with their own development learn firsthand how standards of quality and excellence apply to themselves. Through recognizing their own improvement, they can set higher goals for themselves that are also within their reach.

> I discovered that the students knew themselves as learners better than anyone else. They set goals for themselves and judged how well they had reached those goals. They thoughtfully and honestly evaluated their own learning with far more detail and introspection than I thought possible. Ultimately, they showed me who they were as readers, writers, thinkers and human beings.
>
> *(Rief, 1990, p. 29)*

Supporting Activities

1. Create a documentation portfolio for yourself, selecting and storing materials you produce that document your preparation for teaching. Include specific goals you set for yourself and periodic self-assessments.

2. Conduct an inquiry with young adolescent students to find out what they are learning, their thoughts about the evaluation strategies used in their school, and their perceptions about quality and standards. Ask them to "tell you what they've learned" or "tell you about their work."

3. Conduct an inquiry with middle grades teachers to learn their practices with regard to assessment and evaluation, how they teach students to be responsible, and their perceptions about quality and standards.

4. Design a learning contract for use in a unit you've observed or for one you expect to teach.

REFERENCES

Ausubel, D. P. (1963). *The psychology of meaningful learning.* New York: Grune & Stratton.

Bloom, B. S. (ed.). (1956). *Taxonomy of educational objectives: Handbook 1: Cognitive domain.* White Plains, NY: Longman.

Costa, A. L. (1989). Re-assessing assessment. *Educational Leadership, 46,* 2.

Gagne, R. (1965). *Conditions of learning.* New York: Holt, Rinehart, & Winston.

Honig, B. (1987). Foreword. In *English-language arts framework.* Sacramento, CA: California State Department of Education.

Kenny, M., O'Donnell, M., & Smith, C. (1995, October). Student-led parent conferences. *VAMLE Focus, 1*(2).

Rief, L. (1990). Finding the value in evaluation: Self-assessment in a middle school classroom. *Educational Leadership, 47,* 24–29.

Rogers, V., & Stevenson, C. (1988). How do we know what kids are learning in school? *Educational Leadership, 45*(5), 68–75.

PART THREE

About Being a Teacher

INTRODUCTION TO PART THREE

The previous two sections of this book have been introduced through aquatic metaphors, and so it is with this final segment. I've already emphasized some similarities between teaching well and sailing well. I also proposed that we should think of the middle level curriculum in terms of a healthy estuary. In these final three chapters I want to emphasize the urgent necessity of collaboration with colleagues, with our students, and with our students' parents. Every teacher works with each of these constituencies, and my purpose is to raise the reader's consciousness about the possibilities for developing collaborations that go well beyond the ordinary condition of "working alone together" that is so often the accepted norm in our schools.

Prudent sailors watch the weather carefully. Changes in cloud shapes and configurations as well as sometimes subtle wind shifts usually herald meteorological changes and sometimes dramatic surges of winds and sea that threaten safety and even life itself. Barometer and thermometer are watched carefully. Wizened coastal sailors heed the caveat to "keep a weather eye to leeward." Some of the most dangerous weather comes from behind, building up suddenly and sometimes violently.

Teachers need to stay vigilant, observing and even studying the school equivalents of weather signs. Just as certainly as storms arise on the sea, tempests also rise within schools. The business of growing up often affects youngsters' readiness for the educational processes we plan, and such contingencies are not always predictable. A real potential for division within a faculty is always present. Parental unrest can explode in the face of even the most conscientious teacher. Most of the potential for such storms can be offset by everyone's investment in teamwork. When we understand each other's purposes and we share responsibilities, we not only have much less occasion to work at cross-purposes—we also learn to recognize opportunities to help each other.

Years ago, when I had begun to grow more consciously and deliberately as a teacher but was yet a novice sailor, Nathaniel French, a cherished friend and mentor in both enterprises, shared an anecdotal piece that has served me well on countless occasions in school and on the sea. I recall him saying that the handwritten copy he gave me came from something he had read. Nat died years ago without divulging the source, but I suspect that in truth the piece was his own.

A Crew Without Orders

"All hands on deck! Douse sail for a squall!" This was the shout down the hatchway that roused us from our predawn slumbers. We were crossing the Gulf Stream on the way to Bermuda. Such a call was not unexpected, for before the last watch was relieved, gorgeous piles of bubbling clouds had begun to grow on the horizon. In less time than it takes to tell it, five pajama-clad figures joined the two men on deck, who were already busy with sheets and halyards.

The interesting thing to note was that no further words were spoken. No instructions or commands had to be issued. Every crew member took in the situation at a glance. Each one went directly to a vital spot and began to do what was needed. The mainsail had to be lowered away, the boom sheeted in and placed in the crotch, stops quickly fastened around the bulging canvas—no time for a neat harbor furl! The foresail and headsails had to be gotten down in a hurry—hands, feet, body weight, even teeth to hold the stops were all busily employed. With not a moment to spare, all was secure, and with a gust of wind that whistled through the rigging, the rain came, big pelting drops that soon had all the scuppers running rivulets.

Of course the reason why there was no confused shouting and panic was that we all had an active and intelligent concern for the total setup. We all knew without being told just what had to be done. We all wanted it done quickly and correctly. And we all had confidence in one another. We had sailed together so long that we were a crew who could always act without orders. The only thing we needed was a situation!

And so it is when any team works well: a surgical team, a sports team, a family, a school faculty. Those of us who choose to be a part of the exciting but unpredictable voyage with youth across the challenging seas of early adolescence must invest ourselves first and last in building strong relationships with each other, our students, and their families. Our safety and our successes rest on the quality of trust that holds us together. These final three chapters present strategies by which we can achieve partnerships—alliances of adult mentors to support the children they share.

Chapter 9

Successes and Satisfaction through Teaming

○ *What are the benefits of team organization for students? Teachers?*

○ *What are the other teachers' priorities?*

○ *What do they expect from our kids? From me?*

○ *How do they do things? Why?*

○ *How will we share responsibilities and work together?*

The distinctive goals and purposes of the middle level school reported in Chapter 1 are difficult at best to achieve in a conventional departmentally organized school. Decades ago, insightful leaders recognized that the middle level school needed to be organized differently in order to pursue a wider range of educational outcomes. Interdisciplinary Team Organization (ITO) is the distinctive structural breakthrough for middle level schools, and teacher expertise is steadily growing (Arnold & Stevenson, 1998; Dickinson & Erb, 1997). Although schools have traditionally been based on departmental configurations more appropriate to high schools, state-of-the-art middle schools have reconfigured themselves into formally organized interdisciplinary teams that can function more responsively to the needs of their young adolescent students. Teams that function well devise and implement educational programs that embody consistency, continuity, and coherent linkages between goals, learning programs, and evaluation procedures.

Through well-designed teams, enterprising teachers can best match academic programs and operating procedures with students' interests and backgrounds. A cadre of teachers working cooperatively with each other and a common group of students can create original curriculum in a schooling context they understand and for which they feel ownership and empowerment. Adults and children come to know each other better in these circumstances, and teachers are thus able to better understand and accommodate the needs and circumstances of their students. When they work closely together throughout the school day, common goals, expectations, and standards can become clearly defined to students, to the teachers, and to others outside the team. Excellent teams become known to others by what they do.

Teams may be organized in a variety of sizes. Some may be as small as two teachers and 40 students (see Partner Teaming, p. 296), but large schools, especially in urban areas, may have teams of up to five teachers and 100 or more students. While four-teacher teams and a proportional number of students are most common, smaller teams are increasingly preferred. Regardless of numbers, however, the dominant emphasis is on defining and building a powerful, convincing sense of community where membership consists of young adolescents and a few teachers who lead, teach, and are accountable for their students and each other. Although student team members may have an exploratory class or elective course under a teacher who is not on their team, teacher members generally teach only the students who are on their team.

There are many ways to organize teams, but to ensure that the full potential of this organizational plan is achieved, eight basic issues must be carefully addressed. Thorough planning is critical for successful implementation, and once in place, the program should be evaluated just as one evaluates any other aspect of a school program. The eight essential issues are

1. *Governance:* how the team is organized for decision making
2. *Team Identity:* what the team stands for
3. *Operating Procedures:* daily, monthly, or term calendar and schedule
4. *Communication:* how decisions are conveyed within and beyond the team
5. *Recognition:* how accomplishment is recognized
6. *Curriculum:* what is to be taught and learned
7. *Accountability:* how evidence about team effectiveness is collected
8. *Teacher Efficacy:* benefits to the adults involved

It is essential to effective teaming that issues relating to each of these areas be resolved to the satisfaction of the teacher team members. It is also essential to be persistent and patient, ever mindful that excellent teaming is not ordinarily accomplished quickly. The most notable exemplars of this organizational concept that I have seen have always had two or three years of successful functioning, and they continue to evolve, refining their programs as they grow. Teams grow stronger and increasingly responsive as teacher members learn more about how to collaborate and as students become more fully acclimated. Evolution may pass through a series of phases, growing from initial organization into a community stage, then on to team teaching and self-governance (George, 1982). Studies of especially effective teams have provided valuable insights incorporated in the eight essential issues outlined in the following pages (Arnold & Stevenson, 1998; George & Stevenson, 1989; Erb & Doda, 1989; Larson & LaFasto, 1989).

ESSENTIAL AGREEMENTS FOR INTERDISCIPLINARY TEAMS

Casey Stengel, the legendary baseball player and manager, warned, "If you don't know where you're going, you'll wind up somewhere else." The first rationale for teaming is to establish effective communication, clear understanding, and mutual commitment about shared educational goals and a program calculated to achieve those goals. Interdisciplinary Team Organization is the very best opportunity yet devised for educators to create a distinctive context and climate that will provide the greatest promise for influencing learning of the types described in the previous four chapters.

Teachers responsible for the team must enter their work with clear commitment to a shared vision of what their team can become, and they must contribute their moral support, energy, and ideas for strategies that promise to help them move deliberately toward realization of the vision. Team leaders must be committed to forwarding the team's collective agenda and avoid trying to make the team their own. In order to accomplish this ideal, team members must make specific, detailed plans for their work—a design so encompassing yet precise that the team exists virtually as a school itself within the larger school.

Governance

How Do Team Members Reach Decisions?

Governance is the heart of any viable plan for teaming. In order to agree on policies as varied as a schedule for homework and the composition of parent night presentations, adult teamers must work out an explicit way of making team decisions. Most teamers hope for consensus on every issue, and I have seen many teams whose decisions seem to flow easily, almost effortlessly. However, such a quality of trust in each other's judgment isn't automatic or guaranteed. Where a team is composed of adults whose basic values are dissimilar, a mutually agreed-upon procedure for achieving decisions is especially critical. I know teams that have decided that in anticipation of being deadlocked on an issue, they'll simply take turns deciding. Other teams decide to table decisions about conflicted issues until they can reach consensus. Other teams agree to flip a coin to break deadlocks. Simply voting one's preference may be acceptable to everyone. What is most important for every teamer to remember is that no single decision they will make is more important than their remaining committed to each other and to an agreed-upon governance procedure.

Clarifying individual responsibilities is likewise urgent. Every team must designate a leadership role and agree about who is to fill that role. Even if there are just two members, one must be team leader with specific responsibilities. The leader's primary task is to see to it that the team accomplishes its goals and responsibilities, maintaining the larger, conceptual perspective as well as tracking the nitty-gritty details that are so crucial to daily functioning. The team must meet daily about team business, following an agenda created by the leader with input from colleagues and, as circumstances dictate, the principal. Of similar importance is the role of recorder, the member who promptly produces minutes of team meetings and maintains a written record of team decisions. One teacher member may be designated the parent liaison. Others may also serve specific roles as needed. What is absolutely essential for team effectiveness, however, is daily, agenda-guided team planning sessions where decisions are promptly documented and shared with the principal and other teachers who may not be full-time members but who work with that team's students.

There is no way to guarantee that a team will function effectively and will be a salvation for teachers who would otherwise be isolated from each other. On the other hand, teaming provides by far the best opportunity I know of for educators to collaborate around an educational vision and to see that programs makes sense to students and to themselves. In order for this essential condition of responsive schooling to be achieved, the team plan must first be well thought out, then conscientiously implemented through a decision making process that is supported by each team member.

Team Identity

What Does Our School and Our Team Stand For?

Students in schools without teams usually respond to this question with blank faces and a stammered "What do you mean?" On the other hand, when I visit a well-developed middle level team and ask students the same question, I receive thoughtful explanations of what the team is, what its name means, some explanation of how they do things, and an assortment of characteristics and activities that illustrate their team's identity. During this time of life when youngsters tend to be so preoccupied with their own self-definition, it is especially appropriate to organize them according to teams with clear goals, expectations, standards, and procedures. Excellent teams clearly articulate educationally sound expectations that students can understand and that they can make the basis of their individual choices. Such clarity not only defines the team but may also help youngsters resolve pressing personal concerns as well. Although every person's ultimate self-definition is an ongoing, incremental process that continues well into adulthood, it is prudent for middle level educators to help emerging adolescents achieve degrees of healthy resolution to identity questions through their associations with their team.

Fully developed teams define themselves by an articulated statement of beliefs such as this excerpt of a team philosophy in a handbook prepared for parents by teachers on a multiage team:

> We recognize the uniqueness of each student at [our school] and our responsibility to assist the development of each individual's abilities. We employ conventional and innovative learning activities designed to insure the development of social, intellectual, and living skills necessary to succeed in a changing society.
>
> We further believe that the unique needs of early adolescent learners are best addressed in a multiage environment, one that provides opportunities for children to grow at their own pace while developing valuable interpersonal skills.

Often such a statement of belief is augmented by further value statements such as "a commitment to preserving our environment" or "working to protect endangered species." A pledge, a motto, even a team song may further define what the team advocates and articulate a higher commitment such as those more commonly associated with scouting.

The team's name is probably the foremost outward representation of its values. For example, my last team was known as The Unit, because we wanted our members to see themselves as united: "all for one and one for all." Another team in another school, Uno, teaches essentially the same idea. Sometimes the name conveys a theme, such as Bios and Enterprise. Other names may be couched in mythology, such as Odyssey and Pegasus and Phoenix. A Native American name from the area served by one school, Songadeewin, serves particularly well as a conscious cultural linkage. Still others are selected because they represent important ideas: Paradise, Challenger, Chrysalis, Discovery, Quest, Esprit. Sometimes teams create an acronym that stands for their values: U.P., P.R.I.D.E., B.I.G. Animal names are also popular. The point of emphasis here is that team names embody an identity that goes far beyond simply "the sixth grade team" or "Team 7-C." Identity is further defined through team colors that are used when possible to decorate the team's home base in the school. Some teams choose a mascot, others opt for a logo. T-shirts imprinted with the team's logo in the team's colors further clarify membership. Buttons, stickers, pencils, socks—even lunch boxes in one school I visited—help youngsters identify for themselves and others their primary membership in the school. Simply wearing the trappings of a team doesn't count for very much, however, unless they represent real values and activities.

Rituals and traditional activities further develop team identity. Regular team meetings, celebrations, observing members' birthdays, holiday activities, service projects, and fund-raising activities to help finance team projects are common ways by which the team's identity is further defined. Teachers on one team created a fictional student (Herman Clack) who never actually appeared but who in spirit was part of many team activities. He was often the author of memos and articles in the team newsletter. The Unit team of which I was a teacher member was joined for an entire school year by Jason and Clara, two "spirits of children" who created a memorable intrigue (see this volume's Epilogue). It is through teams' family-like activities that children learn interpersonal and community values most convincingly.

In both academic and social terms, teams also represent identity through expectations and standards. One team that has emphasized journalism produces several publications each year. Each issue is composed of the best writing from current team members, and the accumulated volumes over the years make that team's standards of quality clear to everyone. Another team teaches its commitment to citizenship through a blanket expectation that every team member chooses and renders service to his or her family, school, and community every term. Young adolescents require clear, concrete examples of what is expected of them and what constitutes exemplary performance. Teams have a unique opportunity to provide these examples and to recognize youngsters' emulation of those standards.

Operating Procedures

How Will Our Team Function Day to Day? Week to Week?

The effectiveness of any program is closely related to how well the effort is organized. Decisions having to do with everyday activities should be made at the team level as much as possible. Plans should always be reviewed with administrators, of course, but curricular goals, academic scheduling, and the nitty-gritty details that spell out how the team works should be handled by those people closest to the actual program—the teachers. It is they who will experience the effectiveness of planning, and it is they who understand the context well enough to make adjustments as necessary.

Organizing time is most often the first crucial issue. Time is always finite, and there are always more appealing options that can be accommodated. Ordinarily teachers, students, classes, and activities are organized according to a master schedule that is usually the principal's responsibility. Where people have been reorganized into teams, however, teachers must take on some of that burden, deciding how much of the available time should be apportioned according to their particular curricular goals. The effectiveness of the team leader in managing scarce time and limited resources is extremely important. One very successful team provides two large blocks of at least two hours per day during which their students take minicourses according to their needs in basic academic areas, carry out independent/Orbital studies, and/or do the work associated with integrated interdisciplinary units. What every team needs from the principal is a master schedule that stipulates only those times that must be observed in order that all teams' needs are served. Lunch period and classes that are taught by teachers not on the core team are all that must be scheduled in advance. These classes usually consist of physical education, the arts, and electives.

Essential to successful teaming is time for teachers to create their team plan. Before a new team is launched, a written team plan created by the teachers and evolved from discussion and agreement is absolutely necessary. It is not enough to wing it in good faith that all important decisions can be worked out on the run. These beginning blueprints are best prepared during the summer. They clearly spell out the team members' decisions about how they will function at the beginning of their work together as a team. As they gain experience, their plan will evolve as they see fit. Included in this initial design are agreements about core academic goals, scholarship standards and grading criteria, a schedule for assigning homework and tests, student responsibilities, grouping strategies, plans for dealing with citizenship or disciplinary issues, and so on. The emphasis of the plan must be on reaching agreements about both basic and more peripheral operations of the team in order to ensure a common ground for subsequent individual decisions and implementation.

Successful teaming also requires a common planning period *every day,* during which the teachers address the multifarious details of teaming. Ongoing team business requires that teachers come together to see to it that the academic program is coordinated. Inevitable but unpredictable transient issues also require prompt, united responses. And perhaps most importantly, team members need time to talk about individual students. The best teams make sure that they are informed about each one of their students, not just those who are having academic difficulty or who are disciplinary problems. Much of the credibility of teaming lies in how well each teacher knows each student member of the team (George & Stevenson, 1989).

Communication

How Will Everyone Be Kept Informed?

Accurate communication has long been a problem to schools. Wherever lots of people are involved in almost anything, rumors and misrepresentations will almost certainly abound. Another benefit of teaming is the opportunity to correctly communicate team expectations, activities, and other business to the team's several constituencies.

Within the Team. A compelling feature of working with young adolescents is their readiness for experiencing democracy as a "participation sport." These youngsters are generally very interested in expressing their viewpoints. Building on this interest and energy, responsive educators model the democratic process by ensuring that students experience and enjoy some meaningful authority in their team life. Although classic schemes in which students are represented by elected representatives to a student government are also appropriate, the essence of young adolescents' conceptualization of democracy lies in their ability to talk, to learn about other kids' and teachers' points of view, and to figure out solutions. In my teaching experience with young adolescents on a well-developed team, only occasionally were ideas or disputes resolved by voting. It became much more common that once kids had their say and explored all the options they could imagine, they came to consensus. Furthermore, such resolutions tended to be very conservative and also forgiving. It makes excellent sense for a team to teach democratic values through a town meeting form of government in which students learn how to take turns speaking on an issue, how to use committees to work out details or to propose policies, and how to build consensus (Social Responsibility, 1990). As teams evolve, their design reflects students' involvement in making decisions.

Within the School. The first line of communication outside the team is with the administrators most directly responsible, usually the principal. It is important for that individual to visit team meetings as often as possible, usually once a week. But beyond that face-to-face meeting, it is the team's responsibility to convey its activities to the administration. An excellent way to accomplish this vital function is to keep a daily written record of all team decisions in a central notebook that is shared with the principal at whatever intervals suit his or her schedule. Not only does the notebook document the team decisions, but it illustrates appropriate levels of professional attention and communication.

As already described in treating matters of governance, each daily team meeting should include a written agenda and a written record of decisions. It is also important to see that these written records are distributed to teachers who work with students on the team but who may not be able to attend daily meetings of the core team members: counselors, physical education teachers, specialist teachers, and teacher-advisors who may be administrators, librarians, or other primary staff members in the school. These people have a vested interest in the team, and they need to be kept informed.

Periodic faculty meetings continue to offer a vital opportunity for teams as well as individual teachers to share their work and learn from each other. However, another communication link is essential in schools organized by teams: team leader meetings. At no more than two-week intervals, team leaders should meet with the principal to share both activities and team-related issues. These sessions also provide the important and often necessary context to deal with issues of potential rivalry among teams that can become destructive to the whole school.

With Parents. Parents constitute a huge, usually untapped resource that if cultivated intelligently can extend a team's constructive influence on students. While much more is written about working with parents in Chapter 11, it is important here to point out how very important it is to a team's success that this valuable constituency be kept well informed. In many school communities there is an informal network of parents swapping school-related information on the telephone or over the back fence. A parent advisory committee that meets periodically with the teachers to learn what is going on not only helps defuse rumors but goes a long way toward building trust among adults. The effectiveness of such a committee for the team on which I taught was so great that my teammates and I often felt overrated by our students' parents.

A regularly published team newsletter is also an excellent way to keep this critical constituency informed. The publication can include students' accounts of academic studies and projects, special team activities, results of inquiries, students' essays on issues that they're deliberating, cartoons, and so on. It might also include a calendar of upcoming events, requests for help on projects or field trips, and reminders about school events. The facility of microcomputers, word processing programs, and photocopying technology mean that middle level educators and their students can publish excellent accounts of their school lives every month when it is incorporated in the language arts curriculum.

Occasional publication of a literary magazine or accounts of an IIU also contribute mightily to parents' understanding of their children's school lives. The most essential element is that all of this work is done by students under teacher guidance, and that over a year every student's work appears more than once. Otherwise, such publications merely become another chore and an inappropriate burden on teachers.

One other critical communication vehicle from team members to the parents is periodic evening meetings during which teachers convey team accomplishments and plans. Parents need to understand the team's academic and development agenda, and they enjoy seeing slides or videos of their children in action. I suggest that the focus of the session be broad. Individual conferences aren't practical on such occasions. A prudent team will make a point of offering individual conferences either in person or over the telephone at some other time. It is also advisable that team members take the initiative in telephoning parents about their child's work, especially when the student has done something well and the call is authentic rather than perfunctory.

With the Community. Few middle level teams have targeted the community beyond the school and the parents as an interested constituency. Yet, if we are to cultivate public confidence in our work, teams and individual schools must develop these critical benefactors (Carnegie Corporation, 1989). While public trust probably derives most authentically from personal involvements through apprenticeships or community service projects, one certain avenue for communicating a team's activity is through local media. Feature stories, letters to the editor from students, and invitations to radio and television stations to include students' activities and opinions in their news coverage help put the school before the public in a positive light, and teachers must be savvy and aggressive in developing these forms of communication with their community. For a year my team provided "The Wrong Number," a community service promoting local activities for students from elementary to high school. This brief program of announcements was recorded on a 90- or 120-second tape loop cassette that was played on an answering machine connected to one of our two classroom telephone lines. Not only did the show provide interesting and useful information, it engaged our students in conceiving, producing, and writing brief equivalents of a radio program.

Even with all of these deliberate communication activities in place, outsiders may still charge that "there's a communication problem." Teachers mustn't shrink from this perhaps inevitable accusation—we must acknowledge it as a societal flaw and then carry on to the best of our ability to inform our most critical constituencies about our procedures, accomplishments, and aspirations.

Recognition

What and How Do We Celebrate?

Young adolescents' most frequent descriptor for an experience that has been meaningful to them is *fun*. Adults need to be wary of a tendency to equate *fun* with *trivia*, therefore failing to adequately recognize its underlying meaning and significance. Something that is "fun" is associated with success, is personally affirming, and is usually shared by other kids. There is also an aura of good feeling and good will surrounding experiences they describe as fun—hence the urgency that teachers make celebration a central component in our youngsters' lives as well as in our own.

A spirit of belonging and celebration begins with the decoration of team spaces. Team members need group identification as well as representations of themselves individually through posting of their names and work. The team's identity is spelled out in the physical spaces they inhabit by painting with their chosen colors and depicting the team mascot and logo. Selected noninstitutional furnishings such as a couch, loft, display cabinets, even in a few cases an old bathtub equipped with pillows further personalize their space. Bulletin boards maintained by team members call attention to students' work or teach concepts. Past activities and adventures are documented through photographs and artifacts. One team I know displays an accumulation of twelve years of snapshots of every student member, including his or her name and dates. These details project the value that simply being on this team is in itself good fortune.

Every student has a birthday, and young adolescents appreciate having the recognition that that occasion brings. Consequently, everyone is celebrated. Even those students whose actual birthdays occur in the summer or on weekends or holidays should have surprise birthday celebrations planned by teammates. One team awards students special privileges on their birthdays: permission to go to the front of lines, a class period off, and a daily bonus grade of A in the celebrant's chosen class. Student-of-the-Week or Student-of-the-Month observances are also common in teams. Savvy teachers recognize that these small ways of giving attention and support to every student pay off in the long run. All youngsters want to feel recognized and appreciated by other kids, and these steps constitute a starting place.

The recognition of awards affects many youngsters' motivation to do well. Ribbons, buttons, or certificates that are given out regularly to team members for both academic accomplishment or improvement and contributions to team life are especially prized. Awards may be given at either weekly team meetings or special monthly recognition meetings, so long as everyone on the team is together to take stock of their accomplishments. Commendations should be given so that they ensure initiative or incentive as well as acknowledgment of past accomplishments. One team's most prized award was known simply as EKPTP, for Exemplary Keeper of PRIDE Team Promise. It was not a certificate or pin or trophy but simply the recognition of the student for embodying that team's identity.

Traditions and simple rituals further spell out a team's identity and add importantly to the "fun." When the school climate supports and even encourages individual initiatives, teachers learn to expect originality. Years ago, three students on my team constructed a top hat from black cardboard, decorating it with scraps of costume jewelry and gold braid left over from a Christmas decoration. They suggested that the hat be worn by whoever was in charge of our team meetings. The other students and we teachers quickly agreed, and for the rest of the year on that team, our team meeting moderator always wore the hat as a ritual.

Our team also sponsored an annual Halloween carnival aimed at promoting a good time but also demystifying the holiday for the youngest children in our school. Preparations for that event began early in October, and students' enthusiasm in planning always helped build our team's interpersonal bonds.

Since ours was a three-year multiage team, each year a third of our students left us to go on to high school. We celebrated their presence and contributions at our final team meeting. My co-teachers and I read aloud short pieces we'd written about each graduate, then presented the copy and a modest gift of something we associated with that student, such as a book or record. These occasions of family-like celebration contributed significantly to our team members' congeniality and respect for each other. The celebrations also had a great deal to do with our team's scarcity of disciplinary problems—an attribute of the very best teams (George & Stevenson, 1989).

Yet another way of celebrating team membership is through service projects that teach citizenship and responsibility. Whether the project is a walkathon to raise money for a charity the kids care about or participating in a community cleanup day, a palpable aura of good will abounds when young adolescents and teachers as well as other community members make commitments to each other around a common good. The simple fact of acceptance of children into more adult responsibility and status is in itself a rite of adult recognition and, therefore, celebration.

Note that in this discussion of ways teams celebrate, there has been no mention of parties—perhaps one's first thought about how people celebrate. Parties (much preferred to only dances for this age group) remain a vital, central way of celebrating the good fortune that constitutes team membership. Periodic team or school parties serve the diversity of differences among young adolescents best when they provide a wide variety of activities such as games, contests, and other activities students choose or invent. These parties still provide music and the option of dancing, but the social context is defined more broadly to allow for differences in kids' interests and their readiness for a more purely dance-oriented event. Charades, Ping-Pong tournaments, a paper airplane contest, even a dance contest, and an infinite number of games create an important balance of activities that ensures much greater participation than when the social event is defined more narrowly as simply a dance. The underlying principle for celebrations must be to provide activities for everyone and to recognize everyone's accomplishments, regardless of the specific area of achievement. Every student needs to have successes and be recognized for those successes as often as possible if we're to develop the very best potential of each child.

Curriculum

What and How Do We Learn?

Team collaboration is the only format that has a realistic chance of demonstrating coherence in the school's curricular offerings. Teachers today face an extraordinary array of curricular options that is far more attractive than any that has ever existed. Therefore, the likelihood of disjointed subject matter units that represent an individual teacher's preferences is also greater than it has ever been. The only ways I know to ensure that coherence in light of this condition are two contrasting responses. On one hand, what students are taught is often mandated from above (or beyond) the level of teacher decision making. Subject matter experts rule this domain of curriculum designation, sometimes referred to as "ideological" and "formal curriculum" (Goodlad, 1979). On the other hand, the most comprehensive study of American schooling ever carried out shows that once the classroom door closes, teachers working alone almost exclusively make individual choices about what to teach (Goodlad, 1984). Even the most precisely detailed, carefully sequenced curriculum packages wind up being represented eclectically. After all, teachers reason, "the designers don't know my kids!"

The second and most responsive approach to developing curricular coherence is through a quality of teaming in which the adult members forge a shared curricular plan. When such teams are at their best, teachers agree about some common goals and ways to collaborate in moving toward those goals. There is also critical unanimity about standards—the attributes of excellence teachers agree among themselves to represent. Innovation grows out of teachers' pondering possibilities and creating what they believe are the most fruitful ways to work collectively toward achieving some agreed-upon destinations. And the constant theme in the very best of teams is ongoing concern that every student becomes a successful learner.

Educational organizations include many learned societies that recommend particular concepts, knowledge, and skills distributed across the range of ages and grades that constitute public education. Scope and sequence documents constitute a thoughtful organization of burgeoning fields of knowledge. Yet, on the basis of many years as a classroom teacher and countless formal interviews as well as informal conversations with teachers, I believe these epistemologies only now and then complement the accomplishments of particular classes or teams of what teachers often refer to as "real kids." And that result is predictable, after all, because members of learned subject matter organizations think primarily in terms of a subject matter discipline rather than the developmental nature and needs of young adolescents. The most appropriate curriculum decisions are made by small teams of teachers who are knowledgeable about both their particular group of students and the possibilities as presented by subject matter specialists.

Accountability

How Will Everyone Know What Is Being Accomplished?

This is the evaluation question, and it is twofold. First, it pertains to the learnings and growth of individual students. As already emphasized in the previous chapter, it is necessary that young adolescents learn how to take greater responsibility for their education than was expected when they were younger. By setting personal goals, documenting work and experiences, and conducting periodic self-evaluations, students gain a much fuller sense of what they are accomplishing. Second, the evaluation question refers to the progress of the total team program. Program evaluation provides essential evidence on which subsequent changes can be planned so that the team can try to better accomplish those goals toward which progress appears to be falling short. It is likewise important for teams to document their progress toward goals as part of an ongoing self-evaluation. Insights gained may become the basis for changes designed to bring further improvement, a use generally referred to as *formative evaluation*.

Let's first consider the evaluation function as it relates to individual students. Customarily, each teacher working on a team gives particular attention to portfolios being kept by a subset of the students on that team. Those students who function most marginally are divided equitably among the teacher team members to assure that work is being carried out and accomplishments are being regularly monitored. The teacher-monitor also functions as the team's primary liaison with that student's parents, unless teacher advisors serve as liaison (see Chapter 10). One of the functions carried out during team planning time is to examine folders, exchange observations, and record ideas or conclusions. Those discussions are then conveyed to the student, and a brief annotation is included in his or her folder. My teammates and I learned that when we establish such coordinated attention between home and school, our least responsible students almost always became more conscientious about their schoolwork.

Teachers who have been a part of an active team know very well the challenge of judging the extent to which the team is accomplishing its educational goals. It is common to report that "things are going well" or "they aren't going well" on the basis of day-to-day impressions and anecdotal accounts. However, in order to more comprehensively and objectively judge the team's effectiveness as well as to continually improve the program design, the team teachers will find it prudent to routinely collect data.

Daily attendance information is one of the simplest data forms every team should keep, especially in the early stages of change from a departmental format to teaming. A shift in students' collective attendance patterns may be related to the team's influence. Attendance records for individual students may also signify a student's responsiveness to the team. When a student's attendance has significantly improved, further inquiry about this change usually confirms that being connected to the team has been part of the change. When overall attendance figures show appreciable gains, it is usually reasonable to conclude that team membership and activities have been influential.

"Very best teams" experience a marked decline in disciplinary problems requiring administrative intervention (George & Stevenson, 1989). This is in large part because such teams handle run-of-the-mill behavioral problems internally. Data should be kept on the incidence of significant disciplinary problems in order to understand the extent to which effective teaming may be affecting youngsters' attitudes toward school and, therefore, their willingness to be cooperative. My experience is that where teaming is done well, the only notable disciplinary problems occur with students whose behavioral disorders are more deep-seated than a benefit such as teaming can resolve. The overall effect is a dramatic reduction in the amount of time and energy adults have to give to keeping order among youngsters who are capable of conducting themselves responsibly.

Another data source that can be useful in judging the team's effectiveness is in terms of students' gains on standardized tests. Almost all schools annually employ some form of achievement test that is scored outside the school and reported in terms of national norms. Although it is inappropriate to use nationally normed tests to judge individuals or even a team's achievement, the data do give a general indication of how well student performance compares with that of other students of the same age or grade. When individual tests are administered to estimate a child's academic needs and progress, changes in individual performance (considering the reliability of the test) can be indicators of the extent to which being on the team is affecting performance. In general, students on teams should perform as well or better, as a result of participation on an effective team.

Additional useful information about team effectiveness can be drawn from the students themselves, from off-team teachers such as the librarian and special subject teachers who work with the team's students, and from parents, visitors, and administrators who periodically join the team as participant-observers. Shadow studies described in Chapter 2 present a broad picture of the involvement of a representative student over the course of a day. Several shadow studies can add even more to our understanding of what students are doing. Inquiries in the form of questionnaires constructed specifically around a particular team's goals generate information that helps teachers understand the effectiveness of their design. Inquiries conducted to gather perceptions from parents are also especially helpful.

It isn't possible, of course, to precisely evaluate a phenomenon as multifaceted as an interdisciplinary team in a middle level school. Perhaps a sales team in business can be evaluated in terms of new accounts generated, or a surgical team can be critiqued on the basis of the patient's recovery. Teaming in a school, however, is affected by a great many variables over which the team has no control. Yet, it is possible and appropriate that teams of teachers working together collect the very best information possible in order to gain insights about the viability of the design they have created. Professionalism requires such self-examination.

Teacher Efficacy

What's in It for Teachers?

This is the critical issue of teacher efficacy—the personal payoff for being part of a team. I'm convinced that with few exceptions, teachers earnestly desire to find meaning and personal enjoyment in their work. Over the thirty years I have been a middle level educator, I have met very few teachers who didn't seem to care whether or not their careers were personally satisfying, fulfilling a need to make differences in kids' lives. Those few teachers seemed to have shut out any possibilities for their own renewal and growth through collaborative innovation; they seemed content to bide their time until retirement. On the other hand, the overwhelming majority of teachers I've known and with whom I have worked on teaming issues place a great deal of value upon having close, mutually supportive professional relationships that lead to partnerships in creative teaching. They value opportunities for shared work with fellow teachers, and they appear to draw courage if not reassurance from each other.

At its very best, teaming effects a synergy that enables the participating teachers to transcend ordinariness. I know teams of teachers whose collective work is of considerably greater consequence for their students and for themselves than their individual work was before they were a team. I also know teams in name only—groups of teachers who show several of the trappings of teaming but whose relationships remain essentially independent—each one doing his or her own task alone, yet in the company of others. Teaming at its very best helps adults grow into a closer coterie of colleagues and friends, bound together by mutual respect and a common purpose. As opposed to working more or less in isolation from other teachers, collaboration and reciprocal support become the rule in relationships among fully teamed teachers.

The advantages of teaming to teachers rest squarely on the issue of trust. Where there is a climate of trust, teachers collaborate, communicate openly, and rise to their challenges together. Four themes explain why trust fosters teamwork (Larson & LaFasto, 1989):

1. Trust allows team members to stay problem focused.
2. Trust promotes more efficient communication and coordination.
3. Trust improves the quality of collaborative outcomes.
4. Trust leads to compensating, that is, one team member picks up the slack when another falters.

It is axiomatic that professionals need to believe in their work, knowing that what they do is making a difference in the lives of others. When the evidence is to the contrary, the likelihood of redirection is greater with a team where daily discussions about the efficacy of the program is in order. There is also the benefit that two (or more) heads are better than one. When things are going well, everyone recognizes it and benefits. When things are not going as well as intended, a team responds quickly and collaboratively to reconsider their expectations or the strategies being used. Confidence as well as trust grow from a context that truly embodies the promise of "all for one and one for all."

PARTNER TEAMING

Although two- and three-teacher teams have not been uncommon during my career in middle level education, the most common form of team organization has consisted of four to five teachers and 100 to 125 students. More recently, however, versions of what I have elected to dub as "partner teams" are making an important new presence (see *Partner Teaming* video, NMSA, 1995; Stevenson, 1996). The central feature of these teams is the presence of a palpable state of partnership among the three crucial constituencies: teachers, students, parents—hence, "partner teams." While the vision, organization, and administration rest primarily on the two or three teachers involved, the team meeting is the rootstock of a team governance process that engages students in making real decisions about selected policies, curriculum goals, activities and responsibilities that affect them. In effect, students have a significant say in *democratic* education, and they grow in their understanding and commitment to democratic processes. Further, they appear to be increasingly more willing to trust their teachers' advice and decisions.

Here are some further distinctive features of these partner teams:

- Two or three teachers and 40–75 students work together up to 90% of the school day.
- Teachers choose each other, and students and their parents choose the team.
- Students usually stay on the team two or three years (multigrade).
- Teachers share mathematics, writing, and reading instruction.
- Direct instruction is balanced by integrated and independent studies.
- Team identity is distinguished by high standards, traditions, and publications.
- Students learn to define and achieve personal learning goals and team goals.
- Parents often participate in instructional programs.

One of the most easily available and best-known versions of a highly successful partner team is Watershed, carefully detailed by Mark Springer, one of the two teachers (1994). This remarkable team's vision is built around five values referred to as their "5 Cs": Cooperation, Commitment, Courage, Caution, and Caring. Utilizing an integrated curriculum approach, they investigate in remarkable depth one major watershed for an academic year. Core scholarly skills and insights from the separate disciplines are clearly evident in the high quality of work they produce. Most compelling of all, however, is the responsibility and accountability students demonstrate toward their work and each other. Were it not for their young adolescent appearance, one could believe these youngsters had already advanced to adulthood.

Additional successful partner teaming is reflected in Alexander's account (1994) of the curriculum integration initiatives of two Maine teachers, Kathy McAvoy and Dennis

Carr. By convincingly conveying their trustworthiness through shared decision making about important academic choices, these teachers have seen students in small rural communities grow in understanding, scholarship, and sophistication about forming and addressing important questions. It is increasingly clear that there are middle level educators working closely together with each other, their students, and their students' parents to achieve notable gains.

One single advantage of these teams that should not be overlooked is size. There appears to be an optimal size for a close, mutually supportive community of students and teachers, and that size appears to be closer to 50 than 100 students and two or three adults than four or five. Concomitants of size are efficiency of planning, communication, and program continuity and coherence. All three constituencies—especially the students—understand the educational goals, programs, and expectations and how they can be successful within it. Especially notable to the casual observer are expressions of confidence, respect, and trust among the three groups. Partner teaming offers special opportunities for teachers to have enduring impact on themselves, each other, their students, and the families in their community.

THE CRUCIAL ROLE OF TEAM LEADER

> One thing I've learned is how to be a good leader, which is not dominating the group but leading the group in a way that everybody adds ideas and makes input in an organized way. That's the way to get the job done.
>
> *Sarah, age 13*

Sarah learned about being a good leader from the example of the team leader and teachers on her team, which operated smoothly with effective and efficient leadership. Her teachers also recognized the opportunity to teach students how to lead successfully. I know of no more convincing argument for team leadership than to witness those insights and qualities as they are manifested in students' understanding of "how to get the job done." Every team must have a teacher designated as the team leader, even when there are only two teachers, as is common in partner teams. Sometimes leaders are appointed by the principal or elected by teammates, or the role may be assumed voluntarily with colleagues' consent. Often teams decide to rotate leader responsibilities, each person serving as team leader for a semester or year. After all, some aspects of effective leadership may be tedious. What is crucial in designating a team leader is to assure that particular responsibilities appropriate to the leadership function are accomplished. Some of those duties are

1. *Leader and spokesperson*
   - administer the school philosophy and oversee the team plan
   - prepare daily meeting agenda; lead discussion and decision making, involving every member
   - oversee team budget
   - support/affirm individual teachers and utilize team-building/morale activities as needed
   - seek consensus and resolve interpersonal conflicts
   - nurture a climate that respects all teachers and students

2. *Liaison with administration and other teams*
   - meet regularly (weekly, if possible) with principal and other team leaders for communicating all team plans and activities
   - coordinate information exchange between team members and teacher advisors
   - respond to information requests from principal, central office
   - coordinate school calendar and activities affecting all teams
   - ensure that accurate and up-to-date team records are maintained

3. *Curriculum coordination*
   - coordinate curriculum implementation and evaluation
   - ensure continuous assessment and evaluation of student progress
   - monitor calendar, daily scheduling, and grouping affected by curriculum
   - oversee coordination of curriculum with team goals and/or mission
   - assure regular meetings with parents to focus on team and student progress

Additional possibilities for team leader responsibilities include the more expansive "establishing a vision of the future" and "unleashing the energy and talents of contributing members" (Larson & LaFasto, 1989, pp. 119–129) as well as much more businesslike details like "informing special area teachers of team activities" and "providing assistance for substitute teachers" (Merenbloom, 1991, pp. 112–117). The essential idea in all of this discussion is that from the outset team members should conceptualize their team plan and various needs so comprehensively that various crucial roles will emerge inductively. In the meantime, all members need to invest themselves earnestly in a spirit of collaboration, sharing ideas and the multifarious responsibilities of effective teaming, remembering that they become true colleagues as they "work together, debating about goals and purposes, coordinating lessons, observing and critiquing each other's work, sharing successes and offering solace, with all the triumphs of their collective efforts far exceeding the summed accomplishments of their solitary struggles" (Johnson, 1990, p. 148).

TOWARD BECOMING AN EFFECTIVE TEAM MEMBER

Whether or not one person should trust another is a decision made on a personal assessment of some prior experience. There are attributes of character manifest in day-to-day interactions that invite trust, and there are others that make it difficult to confidently rely on other people. Since successful teaming relies so heavily on the trust that team members have for each other, it is appropriate to examine some of the human characteristics that contribute to our judgments of trustworthiness.

Commitment to Each Other and the Team Agenda

It is very rare for the several teachers on a team to agree about everything. What is common on ideal teams, however, is that the teachers support all aspects of the team agenda, regardless of what may be one individual's personal indifference or preference toward a particular activity or detail. Loyalty to each other's priorities regardless of self-interest invites trust, because it demonstrates personal and professional maturity—hence, trustworthiness.

Compromise

Few concepts are as vital to the progress of any collective effort as compromise. Although most of the decisions made in a team will derive from consensus, some fundamental differences of philosophy or interpretation may arise. Working for compromise becomes the order of such days, and every teacher can and should look for compromise solutions. When there is an impasse, delay a final decision until compromise can be worked out.

Initiative

Volunteering for those team-related duties or details often referred to as "dirty work" shows one's readiness to work for the team's success. This kind of initiative sets an example and stimulates others to be enterprising. Trust is encouraged when a colleague offers genuine interest beyond just the work of the team. Whether sharing a meal, remembering a special event in a colleague's life, or offering to help on a task out of school, such bids express respect and extend friendship.

Dependability

Whatever the collaboration may be—in business, on an athletic team, within a family—one who consistently delivers what was promised earns the respect and trust of those who depend upon him or her. It is essential, therefore, that whatever task one is given or agrees to take, the result is delivered on time and embodies the expected quality. Unexpected events occur, and sometimes tasks turn out to be more complex than originally conceived. These are occasions for the extraordinary effort that stands as evidence of one's commitment to the team and each other.

Patience and Tenacity

A close friend and fellow teacher has worked very hard for several years trying to teach me how to hit golf balls properly. Alas, my failures vastly outnumber an occasional successful stroke. Yet he persists, exuding confidence that I can become his golfing peer. He emulates the qualities of patience and determination I have learned to prize in teammates. When people accept each others' limitations or deficiencies and adjust their efforts without giving up on the goals, eventual success is certain.

Collegiality

Virtually all of the most outstanding teachers I have known on teams have made distinctive efforts to be a trustworthy colleague not just to their teammates but also to off-team colleagues. They understand that preserving mutually positive relationships with teachers on other teams and with teachers who have all-team responsibilities is an investment in everyone's welfare. Occasionally team members look only to each other for collegial friendships, and their ties appear exclusive to others, breeding destructive rivalry and distrust.

Sense of Humor

Four of us who work closely together met for breakfast recently, and by chance a couple of us were in something of a zany mood. One particularly witty colleague was in exceptional form—even for him. Fortunately our agenda was brief, because we spent most of the hour swapping anecdotes and laughing. Near the end of the day we met again, and each of us commented about what a wonderful day it had been. We agreed that the breakfast session had a lot to do with our individual frames of mind as we approached our day's work. We also realized how fortunate we are not only to work together but to enjoy each other, and we resolved to preserve the shared humor that is our team's glue. And a precious bonus is that it benefits our students to see us enjoying each other, sharing our good humor with them as well.

WHEN TEAMS FAIL

Casey Stengel, something of an expert on teaming in baseball, is reported to have responded to a question about how to build a successful team by saying, "Getting good players is easy. Getting them to play together—that's the hard part."

Failure in teaming almost always rests on one or more of several factors. One factor is failure of an administrator to adequately empower the team. Little is accomplished if a team is formed without the requisite authority, time, and supportive resources that must follow. It is critical to effective teaming that principals trust teachers to make wise decisions and then demonstrate consistent support for that authority.

A second and major cause of failure in teams is a failure of trust. According to a major study of successful teams in a variety of professions, trust derives from a climate that includes four essential elements:

1. *Honesty:* integrity, no lies, no exaggerations
2. *Openness:* willingness to share and receptivity to others' ideas
3. *Consistency:* predictable behaviors and responses
4. *Respect:* treating people with dignity and fairness

(Larson & LaFasto, 1989, p. 85)

It is problematic to put together a group of adults who will simply like each other, much less preserve these interpersonal qualities necessary to develop an enduring trust. Teaming teachers must be especially alert to see that differences in personal tastes, lifestyles, politics, and so on don't prevent their creating a professional context built upon mutual trust. When teachers have not been accustomed to working as closely on a daily basis as is necessary for a team to thrive, it is easy for interpersonal differences to become magnified and divisive.

Another significant cause of difficulties in teaming has to do with how the adult team members perceive themselves and identify themselves. For example, a team member says, "I'm a seventh grade math teacher." If that is the limit of that teacher's self-definition, the other team members will have to compensate for that colleague. Seeing oneself as a team member first and subject matter specialist second is vital to the team's success. Working successfully on an interdisciplinary team requires commitment and responsibilities that go far beyond the traditional departmental specializations familiar in junior high and high schools.

There are often situation-specific hazards to successful teaming, but almost everything can be overcome by teachers whose active commitment to a vision of collaboration for the welfare of their students and themselves is professionally strong and mature. It is through such teaming that we teachers can find more satisfying relationships with our peers. Just as our students need to feel safe at school, belonging to a program and people that are worthwhile, we too have the same needs. After all, one of the greatest things teachers have to teach is their humanity, as revealed in how they work with and relate to other people. Interdisciplinary Team Organization is vastly superior to any other way I have seen students and adults organized in a middle level school.

OBSERVATIONS AND STUDENT INTERNSHIPS

Teacher education apprenticeships traditionally have been arranged so that an individual student is paired with one experienced teacher. When such an arrangement includes continuing, candid communication between the intern and the mentor, the student learns a great deal about that teacher's technique, style, and values. I have witnessed many student teachers patterning themselves according to the professional manner and pedagogy of their cooperating teacher. No matter how valuable such an experience may be, such an arrangement limits a student's opportunity to observe and reflect on the styles of several teachers.

Apprenticeships providing the most comprehensive opportunity to learn about teaching occur when the apprentice is attached to an interdisciplinary team that functions effectively. Observation and learning from the professional discourse that occurs during daily planning periods ensures that the apprentice benefits from a variety of points of view—not just the opinion of a single teacher. Linkages between goals and procedures can be seen more clearly as the apprentice sees team members working collaboratively toward common purposes. Although the apprentice is attached to a team rather than a single individual, it is important that he or she work closely on an assortment of projects with each teacher over the course of the internship. Realizations of just how multifarious the role of a responsive teacher must be are guaranteed when the apprenticeship occurs in an effective team where the teachers welcome the opportunity to contribute to the education and development of a new colleague.

Supporting Activities

Preliminary: Organize into two-, three-, or four-member Simulation Interdisciplinary Teams (SITs). Provide basic information about the young adolescent students for each SIT: number of students, ages/grades, male/female ratio, brief characterization of the community (if other than from the immediate one). Note: These data may be obtained from actual teams operating in neighboring schools.

1. In accordance with the questions discussed in this chapter, each SIT must articulate at least three overarching goals for the team. Then, create a team notebook that includes a table of contents and a negotiated plan for deciding each of the questions raised in the body of this chapter.

2. Visit a school organized by teams. Study in advance whatever descriptive material may be available about one team. Working as a shadow team, arrange for one of your own

SIT members to shadow one of the teachers on the team throughout the day. Share your observations about matches between goals and observed activities. Ask students selected at random what the team stands for and how it works. Create a list of questions to explore with the teachers as follow-up.

3. Each SIT member is responsible for learning the rationale and content of the scope and sequence recommendations of the following organizations:

NCTE   National Council of Teachers of English

NCSS   National Council for the Social Studies

NSTA   National Science Teachers Association

NCTM   National Council for Teachers of Mathematics

Design one curriculum unit that integrates selected components of each learned association's scope and sequence recommendations.

4. Identify nonschool teams in your community in industry, commerce, architecture, medicine, public service, or professional sports. Interview a representative member to explore characteristics of the team when it is working at its best and worst. What parallels are there between these examples of functioning teams and those in your school? your SIT?

REFERENCES

Alexander, W. M. (1994). *Student-oriented curriculum: Asking the right questions.* Columbus, OH: National Middle School Association.

Arnold, J. F., & Stevenson, C. (1998). *Teachers' teaming handbook.* Fort Worth: Harcourt Brace Jovanovich. (1998)

Carnegie Corporation. (1989). *Turning points: Preparing American youth for the 21st century.* Washington, DC: Carnegie Council on Adolescent Development.

Dickinson, T. S., & Erb, T. O. (Eds). (1997). *We gain more than we give: Teaming in middle schools.* Columbus, OH: National Middle School Association.

Erb, T. O. (1987). What team organization can do for teachers. *Middle School Journal, 18*(6), 3–6.

Erb, T. O., & Doda, N. M. (1989). *Team organization: Promise—practices and possibilities.* Washington, DC: National Education Association.

George, P.S. (1982). Interdisciplinary team organization: Four operational phases. *Middle School Journal, 13*(3), 10–13.

George, P. S., & Stevenson, C. (1989). The "very best teams" in "the very best schools" as described by middle school principals. *TEAM, 3*(5), 6–14.

Goodlad, J. I., & Associates. (1979). *Curriculum inquiry: The study of curriculum practice.* New York: McGraw-Hill.

Goodlad, J. I. (1984). *A place called school.* New York: McGraw-Hill.

Johnson, S. M. (1990). *Teachers at work: Achieving success in our schools.* New York: Basic.

Kerble, M. (1988). Incorporating special education teachers into teams. *Middle School Journal, 19*(4), 18–19.

Larson, C. E., & LaFasto, F. M. J. (1989). *TeamWork: What must go right/what can go wrong.* Newbury Park, CA: Sage.

Merenbloom, E. Y. (1991). *The team process: A handbook for teachers.* Columbus, OH: National Middle School Association.

Partner Teaming (video). (1995). Columbus, OH: National Middle School Association.

Plodzik, K. T., & George, P. S. (1989). Interdisciplinary team organization. *Middle School Journal, 20*(5), 15–17.

Social responsibility [Special issue]. (1990, November). *Educational Leadership, 48*(3).

Springer, M. (1994). *Watershed: A successful voyage into integrative learning.* Columbus: OH: National Middle School Association.

Stevenson, C. (1996, January). Partner teaming. *VAMLEFocus 1*(5).

Chapter 10

Advocacy and Alliances through Advisories

○ *What do I have to offer these young people?*

○ *What activities can I do with them?*

○ *How can I show my concern? My trustworthiness?*

○ *Will they take me seriously?*

○ *Will they like me? Allow me to help? Depend on me?*

○ *How can I be a friend, yet still be their teacher?*

Nell Noddings argues clearly and convincingly that in its response to existing social problems, our traditional paradigm of schooling is "intellectually and morally inadequate for contemporary society." She suggests that schools should be organized around "themes of care" (1992, p. 173). Fortunately, middle level educators not only have recognized the veracity of her synopsis but have taken initiatives to more effectively guide and support their students. Although many middle level educators have argued that this level of schooling should be embedded in a guidance philosophy, the single most notable organizational feature that has emerged is a teacher-based program most commonly referred to as teacher advisories, which are common in exemplary middle level schools. An advisory is an organized group of one adult and a dozen or so kids that serves as the students' first line of affiliation with their school. The group meets at least once daily, usually for the first 20 minutes or so of the day, and they often collaborate on projects at school or get together for outings away from school. Every student and staff member in the school is an advisory member, and the program is recognized as one of the most tangible evidences of the school's commitment to caring about and being responsive to kids' needs.

The purposes are manifold, however: to ensure that each student is known well at school by at least one adult who is that youngster's advocate (the advisor), to guarantee that every student belongs to a peer group, to help every student find ways to be successful within the academic and social options the school provides, to promote communication and coordination between home and school. More than any other feature of responsive schooling for young adolescents,

The irreducible essence of teacher advisory is a caring commitment to kids.

From a student:

There were times when I would stumble and fall. These were the times when a person treasured in my heart forever would be present—my adviser. In his own special and unique way, he would encourage me never to lose sight of my goal and to press on to the top. He taught me to believe in myself; to believe that I have the destiny, the innate ability, to become all I expect in life. My adviser became more than an inspiration; he became a friend. If it weren't for people such as my adviser, I might never have picked myself up after one of my falls, and I might have lost sight of my vision.

(Dyer, 1990, p. 2)

From a teacher:

My first advisory was made up entirely of 8th grade girls. They personified diversity; one summered in France with wealthy relatives; one slept on her grandparents' sofa rather than live with her manipulative mother; another struggled with an alcoholic father. They came to our union school from five different towns, and although they differed greatly in academic ability, they became good friends during the year. All were very young and relatively cloistered for their age, and in them I saw much of my own early adolescence. They came to treat me like a friend, even giving me a baby shower before Anna was born. I felt comfortable with them. I'd read passages to them from books I was reading, and I'd try to help them with science projects or a history quiz. There were algebra problems to unravel or school rules to discuss. Once we'd warmed up to each other, concerns about boys came to the fore. From local issues and national headlines they frequently wanted to talk about AIDS, drugs, alcoholism, and poverty. We talked about differences between rape and seduction, the risk of reading too many Harlequin romances or, for that matter, too much of any one thing. We talked about how to become close to a boy and still keep self-respect, how to diplomatically help a teacher make a boring class more fun. Topics came up such as mental retardation, the effects of divorce on a family, how to stay safe from a "funny uncle," how to choose a career, what to do with free time. Some days no one had much to say; other days were filled with chatter, laughter, rage, or tears.

Inland country women, I believe, need intermittent contact with the ocean. It is a natural, feminine link that urges periodic rejuvenation, as described in Anne Morrow Lindbergh's *Gift from the Sea*. Perhaps the link is even more basic, a primitive echo of our life eons ago as amphibians. Whatever impels us to the ocean, it also causes us to dream while we are there, to aspire, to envision new and wonderful possibilities. It dawned on me that these girls, so exuberant and idealistic, so vulnerable, idiosyncratic, and needy of validation could use a little dream-fodder. They were late bloomers. An ambitious, crazy trip might convince them of their worth, to believe in themselves as well as lots of possibilities for them. They unanimously agreed—an overnight camping trip to a distant and exotic spot: Cape Cod. Immediately they plunged themselves into planning, volunteering equipment, labor, provisions, and even their parents! I was amazed. The girls *wanted* their parents to share the adventure with them, and the four parents who joined us were a delight.

A stormy beach front presented an exciting encounter with wild surf, where my Green Mountain girls waded waist-deep. Meeting boys raised urgent questions; how far can one go to express interest without it being embarrassing? How do you know if strangers' gestures of friendliness are safe? And as the weather changed, how do we keep a campfire going and cook meals in the rain? Inevitably the girls argued over petty things, cried, hashed out old jealousies and slights, sulked, comforted one another and were reconciled. A walk through Provincetown offered colorful people, fishing wharves, the Pilgrim monument and museum, boutiques and new foods along with new puzzles.

How did such different kinds of people come to live here? How did that fisherman get so wrinkled? How is Portuguese pastry made? Are gay people dangerous, or like us? What can I get for my dad's birthday with $10? If we sailed from here, would we land in Europe? Through each other's eyes, the girls were seeing themselves as valuable, unique individuals. And not only was a link with the ocean being forged for these young rural women, but also links among themselves.

(Susan Rump, teacher-advisor in Thetford, Vermont, personal correspondence)

From a parent:
We started worrying about Walter, Jr., when he was in kindergarten. He never seemed to understand how to play with other children. Later in elementary school he had even more social problems, and his teachers said that he needed our help learning social skills. We tried to teach him how to get along with other kids, but it didn't help. Maybe it was because we're older parents and he is our only child. We even had him tested in 4th grade, but no one could figure out what was wrong. Then he went to the 6th grade in middle school where Mr. Smith was his adviser. All the kids liked Mr. Smith, but he took a special interest in Wally. That was two years ago. His dad and I can't get over how much he's changed in that short time. Now he has lots of friends, and he seems to be more confident, too. Mr. Smith deserves all the credit. He worked magic with Walter, Jr. My husband and I believe what he did probably saved our son's life.

(Anonymous parent, personal correspondence)

These excerpts testify to the value of teacher advisories as experienced by people representing each of the major constituencies in a middle level school. On the several occasions when I have visited the Shoreham–Wading River Middle School for a couple of days, I have informally inquired of students I meet randomly, "If your school was going to be moved to another place and you could take only one thing, what would it be?" Every answer but one has been the same: "Teacher Advisory." My subsequent question, "Why?" has provoked a host of testimony and anecdotes about how "my advisor cares about me . . . helps me . . . knows how to talk to my teachers," and so on. It is clear that both the spirit and purposes of this teacher-based guidance system are valued. There's also ample evidence that students in this exemplary school reciprocate these values in their interpersonal relationships in general (Lipsitz, 1984).

PERSONAL NEEDS OF YOUNG ADOLESCENTS

The developing interpersonal needs of young adolescents have already been described in general terms in Chapter 4. Through the fraternal atmosphere that can be developed within small groups such as advisories, educators have their best chance to successfully respond to many of those needs. Regardless of a youngster's academic or athletic interests, teachers can be absolutely certain that every child needs to have mutually satisfying relationships with other people, adults as well as peers. There is no guarantee, of course, that the specific mix of personalities in an advisory will fulfill the needs of everyone involved, but we should have confidence that when we commit ourselves to searching out feasible matches, few if any children will remain alienated from school. Kids recognize when teachers are listening authentically to them, looking for ways to help them have a better time being a student. And the fact that the effort is being made is persuasive in itself, whether or not that student has things exactly as he or she might want them.

Adolescents who are high achievers in academics and other school activities demonstrate some notable specific behavioral attributes worthy of advisory teachers' incorporation. Some of those behaviors that are suited to an advisory curriculum are shown by students who

- spend significant time in conversation with their parents and other adults
- have learned to do some things very well—computers, carpentry, sewing, etc.
- have regular behavioral patterns, including plans to do specific things
- engage in constructive learning besides homework—hobbies, games, music, etc.
- describe themselves as doing things that are important and worthwhile
- participate in activities that extend their opportunities to read and write

(Clark, 1986)

RESILIENCY IN ADOLESCENTS

Presumably everyone knows or knows of people who have overcome formidable adversities and who continue to be caring, productive, responsible adults. Some of the heroes and heroines we teach our children to emulate exemplify these qualities: Helen Keller, Franklin D. Roosevelt, and Martin Luther King, to name just three. Many of us who teach have also observed as well among our students a mature determination to overcome particular adversities. We know kids who have overcome physical illnesses or family stresses that might easily have overwhelmed them. Jamie Rogers was born with multiple birth defects, and her childhood was punctuated by a series of major corrective surgical procedures, the last of which was a leg amputation. During the sixth, seventh, and eighth grade years that Jamie and I were together on our team, I marveled at her courage and determination. I'll never forget her successfully imploring her father to fashion an ice skate for her prosthesis so she could be part of the lunch-time skating her classmates enjoyed.

An important body of research describes the qualities of character that Jamie and other young people sometimes demonstrate as *resilience*. Children who are able to deal with sometimes immense challenges in their personal lives while continuing to develop as caring, responsible, successful students show high degrees of resiliency. Furthermore, we have learned that these qualities are important to the success of *all* young people as they make their way through the complexities of adolescence, whether or not their experience includes the kind of circumstances Jamie and others must endure. In brief, all of us—kids and adults—benefit from developing high degrees of personal resilience.

Fortunately, research has also shown that personal resilience can be taught and learned by young people. Strengths that foster resiliency in youth include insight, independence, relationships, initiative, creativity, humor, and morality (Wolin & Wolin, 1993). What more perfect school context could there be than the teacher advisory for cultivating individual awareness and personal growth? Consider these teacher advisory values as adapted from strategies by others' recommendations for assuring positive outcomes for children:

1. Show all students in the advisory caring, support, listening, and encouragement; make the advisory an authentic source of unconditional commitment and love.

2. Develop high citizenship expectations and high but achievable standards for academic success.

3. Assure every student with frequent opportunities to contribute to the advisory (Benard, 1991).

4. Develop close interpersonal bonds among students and between them and adults

5. Teach survival skills such as how to say "no," how to make friends, decision making, and mediating conflict between or with others (see Chapter 6).

6. Negotiate and enforce consistently advisory rules and expectations.

(Hawkins, et al., 1992)

Young adolescents are the targets of society's often highly confused and mixed messages. Equally common are family circumstances that fail to either affirm the individual or provide solid guidance in the choices and decisions kids face. They need help—our help. I have found no better context for providing that kind of support at school than a well-conceived, conscientiously provided teacher advisory program. Alas, too few middle level schools have developed their full potential in this domain of our professional responsibilities.

TEACHERS' NEEDS

In my experience, teachers who have really loved their particular subject matter and whose dominant motivation is to teach that subject matter choose secondary schools or higher education. On the other hand, those who deliberately choose to work with young adolescents do so because they are drawn to the youngsters themselves (Carr, 1990). These teachers derive personal satisfaction and meaning in their work from associating with the curiosity, energy, and idealism of these children. They report personal satisfaction and a sense of contribution from witnessing kids' healthy changes and growth. The advisory is a context perfectly configured for enabling teachers to observe a few kids at close range and to be a particularly constructive influence in their development. My teacher education students who intern in schools that include advisories express more eagerness for that role than for any other aspect of being a middle level teacher. It is that particular program innovation that appears to hold the greatest potential for them to make a difference in kids' lives—their most frequently expressed reason for being a middle level teacher.

What Are the Goals of a Teacher Advisory?

It is not uncommon to hear murmurings of discontent from at least a few teachers in schools considering adopting an advisory program for the first time. Naysayers tend to be teachers with the most years of experience, although the most enthusiastic supporters may also come from the school's most experienced staff. It is important to remember that as teacher education students, they were not prepared for such responsibility. Advisory in middle level schools is an innovation that has come along more recently, and its goals must be clearly stated. There also must be a strong support system for all teacher advisors, especially in the initial stages of implementation. The following advisory goals are appropriate for every middle level school.

Advocacy

The most evident and certain attribute of an advisory is the teacher's advocacy for the students in his or her group. In this setting, the teacher takes the student under his or her wing, assuring that the youngster has the adult's attention and commitment of support. One teacher friend made it clear when she asserted to her advisees at their first meeting, "You're all mine, and I'm all yours! Whatever it takes for you to succeed and be happy, I'll deliver! No one here is going to fail." She couldn't guarantee success, of course, but she could and did assure her kids about her confidence in them and in herself. And she did deliver indeed, as is evident in her Advisory Activity Report for the 1989–90 school year, included later in this chapter. What is significant here is that in what she said and demonstrated, the message of "advocacy" was fundamental.

Academic Guidance and Support

What makes an advisory a distinctly educational innovation is the way it helps students become more successful in their academic work. Teacher-advisors continually monitor their kids' performance in their schoolwork by both group discussion and private discussion, examining work samples, helping to clarify confusions or uncertainties, mediating with other teachers on behalf of an advisee who is having difficulties, arranging tutoring or peer instruction as needed, and so on. The essential idea here is that the advisory ensures that no student slips through the cracks in terms of academic work for want of attention and interest from a responsible adult.

Belonging

Perhaps no other word has been used more than *belonging* in reference to a primary social need of young adolescents. Every youngster needs to be connected to other kids, and although team membership can help fulfill some of this concern, there remains a need for an even smaller, more familiar association like that provided through an advisory. Regardless of other group affiliations individual students may enjoy, such as a sports team, scouts, or a clique of self-chosen buddies, the advisory at its best stands as a certain resource for every student. It guarantees that every student has a peer group for more casual and serendipitous friendships, and it assures that regardless of how things are going in the rest of a youngster's school life, the advisor is "always there for me."

Communication

A critical three-way communication network should be established and maintained in every middle level school. That network connects the student, the adults inside the school who are responsible for the student, and the responsible adults outside the school. Advisory is easily the most dependable way of making sure that good communication occurs. Where schools are organized according to departments and home rooms, teacher–student odds work against this quality of communication. Advisories, on the other hand, make sure that advisors are responsible for a manageable number: a dozen or so students whom they see daily. Good communication begins within the advisory group among students and with the advisor. From that foundation the teacher is able to model standards of communication *outside* the advisory, especially with other teachers and with parents.

Administration

A necessary dimension of the life of every school is what may sometimes seem to be an un-ending assortment of administrative details. Daily attendance records, legal forms, an-nouncements, reciting the Pledge of Allegiance, lunch counts, medical excuses, bus route changes, and so on are important but mundane details that need to be handled as effi-ciently and unobtrusively as possible. My teacher friends tell me that they prefer anything else to the dreaded announcements and interruptions that come over the intercom system. The advisory becomes the context for these details in much the same way that home rooms function in high schools. The difference is that because the advisory emphasizes developing thorough acquaintance with a small number of students, handling these de-tails can provide additional insights about individual children's life patterns and possible needs.

Ownership

It is a given that the teacher advisor must be strongly connected to both the concept and to a particular group of students. It is likewise crucial that students feel strongly connected to and responsible for their advisory. One eighth grade advisor in her first year told me that her advisees didn't take the program seriously the first months of the year; they seemed to be just going through the motions of advisory. The preplanned advisory curriculum that she had been using wasn't apparently authentic enough to induce them to invest themselves. When the teacher decided to abandon packaged materials in favor of what the students saw as "real things," the mood changed. In short order the group decided to adopt an elementary student, first as a Christmas project and later from the perspective of big brothers and sisters. One experienced teacher advisor advises, "Make TA about them. Our most stimulating conversations happen when they begin with them. Most students just want someone to ask them about themselves. Make sure to include everyone as often as possible" (Myers & Stevenson, 1993, p. 20).

Recognition

As this book has emphasized repeatedly, recognition is essential to the good life for young adolescents. Advisory is a context where the adult in charge can be sure that every advisee is commended and celebrated in assorted ways. Whether it is observing a birthday, recogniz-ing improvement in spelling, or calling attention to a student's part in a play or on the bas-ketball team, the advisory assures that recognition and celebration come to every student, over and over. And where teachers model recognition well, students also recognize these values and reciprocate them in their relationships with each other. In short, adults can change the character and atmosphere of their school through active, responsive advisories.

Citizenship

If educators assume that children learn citizenship by engaging in active, responsible par-ticipation in the affairs of their community, then an advisory goal might so stipulate. Stu-dents would learn what it means to be a responsible participant in our democratic society through firsthand participation. We know how much youngsters need and value opportunities to do things that are worthwhile in the sight of others. What better school opportunity is there, then, for adults and students to collaborate in concrete ways to contribute to the public welfare as well as learn what it means and feels like to be a responsible citizen, even at ages ten to fourteen?

What Is Essential for Advisories to Function Successfully?

No feature of middle level school organization is more vulnerable to teachers' dispositions than a teacher advisory program. Their positive, proactive attitudes and behaviors are essential to ensure that children will be supported in the ways they most need adult advocacy and support. While only a few preconditions are essential for advisories to function successfully, the absence of any one of them constitutes a serious threat to successful implementation.

Teacher Commitment

Regardless of everything that can be done to establish and maintain an effective advisory program, it will fail unless those people who will serve as advisors commit themselves to the program. More than one effort has failed as a result of one or more teachers' indifference and, I'm sad to say, instances when a teacher or two deliberately sabotaged a nascent effort, apparently because they interpreted the work as outside their contractual obligations or because they didn't want the bother. Consequently, it is vital that teachers participate from the beginning in learning about this innovation through reading, visiting schools where advisories are already in place, and participating in both the initial design and the ongoing evolution of the program in their school. Given that they have this say in their own professional life, it is then incumbent on everyone to see that the program works.

Preparation through Planning

Closely akin to commitment is having an understandable plan for how advisories will actually work in practice. Therefore, teachers need to have as much involvement as they desire in developing overall advisory goals and a schoolwide plan. Beyond this involvement, however, they must also establish personal advisory plans. Just as one prepares instructional units and individual lessons, advisory work requires thoughtful planning. Although it is prudent to ensure that the advisory includes casual or circumstantial conversation, chatting is not enough. Discussions are vital, but they constitute only one function of an effective advisory. The initial phase of preparation is accomplished by developing an activity calendar, collecting ideas for activities, and organizing a record keeping system. The initial term and year of advisory are likely to be the most challenging, but as in all things teachers do, successful experience breeds confidence.

Support

The guidance counselor is usually the most appropriate person to take primary responsibility for both preparing people to be advisors and supporting them with helpful resources once a program is under way. Counselors are familiar with small group dynamics and guidance resources that can also be used by teacher advisors. When teacher advisors are concerned about or need help working with particular advisees, counselors usually have the background and specific training to support such needs. However, fellow advisors are also a rich source of support. Advisory is a shared educational program, and everyone is likely to have ups and downs. It is important that faculty meetings include discussions and sharing pertinent to the advisory. Finally, building administrators not only should be advisors but also must take responsibility for promoting the program among all teachers and parents.

What Does a Typical Advisory Do to Accomplish Its Goals?

Although the preceding essential conditions must be in place to offer the greatest chance for effective advisories, there is no single recipe dictating how every advisory must work on a day-to-day or term-to-term basis. Since the rationale is articulated through educational goal statements, what is central is that whatever activities one may undertake, they derive from and are evaluated according to a clear expression of purpose.

Consider the following example of the variety of activities of one advisory. The excerpts have been taken from a year-end summary written by the teacher from her advisory log. A member of "Wildthings," a seventh–eighth grade interdisciplinary team, she was advisor to the same students for two years. In this particular year her group included seven seventh graders (four boys, three girls) and six eighth graders (three of each). One eighth grader (Barry) was new to the school and therefore new to the team and the advisory.

Teacher Advisory Activity Report for 1989–90

Martha Melton, Wildthings Team

August: Sent postcards to kids inviting them to a cookout at my place on the 30th, asked each to bring a specific thing.

Cookout was a bit awkward at first, but once we played Pokey, everybody warmed up and had a good time. Barry is a new 8th grader from [city] and seemed hesitant/suspicious. Wonderful Joe, Sarah, and Marty from last year are our strength. Their leadership will make it a great year, but I'll need to try to bring out more initiative and leadership from other 8th graders.

September: Got through the school handbook in two days—a world record!

Solved band practice–soccer conflicts for Joe and Jerry.

Sat together at the Central soccer game, cheered our 3 players. Barry got an assist, and we chanted Baa-ree! Baa-ree! He looked embarrassed, but I think he liked it.

October: Mark's great aunt (Mrs. McKay) is in Cedarwood Convalescent Home. We visited her on the 11th, met other ladies, took their pictures, and will keep up contact with notes and visits. Our kissing booth (hands only!) at the Halloween Party was the hit of the evening; we took in $9.22 for 461 kisses sold!

Phil is struggling with 7th grade math. Barry offered to help him after school. *Yahoo!* Barry is becoming one of us!

November: We're making a Thanksgiving mural-collage for our friends at C'wood; it was Suzy's idea—her first responsible suggestion. She's agreed to plan everything, including our visit.

All 8th graders except Marty got PARs (Principal's Academic Recognition), but none of my 7th graders made it. RATS!

Mrs. Woodward died 2 days before our visit to C'wood. Kids were quieter at first but warmed up quickly. The ladies loved the mural, so we hung it in the dayroom.

December: What to do for C'wood for Xmas? Barry suggested we make journals for them—a bookbinding project. All agree, Suzy and Mark to buy materials, we'll do it at my place Sat.

The Quest materials we're going through are well received.

Kids gave me a Nat King Cole record—they knew I'd love it!

January: Marty proposed we offer to do another mural at his little sister's day care center. He, Mark, & Suzy visited and made the offer. Director asked for animal paintings on the walls instead, so we're starting our second decorating project.

The boys wanted to get together to watch the Super Bowl, so I invited them to my place—Tom (my husband) enjoyed them, and they like him, too.

Mrs. Baird called to say that Janice might be a bit upset; she's having her first menstruation. Janice seemed fine, even especially happy in school today, tho.

February: Spent 3 days making Valentines for C'wood ladies.

Barry's mom called for a conference. Finally she explained what I've suspected for a long time: the parents are divorcing.

Barry's tutoring has worked—Phil made a B this term. We all complimented both of them as a great team.

March: We had a blowup between Colleen and Suzy, who is sooooo needy of attention. Colleen is still angry, but Suzy seems to be over it. Colleen has been very quiet for over a week.

The group surprised me with a birthday party although my birthday isn't until July. I loved it!

Colleen told me in her monthly conference that she wanted to change advisories next year. She hasn't admitted it yet, but I think she's still upset at Suzy. How to patch them up?

April: Mrs. McKay died during spring break. We had a long talk about what to do and decided to plant a memorial tree at C'wood. Mark's parents will make arrangements with their minister, and we'll participate in a small service.

Track season and softball have started, and all 13 of my kids are involved. How can I see them all play? I must find a way!

Colleen has finally warmed up to her old self. I'm glad I have another year with her without Suzy. She'll shine next year.

May: The Wildthing Family Fair was a great success. Four ladies from C'wood joined us, and my kids were *Wonderful!* The kids were excellent hosts, and two ladies got teary.

Eight of my TA had their best grades ever, six had perfect attendance, and no one ended with less than C for the year.

Tom is talking about taking some courses to get certified as a teacher; where did this come from????

How Should the Advisory Be Organized and Scheduled?

There is no single recipe to dictate exactly how advisories should be arranged schoolwide. If the program is to provide the qualities of advocacy and guidance illustrated in the preceding examples, however, the plan must guarantee the numbers, time, and resources that are necessary to accomplish the goals. Common sense and my experience with advisories in a variety of middle level schools emphasize that three issues must be worked out thoughtfully in light of program goals.

Composition

I have observed effective advisories ranging from as few as seven students to as many as fourteen, but I have never seen larger groups accomplish much more than a rather perfunctory homeroom period. When all of the adults on the school staff serve as advisors, it is usually possible to have advisor-advisee ratios of 1:10 or 1:12. There are schools where secretarial, kitchen, and custodial staff have served as advisors. After all, an advisor's primary responsibility is to be an adult friend and advocate. Although one should explore school system regulations before including noncertified staff members, advisory truly becomes a schoolwide program when everyone participates.

Advisors I know who do a particularly effective job in this role tend to have strongly held preferences about the mix of ages and sexes. Some prefer to have a group from one grade level for a single year; others believe it is valuable to work with each student for at least two years; others think it is best for all the advisees to be of one sex or the other. Existing data don't prescribe a single formula, although the most common configuration by far is for groups to be composed of boys and girls for at least one year if not more. In most schools it is feasible for advisors to choose whether to keep some or all of their advisees for a second year.

One of the crucial issues to be resolved early in planning is how to go about assigning students to advisories. Should students have a choice? How should parents' requests be handled? What is the role of the advisor in choosing students? Again, there is no single formula, since schools handle these issues idiosyncratically. What seems to be most common, however, is that either the administration assigns advisories or the faculty negotiates the composition of their groups. It is natural to have a few difficult students that many teachers may not want in their advisory. One school handles that problem successfully by first identifying the most challenging students. Teachers who volunteer to take those students are then compensated for their initiative by being allowed to choose some or all of their other advisees. Whatever the system may be, there needs to be built-in flexibility for resolving intractable personality clashes.

Scheduling

For any educational program to be effective, there must be adequate time to do the things that need to be done. Advisory is at the very heart of responsive middle level schooling, and its importance in scheduling decisions is equaled only by teaming. It is, after all, the foremost guidance program in a responsive middle level school.

Just as teaming replaces departmental organization, advisory replaces the homeroom, the traditional functions of which are being supplanted. Therefore, the obvious beginning for each school day is the advisory, handling administrative details such as attendance accounting, announcements, and reciting the Pledge of Allegiance. While advisory accomplishes such housekeeping, the heart of the program is in the quality of relationships and communication that emerge from discussion, planning, and projects such as those listed previously in Martha Melton's account. In order to achieve such quality and diversity of activity, the daily opening advisory period must provide 20 to 30 minutes, plus at least one additional afternoon period of up to 45 minutes. Sometimes advisories rendezvous for lunch once a week for a "business luncheon." Again, there is no single formula for apportioning time, but a common cause of advisory failure is insufficient allotment and expenditure of time.

In addition to these group meetings of the advisory, each advisee and advisor should have one private meeting a month to discuss the student's school progress. These meetings should follow a regular schedule, and the initiative for setting the agenda should come from the student. This meeting guarantees that each student regularly reports his or her school progress, spelling out difficulties as well as accomplishments. These sessions also ensure a student's opportunity to have the undivided attention of his or her primary adult advocate at school.

Accountability

A simple but accurate accounting system for the advisory is necessary. Its expected that every advisor will become thoroughly knowledgeable about each advisee; a log kept in a three-ring binder or a simple folder system will do the job nicely. After all, the typical advisor is responsible for only a dozen or so students. The same kind of anecdotal records described in Chapter 8 also serve the documentation functions of advisory accountability. Several advisors I know like to keep everything in a single binder that is tabbed for group activities and individual records.

Another dimension of accountability has to do with advisors gaining access to colleagues who are working with their advisees. Team meetings provide time for discussions about individual students, and where advisors are present, much of the communication can be accomplished there. Advisors who are not part of daily team meetings, however, will require additional ways of making regular contact. Much of the success of advisory lies in how effectively the key people are able to maintain regular communication, especially when a student is having difficulty.

What Are Appropriate Advisory Activities?

One appeal of advisory to many teachers is the opportunity to follow the interests and energies of the youngsters in a single advisory group. Kids' ideas and questions about their world lead in directions that matter to them. Furthermore, such energy and ownership are essential if the advisory is to be ultimately meaningful. On the other hand, few teachers have been prepared to be advisors, and many of us are immediately uneasy at the prospect of having to invent ways to make the program work. What follows is a collection of possible activities to guide the novice advisor's planning.

Customary Advisory Management

Assuming that the goals of the program include providing an adult advocate and academic guidance, there is routine but general discussion about how the kids are doing. The advisor solicits difficulties as well as successes, using the group session to get clues about how a student's academic life is in fact working out. When the advisor suspects problems, he or she follows up at a later time with more private conversation. Specific accomplishments and overall progress are the kinds of reports that get shared with the whole group.

In order to help advisees develop a game plan to work successfully in the academic program, teachers often use advisory time to teach specific strategies:

How to keep a daily assignment notebook and a monthly calendar
Review of schedules for upcoming tests, due dates on papers or projects, and extra help sessions if available
How to take notes in an organized manner
How to go about proofreading and using peers as editors
How to study for tests in particular subjects
Mnemonic devices that work for others
Strategies for studying together or doing homework together
General study skill suggestions
How to recognize differences in standards of schoolwork

This daily setting also presents opportunities to explore issues related to individual interests and ideas about how knowledge can be used. One of the special benefits to students is the interest and aid of the advisor in determining goals that are realistic for the moment and that are therefore achievable. Teachers must not lose sight of how fundamentally important it is for every single youngster to know as often as possible what it means to be a successful student, and both the fact of accomplishment and the personal empowerment that success brings should be the advisor's constant mission.

It is also part of the advisor's role, as an aspect of monitoring and supporting advisees' academics, to receive grades and comments from colleagues, to compile report cards, and to hand them out. This function ensures that each advisor is familiar with how each advisee is doing in all classes, and it also signals problems to attend to in seeking ways to be helpful. This reporting function also designates the advisor as the faculty member best informed to communicate with parents. Parent conferences with advisors should occur twice a year, but when a conference with another teacher is needed, it should be arranged and attended by the advisor to facilitate the best possible communication. If any tension surrounds such conferences, the advisor becomes even more important, not only as an advocate for the student but also as an intermediary, since it is the advisor who has prior acquaintance with both parents and other teachers.

There are also what might be referred to as "housekeeping" functions:

Taking and sending daily attendance information to the office

Reciting the Pledge of Allegiance

Reviewing announcements, reminding about upcoming events such as school picture day, games, plays, assembly, field trip, and so on

Taking lunch orders and collecting money

Sending and collecting forms from parents (medical, transfers, etc.)

Reviewing the school or team handbook

Working out schedule conflicts, electives choices, bus changes, and so on

Even when the advisory agenda is as businesslike as simply handling housekeeping tasks, however, the gist of the dialogue has a great deal to do with the credibility of the content. Where students are encouraged to handle some of the chores, record the activity in the advisory log, and keep up with themselves and their schoolwork, the authenticity of mundane tasks is enhanced. The advisory is a setting that thrives on discussion in which youngsters learn how to speak, to listen to each other, to contemplate issues, and to reflect on related experience. It is also a supportive context for hashing out personal issues with the school's bureaucracy and differences with each other. A valued benefit of advisory for many youngsters will be simply the opportunity to talk with peers and an interested adult who cares about their point of view, whether or not the adult shares it or agrees with it.

Significant Occasions Outside School

In lamenting "the absence of a special place for teenagers in society," David Elkind has pointed out the "progressive erosion of markers of their transition status" (1984, pp. 93–113). These markers are those recognized events or accomplishments by which their progress from one level to another is publicly recognized. Some kids receive approval through religious rituals such as confirmation and bar or bas mitzvah. Scouting also employs ceremony and ritual to acknowledge a youngster's achievement and movement from one level to another. Even though such events may occur outside the school, they are nonetheless important to young adolescents. It is appropriate for them to share those events with peers at school, too.

The annual event in the life of every youngster that is cause for recognition and celebration is, of course, his or her birthday. In the primary grades parents often bring cupcakes and see to it that birthdays are celebrated. By the middle grades, however, kids have usually outgrown the propriety of their parents' initiative, but they still appreciate being celebrated. The advisory is a perfect setting for some kind of observance and refreshments.

Other events in kids' lives outside school often become part of the exchanges in an advisory where trust is high: family rituals, traditions, and activities; relationships with siblings or step-siblings; the birth of a sibling; the separation, divorce, or remarriage of a parent; the death of a relative or neighbor. It is not the business of the advisor to pry, of course, but when youngsters have issues on their minds that they wish to share and process with each other or with the advisor, there must be a sanctuary where that can happen. The advisory at its best is just such a sanctuary for the youngster who wants to use it accordingly.

Discussion Topics

Although the best discussions generally emerge organically from the day-to-day issues in kids' lives, there are reliable topics that can be suitable at any time the advisor feels a need to generate dialogue. Many of the inquiry possibilities identified in Chapter 3 are appropriate for thoughtful discussion and reflection. Some topics that are likely to engage early adolescents in such talk are these:

> Favorites (foods, books, music, sports, movies, television, actors, actresses)
> Thoughtful critiques of books/stories, movies, music, television
> Hobbies, especially those they can bring in to share
> Pets, pet stories
> Travel, photographs, scrapbooks, other artifacts
> Puzzles, riddles, jokes
> Boy–girl issues, parties, bedtime, curfew, cliques, clothing styles, dating, chores, allowances, rules at home
> Issues reported in the media, current events
> Thoughts about high school, reflections on elementary school
> Career ideas, things they might like to do as an adult

One teacher has students take a camera home overnight in order to "take a picture of yourself without being in the picture" (Bergmann & Rudman, 1985, p. 22). The purpose of the task is for each student to think about those things that represent him or her, then take a photograph of those items. The photographs provoke a lot of speculation and dialogue as kids study each other's representations.

Another way to establish better acquaintances among kids in an advisory is for each student to have one advisory period early in the year to make an autobiographical presentation. These presentations are often augmented by photographs and artifacts that are the props for a youngster to present himself or herself to classmates. These ways of helping youngsters describe themselves to each other help them resolve that pressing existential question of this time of life: "Who am I?"

Curriculum

In some schools the advisory program has a specific curriculum to be accomplished over a year's time. It becomes extremely important, however, that all of the time for such special guidance opportunity not be usurped by an externally prescribed set of activities. To do that is to eliminate exactly the kind of interpersonal exchanges that advisory offers for every student.

Two broad, related areas are often established as curriculum in teacher advisory: personal health and wellness, and decision making. There is no question that a critical change from earlier childhood into adolescence is marked by the larger array of choices kids make that have perilous consequences. For example, the average age of first use of alcohol and marijuana is twelve—the sixth and seventh grade years (Koerner, 1990). Particular hazards to kids' health during this exploratory and experimental developmental period are tobacco, alcohol, drugs, and sex. And whether or not the children in a particular advisory are involved with any of these activities, they are part of a culture where participation has become almost the norm. Nutrition, eating disorders, and exercise are additional critical issues related to the health of children at this time. Much of their nutritional lifestyle is well established by the time they go into high school, and it is urgent that we help them make wise decisions. We must replace traditional candy sale fund-raisers with other ways to both generate funds and promote responsible nutritional habits.

Unsafe choices our students contemplate are often influenced by what selected peers think, what they do themselves, and the pressures they often put on each other. It is common for young adolescents to take their own well-being for granted and to act as if they believe they are immortal. Not to get these issues out into the open as subjects for the most serious dialogue is to sacrifice students' welfare to often dangerous menaces. If children are expected to make responsible decisions, we must see to it that we have done everything possible to point out the risks to them, showing them how to make comparisons and judge for themselves. They need our experience and help in learning how to clarify and judge the quality of the information they receive, how to put all the facts together, and how to make a well-informed decision. Then we must teach them how to take personal positions that will stand up against peer pressure. No single issue is more important to teach successfully to our children than how to become responsible choosers as they shape their own destinies.

The key to an advisory's effectiveness is how much youngsters are able to trust the adult and other advisory members and choose to talk about the issues on their minds. It is to be expected, of course, that they will exercise discretion about just how open and candid to be, but as concerned and committed adults we must do everything we can to convey our trustworthiness and loyalty. We can be sure that our advisees are increasingly aware observers of the human condition, and they have their own thoughts about themselves in relation to an abundance of portentous personal issues such as feelings of helplessness, loneliness, failure, and humiliation. Parental rejection and abuse may lead to life-threatening choices. We know that some of our youngsters contemplate running away or committing suicide. We also recognize their vulnerability to exploitation by others through drug dependency or cults. Our children are simply not yet worldly enough to comprehend and handle choices that are so often self-destructive. We mustn't miss any opportunity to build and nurture their trust, convincing them that we care about them and are their advocates. Their well-being must be the priority that drives everything we do in a teacher-based guidance program.

Games and Puzzles

Games are a natural currency in the interpersonal transactions of children. How many times do we see kids using rock, paper, scissors to settle an issue of "whose turn?" Left to their own devices, children may invent games and puzzles as well as play the ones they already know. Whether it is five-year-olds playing I Spy or fourteen-year-olds bantering with riddles, their routines of matching intuition and wits contribute to the good humor of any group experience. Such activities that have a distinct element of fun help cultivate confidence and feelings of safety and belonging within a group. Advisory is a perfect setting for such exchanges, and teacher advisors are well advised to build a personal collection of successful amusements.

The collection should include both indoor and outdoor games that include physical activity such as a trust fall, perception games and puzzles, dramatic games such as charades, a scavenger hunt, simulation activities, and commercial games such as Trivial Pursuit or Clue or Jeopardy. Old and established favorites I have used successfully include

Twenty Questions, knock-knock jokes, Hangman, Grandma's Picnic, and an ever-growing collection of perception riddles I've taken from readings and exchanges with kids and other teachers.

Young adolescents also have talent for creating games. Early in my career I gave pairs of my students either a die or a spinner plus small bags containing an assortment of three or four various items I found around my house or the classroom. Their task over three days was to use at least one of the items from the bag to invent a game—writing down the rules, testing it on classmates, and refining it to a degree that might make it marketable. Part of the assignment was to write advertising copy. One of those games, dubbed "Corker" by combining "Corinne" and "Kerry," was an immediate hit, and students played it at every opportunity over several months. Another game created by another group of students as part of a different project required role playing. It was named "Flinch" for reasons I cannot recall, and its popularity was so great that it soon became part of the school's culture. During a semester break some six or seven years after this game's creation, a dozen or so students came to my house for a potluck reunion. Not more than an hour passed before someone suggested a game of Flinch. We played Flinch off and on for much of the rest of the evening, reclaiming a piece of childhood that still bonded us in their young adulthood. I remain very impressed by the value those college students placed on a simple game they had invented years earlier, even before they entered high school. There is something about games, especially original ones, that seems to stick close to what we hold to be meaningful during these years.

A teaching principal in a small, rural, middle level school was concerned about the decline of games in family life and their replacement by the ubiquitous television. She created an original social studies unit through which her middle level students solicited favorite games and puzzles from their parents', grandparents', and other senior citizens' childhoods. Once students had mastered the games or puzzles, they constructed whatever game board or pieces were required, wrote descriptions and rules, and taught them to classmates. Eventually they published a small book for their community that preserved their elders' heritage of games and puzzles. Later they invited students to visit from a neighboring school in order to share their work and teach others what they had learned.

Our culture contains an exceptionally rich variety of games of all kinds—puzzles, riddles, role-plays, and so on—that can be used to cultivate good will and simple fun within an advisory group. Building a dossier of activities that contribute to the advisory quality of life is part of being a teacher advisor. A list of resources for games and puzzles is included at the end of the chapter.

Advisory Projects at School

Advisory groups can contribute in countless ways to the quality of life in the school. Projects can be satisfying for the group to plan and carry out as well as a source of compliments from other students and adults. In one survey, students reported that their favorite activities were athletic games, field days, and parties (Maynard, 1985). These popular activities can be shared by advisory groups. Beyond these familiar sources of enjoyment, however, there are lots of additional things kids can do that are worthwhile for their school and also satisfying to provide:

Taking responsibility for a classroom/hallway bulletin board or display case
Writing a column or feature piece for team/school newsletter

Helping younger students by serving as a teacher's aide: reading, tutoring, leading games, helping with coats and mittens

Performing a play or skit at a team meeting or school assembly

Hosting visitors

Sponsoring a team or all-school event such as a spelling bee, geography bee, paper airplane contest, poetry contest, lip-sync contest, dress-up day, talent show, hat day, poetry or short story award, holiday celebration, pep rally

Sponsoring a school service event such as cleanup day, canned food drive, recycling projects, parent/grandparent/community person appreciation day, wellness/fitness promotion, school birthday party

Recognizing other students' and adults' accomplishments or special events in their lives through a letter or ribbon

Sponsoring a spirit award to give to the Advisory-of-the-Month

Advisory Activities and Projects Out of School

A distinct treat cherished by my seventh and eighth grade male peers when I was a young adolescent in a small Alabama town was to be invited by Miss Lila Mae Schuessler, our science teacher, to travel with her to a high school football game in a neighboring town. Five times a year she'd invite three or four of us who loved football (as she did) to pile into her ancient Packard for an hour or so drive to games with rival high schools. We didn't actually sit very long with Miss Lila Mae at the game because we were eager to explore the alien stadium and prowl the sidelines and the end zone during the game. While I don't recall anything of the science curriculum from those two years, I have warm memories of the game trips. Miss Schuessler entertained us with stories of great games from past years, and she proclaimed her confident expectations for what a great team ours would be when we were in high school. She also loved fishing, knew a great deal about what was in those days a masculine domain, and had vivid stories of big ones that got away. I appreciated her surprising love of things we also loved, her civility in talking with us rather than at us, and the generosity she extended to us when she knew just how much we wanted to attend a game we had no other way to see. I also recall being aware of how important it was for us to be patient about taking turns; she couldn't take all of us to every game. Furthermore, while I can still name six other teachers from those years, I don't recall much of anything about who they were as people or what they believed in.

Activities away from the school campus are especially helpful in building both interpersonal bonds and confidence among young adolescents and with their adult mentors. As one student expressed this actuality in a commencement speech, "I learned that my teacher didn't just talk that talk—he walked that walk." These are the learnings that derive from activities and experiences in which the adult and students share or explore their interests. Early in each new year, one friend takes her advisory to the fitness center where she is a member. Kids see a new place, try out the equipment, go for a swim, and—best of all—get to know their teacher in a way that isn't possible back at school. Another advisor attends most of the sports events at the local college, and several times a year he invites his advisees to join him. Another teacher is a part-time candymaker, and once or twice a year he takes his advisees on a tasting trip to the candy kitchen. Another advisor has each of her students meet her once a month for breakfast at a fast-food restaurant two blocks from the school. Not only do they have the treat of sharing breakfast, but they are able to have a one-to-one conference outside the school grounds. Other teachers share their avocational interests by inviting students to attend a movie, take a day-long bicycle ride, go fishing or camping or bowling or skating, attend a concert or play in the community, or meet at the teacher's house for a cookout. It is through these activities away from school that our students gain fuller understanding of who we are and the values we live, and satisfy the natural curiosity students have about their teachers.

Just as the advisory is an appropriate group to sponsor service projects within the school, it is also a natural group for service activities that benefit the community. Remember the earlier example of Martha Melton's advisory establishing relationships with lonely senior citizens in a local convalescent center. Every community has homes for the elderly, and some version of an adopt-a-grandparent program can be carried out.

Participation in community events such as the town's birthday, a walkathon, a paper drive, community cleanup day, and Veteran's Day can easily be done through advisory groups. Kids may want to promote recycling or adopt a community beautification project by making posters for stores to display or collect funds to support needy projects such as the local food shelf or the humane society. National fundraising efforts to fight dread diseases such as AIDS, muscular dystrophy, and multiple sclerosis also appreciate help from children. A final suggestion to the teacher advisor is to look for opportunities to connect these experiences with the academic curriculum, especially writing. It is appropriate for kids to write letters of appreciation to community people and letters that express their viewpoint on community issues to the local newspaper. Many local newspapers are also eager to publish kids' writing and photography that addresses community events.

In my years of working with young adolescents I learned that many if not most of them were deeply interested and thoughtful about pressing issues in the larger community, too. They are quick to advocate for animals, especially species whose existence is in jeopardy from changes in their habitats wrought by various human enterprises. Their developmental idealism also influences their tendencies toward conservation consciousness, and they are typically ready to lend a hand in protecting our environment. "Youngsters are picketing supermarkets, boycotting restaurants and writing Congressmen, sometimes on recycled paper they have painstakingly mixed, pressed and dried themselves. The White House reports that it receives hundreds of environmental entreaties every day from citizens too young to make their views known at the ballot box" (Dewitt, 1990, p. 51). John Arnold (1990) reports an example of eighth graders and their teacher looking into local drought conditions that resulted in their actually proposing legislation to the state legislature. The result was passage of a bill requiring xeriscape landscaping, a technique that saves the state money and countless gallons of water. Children naturally have the interest and energy to improve conditions, and when teachers harness those resources, remarkable things become possible.

Activities with Families

Perhaps the communication link most vital to a child's success at school is that between the teacher advisor and the child's parents. Advisory offers teachers the opportunity to know a small group of children very well, and because of the small ratio, it is additionally feasible to become better acquainted with their parents. That connection has to be developed, however, through initiatives that reassure the parent of the teacher advisor's sincerity and trustworthiness. Parents will not typically take initiatives on their own unless they have been put at ease and are assured that the advisor wants their communication. Teachers need to remember that those parents also spent many years as students and may retain some doubts from those years regarding teachers' commitment and dependability.

There is nothing mysterious about establishing the credibility of the teacher advisor's interest. It begins when the advisor makes an introductory telephone call early in the school year to express interest in the child and to encourage the parent to keep the advisor informed as the year develops. Once these introductions have been accomplished, it is a good idea to schedule some kind of social gathering such as a cookout that includes advisees and their parents. By the time the fall open house is held, adult acquaintances are well established. As the year passes, a periodic note and/or phone call to maintain contact helps keep communication channels open. By the time the first half of the year has passed, it is wise to invite parents back for another advisory conference. Certainly by that time the advisor knows the student's school performance well, and by then the student should be in a position to take an active part in the conference.

It is essential through all of these contacts for teachers to keep in mind that both the parents and the advisor want the child to succeed. All of the adults immediately concerned share a personal investment in the youngster's welfare. When a difficulty arises, similarly motivated advocates are able to communicate more clearly and coordinate their efforts to help the youngster. We must not forget that the original and ongoing purposes of the advisory are to help every youngster be a successful learner and good citizen.

What Are Hazards to the Success of Advisories?

Far and away the single most crucial element to the success of a teacher advisory program is the teachers' commitment. When teachers either are disinterested or go through the motions, it flops. It is critical, therefore, for every person in a middle level school that adopts a teacher advisor program to be committed to doing whatever is necessary to make the program successful for every student.

A second common hazard to successful advisories is inadequate apportionment of time. At the risk of being repetitious, let me stress this important point again: No less than 20 minutes should be scheduled every day, preferably first thing in the morning. In order for groups to develop projects and contribute to the whole school, they need at least one additional meeting of 30 to 45 minutes a week. These times are minimal, however. Other advisory meetings should be held when possible, for example, one lunch meeting per week. Time must also be found for monthly private meetings as well, whether they are scheduled during the day or before or after school. These one-to-one meetings are essential.

Once these commitments of disposition and time have been made, there are measures that can help teachers acquire the background and repertoire of activities they may need to provide students with experiences such as those described in this chapter. Ample teacher preparation time is also essential. I recommend at least a week of study and program development before the opening of school, augmented by monthly faculty meetings aimed solely at troubleshooting advisory problems. Individual faculty requiring additional assistance should meet on an as-needed basis with the guidance counselor. It should also be remembered that this program is much more time consuming in its initial stages of implementation. Once it has been in place for a year, everyone feels considerably more comfortable with it, and an even greater potential for mutual support and success becomes achievable.

Finally, there is no single advisory program every school should have. The essence of advisory is a commitment to kids. The concept of advisory should permeate all our dealings with children at the middle level. As Sandra Caldwell of Kennebunk Middle School in Maine is fond of saying about "Prime Time," their advisory program, "We concentrate on concept transplants rather than program transplants." That expression captures a deliberate theme in this chapter, namely that however an advisory program is crafted, it should reflect the ideas and inspirations of a faculty motivated by common goals.

Conclusion

I have come to believe that the teacher advisory is the very best idea in the middle level concept that has been poorly and/or inadequately implemented. Too often advisory groups are too large (more than twenty students) and the period of time is too brief (less than 20 minutes). It is not unusual to find that little or no in-service preparation was invested in preparing teachers and the program, resulting in highly diverse commitments. In an occasional case, contract negotiators have attempted to renegotiate contracts to include advisory as an extra responsibility to be further compensated. Yet, the teacher advisory remains the soul of the middle level movement, for in that context more than any other, teachers can act on their commitment to education based on the nature and needs of young adolescent children. As one experienced middle level educator observed, "We may be a long distance away from having all teachers serving as advocates across the entire school day for students, but it is time in our journey to move towards that goal" (Van Hoose, p. 7).

Supporting Activities

1. Arrange to visit an advisory group every day for a week. Record the activities and topics of conversation. Ask students at the end of the week to tell you about the benefits of their advisory as well as those of their friends. Ask them also how the advisory could be improved.

2. If an accessible school does not have teacher advisories, explore with the principal and college coordinator the possibility of having university students serve as advisors. It might be possible to arrange a group of ten to twelve young adolescents who could meet for a 30-minute period two or three times a week. These groups could be a source for inquiries and could enable aspiring teachers to try out advisory activities.

3. Develop a school year calendar of annual events likely to hold interest for all or a few young adolescents, for example, the school or town's birthday, the opening of the fishing season, the Super Bowl, and so on. Create activities around those events that you might use with an advisory group.

RESOURCES

Prevention of Drug Use

Elks Drug Awareness Programs, P. O. Box 310, Ashland, OR 97520
Kiwanis International, Public Relations, 3636 Woodview Trace, Indianapolis, IN 46268
Lions International, 300 22nd Street, Oak Brook, IL 60570
National Federation of Parents for Drug Free Youth, 1423 North Jefferson, Springfield, MO 65802

Curriculum

Quest: Skills for Adolescence is a decision-making curriculum designed for adolescents available from Quest International, 537 Jones Road, PO Box 566, Granville, OH 43203–0566.

Guidance Activity

Bormaster, J.S. & Treat, C.L. (1982). *Building interpersonal relationships through talking, listening, communicating.* Austin, TX: Pro-ed.

Canfield, J., & Wells, H. C. (1976). *100 ways to enhance self-concept in the classroom: A handbook for teachers and parents.* Englewood Cliffs, NJ: Prentice-Hall.

Casteel, J.D. (1978). *Learning to think and choose: Decision-making episodes for the middle grades.* Glenview, TX: Scott, Foresman.

Chase, L. (1975). *The other side of the report card.* Pacific Palisades, CA: Goodyear.

Chesler, M., & Fox, R. (1966). *Role-playing methods in the classroom.* Chicago: Science Research Associates.

Javna, J. (1990). *50 simple things kids can do to save the earth.* (The Earthworks Group). Kansas City, KS: Andrews & McMeel.

Morganett, R. S. (1990). *Skills for living: Group counseling activities for young adolescents.* Champaign, IL: Research Press.

Palmer, P. (1976). *The mouse, the monster, and me: Assertiveness for young people.* San Luis Obispo, CA: Impact.

Putbrese, L., & Putbrese, *The Weekly Advisor.* Available by subscription from Early Adolescent Connections, P.O. Box 1844, St. Cloud, MN 56302.

Simon, S. B. (1974). *I am lovable and capable.* Chicago: Argus.

Simon, S. B., Howe, L. W., & Kirchenbaum, H. (1972). *Values clarification: A handbook of practical strategies for teachers & students.* New York: Hart.

Spencer, C. (1990). *One TA to grow on, please.* Available from VAMLE, P. O. Box 664, Middlebury, VT 05753.

Games and Puzzles

Fluegelman, A. (Ed.). (1976). *The new games book.* Garden City, NY: Doubleday.

Fluegelman, A. (1981). *More new games.* Garden City, NY: Doubleday.

Kohl, H. (1986). *The book of puzzlements.* New York: Random House.

Manchester, R. H. (1976). *The mammoth book of word games.* New York: Bristol.

Pentagram. (1990). *Pentagames.* New York: Simon & Schuster.

Rohnke, K. (1984). *Silver bullets: A guide to initiative problems, adventure games, and trust activities.* Project Adventure, P. O. Box 100, Hamilton, MA 10936.

Rohnke, K. (1981). *Cow's tails & cobras.* Project Adventure, P. O. Box 100, Hamilton, MA 10936.

Rubin, D. (1988) *Brainstorms. Real puzzles for the real genius.* New York: Harper & Row.

REFERENCES

Arnold, J. F. (1990). *Visions of teaching & learning: 80 exemplary middle level projects.* Columbus, OH: National Middle School Association.

Benard, B. (1991). *Fostering resiliency in kids: Protective factors in the family, school and community.* Portland, OR: Western Regional Center for Drug-Free Schools and Communities.

Bergmann, S., & Rudman, G. J. (1985). *Decision-making skills for middle school students.* Washington, DC: National Education Association.

Carr, J. F. (1990). *There by choice: Teachers who prefer to teach in the middle grades.* Unpublished doctoral dissertation, University of Vermont.

Clark, R. (1986). *Family life and student achievement.* Chicago: University of Chicago Press.

Cole, C. G. (1988). *Guidance in middle level schools: Everyone's responsibility.* Columbus, OH: National Middle School Association.

Dewitt, P. E. (1990, December 24). The ecokid corps. *Time, 136*(27), 20–24.

Dyer, T. J. (1990). Opinion. *NAASP NewsLeader, 38*(1), 2.

Elkind, D. (1984). *All grown up & no place to go: Teenagers in crisis.* Reading, MA: Addison-Wesley.

Hawkins, J.D. et al. (1992). *Risk-focused prevention.* University of Washington: School of Social Work.

Koerner, T. O. (Ed.). (1990). Striving for drug-free schools. *The Practitioner, 16*(3), 2.

Lipsitz, J. (1984). *Successful schools for young adolescents*. New Brunswick, NJ: Transaction.

Maynard, G. (1985, April). *Middle level students suggest social activities. Schools in the middle: A report on trends and practices*. Reston, VA: National Association of Secondary School Principals.

Myers, D. & Stevenson, C. (1993). Some truths from a terrific T.A. *VAMLE Journal* 6(1).

Noddings, N. (1992). *The challenge to care in schools*. New York: Teachers College Press.

Van Hoose, J. (1991, Fall). The ultimate goal: A/A across the day. *Midpoints* (2) 1.

Wolin, S. J. & Wolin, S. (1993). *The resilient self: How survivors of troubled families rise above adversity*. New York: Villard.

Chapter 11
Partnerships with Parents

○ *Who are my students' parents? What are their interests? Priorities?*

○ *How do they relate to their children?*

○ *What do they want for them? Expect of them?*

○ *What do they count on from me? From us? From the school?*

○ *How can we work together to achieve some common goals?*

I had been a middle grades teacher for several years before I consciously acknowledged the absurdity of my understandable but misguided assumption that my teammates and I bore full responsibility for our students' education. Although I recognized that our students' parents had a great deal to do with how seriously their kids responded to schoolwork, I felt deficient when kids were indifferent or just plain bored. I also felt inadequate when my students misbehaved, especially those who conducted themselves properly for other teachers.

I learned the amazing power of teacher–parent collaboration by chance. While teaching in New York City, I planned and led a camping trip during the summer for two families that had always lived in the city and had never been camping or fishing, didn't know how to cook over an open fire, and had never slept on the ground. I found myself teaching my kids' parents, showing them how to do things, and telling stories of such outings from my boyhood. They, in turn, taught me, willingly tackling new tasks and sharing wonderful anecdotes from their childhood in the city. Storytelling around the campfire became a bond, assuring each of us of our relationship and credibility with the others. Those three days together on Lake George a quarter century ago stand out in my mind as a time of sudden insight about how valuable it is for a teacher and parents to know each other and to work together both with and for their children.

Conveying the depth of our thought and commitment to our work and to their children in particular is the key to gaining credibility and trust with parents, and scheduling regular communications, collectively and individually, is essential. By simply becoming acquainted with them as adults, I learned about their hopes for their children. As we swapped ideas about a variety of mutually interesting topics, I came to realize the potential of our partnership—a potential I'd done little to cultivate in the past. When we could agree about expectations and standards and when we worked together on educational projects and programs for all the children on the team, our combined influence on the kids was considerable. And an unexpected dividend was that I came to value parents as friends and colleagues independent of our professional school-based relationships.

One teacher friend, Jane Vossler, has cultivated parent participation and trust in her Odyssey team by promoting parents and students reading together (Vossler, 1996). She prepares a list of books parents and students can read together, and she collects multiple copies of as many as possible for them to borrow. Survival books are particularly popular. Periodically the readers come to an evening meeting to talk about the books they have read, discuss personal reactions, relate particularly popular scenes, and speculate about the authors' motives and decisions. Students prepare refreshments in advance, and Jane acts as the primary hostess for the evening. She moves among the several groups of six to ten people, helping get discussions under way as needed and "creating a little controversy if things seem too bland. Get an argument going and then move on," she encourages.

Another intriguing sixth grade team whose name, "Kingdom of Well," suggests a central theme of wellness, publishes every Friday a two-page newsletter titled "Kowbell." Every issue includes brief pieces by various students and one or more of the three teachers. From time to time parents have talked about matters such as the team's homework expectations or whether or not the team should go on an overnight field trip. On such occasions Kowbell defines the issue and serves as a formal inquiry to solicit parents' opinions. The following issue reports the results, followed by a statement from the teachers. When there was controversy among parents about the amount of assigned homework, for example, the inquiry revealed that 85 percent of the parents believed that it was "just right." No one could argue that the parents' perceptions did not count. Furthermore, the teachers report that they have never before enjoyed such comfortable relationships with their students' parents, and they attributed the good citizenship of their students in part to this cultivation of their parents' support.

As every teacher who solicits parents' opinion discovers, however, there are also some loose cannons out there. I have known the struggles with parents who disagree with me, and I have also known the personal pain of trying to work with someone who simply disliked me. During the last half dozen years that I taught in a particularly dynamic university-dominated urban community, I contended with parents who charged that our program was too "unstructured" or "progressive" as well as some who assaulted us for being what they described as "too conservative." One father stood up in the first parents' meeting of the year and threatened to sue if we didn't promise to use a particular basal reading text with his son. I spent a good bit of time that year meeting with him and his son, reviewing Andrew's portfolio, examining his reading and writing work, talking about books and stories and movies and ideas, and listening to Andrew. Three years later that same father demanded that Megan, his daughter, be placed on our team. He had become more vocal as our advocate than he had been earlier as our critic. Such experiences taught me the extremely valuable lesson that while my professional decisions must not be geared to pleasing parents, I must understand them and their manifold expectations if my efforts with their children are to have support and continuity in the home. We cannot be certain of enriching or salvaging youngsters' lives unless we understand their personal, familial contexts.

The validity of my assertion about the propriety of building partnerships with our students' parents is also strongly supported in the professional literature. From his work as a site visitor to twenty-two unusually effective middle level schools, Garvin found "parent involvement crucial to school effectiveness" (1984, p. 33). His work further specified nine priorities parents have for their children during the middle years (1988; Melton, 1987). Explicated and paraphrased, those priorities are as follows:

1. When their child goes to school, parents want to know that he or she is safe, especially about things like the bus, changing classes, the cafeteria, and free time. They want to be assured that their youngsters will feel safe and be safe throughout the day.

2. Parents want their child to know at least one adult to approach when problems develop and have that adult know the child well enough to be of help with those problems.

3. Parents expect the school to see that constructive interpersonal relationships are emphasized.

4. Parents associate their children's happiness with the degree to which youngsters feel they belong to the total school program.

5. They want their youngsters to have enough successful experience each day to reinforce their good feelings about returning the next day.

6. Parents want their children to be challenged academically and to achieve, but they want learning goals to be realistic.

7. Parents want teachers to see that their children are informed about their progress, and parents value opportunities to work in concert on problems. They especially want to know their role in homework.

8. Parents want to feel welcomed at the school, known by their names, and invited for more than just parent conferences.

9. They want schools to help them learn more about what youngsters are like at this time, providing seminars, support groups, and access to resources and professional organizations.

Although it is common for parents to have their hands full with both career and domestic responsibilities, I have learned that with rare exception they care about their children's schooling and life beyond the classroom. They also have idiosyncratic values, but in my experience there has been a good bit of common ground.

SOME ASSUMPTIONS ABOUT PARENTS AND WHAT THEY VALUE

In the decade that I have been a university teacher I have visited lots of middle level schools to make presentations to parent-teacher groups about young adolescent development and how schools can be responsive to children's needs. The sessions I find most personally insightful are those where the numbers are small enough to let us shift from my doing all or most of the telling to more informal discussion in which people swap aspirations, ideas, and concerns. Such sessions almost always constitute a wonderful context for inquiry where I can use small group interview and discussion techniques around several questions.

What do we want our kids to know and be able to do by adulthood? I jot down the things people offer, and when we have what seems like the items most on their minds, we classify them. The most common and predictable categories have to do with self-sufficiency, responsibility, the ability to adapt and get along with others, and high standards. Not every response falls into one of these four categories, of course, but they are by far the dominant ones. The next questions, then, are: How do people learn these things? How did *you* learn how to be responsible, self-sufficient, and so forth?

It quickly becomes evident that parents report having learned responsibility, for example, by having real responsibility, by being accountable to other people in circumstances where the consequences are real. An appreciation for responsibility grows out of having been responsible and having enjoyed being successful at it. Invariably, participants provide personal anecdotes that confirm having the kinds of experiences this book proposes for middle level schools. However, more often than not parents report significant experiences outside of school. Our ignoble tradition is that school curricula are abstracted from the real, firsthand experiences that teach the very qualities we see as critical to future success and personal satisfaction. The final question then becomes: What do we need to do at school to achieve these learnings?

Each of the two-hundred-plus groups I've worked with around Vermont on these questions has contributed new ideas and propositions, but four general themes remain constant. While these small group interviews have not been nearly so systematically documented as those previously cited by Garvin, I include them here because they are also highly consistent with what I learned about parents while teaching in urban settings.

Assumption 1

Parents want to feel confident that their children are and will be "happy." Happiness appears to be associated with successful relationships with others even more than academic success. I can't recall anyone ever suggesting that academic success was not important and desirable, but the sheer volume of expressions having to do with interpersonal happiness outweighs virtually everything else. Grownups old enough to have young adolescent children are amply experienced in the adult world to appreciate the vital connection between personal fulfillment and a satisfying sense of community.

Assumption 2

Parents want very much to trust teachers, but they are often uncertain, if not suspicious, about our trustworthiness. Every parent has also been a student during these vulnerable years, exposed to all kinds of teachers' dispositions. They are also sufficiently experienced in the adult world and with their own children to understand just how fragile adult equilibrium can be. They know a great deal about just how complex our work is, perhaps more so than I think we often give them credit for understanding. When teachers optimistically share their aspirations and plans as well as competent professional assessments of kids' work, anxieties about trust and their kids' futures dissipate. I also know personally as a parent of four children just how much importance parents attach to believing that our children's teachers care about their happiness and do what they can to support their needs.

Assumption 3

Parents know a great deal about their children, and they want to share their insights with teachers who listen thoughtfully, take their perceptions seriously, and look for ways to use that knowledge. Parents also know their children are changing. After all, they buy the groceries and clothing. They are the experts about their child's transition insofar as it is signaled by physical changes, disposition, work habits, and many other aspects of childhood they see at home. Parents don't necessarily understand change in broader terms of child development, and they may have overlooked some important dimensions of their child's changes. However, teachers should assume that by virtue of their closer observations of their child, parents are in a position to teach us some valuable things. We do well by them when we ask and listen and learn.

Assumption 4

We teachers must never forget that many of our students' parents have serious problems of their own, often rendering them reticent to disclose very much about themselves and their family life. Teachers must approach parents with the same professional dignity and demeanor our society expects from a family physician. In order to serve children well, we must convey earnest concern that helps offset our adult constituents' apprehensions. We must also remember that we will work with parents who are self-conscious about their children, especially when the child's problems or deficiencies might be construed as a reflection of home life or the parents' career accomplishments. We must be careful to be supportive and nonjudgmental in the face of issues that may be sensitive for adults.

While many parents have authentic interest in their children's general welfare, they have historically been included only peripherally in their children's lives at school. The Carnegie Council laments that "despite the clearly documented benefits of parental involvement for students' achievement and attitudes toward school, parental involvement of all types declines progressively during the elementary years" (1989, p. 66). According to one report, when parents are required "to pick up their children's report cards in person . . . some report cards go unclaimed for months" (Maeroff, 1989). The priorities and assumptions previously cited, combined with some parents' indifference or preoccupations with other problems, constitute an admittedly substantial but vital challenge to middle level educators.

FAMILIES IN TRANSITION

The personal developmental changes children experience during early adolescence have been summarized in previous chapters, and some of the influences of those changes in family life were discussed briefly in Chapter 4. We must also consider the changes in family composition and organization that have been occurring in the post–World War II years. This evolution of family structures is evidenced in a wide variety of residential configurations that include middle level students.

Parents of young adolescents tend to be in the age range of thirty-five to forty-five, generally referred to as a time of mid-life changes. Thus, parents are often contending with their own personal developmental changes. "A mid-life parent who is especially concerned over changes in his or her physical appearance and attractiveness may greet the adolescent's new social life with ambivalence" (Steinberg, 1980, p. 12). Adult development issues appear to follow patterns that affect mothers and fathers similarly, as well as others that are specific to sex and age (Erikson, 1968; Levinson, 1978; Gilligan, 1982). It is not uncommon for those changes in adults to have dramatic effects on the children and family. Like their children (and teachers, too!), parents handle personal changes in a variety of ways, sometimes causing problems for those who have been closest to them. While this is not the place to delineate adult development issues, it is nonetheless extremely important for middle level teachers to be sensitive to the possibilities of issues in parents' lives that are in turn affecting their family and therefore our students.

Contemporary trends in family composition are moving away from the traditional definition as "a group of people related by blood, marriage, or adoption" (Cole, 1990). While there will continue to be many traditionally composed families, teachers should expect that some of their students will come from variously organized living units headed by single parents, grandparents, and sometimes adult siblings or other relatives. Many children will live in so-called blended families composed of one parent, a stepparent, and children from a previous marriage or relationship. Some children may live with a parent who was never married. Other kids live with a parent who has had multiple transient relationships, and many have a surrogate parent figure. There may also be kids living in domestic partnership units formed by gay or lesbian parents.

The blending of contemporary American culture has also raised important questions for young adolescents about their racial and ethnic identities. Our nation's population is undergoing rapid change toward far greater pluralism than has been the case in the past. Youngsters who live in large inner cities are especially influenced by ethnocentrism and discrimination, and it is incumbent on middle level educators to help children understand and process these issues. As teachers of all these children, we must be sensitive to the variety of family configurations and cultural influences in which our students are living.

Teachers must remember, nonetheless, that while all parents have some kind of influence on their children, we must make sensitive, thoughtful assessments of that influence. We've all worked with students whose relationships with either parent or both parents was tense and acrimonious. Taking sides on an issue risks losing trust and credibility. Sometimes we see family circumstances in which the youngster suffers from neglect or abuse. There have been a few kids for whom my teammates and I served informally as surrogate parents, providing a respite from rejection and abuses at home. In these cases, simple neglect would have been an improvement over their deleterious circumstances. For better or worse, the parents our students have are the ones that matter, so our task is to do the very best we can with each situation as it is.

FOSTERING UNDERSTANDING AND BUILDING TRUST

Our overarching goal must be to gain our students' parents' trust, because whatever we try to do to educate their children will be affected in some way by their opinions. In order for them to trust us, they need to understand both our commitment to their children and the work we are doing to educate their children. I benefited enormously as a teacher from the trust my students' parents demonstrated in countless ways, many of which are included in the following recommendations.

School–Home Communication

Good communication rises from effective listening and thoughtful responses. The key with parents is in being a good listener, and as teachers it is up to us to take the initiative in creating contexts where effective exchanges are most likely to occur. Parents know a lot about their children, and although teachers often have to carefully sort actualities from opinion, the investment of initiating regular effective communication pays large dividends. And unless we establish regular ways of informing parents and opening ourselves to their feedback, contact will be left solely to open house night and routine conferences. After all, realizing the possibilities of a partnership with parents depends on success in establishing effective dialogue between home and school.

1. Telephone three parents each afternoon, evening, and weekend to share some supportive observations and encouragement about their children. Limit the calls to 5 minutes or less, and this small investment of time will bring great returns—guaranteed!

2. If your school has teacher advisories, be sure to include advisees' parents in these calls, contacting them at least once a month.

3. Give your home telephone number to advisees and their parents, encouraging them to initiate the call in the event of an urgency.

4. Invite advisory parents to an initial conference one day after school early in the year.

5. Publish a team newsletter at least monthly to communicate current activities, to describe upcoming studies and events, and to solicit parents' help.

6. Conduct inquiries to find out about parents' careers, hobbies, travel, interests, and other information of possible use.

7. Hold special gatherings such as culminating events for curriculum studies, reading groups, parent advisory council, field trips, and so on where parents will be able to learn more about the educational program and participate in supportive ways.

It is important to the climate of both telephone conversations and face-to-face meetings that the teacher conveys a sincere attitude of advocacy for the child. It is especially prudent in the first meeting to let the parent do most of the talking, using the meeting to learn as much as possible about the child's life out of school. I recommend taking occasional notes, requesting examples of generalizations that may be unclear, and giving direct answers to parents' questions about details of how the program works. It is extremely important not to introduce one's own uncertainties or frustrations into this dialogue. Parents expect us to be professional, just like their dentist or family doctor. We need to convey our competence and maturity to them.

There are also communications from the team or school that are important for us to support. Make certain that the newsletter informing parents about team and advisory activities is published and distributed according to a regular schedule. Emphasize both students' and teachers' accounts of their experiences. Plan open house or parents' night presentations thoroughly, making sure that parents see numerous examples of high-quality student work.

Invite Parents to Visit

"The more parents actually see kids in the school setting, the more they appreciate teachers."

(Spear, 1994)

Parents of primary school children often see their children in school. It is common for parents to serve as helpers in the early years. One could argue that owing to the general lack of parents' knowledge about early adolescence, parents ought to be involved at least as much in the middle years. Although some middle level teams have created important active roles for parents, it is far less common for young adolescents' parents to be at school.

Parent visitors are better off if they have something to do when they visit. One team organized book groups with one parent in each group (see Chapter 6 on book groups). Once a week the parent would come for lunch to talk with his or her book group about the book they were currently reading. This arrangement enabled the parent to have a broad perspective on the team plus an up-close involvement. Parents may also work on basic writing or mathematics skills or help with the newsletter. Parent mentors for individual students who want a mentor can help everyone. Parents may conduct shadow studies for the teacher, or they may be particularly useful in helping with small groups in a larger curriculum project.

Perhaps the most preferred way to welcome parents during the school day is to invite them to come for lunch with their child. Although this thought may horrify some students (and their parents), early adolescence is often a time when a counterproductive intergenerational gulf may emerge. Often teachers, more than anyone else, can create opportunities to bridge such difficulties and provide the savvy guidance needed to help keep communication flowing.

Recruit Parents as Teachers

There are certainly some parents who don't belong working with young adolescents. On the other hand, these exceptions are vastly outnumbered by parents who know a great deal and who can be extremely helpful to the instructional program. Compile a Rolodex or a computer file accessible to students that incorporates information gathered through a parent inquiry. Organize the file around topics parents have identified as interests or areas of expertise. This file then becomes a regular resource in several ways.

1. Students can contact parents whose names appear in the file related to a topic the student is studying.

2. The teacher can also identify parents whose interests or background are connected to a unit being planned.

3. Teachers may wish to invite a parent to teach a workshop or minicourse about an area of his or her interest or expertise. Parents of my students have presented single lessons to small groups of students about interests such as baking and fly-fishing, while others have taught more specialized short courses of a week or more about basic electronics and the opera.

4. Parents who enjoy reading can be especially valuable as book group leaders, so long as they are given some direction about how to lead a small group of young adolescents. In my experience, employers will allow the parent a couple of hours of leave over a week or so to participate in the school's instructional program.

5. Parents can be especially helpful for tutorial sessions with children needing a good bit of individual help, such as work that focuses on basic literacy skills. Again, time needs to be set aside after school so the teacher can give the parent-tutor guidance.

6. Although I've usually preferred to conduct field trips on my own with groups of a dozen or fewer students, there have also been occasions when contributions by parent chaperones made a huge difference in the quality of the experience. A trip to a fiberglass boat factory stands out in my memory. The grandfather chaperone had done his homework thoroughly, and his knowledge of the operation we observed made those three hours especially significant. In fact, I recall feeling that I was virtually superfluous; it became very much his trip. The essential thing for teachers to remember, however, is that the trip's purposes and expectations for students need to be communicated to the chaperone-helper clearly and succinctly in advance.

7. On a few occasions a parent volunteer has informally become an adjunct member of our team. One mother shared her fluency in Italian and German by teaching small exploratory classes to interested students. Other parent volunteers initiated classes about decision making that have endured for more than a decade (Bergmann & Rudman, 1985).

8. Arguably, the most delicate curricular topic young adolescents need to study brings particularly volatile value content: adolescent sexuality. A variety of sectarian policies and personal viewpoints makes it extremely important that teachers and parents work together. Some schools address this issue by involving selected parents as adjunct teachers and small group leaders so long as they participate in a preliminary training program and conform their sessions to the professionally prepared curricular design.

When collaborations of this quality occur between teachers and parents, people don't just benefit, they *thrive*. Sharing responsibility for educating youth becomes coordinated and more consistent, presenting our students with at least an approximation of a solidarity found in culturally homogeneous societies such as that of Japan (George, 1989). Our considerable challenge is to present students with as much consistency in values and standards as is practical in our pluralistic society.

Parent Connection to Community Resources

The fastest way to develop particular community resources is to go through students' parents. Whether the need is for recyclable materials or sites for apprenticeships, parents frequently already have connections that can benefit your program. Two parents of kids on our team were dubbed our official Rag & Bone Committee. These two moms supported our efforts by collecting an amazing assortment of consumable materials we were able to use, such as a variety of types, colors, and grades of leftover paper from several print shops and foam sandwich board from an architectural model company. They located an industrial recycling center from which we received such diverse materials as paper tubes from newsprint rolls, ball bearings, tiny DC electric motors, plastic tubing, small spirit levels, plastic prescription bottles, and rubber straps. What made their help additionally welcome was that the materials were entirely free. Furthermore, by recycling these materials we were helping in a small way to protect our environment. Our only challenge lay in storing materials, so we invented more efficient ways to use high wall space and labeled storage bins.

Parents are also direct links to extremely valuable human resources in the community. One school encouraged personal improvement each month by having teachers identify as many students as they wished for a drawing for the Limo Lift award. The only criterion for nomination was that the student had worked consistently to be a credit to the school. The student whose name was drawn was met the next morning by a chauffeured limousine for the trip to and from school. The service was provided free of charge by a limousine service that had been approached by a parent. Not only did the company make a valuable contribution to the school, but it benefited from advertising and positive publicity.

A committee of parents in another school, working with teachers, the principal, and one teacher-coordinator, formed partnerships with community businesses in order to create incentives for students. Students who handled a project particularly well in class or who showed positive initiative in terms of citizenship or who performed well in a drama or sports event could receive a VIP card from any teacher who wished to recognize that student. The card was a business-size card imprinted with the school and team logos and showing a teacher's signature and date. These cards could be used for a twenty-five-cent discount at several local merchants and the movie theater, or they were redeemable as tickets of admission to a variety of lunchtime activities at school, such as a dance contest or lip-sync competition. Both the program and the activities were planned and carried out by the parent committee. The morale of both students and teachers was clearly lifted.

These several examples of parents' contributions to the life of a middle level school grew out of trusting communications with teachers when everyone looked together for ways to provide positive support for children. They were drawn together by common concern, and they applied imagination and ingenuity to invent ways to encourage and support their children. When grown-ups work together like this, who knows how many creative programs will emerge? The point of emphasis is that the dialogue was initiated by teachers, whose domain the school is—at least in parents' minds.

Parents and Community Service Projects

The many benefits to young adolescents of being involved in school and community service have already been discussed here and elsewhere (Carnegie Corporation, 1989). However, a persistent problem in setting up and carrying out such projects is time—especially time to make arrangements and to chaperone students as they perform their services in the community. Teachers already have to deal with time-related frustrations in their ongoing efforts to accomplish the multifarious details of being a teacher. Parents are also busy, sometimes even more so than teachers. Yet, early adolescent youngsters need the experience of doing good work for another person alongside an adult who is also committed to being a constructive member of society.

Parents are the primary adult influence on children's values. Because youngsters are changing in how they think about and weigh value-related issues, early adolescence is a particularly important time for them to do things with adults and discuss their ideas and perceptions. Therefore, the ideal way to establish and maintain community service is through parent-teacher–sponsored projects that connect kids in meaningful ways to an assortment of community needs. For example, one community has a joint program called "Builders Club," which engages middle school students working on weekends with members of Kiwanis and Habitat for Humanity. They make repairs or improvements on buildings that house low-income families, help restore public facilities such as parks, and collect food and clothing for the homeless. Virtually every community in America has adult service organizations that can be linked to young adolescents to model the virtues of citizenship we value for our youth and want them to emulate. An organization of parents supported by teachers is the key to bringing about a coordinated influence in the development of children's values.

A sixth to eighth grade multiage team in a K–8 school sponsored an annual family fair. Each family or a combination of families planned and set up some kind of booth or game at the fair. The three teachers on the team arranged for music, and students handled publicity and accounting as part of their instructional program. Each spring the fair raised several hundred dollars, half of which went into the team budget. The remaining half was distributed among charities the students wished to support. Not only did this event engage children and adults in providing a service, the event itself brought both generations closer together around a common purpose and built pride and school spirit.

There are many ways young adolescents can serve others in their community: tutoring or reading to younger children, supervising their play periods, providing companionship for senior citizens, working on projects designed to benefit the community, assisting with meals at a convalescent center, helping the elderly who live at home with maintenance chores. Many of these services already occur within single families, but when parents and teachers collaborate to see that strangers also benefit, value statements about citizenship are made. Teachers are, once again, the key to initiating the dialogue with parents that can lead to a coordinated, unifying effort.

Parents as General Helpers

Parents who have the time, inclination, and occasionally specialized skills have for years provided valuable assistance with school needs. Many elementary school playgrounds, for example, have been constructed on weekends with parents' labor. Fundraising projects such as a pancake breakfast or spaghetti supper frequently rely upon the parents' organization for success. Several well-known schools that receive numerous visitors provide a visitor program conducted by parent volunteers.

This need has proved to be so great at Shoreham–Wading River Middle School that eventually parents were employed by the school system to operate their visitor program. When typing is needed for a team or school publication such as a literary magazine and students' skills aren't adequate to accomplish the task on time, parents are often called upon for help. My teammates and I asked parents to subscribe to particular magazines we wanted in our classroom but couldn't afford; the parents received them, read them, and then sent them to school. Once communication has been established and nurtured, parents look for ways to help teachers accomplish their programs.

LEARNING WITH PARENTS

On the several hundred occasions I have spoken to parent groups in schools over the last two decades, I have always urged parents and teachers to read about young adolescent development and middle level schooling *together*. While I have no data about how much that advice has been heeded, I do know anecdotally that many schools and more often successful teams have formed some kind of adult reading groups to explore related literature and video materials together. Middle level education is a steadily changing knowledge base, and a very useful way of staying abreast of those changes is to invite parents' participation in a group that meets periodically to examine developments pertinent to parenting and teaching young adolescents.

One particularly useful publications to provide content and guide adult groups' discussions is *The In-Between Years,* a quarterly newsletter published by Connie and Ed Brazee, two richly experienced middle level educators, parents and scholars. Each issue addresses an issue that is important to everyone involved at this level. Topics such as communication, expectations, decision making, summer activities, allowance, and talking with kids about human sexuality are thoughtfully organized and augmented with sound advice.

Informational resources about young adolescent children that are appropriate for use by parents and teachers are better than they have ever been, and that body of work is steadily growing. Some of those resources are listed at the end of this chapter, but every chapter is concluded with suggested activities and resources that may be useful in getting under way with a form of parent–teacher collaboration that will benefit everyone.

PRESERVING PARTNERSHIPS

Establishing communication with parents is just the first step toward collaboration. Once projects are under way, it is essential that teachers and students do all that they can do to let parents know that who they are and what they do is recognized and appreciated. After all, parents have human ego needs just as teachers and students do. When they are recognized for their efforts, they usually reciprocate by expressing their appreciation and loyalty as well as showing further initiative. An excellent subject for students' discussion and planning has to do with how appreciation can be conveyed to adults. Establishing a routine that makes sense to the kids and is reasonable from the teachers' perspective is an important detail of team governance and functioning.

There are several simple ways both to let parents know they are appreciated and to teach our students the importance of such acknowledgments. These examples can be options for youngsters to consider in working out a team routine.

1. Whenever a parent or other community member contributes material or provides a singular service to the team or school, it is essential that one or more students promptly write a letter of appreciation. Teachers should likewise follow up with a brief note or telephone call to ensure the adults' awareness and appreciation of the donor's contribution.

2. Many teams create a special certificate to award to off-team people who have provided some kind of service. The certificate bears the team name and logo, is usually decorated with filigree that ornaments it with an air of formality, and bears signatures of teachers and team members or officers. The value adults place on receiving such certificates has been evidenced by their display in offices and homes.

3. Similar to awarding certificates is the practice of presenting a team T-shirt, button, bumper sticker, or other representation of the team's appreciation to a parent or community member who has supported a team project.

4. Occasionally a parent's support is especially benevolent and justifies more singular public recognition. Our team gave a surprise party for the two mothers who were our Rag & Bone Committee. They came to our team room on a Friday afternoon in early

November, ostensibly to meet with a student committee planning a project of making tree decorations to be sold at a school Christmas fair. The mothers came expecting to share some ideas and show some scrounge materials they believed could be used in the project. The party included a riotous skit written and performed by students as well as testimonials, singing, and refreshments. The culminating event was the presentation of a canvas bag on which some students had silk-screened each mother's first name and "OUR-BC," an acronym for "Out Unit Rag & Bone Committee."

5. One more easy but certain way to confirm appreciation for parents' help is to mention them in the team newsletter. Parents have a keen interest in that publication, since it is written by their children and it tells about team activities beyond what one child may be sharing in conversation at home.

The ultimate and absolutely essential expression of appreciation is, of course, the accomplishments of their children and our students. There is no question that parents' greatest satisfactions lie in seeing their children growing up as intellectually thoughtful, responsible, appreciative young people—a credit to their gene pool. And after all, that is also the ultimate payoff for us, too.

Supporting Activities

1. Design and administer an interview inquiry with parents to explore their hopes and expectations for their young adolescent children.

2. Survey your school community for possible community resources that might be developed through parent initiative.

3. Visit a functioning service project and interview providers and beneficiaries to see how young adolescents might be useful.

RESOURCE ORGANIZATIONS FOR PARENTS

Family and Community Advocacy Committee, National Middle School Association, 2600 Corporate Exchange Drive, Suite 370, Columbus, OH: 43231–1672. 800–528–NMSA

Carnegie Council on Adolescent Development, 11 Dupont Circle, NW, Washington, DC 20036. (202) 265–9080

Children's Defense Fund, 122 C Street, NW, Washington, DC 20001. (202) 628–8787.

Constitutional Rights Foundation, 601 South Kingsley Drive, Los Angeles, CA 90005. (213) 487–5590.

Early Adolescent Helper Program (CASE), City University of New York Graduate Center, 25 West 43rd Street, New York, NY 10036. (212) 642–2946

Massachusetts Advocacy Center, 76 Summer Street, Boston, MA 02110. (617) 357–8431

National Center for Service Learning in Early Adolescence, CASE: The Graduate School and University Center of CUNY, 25 West 43rd Street, Suite 612, New York, NY 10036–8099. (212) 642–2946.

National Coalition for Parent Involvement in Education, Box 39, 1201 16th Street, N.W., Washington, DC 20036.

National Committee for Citizens in Education, 10840 Little Patuxent Parkway, Suite 301, Columbia, MD 21044. (301) 997–9300, 800-638–9675

National Helpers Network, 245 Fifth Avenue, Suite 1705, New York, NY 10016–8728. 800-646–4623.

National PTA, 700 North Rush Street, Chicago, IL 60611–2571. (312) 787–0977.

Search Institute, 700 S. Third St., Suite 210, Minneapolis, MN 55415. 800-888–7828.

ADDITIONAL RESOURCES FOR PARENTS AND TEACHERS

The In-Between Years, a newsletter for parents and caregivers of ten to fourteen year olds, published quarterly: *The In-Between Years,* P. O. Box 575, Orono, ME 04473.

Carnegie Corporation. (1995). *Great transitions: Preparing adolescents for a new century.* New York: Carnegie Corporation of New York.

Feldmeyer, D., & Roehlkepartain, E. C. (1995). *Parenting with a purpose: A positive approach for raising confident, caring youth.* Minneapolis, MN: Search Institute.

Freeman, C. G. (1996). *Living with a work in progress.* Columbus, OH: National Middle School Association.

Gordon, S. (1981). *The teenage survival book: The complete, revised, updated edition of you.* New York: Times Books.

Hechinger, F. M. (1992). *Fateful choices: Healthy youth for the 21st century.* New York: Carnegie Corporation of New York.

Johnston, J. H. (1990). *The new American family and the schools.* Columbus, OH: National Middle School Association.

Living with 10 to 15 year olds: A parent education curriculum. Available from Search Institute, 700 South Third Street, Minneapolis, MN 55415. 800-888-7828.

Myers, J., & Monson, L. (1992). *Involving families in middle level education.* Columbus, OH: National Middle School Association.

Showalter, J. E., & Anyan, W. R., Jr. (1979). *The family handbook of adolescence.* New York: Knopf.

REFERENCES

Barrish, I. J., & Barrish, H. H. (1989). *Surviving and enjoying your adolescent.* Kansas City, MO: Westport.

Bergmann, S., & Rudman, G. J. (1985). *Decision-making skills for middle school students.* Washington, DC: National Education Association.

Berla, N., Henderson, A. T., & Kerewsky, W. (1989). *The middle school years: A parents' handbook.* Columbia, MD: National Committee for Citizens in Education.

Carnegie Corporation. (1989). *Turning points: Preparing American youth for the 21st century.* Washington, DC: Carnegie Council on Adolescent Development.

Clark, R. M. (1983). *Family life and school achievement: Why poor black children succeed or fail.* Chicago: University of Chicago Press.

Cole, C. G. (1990). 2001: A middle school odyssey. *Middle School Journal, 22*(2), 3–6.

Dorman, G., Geldof, D., & Scarborough, B. (1982). *Living with 10 to 15 year olds: A parent education curriculum.* Carrboro, NC: Center for Early Adolescence.

Erikson, E. (1968). *Identity, youth, and crisis.* New York: Norton.

Farel, A. M. (1982). *Early adolescence: What parents need to know.* Carrboro, NC: Center for Early Adolescence.

Garvin, J. P. (1984). In search of excellence: *The national reports—implications for middle schools.* Columbus, OH: National Middle School Association.

Garvin, J. P. (1988, March). What parents expect from middle schools. *Principal, 67*(4), 55–56.

George, P. S. (1989). *Inside the Japanese junior high school.* Columbus, OH: National Middle School Association.

Gilligan, C. (1982). *In a different voice.* Cambridge, MA: Harvard University Press.

Lefstein, L. M., Kerewesky, W., Medrich, E. A., & Frank, C. (1982). *3:00 to 6:00 P.M.: Young adolescents at home and in the community.* Carrboro, NC: Center for Early Adolescence.

Levinson, D. J. (1978). *The seasons of a man's life.* New York: Knopf.

Maeroff, G. I. (1989). "School Smart" parents strengthen education. *Education Week, 9*(8), 32.

Melton, G. E. (1987). Middle level schools as perceived by parents. *NASSP NewsLeader 35*(1), 4.

Myers, J. W. (1985). *Involving parents in middle level education.* Columbus, OH: National Middle School Association.

Spear, R. C. (1994, Spring). "A conversation with John Lounsbury." *Journal of the New England League of Middle Schools, 7*(2), 29–32.

Steinberg, L. D. (1980). *Understanding families with young adolescents.* Carrboro, NC: Center for Early Adolescence.

Vossler, J. M. (1996, February). Parents and students read together. *VAMLEFocus, 1*(6).

Epilogue

The first letter was delivered to our classroom on the second Monday of the new school year. Neatly typed on note paper, it read:

> Dear Unit,
>   I am the spirit of a child. Today I was going past your school, and I decided to drop in for a visit. I really liked what I saw. In fact, I've decided that I want to become a member of your class. There's just one problem. Spirits aren't supposed to contact mortals, so if I get caught I will be in a lot of trouble with Malcolm. He's the Keeper of Children's Spirits. On yeah, there's another problem, sort of. I can see you, but you can't see me (because I'm a spirit). But I can send you letters, which I will do. So long for now. I'll write again soon. Ta Ta!
> Love,
> Jason

Forty-four children (eleven to thirteen years old) plus two teachers made up the Unit. We began each school day with a class meeting in which we'd swap experiences from the previous day, discuss the day's agenda, and talk over any issues that concerned the group. As part of that routine, Jason's strange letter was read aloud by the student in charge. Kids reacted with indifference. In their own eyes they were worldly-wise Cambridge kids—street smart, sanguine, the personification of "cool." They also knew well that in their innovative school, teachers worked hard to generate intriguing, stimulating circumstances for learning. For them the incident was just another teacher's effort to bring something mystical and amusing into their school lives.

Two days later, Jason's second letter arrived. Again it was read aloud in the morning meeting, Jason wrote about his excitement at finding a school he really liked. He cited as an example Todd helping Melissa with a math problem: "It's great to see boys and girls help each other sometimes."

Again, the students' reactions were nonchalant. Except for Willy Claflin, my co-teacher, and me, no one seemed to take much notice of either letter. The kids were preoccupied with settling into routines and reestablishing friendships. This Jason business was casually dismissed, apparently in confidence that it was our chicanery. They began to question us sarcastically: "Who do you guys think you're fooling? We know you're Jason. Why don't you can that jive, man?"

For the fifteen years I had worked with middle school children, I had prided myself on being able to arouse genuine interest, to inveigle kids into making serious intellectual commitments. I worked hard at conceptualizing, designing, and implementing high-interest challenges that would teach—connect students to the world outside and satisfy their need to know. Consequently, I found the Jason letters intriguing. I was certain that someone I knew was writing them, and it became important to me to know who it was if for no other reason than to offer my congratulations.

I questioned Willy; he pleaded innocent. So did my other colleagues. Someone, I began to feel, was copping my act, and in spite of their repeated denials, I figured it had to be one of my colleagues. It was no puzzle to the children; they were quite satisfied that I was responsible. I continued to press Willy. He seemed puzzled by my grilling, being all the while certain that I was behind Jason. Eventually it began to sink in that neither of us was responsible, nor did either of us have any clue to whose work it was.

Jason's third letter began to compel the students' attention. He wrote with insight about some of the interpersonal dynamics of our group, and he was straightforward in articulating his observations and opinions. He explained that Ethel, a new student, was feeling shy, afraid of joining into activities with other girls, afraid they didn't like her. He urged us to invite her participation. He also wrote of how much he liked Carol, Diane, and Becky, in spite of the fact that they were leaving caustic, anonymous notes in Susan's desk. The three girls blushed immediately; Jason's reproof was understood. The intimate nature of these expressions made everyone suspicious of just how Willy and I were managing to get such remarkable inside information. Their previous teasing accusations that he or I was Jason began to give way to queries: "How'd you know about that stuff? Who told you about the notes?"

I sensed an unwanted estrangement arising, and because, in truth, the situation was out of our hands, I became apprehensive about students' reactions to our apparent invasion of their privacy. I renewed my questioning of colleagues and began to speculate about several parents and even a couple of friends who had no association with the school. Everyone came under my scrutiny as I pondered, "Who is Jason?"

As September passed into October, we continued to receive letters at least twice a week. Jason always commented candidly about relationships within the Unit, but he was always optimistic and enthusiastic. When Bob began to complain that parts of his lunches were missing, Jason revealed that Tommy often didn't have a lunch or money to buy one, and suggested that others of us ought to share. Immediately the lunch larceny ceased, and students began pooling their lunches. Jason had an uncanny knack for knowing which people were slacking off in their daily cleanup chores. A word from him served well to remedy the situation. Surprising us further, Jason began to send birthday greetings to class members.

The mystery spread throughout our school community. Children in other classes were asking about Jason, coming to see his letters. More and more I was being addressed as Jason, even by some of the parents. Everyone seemed certain that the letters were all my work. It was strange to receive so much credit from so many people for something I had not done.

A favorite school tradition was the Halloween Carnival. The oldest students in the school—the Unit—planned and conducted the carnival for the rest of the children. Usually there were about fifteen booths at which one could get a face painting, bob for apples, shoot a candle flame with a water pistol, and so on. Each event cost one or two cents, making it possible for children to do as many activities as they wished. At the conclusion of the affair, a schoolwide vote was taken to decide how to spend the approximately twenty-five dollars that had been collected. (Inevitably we opted to donate the money to UNICEF.)

The carnival was always great fun, and the children looked forward to it for weeks ahead of time. Jason was no exception. He wrote of his excitement about attending his first Halloween carnival, and several of his letters included ideas for booths. It seemed fitting that Jason, being a spirit, would have such a keen interest in the occasion.

Since Halloween fell on a Saturday, the carnival was scheduled for Friday afternoon. The plans had been made, the materials for the booths had been gathered, and all preparations that could be made in advance had been completed. After extended discussion, the members of the Unit decided not to provide prizes for participation in booth activities. Initially everyone had favored giving candy prizes, but when the total cost was calculated, we reluctantly decided that the expense was too great. That resolve did not detract from the preparations, however, and when the students headed home on Thursday afternoon, they were excited, looking forward to our carnival day.

When I unlocked our classroom early Friday morning, I was startled. Sitting on a table in the middle of the room, surrounded by cut-out pumpkins, black cats, and broomsticks, was a ten-pound box of candy corn. Taped to the box was a sign that read: "This candy is for prizes at the carnival. Hooray! Love, Jason."

Word spread quickly throughout the school that Jason had contributed prizes for the carnival. Soon children were thanking me profusely for using Jason as an excuse for donating the candy. What was particularly unnerving to me was knowing that some unknown person must have a key to the school. The idea crossed my mind to have the locks changed. But how would I explain such an expense to the board of trustees? They were already aware of the Jason mystery (I had actually suspected a couple of them as the perpetrators.) Several had even complimented me on my "clever idea." I was beginning to experience mild panic. When, I wondered, was this ruse going to end?

The trustees did indeed express concern about Jason's ability to get inside a locked school, although their concern was tongue-in-cheek. Convinced that I was behind the whole caper, one trustee remarked that since Jason was a spirit, he didn't need a key; he could simply walk through the walls.

Prior to Thanksgiving recess, we were busy completing the first of two issues of our literary magazine, *Facets*. As the student editors began to read through the poems and articles submitted for publication, they realized that almost 75 percent of the pieces were about Jason. He had captured everyone's imagination and was clearly the hottest item in school.

As Jason's popularity, power, and influence grew, so did my apprehension. What would I do if Jason suddenly stopped writing? How would I explain contrary value positions he might take? Suppose he advised children to quit school? Clearly, there was no option but to go with it. Exhausted with denying that I was Jason, I even began to wonder in private moments if indeed I *was*. Could it be that another side of me was operating clandestinely? Jason was beginning to keep me awake at night.

Our first letter after Thanksgiving introduced us to Jason's new friend, Clara. Jason explained that while he was on vacation he had met her, thought her trustworthy and, in confidence, told her about his new school and new friends. Clara begged Jason to let her visit with him; she promised that she would keep his secret from Malcolm so that the "Spirit Keeper" would never know. From that time on, the letters we received included observations and comments by both Jason and Clara.

As Christmas and Hanukkah drew near, Jason and Clara made it a point to pass along their seasonal good wishes to the children. Soon we were on vacation, and as those restful days passed, I began to believe that we would hear no more from our spirit friends. Jason and Clara had had their fun with us, especially with me. This was the logical time for the saga to end. Enough was enough.

No such luck. The first school day of the new year brought fresh news from Jason and Clara. They reported on their holiday with their spirit friends, on the presents they'd exchanged, and on how blissful it had been to sleep late every morning for two weeks. They also shared New Year's resolutions, which included such intentions as becoming more patient with each other, doing their chores more willingly, avoiding procrastination, and being careful not to expect others to see things exactly as they did.

Aside from the continuing flow of letters, Jason and Clara made no other contact with us until February. Then, on Valentine's Day, I unlocked our classrooms to find the rooms festooned with streamers of red, pink, and white. Huge red hearts cut from large sheets of posterboard were scattered on tables and walls; valentines, poems, and other messages were everywhere. On the center table was a huge, heart-shaped cake with pink icing and red lettering bearing the message: "We love all of you! Jason and Clara."

For a week following Valentine's Day, we didn't hear from our spirit friends. Concern began to show in the faces and voices of the students. They no longer asked me why *I* had not communicated; Jason and Clara had become so personified that they were now an independent phenomenon. The second week began with no word. Finally, on Friday, a telegram arrived. It read simply but alarmingly: "Malcolm found out. Have split up and gone underground. Will try to contact you later. Clara."

We were speechless, jolted awake from our delightful dream to face a reality that was cruel and unfair. None of us was prepared for this turn, and we were preoccupied with it as we tried to resume our schoolwork. I watched my students moving about the room aimlessly, whispering solemnly, their strained faces registering their concern. A few asked me what I thought: "Will they be all right? What do you think Malcolm will do to them?" I feigned confidence and said that I couldn't believe Malcolm would punish them severely for something that was so well-intentioned. "I'm sure they're all right. Of course we'll hear from them," I tried weakly.

Three weeks passed with no further word. A pall hung over the class. Children reread old letters, talked fondly of past antics, exchanged hopeful but unsubstantiated platitudes. One Friday morning Randy raced into the room, exclaiming, "Look! Look! It's a message to Clara from Jason!" Randy crumpled under the weight of his forty-three teammates shrieking as one, "Lemme see! Lemme see!"

In the "personals" column of the morning paper was a brief notice: "Clara. Meet me Friday at 3:30 at the corner of Huron and Concord. Jason."

All day long we watched the clock; the day seemed interminable. When three o'clock dismissal finally arrived, our entire team scooted the six blocks to the designated meeting place. Jittery with excitement, they were absolutely certain that they'd soon see their two long-lost friends. Having the excuse of an appointment on the other side of town shortly after school, I drove past the intersection. There was our team, all forty-four eager students searching high and low for a glimpse of Jason and Clara. But how can one see a reunion of spirits?

Monday brought the first letter in almost five weeks, confirming that Jason and Clara had indeed planned a rendezvous. They explained that Malcolm had been furious when he first discovered that they had broken the cardinal rule of the spirit world by contacting us. After a while, however, he'd cooled down and sent out the word that he'd forgive them if they'd come out of hiding. Deep down they really wanted to trust Malcolm and believe in his good nature, so they decided to give themselves up. After reprimanding them for what they'd done, Malcolm asked for an apology and hinted about a surprise present to make amends.

Clara and Jason apologized for upsetting Malcolm—but not for contacting us. (Clara called it "diplomacy.") Malcolm wasn't thrilled, but he was satisfied enough to reward them with a trip around the world. Jason said, "I see through Malcolm; this is just a way to get us out of town and away from you." Malcolm also tried vainly to get them to promise never to contact us again; they agreed to "think it over for a while." Uppermost in our minds was that Jason and Clara were safe. We were also quite happy to know that they were forgiven and about to take off on such a wonderful trip.

For the next four weeks we received letters from all around the world: Montreal, London, Paris, Madrid, Rome, Cairo, New Delhi, Bangkok, Tokyo, Rio de Janeiro. And there was no doubt that the letters had been sent from those cities; the stamps and postmarks were authentic. The two spirits also described with remarkable precision the sights they had seen and the food they had enjoyed. The letter from Paris included what Jason described as "a picture of Clara and me standing in front of the Eiffel Tower." It was, of course, a snapshot of the Eiffel Tower.

Jason and Clara's sense of humor restored us to the happy disposition we'd known before the trouble with Malcolm, the collective temperament of our class being closely tied to the vagaries and adventures of out phantasmic friends. No evidence whatsoever had come forth to intimate that it was all a hoax. I don't know why I couldn't simply let myself go and believe. But it was simply too much. Again I succumbed to the obsession for uncovering who was behind this prank, for finding the "real" Jason and Clara.

As the close of the school year was fast approaching, I had to turn my thoughts to the multitude of details involved with another year's ending. By tradition we presented each graduating student with a modest gift, something specially selected for that person: a book, a framed print, a bit of jewelry. The gifts were presented at our final school meeting, following which we retired to our classrooms for refreshments and final good-byes. It was a sentimental occasion, and the preparation for it distracted me somewhat from Jason and Clara. At the same time, they were also very much a part of my thoughts as I prepared for that final day.

Two days before it arrived, we received a letter from Jason. It was an exciting one, for it promised that if I would read an enclosed poem at our class party, Jason and Clara would appear to us. That was electrifying news.

After all these months of mystery, finally we were going to see, and seeing had become for me the requisite for believing. I recall thinking happily to myself that this was the perfect consummation of our magical year. Whoever had carried out this yearlong mystery was a master. The anticipation of actually meeting Jason and Clara fueled the already considerable excitement that attended the concluding days of school.

Jason's poem consisted of four lines of rhyming nonsense syllables. It reminded me vaguely of Lewis Carroll's "Jabberwocky," but it had not even a hint of a story line. I studied it searching for clues that might help prepare for the revelation. Nothing.

Finally the big day came. Insofar as the concluding litany was concerned, I was essentially going through the motions; the long-awaited meeting with Jason and Clara dominated me. I expected the same intensity to be evident in the students, but they were obviously more involved in the ceremonies.

When at long last the school meeting was over and the younger children had departed for their class parties, our group made its way to our meeting area and we all sat cross-legged on the floor as we had done twice a day throughout the year. I called the meeting to order and asked playfully, "Is there any old business?" Everyone laughed.

There was only one item of business, and we all knew we were at the moment of truth on that matter. With a poorly disguised shaking voice, I began to read the poem. The lines sounded ridiculous, but no one could have kept me mute. On the final syllable I folded the poem shut. Nothing happened. After a few awkward moments the children began to look quizzically at one another. Then, as a group, those forty-four youngsters came to their feet.

I continued to sit, startled. For a moment I felt confused, then awestruck by what I was beginning to perceive. First they smiled, then they laughed, then they cheered and clapped. I was numb. The realization that these youngsters had accomplished such an incredible coup was more than I could fully comprehend.

As my wits slowly returned, I asked the inevitable "How?" They were eager to supply the answers. The scheme had begun spontaneously with three girls. They saw it as a chance to create their own living mystery. As the year progressed they were gradually "discovered" by classmates, one at a time. Rather than expose the scheme, the discoverers were invited to join in the intrigue. By midyear, every student had become part of Jason and Clara.

My first cogent question concerned how they managed to get into the locked building. They responded with peals of laughter. It was well known that I was continually misplacing my keys. Two boys had quietly removed the master key from my mislaid key ring one morning, had it duplicated during lunch, then returned it to the ring before dismissal. With the telling of that detail, the duplicate key was handed over to me with great pomp.

Jason and Clara's trip was the focus of my next question. One student's father worked for a company that had offices in most major cities around the world. Through his cooperation, the students were able to send letters addressed to the Unit to the overseas offices, whose employees stamped the letters and mailed them back to us.

What a beautiful stratagem! These youngsters had created a major intrigue, sustained it for nine months, and kept it virtually to themselves.

Several years have passed since that remarkable experience. That was the last year I worked daily with middle schoolers, but it has left me with immutable optimism about the potential of young adolescent children. Given learning opportunities that truly challenge, the responsibility to exercise meaningful choices, and respect for their ideas and dignity, youngsters are capable of tremendous commitment and dazzling originality. Underneath the confounding, frustrating, often exhausting surface, there lies an indomitable human spirit, capable of the exceptional.

From time to time I still receive mail signed "Jason" or "Clara." It is gratifying to know that they are alive, well, and—above all—continuing to keep the spirit.

I had been aware for a long time that my young adolescent students had the makings to accomplish bigger things than what routine schooling called for. After all, good fortune and personal initiatives had made my own years of early adolescence a time of adventure and accomplishment in spite of what I think of as impotent schooling. I can't recall that the instructional program at school ever drew me into the issues of the time, generating ideas or cultivating a passion for learning. The school curriculum, regardless of whatever good intentions of those who chose it, held virtually no interest for me. It was little more than an obstacle course, and it came very close to alienating me altogether from formal learning. Thankfully, lots of books, initiatives toward personal interests, and a life in what teachers still curiously refer to as "the real world" taught me how much more there was to learning.

Even my most generous estimates of what kids can do fell short, however, of what Jason and Clara taught. Years later, as I choose these final words of urging and counsel for present and future teachers, I hope very much that I am not still selling the kids short, underestimating their capabilities and curiosities. Think about the young adolescents who at this moment are full-fledged soldiers in war-stricken countries, those who are heads of families in developing nations, and those in our own technologically advanced nation who struggle with and bear scars from all kinds of abuses at the hands of tragically confused adults. When such youngsters survive, they overcome fate with their indomitable human spirit to succeed in the face of adversity. It is right for us as teachers to respect young adolescents' circumstances and work with them, aware that although they are not yet adults, neither are they children. If we are patient, encouraging, and responsive to them, they will teach us about themselves—just as Jason and Clara did. Kahlil Gibran reminds us in *The Prophet* that the heart of our challenge is not so much to give our kids our wisdom but our "faith" and our "lovingness."

I have described in this book a host of strategies for working with young adolescents in ways that are responsive to their nature and needs. There is a final caveat. It is crucial to be constantly mindful that such things as shadowing, inquiries, teaming, integrated instruction, advisories, parent partnerships, and so on must not become our ultimate goals. They are means to the greater goal of helping our students be the very best young adolescents they can be. If their lives are meaningful, rewarding, and responsible while we are with them, they will also be far better prepared for challenges ahead.

There is also a payoff for us, too. If we decide to commit ourselves to this work I regard as sacred, we embark on an intriguing course. For in taking care of young adolescents by sustaining their spirits, nourishing their minds, feeding their hunger for self-definition, and affirming their existence, we also take good care of ourselves—upholding our own spirits, stretching our minds, and defining ourselves as "teachers of young adolescents," affirming our own existence.

Note

"Meet Jason, Our Classroom Spirit" originally appeared in *Learning* (April–May 1982), 34–37.

Index